# The Blackwell Encyclopedic Dictionary of Marketing

## About the Editors

**Cary L. Cooper** is Professor of Organizational Psychology at the Manchester School of Management (UMIST), UK. He has also been appointed Pro-Vice-Chancellor at the University of Manchester Institute of Science and Technology (UMIST). He is the author of over 80 books, has written over 250 scholarly articles and is editor of the *Journal of Organizational Behavior*. He is also the Founding President of the British Academy of Management.

**Chris Argyris** is James B. Conant Professor of Education and Organizataional Behavior at the Graduate School of Business, Harvard University. He has written many books and received numerous awards, including the Irwin Award by the Academy of Management for lifetime contributions to the disciplines of management. Recently, the Chris Argyris Chair in Social Psychology of Organizations has been established at Yale University.

## About the Volume Editors

**Barbara R. Lewis** is Senior Lecturer in Marketing at the Manchester School of Management, UMIST. She has published widely on marketing issues in the services sector, and her present research activities relate to customer care and service quality, and consumer behavior in the services sector.

**Dale Littler** is Professor of Marketing at the Manchester School of Management, UMIST. He has published extensively on various aspects of strategic marketing and new product development and his current research is focused on customer behavior towards innovative products and services.

# The Blackwell
# Encyclopedic Dictionary of
# Marketing

Edited by Barbara R. Lewis and Dale Littler

*Manchester School of Management, UMIST*

Copyright© Blackwell Publishers Ltd, 1997
Editorial organization© Barbara R. Lewis and Dale Littler, 1997

First published 1997

First published in USA 1997

2 4 6 8 10 9 7 5 3 1

Blackwell Publishers Ltd
108 Cowley Road
Oxford OX4 1JF
UK

Blackwell Publishers Inc.
238 Main Street
Cambridge, Massachusetts 02142, USA

*Library of Congress Cataloging-in-Publication Data*

The Blackwell encyclopedic dictionary of marketing /
  edited by Barbara Lewis and Dale Littler
      p.   cm.
  Includes bibliographical references and index.
  ISBN 1-55786-939-1 (acid-free paper)
  1. Production management–Dictionaries.        I.
TS155.B525   1996                                                95-37289
658.5′003—dc20                                                   CIP


*British Library Cataloguing in Publication Data*
CIP catalogue record for this book is available from the British Library.

ISBN 1557869391

Typeset in 9½ on 11pt Ehrhardt by Page Brothers, Norwich
Printed in Great Britain by T. J. Press (Padstow) Ltd

This book is printed on acid-free paper

# —— Contents ——

# —— Preface ——

Marketing poses an interesting challenge for the lexicographer: the subject may be long established in practice, but its emergence as a formalized area of academic interest with its own concepts, techniques, terms, and theories is relatively recent. As with other areas of management which are now foci of cerebral scrutiny, there is more looseness than tightness about the terminology and range of its interests. There is, then, much scope still for contention about the essence of the academic discipline of marketing, although the ongoing debate may naturally reflect the evolving nature of the subject as much as the lack of a clear consensus emanating from its limited heritage.

Despite this, marketers in general do tend to employ a core language about which there is, at least, some degree of visible agreement, even though there may, in not infrequent cases, be some lack of precision and even conflict about interpretations that we may not have been clearly able to clarify or resolve. This common ground of the core language has formed the base of this volume, with elements garnered from a wide array of sources, including our residential experts on particular aspects of marketing here in the Marketing Group at the Manchester School of Management. The cull of the resulting long list of terms, concepts, and areas of marketing was to a large extent the result of the arbitrary decisions of the editors. The task was somewhat simplified because for many topics there were several prospective entries used in similar ways, and where this applied we have used extensive cross-referencing.

The result we hope reflects the foundations of marketing, and provides a starting point for further investigation, a means of confirmation, or an easy source of reference.

We are grateful for the assistance, in the development of this volume, of our colleagues in the Marketing Group at the Manchester School of Management, some of whom have subsequently moved on. They are (in alphabetical order): Margaret Bruce, Mike Greatorex, Steve Greenland, Nigel Holden, Fiona Leverick, Vince Mitchell, Dominic Wilson, Steve Worrall, Mo Yamin, and David Yorke.

We are also indebted to Beryl Boswell and Patrizia Venosa for their typing and effective co-ordination of material from diverse sources. Their contribution has been eminently clear to us.

Barbara R. Lewis
Dale Littler

# —— Contributors ——

**Margaret Bruce**
*Manchester School of Management*

**Michael Greatorex**
*Manchester School of Management*

**Steve Greenland**
*Manchester School of Management*

**Nigel Holden**
*Manchester School of Management*

**Fiona Leverick**
*Aberdeen Business School*

**Barbara Lewis**
*Manchester School of Management*

**Dale Littler**
*Manchester School of Management*

**Vincent-Wayne Mitchell**
*Manchester School of Management*

**Dominic Wilson**
*Manchester School of Management*

**Steve Worrall**
*Manchester School of Management*

**Mo Yamin**
*Manchester School of Management*

**David Yorke**
*Manchester School of Management*

# A

**action** The term "action" appears at the CONATIVE (or behavioral) STAGE of models of MARKETING COMMUNICATIONS and refers to positive acts of the buyer/customer/consumer such as seeking further information from the supplying organization, TRIAL of the product or service together with the first (and, ultimately, repeat) purchase of the product or service. Triggering desired forms of "action" is best achieved by specific communication techniques such as ADVERTISING (for seeking further information), and PERSONAL SELLING (for trial and purchase), although more recent developments in DIRECT MARKETING such as DIRECT MAIL, OFF THE PAGE selling, and TELEMARKETING are now being used to generate a complete range of actions.

### Bibliography

Kotler, P. (1994). *Marketing management: Analysis, planning, implementation and control* (8th edn). Englewood Cliffs, NJ: Prentice-Hall. Chapter 22.
McCarthy, E. J. & Perreault, W. D. (1993). *Basic marketing* (11th edn). Homewood, IL: Irwin. Chapter 15.

DAVID YORKE

**adaptive strategy** This is one of three strategic styles, the others being the ENTREPRENEURIAL and PLANNING, suggested by Mintzberg (1973). The adaptive mode is suited to large, often non-profit-oriented, organizations that will tend to be in the public sector. They do not have unambiguous goals and there are many different interest groups within the organization, each with their own objectives and agenda. Consequently, strategy often emerges through a process of bargaining and consensus-seeking, similar to that identified by Cyert & March (1963). This approach to strategy formation can be contrasted with the entrepreneurial style of bold decision-making. This is generally a feature of small organizations dominated by the owner-manager. However, such a perspective ignores research (e.g., Golby & Johns, 1971) suggesting that many small firms tend to be rather conservative, with their owners preferring to ensure continued control rather than engaging in taking significant risks with a view to securing significant growth. Large firms, particularly those with a dominant chief executive, may also engage in entrepreneurial strategy formation. Finally, the planning mode is the traditional approach to STRATEGIC PLANNING and tends to be suited to large, bureaucratic, organizations operating in relatively stable environments with the resources to afford the detailed analysis such an approach requires.

### Bibliography

Cyert, R. M. & March, J. G. (1963). *A behavioral theory of the firm.* Englewood Cliffs, NJ: Prentice-Hall.
Golby, C. W. & Johns, G. (1971). *Attitude and motivation.* Bolton Committee Research Report # 7.
Mintzberg, H. (1973). Strategy making in three modes. *California Management Review,* **16**, (2), Winter, 44–53.

DALE LITTLER

**adoption process** The consumer adoption process is a micro process and focuses on the "mental process through which an individual consumer passes from first hearing about an innovation, to final adoption," i.e., the consumer goes through a series of stages of acceptance in the process of adopting a new idea.

Rogers (1983) defines these stages as the following: Awareness: the consumer is exposed to a product innovation, is cognizant of it, but lacks information about it. Interest: the consumer is stimulated to seek information about an innovation. Evaluation: the consumer considers whether or not it would make sense to try the innovation, a "mental trial." Trial: the consumer tries the innovation on a small scale, if possible, to improve his/her estimate of the product's utility. Adoption/rejection: the consumer decides to make full/regular use of the product.

An alternative model, offered by Robertson (1971), the "acceptance process," has stages of problem recognition, awareness, comprehension, attitude formation, legitimation/conviction, trial, and adoption. This model focuses on the use of particular information sources at the various stages. Typically, impersonal sources (e.g., MASS MEDIA) have most value in creating initial product awareness, and INTERPERSONAL COMMUNICATIONS have most value at the later, evaluative, stages.

Time pervades the adoption process in relation to: the time from awareness of a new product to purchase (for an individual consumer or household); the identification of adopter categories; and rate of adoption. With respect to adopter categories, Rogers (1983) assumed a normally distributed adopter pattern of: innovators, early adopters, early majority, late majority, and laggards. Rate of adoption refers to how quickly a product innovation is accepted by those who will adopt it; for example mobile telephones and video recorders have been adopted much more quickly than dishwashers and electric toothbrushes.

The adoption process is affected by product characteristics (see DIFFUSION PROCESS) and by consumer variables. With respect to consumer variables, a number of researchers have tried to profile early adopters and consumer innovators in relation to: demographic and socioeconomic factors, personality traits, perceptions of risk, product interest, consumption characteristics, media habits, and opinion leadership, but have found varying conclusions.

### Bibliography

Engel, J. F., Blackwell, R. D. & Miniard, P. W. (1990). *Consumer behaviour* (6th edn). Orlando, FL: The Dryden Press. Chapter 23.

Robertson, T. R. (1971). *Innovative behaviour and communication.* New York: Holt, Rinehart & Winston.

Rogers, E. M. (1976). New product adoption and diffusion. *Journal of Consumer Research*, 2, March.

Rogers, E. M. (1983). *Diffusion of innovations* (3rd edn). New York: Free Press.

Rogers, E. M & Shoemaker, F. L. (1971). *Communication of innovations* (2nd edn). New York: Free Press.

Schiffman, L. G. & Kanuk, L. Z. (1991). *Consumer behaviour* (4th edn). Prentice-Hall. Chapter 18.

BARBARA LEWIS

**advertisement**  *see* ADVERTISING

**advertising**  Advertising is a paid form of non-personal presentation and communication about an organization and/or its goods and services, by an identified sponsor, that is transmitted to a target audience through a mass medium.

Advertising is a one-way communication from an organization to a customer and is subject to the consumer selective processes of: exposure, perception, selection, distortion, and retention (*see* CONSUMER PERCEPTIONS, SELECTIVE EXPOSURE, and SELECTIVE RETENTION), i.e., the audience is not obligated to be attentive or respond, which in turn depends on: consumer attributes, needs and values, predispositions, characteristics of the company and its messages, and channels of communications. Key features of advertising are: its public presentation, which confers a legitimacy; its persuasive nature, which is possible through repetition; and its expressive nature in so far as it dramatizes a company and its products or services.

Advertising is an integral element of an organization's MARKETING COMMUNICATIONS (*see also* COMMUNICATIONS MIX). It may be planned and executed within an organization or handed over to specialists, i.e., advertising agencies (*see* AGENCY). Advertising is an industry in its own right although it employs relatively few people, the major expenditures being for media time and space.

The major stages in the development of an organization's advertising are: setting advertising objectives; deciding on the budget; planning messages; selecting the media; and evaluating advertising effectiveness.

Advertising objectives flow from prior decisions on an organization's target MARKET (or segments; (see MARKET SEGMENTATION), market POSITIONING and MARKETING MIX and are various (e.g., Colley (1961) lists 52 possible objectives). They are concerned with informing, persuading and reminding current and potential buyers/customers/consumers, including other organizations in the DISTRIBUTION chain, with respect to products, and organizations/institutions (see also COMMUNICATIONS OBJECTIVES). Product and brand advertising is typically focused on generating or defending sales whereas institutional advertising is usually concerned with promoting an organization's image or reputation, developing goodwill, or improving a company's relationships with various groups to include customers, channels (of distribution) members, suppliers, shareholders, employees, and the general public.

In setting the advertising budget, organizations may take account of factors such as stage in the PRODUCT LIFE CYCLE, MARKET SHARE and customer base, competition, advertising frequency, and product substitutability. These and other variables are built into advertising expenditure models which, as a result of developing computer technology, are becoming increasingly complex. The advertising budget can be established on the basis of what is affordable, as a percentage of sales, on the basis of competitors' expenditures, on the basis of objectives and tasks.

Advertising messages represent the creative aspect of advertising (see MESSAGE) and organizations are concerned with developing messages, evaluating and selecting among them, and executing them effectively.

In deciding on advertising media, it is necessary to take account of the desired REACH, FREQUENCY, and IMPACT; choose among the major media types and vehicles; and decide on media timing.

The choice of media types is influenced by considerations such as the product/service being advertised, target audience media habits, the advantages and limitations of the media, and their costs. Advertising media comprise: TELEVISION, RADIO, NEWSPAPERS, MAGAZINES, TRADE JOURNALS, POSTERS (BILLBOARDS), and DIRECT MAIL. They are distinguished from other forms of communication (see MARKETING COMMUNICATIONS and COMMUNICATIONS MIX), e.g., PUBLICITY, because the time and/or space has to be paid for.

Developing of advertising messages and choice of media is influenced, in part, by product sensitivity and advertising controls. For example, companies need to be aware of the sensitive nature of advertising alcohol and tobacco, the misuse of which may contribute to health and social problems. Advertising controls embrace government (legal) regulations and self-regulation. Various legal statutes impinge on advertising, e.g., the Trades Descriptions Act, the Medicines Act, food and drug labeling requirements, consumer credit regulations, together with restrictions with respect to the advertising of alcohol, tobacco, medicines, professional services, etc. Examples of industry self-regulation may be seen in various CODES OF PRACTICE, the Advertising Standards Authority, and the television advertising standards authorities.

The effectiveness of advertisements may be assessed in two major ways: pre-testing adverts (e.g., copy testing) and post-evaluating their effectiveness (e.g., recall and recognition tests). Advertisers also try to measure the communications effects on awareness, knowledge, preferences, and sales, although it is accepted that relationships between advertising and sales are not necessarily causal due to: the influence of other variables in the marketing mix; competitors' activities; and sales effects over time, e.g., adverts may not be seen immediately, impact may be later, there may be carry-over effects, or sales may be brought forward at the expense of future sales.

### Bibliography

Colley, R. H. (1961). *Defining advertising goals for measured advertising results*. New York: Association of National Advertisers.

Dibb, S., Simkin, L., Pride, W. M. & Ferrell, O. C. (1994). *Marketing concepts and strategies* (European edn). London: Houghton Mifflin Co. Chapter 15.

Kotler, P. (1994). *Marketing management: Analysis, planning, implementation and control* (8th edn). Englewood Cliffs, NJ: Prentice-Hall. Chapter 23.

BARBARA LEWIS

**advertising agency**   *see* AGENCY

**affective stage**   MARKETING COMMUNICA-TIONS models, which state that a target buyer or customer moves along a spectrum from a state of ignorance or unawareness of an organization and/or its products or services to ultimately making a purchase, comprise three principal stages, namely, the COGNITIVE, affective, and CONATIVE (or behavioral).

The affective stage is that which attempts to create a preference for one product, brand, or service in the target buyer's or customer's mind, in relation to all others. In other words, communications at the affective stage are designed to develop, maintain, and reinforce positive attitudes in the mind of the target buyer, customer, or consumer. Investment of resources of time and money in attaining such an objective can be huge, but there is plenty of research evidence to support the notion that it can be achieved, e.g., Volvo is synonymous in many people's minds with security or safety, after spending millions of financial resource and many man-hours both on developing and testing safety features in their cars and also on telling potential customers that they have effectively done so. Currently, major organizations are seemingly attempting to show that they are "environmentally-conscious," i.e., that their concern for reducing the erosion of the Earth's resources is reflected in their product or service offerings.

**Bibliography**

Kotler, P. (1994). *Marketing management: Analysis, planning, implementation and control* (8th edn). Englewood Cliffs, NJ: Prentice-Hall. Chapter 22.

DAVID YORKE

**agency**   An organization can develop its own ADVERTISING and promotional (*see* PROMO-TION) skills or use those of an agency, either in-house, which is owned and controlled by the parent company, or one that is independent. Cost is a major consideration but other factors, such as generating an external perspective and the facility to offer a complete range of services from market research to distribution, may play a role in the client–agency relationship.

Advertising agencies vary, both in size and in expertise. Some are international, others local, some specialize in e.g., BUSINESS-TO-BUSINESS MARKETING, RETAILING, fashion, or finance, others handle a variety of accounts.

Traditionally, agencies have not been considered to be highly business-oriented, preferring to offer creativity without the corresponding and complementary cost-effectiveness. More clients, as a result of greater competition in their own markets, are now seeking a more measurable return for the resources spent by their agencies.

Typically, an agency is organized into three functions, namely, client services (each client has an account manager), creative services (responsible for design and production), and marketing services (market research and media buying). Specialist agencies exist for media ADVERTISING, SALES PROMOTION, PUBLIC RELATIONS, and PACKAGING.

**Bibliography**

Crosier, K. (1994). In M. J. Baker (Ed.), *The marketing book*. Oxford: Butterworth–Heinemann. Chapter 21.

Institute of Practitioners in Advertising (1986). *Some suggested provisions for use in agency/client agreements*. London.

McCarthy, E. J. & Perreault, W. D. (1993). *Basic marketing* (11th edn). Homewood, IL: Irwin. Chapter 17.

DAVID YORKE

**Aida model**   This is one of a number of models of MARKETING COMMUNICATIONS which show how a targeted buyer or customer progresses from a state of unawareness of a product or service to purchase of it. The Aida model is an acronym for: Attention → Interest → Desire →Action.

The first term relates to the COGNITIVE STAGE of the process, indicating a need for the marketing communicator to gain the receiver's ATTENTION before attempting to do anything else. Developing INTEREST and desire (to purchase) are elements in the AFFECTIVE STAGE, i.e., where positive attitudes toward and preference for the product or service are sought. ACTION is the CONATIVE STAGE (the purchase).

Measures taken before and after a form of communication is used will enable objective(s) to be set and the success of it to be analyzed. Progression logically through the stages is not always possible – indeed much depends on the product or service being offered and the target groups of receivers.

*See also* **Communications objectives**

**Bibliography**

Cox, K. K. & Enis, B. M. (1972). *The marketing research process.* Pacific Palisades, CA: Goodyear Publishing Co., Inc.

Kotler, P. (1994). *Marketing management: Analysis, planning, implementation and control* (8th edn). Englewood Cliffs, NJ: Prentice-Hall. Chapter 22.

Strong, E. K. (1925). *The psychology of selling.* New York: McGraw-Hill.

DAVID YORKE

**AIOs (activities, interests, and opinions)** *see* LIFESTYLES

**atmospherics**   "Atmospherics is the tailoring of the designed environment to enhance the likelihood of desired effects or outcomes in users" (Greenland & McGoldrick, 1994). Other definitions focus upon the more subtle design effects that influence consumers at an almost subconscious level: "Atmospherics – the design of an environment via visual communications, lighting, colors, music and scent to stimulate customers' perceptual and emotional responses and ultimately affect their purchase behavior" (Levy & Weitz, 1995).

The term was coined by Kotler (1973) in relation to a retail environment's contribution to its buyer's or customer's purchasing propensity.

It is, however, relevant to a broad spectrum of product retailing and service environments and is an important consideration in both staff, as well as customer, management. Effective use of atmospherics can enhance a retail outlet's designed environment, improving staff satisfaction and performance levels, as well as stimulating favorable reactions and behavior in customers. Such favorable outcomes might include a propensity for customers to spend more time in the store and improvements in levels of impulse purchasing, store patronage, and image.

*See also* **Impulse purchasing; Store design**

**Bibliography**

Greenland, S. J. (1994). The branch environment.In P. J. McGoldrick, & S. J. Greenland (Eds), *Retailing of financial services* (pp. 163–196). Maidenhead: McGraw-Hill.

Greenland, S. J. & McGoldrick, P. J. (1994). Atmospherics, attitudes and behaviour: modelling the impact of designed space. *The International Review of Retail, Distribution and Consumer Research*, **4** (1), 1–16.

Kotler, P. (1973). Atmospherics as a marketing tool. *Journal of Marketing Research*, **49** (4), 48–64.

Levy, M. & Weitz, B. A. (1995). *Retailing management.* Chicago: Irwin.

STEVE GREENLAND

**attention**   Attention is the first stage in the AIDA MODEL of MARKETING COMMUNICATIONS. Depending upon the channel of communication used, various stimuli may be used to gain attention, e.g., in the broadcast media, the first five seconds may need something emotionally appealing; in print media, the use of a dramatic headline or the use of color may have a positive effect; in PERSONAL SELLING, appearance; or in TELEMARKETING, the initial verbal contact may be important.

Cost-effectiveness is vital in gaining attention. Broadly, less personal forms of communication such as media ADVERTISING are more cost-effective at this stage, although personal selling and telemarketing may be of use with higher value products or services.

**Bibliography**

Kotler, P. (1994). *Marketing management: Analysis, planning, implementation and control* (8th edn). Englewood Cliffs, NJ: Prentice-Hall. Chapter 22.

Strong, E. K. (1925). *The psychology of selling.* New York: McGraw-Hill.

DAVID YORKE

**attitudes**   *see* CONSUMER ATTITUDES

**awareness**   Awareness is the first step in the DAGMAR, HIERARCHY OF EFFECTS, and INNOVATION-ADOPTION models of MARKETING COMMUNICATIONS which focus on the consumer purchasing process. At this initial stage in the buying process, the potential customer/buyer is made aware of the existence of the product, service, or organization supplying it. Various stimuli may be used to create awareness in the buyer's or customer's mind, depending on the channels of communication used (*see* COMMUNICATIONS MIX). Awareness is sometimes difficult to achieve due to the consumer's selective processes (*see* SELECTIVE EXPOSURE and CONSUMER PERCEPTIONS).

**Bibliography**

Colley, R. H. (1961). *Defining advertising goals for measured advertising results.* New York: Association of Advertising.

Kotler, P. (1994). *Marketing management: Analysis, planning, implementation and control* (8th edn). Englewood Cliffs, NJ: Prentice-Hall. Chapter 22.

Lavidge, R. J. & Steiner, G. A. (1961). A model for predictive measurements of advertising effectiveness. *Journal of Marketing,* 25, Oct., 61.

Rogers, E. M. (1962). *Diffusion of innovations.* New York: Free Press.

DAVID YORKE

# B

**BCG matrix** The BCG matrix, as its name implies, is the eponymous technique developed by the Boston Consultancy Group, that gained popularity in the 1970s. It was advanced as a technique for assisting companies to analyze their diverse business portfolios. It is based on two major premises. The first relates to what the BCG terms the experience curve effect by which the total costs involved in manufacturing, distributing, and selling a product decline with increased experience in production. The experience is a composite of economies of scale and specialization; the modifications to or redesign of products to obtain lower costs; productivity improvements from technological change and/or learning effects leading to the adoption of new production methods; and the displacement of less efficient factors of production. The effects of experience can be depicted by plotting real unit cost against cumulative production volume as a measure of accumulated experience. If logarithmic scales are used then a straight line is normally obtained. In fact, the Boston Consultancy Group argued that real unit costs fall by 20 to 30 percent for each doubling of cumulative experience. The implication, then, is that businesses should focus on securing high volume, and therefore high MARKET SHARE, through aggressive pricing. The second premise is that the consumption of resources, in particular cash, is a direct function of market growth. BCG developed a four-box matrix (*see* figure 1) with market growth and market share relative to that of the next largest competitor (since this is the true indicator of COMPETITIVE ADVANTAGE) as the two parameters. Each is measured as "high" or "low." Businesses can then be categorized according to whether or not they are "stars" (high market growth, low relative market share); "cash cows" (low growth,

high share); "problem children" (high growth, low share); or "dogs" (low growth, low share). The cash cows should have lower costs than their rivals and demand comparatively lower investment. They therefore generate cash which can be employed to convert some of the "question marks" into "stars" which are essentially cash neutral. The stars of today should become the cash cows of the future. Generally, it is argued that the deletion of the "dogs" should be seriously considered.

### Relative market share

| Market Growth | High | Low |
|---|---|---|
| High | Stars | Problem Children |
| Low | Cash cows | Dogs |

*Figure 1    The BCG Matrix*

The technique has been extensively reviewed and apparently accepted, probably because of its simplicity and easy comprehensibility. However, there have been many criticisms. There may be problems in defining "market" and hence "market share"; the measures of "high" and "low" are subjective and easily manipulatable; the possibilities of external financing are excluded from the analysis; and the influence of NON-PRICE FACTORS on demand tends to be ignored. Moreover, the approach is overly deterministic and the acceptance of its prescriptions could lead to suboptimum and even significantly inappropriate decisions. For example, so-called "dog" businesses might have cost and demand interrelationships with other businesses, and to delete these, as the analysis implies, could have adverse consequences for businesses at present in more attractive quadrants.

In general, the analysis rests on the assumption that businesses' products have a life cycle (*see* PRODUCT LIFE CYCLE), of which, in particular, the "mature" stage is of sufficient duration to enable the company to reap the benefits of its previous investments in current "cash cows." The industry might, however, witness the introduction of a new technology which might give a "groin kick" to the technology of the future cash cow, thereby undermining its future market position. The emphasis on market share can blinker decision-makers to such a possibility and perhaps further the dependence on a vulnerable industry, while rivals may leapfrog the firm by acquiring experience through the purchase of plant and equipment which embody state-of-the-art technology. Finally, cash cows may require considerable investment in order to protect their competitiveness, a fact which the analysis seems to overlook somewhat.

**Bibliography**

Hedley, B. (1976a). A fundamental approach to strategy development. *Long Range Planning*, **9**, (6), 2–11.

Hedley, B. (1976b). Strategy and the "business portfolio". *Long Range Planning*, **10**, (1), 9–15.

Wensley, R. (1981). Strategic marketing: Betas, boxes or basics. *Journal of Marketing*, **45**, 173–182.

DALE LITTLER

**bidding**   Bidding or tendering is a process in which potential suppliers are invited to submit bids or tenders in which they set out their specifications, terms and prices in response to a stated customer requirement. How to decide the price aspect of a bid or tender is made even more awkward by the UNCERTAINTY surrounding rival bids and the need to balance the wish to make a profit (or even just to cover costs) against the wish to secure the contract. Because price is only one aspect (if often the most important) of the bid or tender, the successful bidder will not always be that offering the lowest price, though evidence of a lower bid may be used to renegotiate the price offered by the eventual contractor.

There are several variants of tendering, especially auction bidding and sealed-bid pricing which is used in organizational markets (and Scottish real estate markets). These techniques for soliciting prices have the effect of orienting price decisions more toward competitive issues than toward issues of cost or demand.

There are several advantages to competitive bidding or tendering for the customer: it can help to remove many possibilities for corrupt or unethical practices; it provides important competitive information where this might otherwise be difficult to gather; it helps to ensure value for money and cost minimization; and it provides insight to the costs associated with differences in the terms of the contract (e.g., in delivery arrangements, quality levels, service provision). Because of its apparent efficiency and probity, competitive bidding or tendering is increasingly being used in large-scale tenders where price is a major purchase constraint and/or where it is important to ensure that processes are seen to be equitable and "aboveboard" (e.g., in central and local government purchasing, and in OUTSOURCING).

DOMINIC WILSON

**billboards**   *see* POSTERS

**bivariate analysis**   Bivariate analysis is concerned with the quantitative analysis of data where pairs of variables are analyzed together, usually to see if there is any relationship between the variables.

If both variables are measured on nominal (categorical) scales, CROSS-TABULATIONS (cross-tabs) can be used to summarize the sample data in the form of two or more frequency distributions. A cross-tab is a table with the categories (or values) for the two variables listed on the two axes and the counts of the number of times each pair of values occurs recorded in the cells of the table. The row and column totals are usually calculated and percentages across the rows and/or down the columns are also computed to aid in the interpretation, description, and discussion of the results. In principle, cross-tabs can be formed in more than two dimensions when data for more than two categorical variables are analyzed, but interpretation becomes difficult because the increased number of cells often leaves empty cells or a number of cells with small counts.

If both the variables are interval, the relationship between them can be studied, visually, using a scatter diagram and, numerically, using simple correlation and regression (*see* REGRESSION AND CORRELATION). The product-moment correlation coefficient measures the strength of a linear relationship between the variables: a value close to zero means no relationship or a very weak relationship; a value close to +1 means a very strong positive relationship; while a figure close to –1 means a very strong negative relationship. The regression analysis tells the form of the relationship, i.e., the way one variable affects the other is indicated by the straight line equation estimated using regression techniques.

If both variables are measured on ordinal scales, cross-tabs may be used to summarize the data. Alternatively, correlation coefficients such as Kendall's tau or Spearman's rank correlation coefficient indicate the strength of any relationship between the variables.

When the variables are measured on scales of different types, a range of possibilities arise. For instance, when one variable is measured on an interval scale and the other on a categorical scale, the sample can be broken down into subsamples using the categorical variable and the data for the interval variable can be summarized for each subsample using a frequency distribution, histogram, and/or measures of average and variation. Subsamples can be compared by looking at, for example, the histograms or measures of average of the interval variable to see if and how they change with different values of the categorical variable.

A range of hypothesis tests (*see* HYPOTHESIS TESTING) is available to see if there are any significant relationships between the variables. The appropriate test depends upon the type of measurement used for each variable. For instance, if both variables are measured on categorical scales, either the chi-square test or an exact test using the hyper-geometric distribution is likely to be used depending, among other things, on the size of the sample and the number of categories for each variable. If both variables are interval, the t-test and F-test are two examples involved in testing hypotheses related to simple correlation and regression. When one variable is interval and the other categorical, the t-test is used to test for the equality of arithmetic means of the interval variable when comparing just two subsamples defined by the categorical variable and the F-test is used when there are two or more subsamples. If one variable is measured on an ordinal scale and the other on a categorical scale, then tests such as the Mann-Whitney U test, the Wilcoxon test, the runs-of-signs test, the Kolmogorov-Smirnov two-sample test, the Kruskal-Wallis one-way ANOVA (analysis of variance) test, and the Friedman two-way ANOVA test are used, depending upon the circumstances. Many other tests are available for different sets of situations.

**Bibliography**

Tull, D. S. & Hawkins, D. I. (1987). *Marketing research: measurement and method* (4th edn). New York: Macmillan. Chapter 13.

MICHAEL GREATOREX

**brand** The original thinking behind branding was to take a commodity and to endow it with special characteristics through imaginative use of name, PACKAGING, and ADVERTISING. Aaker (1991) defines a brand as: "a distinguishing name and/or symbol (such as a logo, trademark, or package design) intended to identify the goods or services of either a seller or a group of sellers and to differentiate those goods or services from those of its competitors." Central to the value or equity of the brand is a set of assets, including: BRAND LOYALTY; brand awareness; perceived quality; and brand associations. A manufacturer brand is initiated by a producer, such as Coca Cola, and a private or "own-label" brand is initiated by a retailer, such as Tesco's "Value" product line (*see also* PRODUCT).

**Bibliography**

Aaker, D. A. (1991). *Managing brand equity – Capitalizing on the value of a brand name*. New York: Free Press. Chapter 1.
Macrae, C. (1991). *World class brands*. Reading, MA: Addison Wesley.

MARGARET BRUCE

**brand equity**   There has been increasing contemporary consideration of brand value or equity. This can be regarded as "the incremental cash flow resulting from a product with the brand name vs the cash flow which would result without the brand name". (Schoker & Weitz, 1988) Successful brands generally have a set of powerful associations attributed to them by customers that act to differentiate them clearly from competing products. These qualities embrace intangible factors which collectively form the image of the brand, as well as other aspects of the product, such as performance, which generally reinforce this general brand image.

It is generally argued that there has to be continued investment in the brand through advertising and product development to project and support the brand's values. The returns are in the form of higher margins that customers are prepared to pay for the particular benefits attributed to the brand and BRAND LOYALTY, the latter being especially important given the costs of replacing lost customers, and the additional revenues that can be obtained over the lifetime of existing customers through, for example, cross-selling of other products.

Some companies have attempted to value their brands but to date there has been no agreed methodology for including these values in companies' balance sheets. Firms often seem prepared to pay significant amounts to acquire brands, as the Nestle takeover of Rowntree seemed to indicate. However, in the acquisition of brands, the additional value paid for the perceived value of a brand is, under existing UK accounting practice, written off as "goodwill." Nevertheless, the value of the brand is being challenged. Friday April 2, 1993, which has gone down in history as "Marlboro Friday," appeared to be apocalyptic for the brand. Under pressure from cheaper "generic" cigarettes, Philip Morris reduced the price of Marlboro cigarettes by a fifth. In hindsight, the strategy appears to have been successful since Marlboro's market share and revenues have subsequently recovered. Commentators have argued that in this case, at least, Philip Morris had allowed the price differential between Marlboro and its competitors to increase beyond a level that consumers regarded as reasonable for the image that Marlboro had. Nevertheless, many

retailers market products under their own name which benefit from the perceived values associated with the retailer and which are generally offered at a lower price than manufacturers' brands. The power of manufacturers to influence the channel of distribution through their own brands which have influential customer franchises is being eroded and more manufacturers, in order to ensure continued volume of output, are being compelled to supply retailer branded merchandise.

**Bibliography**

Peters, T. (1988). *Thriving on chaos*. New York: Macmillan, as quoted in P. Doyle (1994). Branding. In M. J. Baker (Ed.), *The marketing book* (3rd edn). (pp. 471–483). Oxford: Butterworth Heinemann.

Schoker, A. & Weitz, B. (1988). A perspective on brand equity – principles and issues. In L. Leuthesser (Ed.), *Defining, measuring and managing brand equity: a conference summary*, (pp. 88–104). Cambridge, MA: Marketing Science Institute.

D. LITTLER

**brand image**   *see* BRAND LOYALTY

**brand loyalty**   Consideration of consumer buying behavior over a period of time involves an understanding of brand loyalty which follows from the formation of brand images and brand preferences.

BRAND IMAGE is a set of associations or perceptions that consumers have for a brand; it is awareness or recognition. It also implies attitudes toward a brand, either positive or negative, which are learned over time.

BRAND PREFERENCE is a definite expression of positive attitude. One would normally expect people to buy a preferred brand or brands, assuming that they are in the market for the product. However, there are occasions when the product may not be needed or the consumer cannot afford the preferred brand, or the preferred brand may not be available.

Brand loyalty implies purchasing the same brand more than once, again assuming that this is the preferred brand, although this may not necessarily be the case. Brand preference and brand loyalty may exist in relation to manufacturers' brands (e.g., Heinz) and distributors' brands (e.g., Safeway), and loyalty may prevail with respect to stores.

Definitions of brand loyalty have evolved and are typically concerned with a degree of consistency in the preference for each brand by a consumer, over a specified period of time. Some definitions also refer to "biased choice behavior" with respect to branded merchandise, or "consistent" purchasing of one brand, or the proportion of purchases a consumer (or household) devotes to the brand most often bought. There are inherent dangers in looking at sequences of purchases to define and measure loyalty as individuals and households may be buying more than one brand on a regular basis (e.g., toothpaste, breakfast cereals).

Further, Day (1970) offers a two-dimensional concept of brand loyalty, bringing together attitudes and behavior. He asks "Can behavior patterns be equated with preferences to infer loyalty?," and distinguishes between spurious and intentional loyalty. Spurious loyalty may just be habit or consistent purchase of one brand due to non-availability of others, continuous price deals, better shelf space, etc. Intentional loyalty occurs when consumers buy a preferred brand, as would be evidenced by some attitude measurement. When a consumer is intentionally loyal and insists on a particular brand, he or she will be prepared to shop around for this brand, or defer purchase if the brand is unavailable – rather than accept a substitute.

Research has been unable to pinpoint particular determinants of brand loyalty, though a number of empirical investigations have suggested and looked for relationships between brand loyalty and: personal attributes, e.g., socioeconomic variables; group influence; levels of demand; sensitivity to promotion; and store factors.

Nevertheless, manufacturers and distributors are concerned to encourage loyalty to their brands and switching away from other brands. Consumers switch brands for reasons of: curiosity with respect to new/different brands; disappointment with present brand; reassurance with respect to a favored brand; chance; inducement; and availability. Additionally, consumers may be multi-brand buyers for reasons of: indifference; perception that brands are perfect substitutes; for variety's sake; several preferences within a household; and as a response to availability and promotions.

### Bibliography

Carmen, J. M. (1970). Correlates of brand loyalty: Some positive results. *Journal of Marketing Research*, 7, Feb., 67–76.

Day, G. S. (1970). *Buyer attitudes and brand choice behavior*. Chicago: Free Press.

Jacoby, J. & Chestnut R. (1978). *Brand loyalty: Measurement and management*. New York: Ronald/ John Wiley.

BARBARA LEWIS

**brand managers**  *see* MARKETING ORGANIZATION

**brand preference**  *see* BRAND LOYALTY

**branding**  *see* BRAND

**break-even analysis**  A break-even analysis is meant to identify the break-even point, i.e., the point in time at which the sum of fixed (or "indirect") costs and variable (or "direct") costs involved in the production and distribution of a good or service is matched by the sum of its accumulated sales. The break-even point can be calculated by using the following formula:

break-even point = fixed cost/(price − variable cost)

Beyond this break-even point the profitability of the good or service will be a function of the excess of sales revenues over variable costs. Break-even analysis is an important aspect of PRICING calculations in that it can help to show the profitability of a product over time according to different assumptions about price, demand, and the allocation of costs (many costs, especially fixed costs, will be shared by several products and allocation can be problematic). The difficulty of anticipating demand response to different pricing policies emphasizes the importance of undertaking extensive break-even analysis for different assumptions.

DOMINIC WILSON

**business-to-business marketing**  Business-to-business marketing refers to the marketing of products and services to organizations rather than to households or ultimate consumers. The implied alternative is CONSUMER MARKETING, although the distinction between the two areas is not entirely clear-cut (*see* CONSUMER MARKETING). Business-to-business marketing has also been termed variously: industrial marketing, commercial marketing, institutional marketing and ORGANIZATIONAL MARKETING.

Although many of the same products will be bought by both business and consumers, it is possible to identify a number of ways in which the emphasis of business-to-business marketing differs from that of consumer marketing and this is reflected in the large volume of literature and research programs devoted exclusively to the business-to-business marketing area (Chisnall, 1989; Gross et al., 1993; Reeder et al., 1991; Webster, 1991). These differences are seen to have considerable implications for the manner in which business-to-business marketing is undertaken.

Market structure is the first of these, with business markets tending to have a greater concentration of both buyers and sellers in comparison to consumer markets. Derived demand is another feature, with the demand for business products and services said to be dependent to an extent on the level of activity the buying organization generates in its own markets, although this will clearly not always be the case. The scale of business purchases is often seen as greater than that for consumers and products are generally held to be more technologically complex although both of these factors are relative and something of broad generalizations (Chisnall, 1989).

The manner in which purchase decisions are made is another area in which businesses are said to differ from consumers. Many organizations employ professional purchasers, or have a purchasing department, although it has been noted that the purchasing department is often not the most powerful influence on supplier choice (Webster & Wind, 1972). Purchases are generally made not for self-gratification but to achieve organizational objectives and are therefore often held to be based more on "rational," "economic," or "task" considerations, such as price, quality, and delivery criteria, than the purchases of individual consumers. Some authors assert that the "rational" nature of business buying behavior has been overemphasized. Chisnall (1989), for instance, refers to the influence of "non-task" factors such as motivation, personal values, or political, social, and cultural influences, as important in business purchase decisions. However, it is widely recognized that business buying is more likely than consumer buying to be guided, at least, by formalized rules, evaluation criteria, or procedures.

Business purchase decisions are also typically seen as a more complex process than those of consumers, involving several people, frequently from different departments. A pioneer study in 1958, for example, showed that in 106 industrial firms three or more persons influenced buying processes in over 75 percent of companies studied (*see* Alexander et al., 1961). A number of researchers have studied the concept of the BUYING CENTER, i.e., all organizational members involved in the buying decision, and have noted that this is likely to vary considerably according to the purchasing situation (*see* for instance, Robinson et al., 1967; Johnston & Bonoma, 1981). Various different organizational purchasing roles have been identified by Webster & Wind (1972), some or all of which may be played by individuals in the buying center. These include "users" of the product or service in question; "gatekeepers," who control information to be received by other members of the buying center; "deciders," who actually make the purchase decision, whether or not they have the formal authority to do so; and "buyers," those who do have formal authority for supplier selection, but whose influence is often usurped by more powerful members of the buying center (*see also* ORGANIZATIONAL BUYING BEHAVIOR).

Finally, and perhaps most importantly, the importance of long-term, relatively stable relationships between buyers and sellers has been emphasized, with extensive work conducted by researchers involved in the International Marketing and Purchasing (IMP) Group (Håkansson, 1982 & 1987; Ford, 1990). This recognition has led to the development of the INTERACTION and NETWORK approaches to business-to-business marketing, where the role of MARKETING MANAGEMENT is seen in terms of the management of a range of individual buyer–seller relationships in the context of a broader network of interconnected supplier, buyer, and competitor organizations.

The various differences in emphasis between business-to-business marketing and consumer marketing have led to attempts to develop the scope of the MARKETING CONCEPT and to reappraise such marketing tools as the MARKETING MIX, which is seen as inappropriate in its traditional form.

*See also* **Marketing; Marketing concept; Marketing management; Marketing mix; Relationship marketing**

**Bibliography**

Alexander, R. S., Cross, J. S. & Cunningham, R. M. (1961). *Industrial marketing.* Homewood, IL: Irwin.
Chisnall, P. M. (1989). *Strategic industrial marketing* (2nd edn). Prentice-Hall.
Ford, D. (Ed.) (1990). *Understanding business markets: Interaction, relationships, networks.* London: Academic Press.
Gross, A. C., Banting, P. M., Meredith, L. N. & Ford, I. D. (1993). *Business marketing.* Boston: Houghton Mifflin Co.
Håkansson, H. (Ed.) (1982). *International marketing and purchasing of industrial goods: An interaction approach.* Chichester: John Wiley.
Håkansson, H. (Ed.) (1987). *Industrial technological development: A network approach.* London: Croom Helm.
Johnston, W. J. & Bonoma, T. V. (1981). The buying center: Structure and interaction patterns. *Journal of Marketing*, 45, Summer, 143–156.
Reeder, R. R., Brierty, E. G. & Reeder, B. H. (1991). *Industrial marketing* (2nd edn). Englewood Cliffs, NJ: Prentice-Hall.
Robinson, P. J., Faris, C. W. & Wind, Y. (1967). *Industrial buying and creative marketing.* Boston: Allyn & Bacon Inc.
Webster, F. E. Jr (1991). *Industrial marketing strategy* (3rd edn). New York: John Wiley.
Webster, F. E. Jr & Wind, Y. (1972). *Organizational buying behavior.* Englewood Cliffs, NJ: Prentice-Hall.

FIONA LEVERICK

**buy-feel-learn model**  The buy-feel-learn model in MARKETING COMMUNICATIONS suggests that in some situations buyers/customers do not follow the logical LEARN-FEEL-BUY sequence. The BFL model typically applies to IMPULSE PURCHASING and/or for new brands, where attitudes, knowledge, and liking/preference are developed after purchase rather than prior to it.

*See also* **Feel-buy-learn model; Learn-feel-buy model**

**Bibliography**

Dickson, P. R. (1994). *Marketing management* (international edn). Fort Worth: The Dryden Press. Chapter 12.
Kotler, P. (1994). *Marketing management: Analysis, planning, implementation and control* (8th edn). Englewood Cliffs, NJ: Prentice-Hall, p. 602.

DAVID YORKE

**buyer behavior models**  Parallel to the development of thought about the variables that are important in understanding CONSUMER BUYER BEHAVIOR have been attempts to organize the variables into models of the buying process and consumer behavior. The purpose of such models is to try to understand the buying process and aid market research. Models serve to simplify, organize, and formalize the range of influences which affect purchase decisions, and try to show the extent of interaction between influencing variables. Some models are descriptive and others decision models.

Descriptive models are designed to communicate, explain, and predict. They may postulate at a macro level some variables and the relationships between them (e.g., sales, income, price, advertising); or, at a micro-level, consider more detailed links between a variable and its determinants (e.g., the effect of advertising on sales). In addition, a model at a micro-behavioral level may create hypothetical consumers and dealers who interact – with resulting behavior patterns being investigated. The well-known, available, models of consumer buyer behavior are descriptive and include those of Howard & Sheth (1969), Nicosia (1966), Andreasen (1965),

Engel, and Kollat & Blackwell (*see* Engel et al., 1993)

The Howard and Sheth model is concerned with individual decision-making and has its roots in stimulus-response learning theory (*see* CONSUMER LEARNING). The focus is on repeat buying, and therefore the model incorporates the dynamics of purchase behavior over time. The model has four central parts: inputs or stimulus variables to include products and social factors; perceptual and learning constructs; output response variables; and exogenous variables to include environment, financial status, and culture. From these elements, it is possible to consider the impact of decision mediators in consumer motivations and brand choice decisions.

Nicosia's model is also focused on individual consumers' decision-making and considers the relation between a firm and its potential customers with respect to a new product. He used computer simulation techniques to explain the structure of consumer decision-making. The consumer starts off with no experience of the product, and from exposure to the environment and the company's marketing effort forms predispositions, attitudes, and motivations which lead, via information search and evaluation, to purchase.

Andreasen's model is a general one based on specific conceptions about attitude formation and change; the key to change being exposure to information, either voluntary or involuntary.

Engel, Kollat, & Blackwell focus on motivation, perception, and learning in the buying decision process and their model has elements such as a central control unit, information processing, decision process, and environmental influences.

In addition to these descriptive models are others which are also predictive, e.g., stochastic learning models and queuing models. Stochastic learning models contain probabilistic elements and consider buying over time, usually purchases of brands in a product category. The basic approach is that an individual consumer learns from past behavior and the degree of satisfaction will influence future purchases. Also, more recent buying experiences with a particular brand/product will have greater effect than those which took place at a more distant time. These models analyze the relative purchase frequencies of brands in a product category and estimate the probabilities of switching brands on the next purchase. If such probabilities are assumed to be constant then market shares, for the future, can be computed.

Finally, with regard to decision models: these have been designed to evaluate the outcomes from different decisions, and they include optimization models to find a best solution, and heuristic ones which use rules of thumb to find reasonably good solutions. They incorporate - differential calculus, mathematical programing, statistical decision theory, and game theory.

### Bibliography

Andreasen, A. R. (1965). Attitudes and consumer behavior: A decision model. In L. Preston (Ed.), *New research in marketing*, (pp. 1–16). Berkeley: Institute for Business and Economic Research, University of California.

Bettman, J. R. (1979). *An information processing theory of consumer choice*. Reading, MA: Addison Wesley.

Engel, J. F., Blackwell, R. D. & Miniard, P. W. (1993). *Consumer behavior* (7th edn). New York: The Dryden Press.

Howard, J. A. & Sheth J. N. (1969). *The theory of buyer behavior*. New York: John Wiley.

Loudon, D. L. & Della Bitta, A. J. (1993). *Consumer behavior* (4th edn). McGraw-Hill Int. Chapter 19.

Nicosia, F. M. (1966). *Consumer decision processes*. Englewood Cliffs, NJ: Prentice-Hall.

Schiffman, L. G. & Kanuk, L. Z. (1991). *Consumer behavior* (4th edn). Prentice-Hall. Chapter 20.

Sheth, J. N. (Ed.) (1974). *Models of consumer behavior*. New York: Harper & Row.

BARBARA LEWIS

**buyer behavior theories**   As the discipline of consumer behavior has developed, various theories have contributed to understanding behavior. These include economic theory. Economists were the first professional group to offer a theory of buyer behavior. The Marshallian theory holds that consumer purchasing decisions are largely the result of "rational" and conscious economic calculations, i.e., the individual seeks to spend his or her income on goods that will deliver the most likely utility (satisfaction) according to his or her tastes and relative prices.

This model assumes that consumers derive satisfaction from consumption (probably not the case with expenditure on insurances, dental treatment, etc.) and seek to maximize satisfaction within the limits of income. The model also assumes that consumers have complete information with respect to supply, demand, and prices; complete mobility, i.e., can reach any market offer at any time; and that there is pure competition. In practice, consumers typically are not aware of and cannot judge all product offerings and may have restricted access. Consequently, consumers may well be "satisficing" rather than "maximizing" their utility.

Economic theory does have a role to play in understanding consumer behavior, in so far as people may be "problem solvers," trying to make rational and efficient spending decisions. However, it is also necessary to consider and understand the marketing and other stimuli that impact on buyer behavior (see CONSUMER BUYER BEHAVIOR), together with buyers' individual characteristics, i.e., to take account of various social and psychological influences on buying behavior.

### Bibliography

Katona, G. (1953). Rational behaviour and economic behaviour. *Psychological Review*, Sept., 307–318.

Kotler, P. (1965). Behavioural models for analysing buyers. *Journal of Marketing*, **29**, Nov., 37–45.

Loudon, D. L. & Della Bitta, A. J. (1993). *Consumer behavior* (4th edn). McGraw-Hill Int. Chapter 19.

Schewe, C. D. (1973). Selected social psychological models for analysing buyers. *Journal of Marketing*, **37**, July, 31–39.

BARBARA LEWIS

**buyers** Buyers are those individuals administering the purchasing policies and practices of an organization. At its best, buying is a professional activity with specialist qualifications and professional bodies, but buying can also be undertaken much more informally (especially perhaps in smaller organizations) and with little specialist expertise. Buyers are also important members of the DECISION-MAKING UNIT (DMU) where they provide much of the background information and analysis. Perhaps the most important (and most often overlooked) role of buyers is in managing the day-to-day relationship between an organization and its suppliers (see ORGANIZATIONAL BUYING BEHAVIOR; PURCHASING PROCESS).

DOMINIC WILSON

**buygrid model** *see* PURCHASING PROCESS

**buying center** In the 1960s and 1970s several surveys of industry purchasing practices in the UK and the USA established, inter alia, that industrial PURCHASING decisions involved many individuals from different functions within an organization in what is now generally referred to as a buying center or decision-making unit (DMU). Webster & Wind identified five buying "roles" within the context of this buying center: USERS, INFLUENCERS, BUYERS, DECIDERS, and GATEKEEPERS (Webster & Wind, 1972). This classification is now widely accepted as a general model though additional roles may be identifiable on closer examination of specific instances. The various roles discernible within the buying center may sometimes be fulfilled by only one or two individuals, while on other occasions these roles may be allocated to different individuals, departments and levels of seniority, according to the circumstances of each purchase. With the development of more collaborative approaches to inter-organizational marketing, such as PARTNERSHIP SOURCING, it seems reasonable to extend the membership of the buying center, on occasion, to include representatives of SUPPLIERS.

Further studies have suggested that the composition of the buying center and the influence of these departments and functions on any particular purchase occasion may vary according to such variables as: buy class (a NEW TASK generally requires a broader membership of the buying center than does a MODIFIED or STRAIGHT RE-BUY); the specific purchase criteria and their relative importance (e.g., an emphasis on technical specifications may require additional technical representation in the buying center); phase of the buying cycle; the complexity of the product/service under consideration; the competitive and strategic significance of the purchase; the cost of the purchase over its useful life; the relevance of the purchase to different departments within the organization; and the cultural attitude of the organization to PERCEIVED RISK. It has also been suggested that the political and cultural "pecking order" of departments and individuals within an organization can be an important variable, allowing some individuals to have considerable influence over purchasing decisions outside their functional areas of responsibility (Pettigrew, 1975; Strauss, 1964).

### Bibliography

Pettigrew, A. M. (1975). The industrial purchasing decision as a political process. *European Journal of Marketing*, 5, Feb., 4–19.

Strauss, G. (1964). Work-flow frictions, inter-functional rivalry and professionalism: A case study of purchasing agents. *Human Organisations*, 23 (1), 137–149.

Webster, F. E. Jr & Wind, Y. (1972). *Organizational buying behavior*. Englewood Cliffs, NJ: Prentice-Hall.

DOMINIC WILSON

**buying operations**  *see*  CONSUMER DECISION-MAKING PROCESS

**buying process**  *see*  PURCHASING PROCESS

# C

**call planning** PERSONAL SELLING (by representatives from supplier organizations to customers) is considered a vital element in the marketing COMMUNICATIONS MIX. However, it is extremely expensive and increasingly so. Cost-effectiveness of the personal selling effort, i.e., making more productive use of salespersons' time, will be enhanced if the schedule for calling on customers, both actual and potential, can be planned. Clearly, two factors are of importance, namely, the time available to the salesperson and the needs of the customer. In today's competitive environment, the latter should predominate. Some customers may need more frequent contact with salespersons, some may even specify the frequency and the times to meet. The objective, therefore, of call planning is to use the resource of personal selling as efficiently as possible with no unnecessary or duplicated calls. Time should, however, be set aside for possible emergency calls as requested by customers.

### Bibliography

Kotler, P. (1994). *Marketing management: Analysis, planning, implementation and control* (8th edn). Englewood Cliffs, NJ: Prentice-Hall. Chapter 25.
Wilson, M. T. (1983). *Managing a sales force* (2nd edn). Aldershot: Gower.

DAVID YORKE

**channels of distribution** Products and services are moved from their source of production to the customer by means of a channel of distribution. The channel may be simple when the producer sells direct to customers (through, for example, DIRECT MAIL) or it can consist of one or more intermediaries, such as agents, WHOLESALERS, and RETAILERS. The form, and complexity, of the distribution channel employed depends on the product (its perishability, bulk, frequency of purchase, whether or not it is an industrial or consumer product), the customers for the product, and their geographical dispersion.

A producer may employ an intermediary because it is the traditional practice of the industry, although often significant competitive advantages can be gained from innovating. Selling direct can be employed by firms selling particular categories of industrial products, such as expensive capital goods or bulk raw materials. Such sales involve high-value dispatches, relatively infrequent purchases, and special pre-sale NEGOTIATION on price and technical specifications. However, direct selling (*see* DIRECT MARKETING) is employed widely in consumer markets, and is gaining more widespread appeal, partly because of the often considerably lower costs.

Where independent intermediaries are used, a distinction can be drawn between those who act merely on behalf of the manufacturer (e.g., selling and distributing the product) without purchasing the product (i.e., they do not take title), and those who take title and undertake all further responsibility for distribution and perhaps other aspects of marketing. Intermediaries who do not take title include brokers and manufacturers' sales agents. A broker will attempt to find possible purchasers of the product and bring the manufacturer and these potential customers together. Manufacturers' sales agents fulfill similar functions, although they will often employ their own sales staff, carry stock on consignment, and provide ancillary services such as financing, installation, and so on. Both brokers and agents receive a commission on any sales.

Intermediaries who do take title include wholesalers and retailers. These both buy and sell. Wholesalers will collect a range of goods from various manufacturers and usually sell them to other intermediaries (e.g., small retailers). Wholesalers are used when, for example, the amount sold per customer is relatively small, or when customers are widely scattered geographically. Generally, wholesalers sell to other companies or to retailers. Retailers, which carry out a similar function, mostly sell to the final customer. Large retailers will generally take delivery direct from manufacturers.

There are various transfers between the different elements of the distribution chain. Five types of transfer can be identified: *physical goods transfers* – the movement of goods, ranging from the initial raw materials, through components and subassemblies, to the final product; *ownership transfer* – as the product passes through the chain, the ownership of the physical goods can change; *payment transfer* – the movement of money for the payment of goods and services; *information transfer* – the flow of information between different stages in the chain; and *influence transfer* – the way in which different elements in the chain attempt to promote themselves and thereby influence other elements in the chain.

**Bibliography**

Dibb, S., Simkin, L., Pride, W. M. & Ferrell, O. C. (1994). *Marketing: Concepts and strategies* (European edn). London: Houghton Mifflin Co. Chapters 10, 11, 12.

McCarthy, E. J. & Perreault, W. D. (1993). *Basic marketing* (11th edn). Homewood, IL: Irwin. Chapters 13, 14.

DALE LITTLER

**cluster analysis**   Cluster analysis refers to a body of techniques used to identify objects or individuals that are similar. Using measurements on several variables for a number of cases, a small number of exclusive and exhaustive groups or clusters are formed. Each cluster has high within clusters homogeneity and high between clusters heterogeneity. Usually a measure of the distance

between individuals is used to build up clusters. When the number of cases is small, the clustering can be observed, but with larger numbers of cases faster clustering is used and less detailed output is provided by the computer packages, e.g., the STATISTICAL PACKAGE FOR THE SOCIAL SCIENCES, SPSS, which are necessary for cluster analysis. Once the sample has been partitioned and the clusters have been identified using some of the variables in the analysis, the remaining variables can be investigated to obtain profiles of the clusters and to see if and where there are differences between the clusters.

Cluster analysis differs from DISCRIMINANT ANALYSIS in that there is no external means of grouping the cases.

The usefulness in marketing to help in segmenting (*see* MARKET SEGMENTATION) populations should be obvious. The variables used to define the clusters could be the needs and lifestyles of individuals and the subsequent profiling may involve demographic, socioeconomic, etc. variables to see where the clusters differ and to see if the clusters can be named. If the researcher has a large sample, a cluster analysis may precede the application of other statistical methods, including other multivariate techniques (*see* MULTIVARIATE METHODS (ANALYSIS)), to each cluster in turn.

**Bibliography**

Hair, J. F., Anderson, R. E. & Tatham, R. L. (1987). *Multivariate data analysis* (2nd edn). New York: Macmillan. Chapter 7.

MICHAEL GREATOREX

**codes of practice**   It is desirable that industries conform to certain rules or regulations in the conduct of their business. Broadly, such regulations may be imposed by external organizations (i.e., by law) or they may be self-imposed (i.e., codes of practice such as advertising industry standards and those enforced by professional service firms). The advantages claimed for codes of practice are: they can help to raise the standards of an industry; organizations within the industry are often happy to accept restrictions imposed by voluntary codes of practice rather than be subject to the law over which they have little control or influence; and codes may offer a cheaper and quicker means of resolving grievances than using more formal legal channels.

Trade or industry associations are encouraged to adopt codes of practice and to update them constantly as the MARKETING ENVIRONMENT changes.

## Bibliography

Institute of Practitioners in Advertising (1980). *Some suggested provisions for use in agency/client agreements.* London.

Runyon, K. E. (1984). *Advertising.* Columbus, OH: Charles E. Merrill Publishing Co. Chapter 23.

DAVID YORKE

**cognitive dissonance**    Individual consumers' cognitions for products which are expressed in terms of values, beliefs, opinions, and attitudes (*see* CONSUMER ATTITUDES) tend to exist in clusters that are generally both internally consistent, and consistent with behavior; and an individual strives for consistency within his or her self.

However, any two cognitive elements or attitudes may or may not be consonant with each other. If such an inconsistency exists in a pre-purchase situation, a consumer has a state of conflict which makes it difficult to make a choice. If after a purchase there is inconsistency between cognitive elements then cognitive dissonance is said to exist, i.e., it is a post-purchase state of mind.

When making choices between alternatives, consumers invariably experience cognitive dissonance as on few occasions do they make a completely "right" decision; consumers may remain aware of positive features of rejected alternatives and negative features of a selected alternative – which are inconsistent/dissonant with the action taken.

Cognitive dissonance will be high when: the buying decision is important, either psychologically or in terms of financial outlay; when a number of desirable alternatives are available; when the alternatives are dissimilar with little cognitive overlap, e.g., the choice between a television or a washing machine; and when decision choice is a result of freewill with no help or applied pressure from others.

The existence of cognitive dissonance is psychologically uncomfortable and so consumers develop strategies to reduce/eliminate it to re-achieve consistency or consonance. These include: eliminating responsibility for the decision, e.g., return the product; change attitudes towards the product to increase cognitive overlap; deny, distort or forget information (e.g., cigarette smokers and health warnings); seek new information to confirm one's choice; or reduce the importance of the decision.

## Bibliography

Cummings, W. H. & Venkatesan, M. (1976). Cognitive dissonance and consumer behavior: A review of the evidence. *Journal of Marketing Research*, Aug., 303–308.

Festinger, L. (1957). *A theory of cognitive dissonance.* Stanford University Press.

Loudon, D. L. & Della Bitta, A. J. (1993). *Consumer behavior* (4th edn). McGraw-Hill Int. Chapter 18.

Schiffman, L. G. & Kanuk, L. Z. (1991). *Consumer behavior* (4th edn). Prentice-Hall. Chapter 9.

BARBARA LEWIS

**cognitive stage**    Models of the CONSUMER DECISION-MAKING PROCESS which suggest that a target buyer or customer moves from a state of ignorance or unawareness of an organization and/or its products or services to ultimately making a purchase comprise three principal stages: COGNITIVE, AFFECTIVE, and CONATIVE. (*see also* MARKETING COMMUNICATIONS.) The cognitive stage is that which draws the ATTENTION of the buyer or customer to an organization, its products, service, or brands, creates an AWARENESS of their existence, and develops a clear understanding of what is being offered.

The cost-effectiveness of achieving this is determined largely by the MEDIA used and the size and type of the target group(s). For example: PERSONAL SELLING is less cost-effective when the number in the target group is large, although TELEMARKETING and DIRECT MAIL can reduce the cost; and ADVERTISING is considered to be relatively successful at the cognitive stage providing there are media appropriate for reaching only the target group.

**Bibliography**

Kotler, P. (1994). *Marketing management: Analysis, planning, implementation and control* (8th edn). Englewood Cliffs, NJ: Prentice-Hall. Chapter 22.

DAVID YORKE

**communications objectives**   The objectives of MARKETING COMMUNICATIONS are concerned, primarily, with information and education about companies and their products and services and, ultimately, with consumer purchase and satisfaction, together with achievement of corporate goals such as profits, return-on-investment, growth, and market shares.

However, "purchase" behavior is typically the end result of the CONSUMER DECISION-MAKING PROCESS and the marketing communicator wishes to move the target audience (e.g., buyer/consumer) through several stages of readiness to buy, i.e., moving them through the COGNITIVE, the AFFECTIVE, and the CONATIVE (or behavioral response) STAGE.

Thus, specific objectives might be to: provide information about a new product/brand and create awareness of the product/brand; generate interest in the product or brand from a target market (or segment – *see* MARKET SEGMENTATION); encourage sales from new customers; increase sales among existing customers; increase MARKET SHARE; introduce price concessions; provide information on product changes and availability; and educate customers or the general public about features/benefits of the product. Communication objectives might also be concerned with providing information and generating attitudes and responses from other organizations in the distribution chain, e.g., encouraging new distributors or improving dealer relationships; or relate to consumers' attitudes and responses toward organizations, e.g., generating goodwill and creating a corporate image.

Marketing communications objectives which are concerned with consumers' responses to products/brands are reflected in various response hierarchy models which have been offered, e.g., AIDA MODEL DAGMAR MODEL, HIERARCHY OF EFFECTS MODEL, and INNOVATION-ADOPTION MODEL. These models assume that a buyer moves through the cognitive, affective and behavioral stages in that order, i.e., the "learn-feel-buy" sequence (*see* LEARN-FEEL-BUY MODEL); alternative sequences, depending on the product category and consumer involvement, are BUY-FEEL-LEARN and FEEL-BUY-LEARN.

As a consequence, communications objectives may be set depending on the product, consumer involvement, and stage in the consumer decision-making process.

**Bibliography**

Colley, R. H. (1961). *Defining advertising goals for measured advertising results.* New York: Association of National Advertisers.

Kotler, P. (1994). *Marketing management: Analysis, planning, implementation and control* (8th edn). Englewood Cliffs, NJ: Prentice-Hall, p. 602.

Lavidge, R. J. & Steiner, G. A. (1961). A model for predictive measurements of advertising effectiveness. *Journal of Marketing*, 25, Oct., 61.

McCarthy, E. J. & Perreault, W. D. Jr (1993). *Basic marketing* (11th edn). Homewood, IL: Irwin. Chapter 15.

Rogers, E. M. (1962). *Diffusion of innovation.* New York: The Free Press, pp. 79–86.

Semenik, R. J. & Bamossy, G. J. (1994). *Principles of marketing.* Cincinnati, OH: South-Western Publishing Co. Chapter 10.

BARBARA LEWIS

**communications mix**   The marketing communications mix is a subset of the MARKETING MIX and includes all the techniques available to the marketer, and which may be "mixed," in order to deliver a MESSAGE to the target group of buyers, customers, or consumers.

Techniques, broadly, may be classified using two dimensions – first, whether they are delivered personally (e.g., PERSONAL SELLING, TELEMARKETING) or whether the medium used is impersonal (e.g., ADVERTISING, PACKAGING, SALES PROMOTION, PUBLIC RELATIONS); and secondly, whether or not the technique involves a payment by the sponsor. All of the first group are thus "commercial." Examples of "non-commercial" techniques are PUBLICITY and opinion leaders (*see* INTERPERSONAL COMMUNICATIONS).

Different techniques have different strengths (and conversely, weaknesses). There is a need for the marketer to define the target groups, to set objectives for each, and to evaluate the most cost-effective means of reaching the target(s) and attaining the objectives. A different mix, for example, would be employed at different stages of the PRODUCT LIFE CYCLE. A similar situation exists for products or services of high or low value (where the degree of PERCEIVED RISK in the target's mind will vary) and depending on whether the target group is concentrated or dispersed.

*See also* **Marketing communications**

**Bibliography**

Crosier, K. (1994). In M. J. Baker (Ed.), *The marketing book* (3rd edn). Oxford: Butterworth Heinemann.
Kotler, P. (1994). *Marketing management: Analysis, planning, implementation and control* (8th edn). Englewood Cliffs, NJ: Prentice-Hall. Chapter 22.
McCarthy, E. J. & Perreault, W. D. (1993). *Basic marketing*. Homewood, IL: Irwin. Chapter 15.
Semenik, R. J. & Bamossy, G. J. (1994). *Principles of marketing*. Cincinnati, OH: South-Western Publishing Co. Chapter 10.

DAVID YORKE

**communications research** Communications research is aimed at optimizing the effectiveness of communications through *ex ante* and *ex post* evaluations of different elements of the COMMUNICATIONS MIX. ADVERTISING effectiveness tends to receive more emphasis because it usually commands much higher expenditures than other elements of the communications mix. Pre-testing (before the communication is used on the public at large) may be employed to assess reactions to different forms of the communication in order to identify the version which is likely to yield the most favorable response. A variety of research techniques may be employed, ranging from the gathering and analysis of attitudes to laboratory tests using equipment to measure physiological responses, such as pupil dilation, heartbeat, and blood pressure. Post-testing can include evaluating consumers' ability to recall or to recognize communications (generally advertisements).

The relationship between sales and expenditure on communications is much more difficult to ascertain. However, by the use of carefully designed experiments (*see* EXPERIMENTATION) it may be possible to measure the sales effect of, say, advertising. For example, Du Pont's Paint Division divided its 56 sales areas into high, average, and low MARKET SHARE territories. In one third, Du Pont allocated the normal amount to advertising; in another third, it allocated two and a half times the amount; and in the final third, four times the normal amount. The experiment suggested that an increased spend on advertising increased sales at a diminishing rate, and that the sales increase was weaker in Du Pont's high market share territories (Buzzell, 1964). Other research on effectiveness has attempted to identify an historical relationship between sales and, for example, the expenditure on advertising using advanced statistical techniques.

Generally, though, there are significant difficulties in assessing the impact of communications on sales. First, without carefully controlled experimentation, one cannot conclude that there is any direct link between the communication and the sales/profits secured; there are too many other variables involved. Even if all the extraneous variables are controlled, there might still be some external influence, unthought of by the experimenters, that may affect the results.

Secondly, the full impact of the communication may be spread over time. Taking the case of advertising, some people who are acquainted with the advertising in the early stages of the campaign may react quickly; others may, for various reasons, delay a response. A further group of people may not learn of the advertising for some time after it starts. In the same way, the full effects of reducing or stopping advertising may not become apparent for some time; there may well be a "carry over" effect. Thus, when considering the impact of advertising at any given time, it is possible to have a distorted picture of its general effectiveness. It may well be that there is a steep rise in sales stemming from the advertising, but this may be because the advertising has *brought forward* sales that, in its absence, would have been made some time in the future; so the total sales may be unaffected. Of course, this may well be what the advertiser desired as he or she will have the advantage of obtaining, perhaps, a higher market share (and earlier); in addition, there will be resulting higher sales revenue in the early stages of the PRODUCT LIFE CYCLE concerned.

Thirdly, the creativity (*see* CREATIVE CONTENT) of the communication can be expected to influence its effectiveness. Thus, spending large amounts of money on advertising will not lead inevitably to substantial sales if the campaign itself leads to resentment, fails to stimulate interest, or lacks credibility. Similarly, of course, any communication will be ineffective, in the medium term, if the product is unreliable, of poor quality, or has undesirable side-effects. Because of the specificity of most of the marketing variables (i.e., the development of a specific campaign for a specific product), it becomes difficult to make general conclusions about the effectiveness of an additional dollar spent on advertising.

### Bibliography

Buzzell, R. D. (1964). E. I. Du Pont de Nemours and Co.: Measurement of effects of advertising. *Mathematical models and marketing management* (pp. 157–79). In Boston: Division of Research, Graduate School of Business Administration, Harvard University.

DALE LITTLER

**competitive advantage**   Competitive advantage may be secured through differentiation of the organization and/or its products and services in some way in order to gain preference by all or part of the market over its rivals. This may result in higher MARKET SHARE and/or margins than competitors. In general, competitive advantage will be obtained through offering higher customer value. Day & Wensley (1988) argue that there is no common meaning of "competitive advantage," it being used interchangeably with "distinctive competence" to mean relative superiority in skills and resources, or with "positional superiority in the market," as providing greater customer value yields high market share.

Resource-based theories argue that there are two related sources of competitive advantage: assets, i.e., the resource endowments the business has accumulated (e.g., investments in the scale, scope and efficiency of facilities and systems, brand equity, etc., and capabilities, defined as "the glue that brings these assets together and enables them to be deployed advantageously" (Dierickx & Cool, 1989). Capabilities differ from assets in that they cannot be given a monetary value. They are, according to Dierickx & Cool, "so deeply embedded in the organisational routines and practices that they cannot be traded or imitated." They include skills and processes, and are often tacit. They have some similarity to the core competencies described by Prahalad & Hamel (1990) except that these are seen as the capabilities which support multiple businesses within an organization.

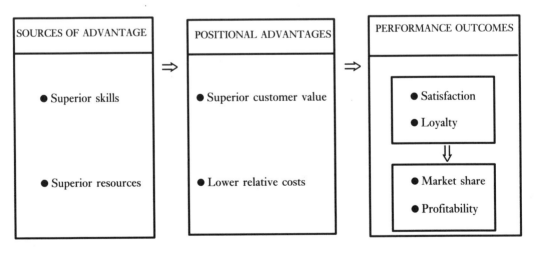

*Figure 1   The Elements of Competitive Advantage*
*Source:* Day & Wensley, 1988

Day (1994) suggests that two capabilities are particularly critical to competitive advantage, namely, market sensing capability, which is the ability to detect changes in the market and to anticipate the possible responses to marketing actions that may be taken; and customer linking capability, which embraces the "skills, abilities and processes needed to achieve collaborative customer relationships so that individual customer needs are quickly apparent to all functions and well-defined procedures are in place for responding to them."

As Porter (1980) argues, it is important to establish a competitive advantage which is *sustainable*, i.e., not easily eroded by environmental changes, or imitated by existing or potential competitors.

### Bibliography

Day, G. S. (1994). The capabilities of market-driven organisations. *Journal of Marketing*, 58, Oct., 37–52.

Day, G. S. & Wensley, R. (1988). Assessing advantage: A framework for diagnosing competitive superiority. *Journal of Marketing*, 52, 1–20.

Dierickx, I. & Cool, K. (1989). Asset stock and accumulation and sustainability of competitive advantage. *Management Science*, 35, 1504–1511.

Porter, M. E. (1980). *Competitive strategy: Techniques for analyzing industries and competitors*. New York: Free Press.

Prahalad, C. K. & Hamel, G. (1990). The core competence of the corporation. *Harvard Business Review*, 68, (3), May–June, 79–91.

DALE LITTLER

**competitive strategy** Widely popularized by Michael Porter (e.g., 1980) during the 1980s, "competitive strategy" tended to be accepted as a new approach to organizational strategy. Its roots are within the traditional area of industrial economics, and particularly the structure-conduct-performance paradigm. Porter argues that there are five major forces which affect the attractiveness of an industry. These are: intra-industry rivalry; the threat of new entrants; the existence, or potential development, of substitutes; the power of customers; and the power of suppliers. New entrants pose a threat as they augment existing capacity and may be disruptive because they will have to secure a market position in order to justify the costs of

entry. Substitutes place a ceiling on the price that can be charged. Supplier power can lead to higher input costs and is increased where suppliers are highly concentrated relative to the customer industries; and they have a unique product and there are switching costs. The power of customers, which can result in downward pressure on margins, is enhanced where they purchase in large volume, the product they purchase is standard or undifferentiated, and the product accounts for a significant proportion of the buyer's cost and, therefore, profits. Rivalry is likely to be intense where there are many firms of equal size, growth is slow, the product is undifferentiated, and there are high fixed costs presenting significant barriers to exit. Porter argues that it is these specific industry factors that are important since macroeconomic and other factors (*see* ENVIRONMENTAL ANALYSIS) will affect all industries equally. The major objective is then for organizations to position themselves favorably with regard to each of these five forces. Thus, they may strive to establish or reinforce barriers to entry; or build in switching costs to reduce the power of customers; or develop alternative sources of supply through collaborative product development with other possible suppliers.

Porter assumes that industries evolve, with distinct phases to their life cycle (nascent, growth, maturity, decline), and he applies the five forces framework to each of these stages. He develops the concept of strategic groups based on the view that industries can be disaggregated into clusters of firms with each cluster pursuing different strategies. There may be mobility barriers inhibiting the movement of firms from one cluster to another. However, the approach is essentially descriptive and, it can be argued, lacks robustness since firms can be clustered in two or more ways depending on the criteria employed to define the clusters.

Porter argues that the major focus of competitive strategy is to provide customer value. This can be perceived in terms of lowering customer costs and/or allowing the customer to secure higher quality, etc. Firms can follow one of four generic competitive strategies (*see* GENERIC STRATEGIES). They can aim at the lowest cost position or differentiation within the market as a whole; or they can strive for one of these positions aimed at a particular segment/or segments of the market (*see* FOCUS STRATEGY). Firms which neither aim at the lowest cost position nor the differentiated position become, according to Porter, "stuck in the middle" with suboptimum returns. However, there is little empirical evidence to substantiate his thesis; indeed, there has been increasing evidence that high performers can follow high levels of efficiency as well as having a significantly differentiated market position (e.g., Hall,1980; Cronshaw et al., 1994).

Porter's work and that of his followers makes at least three important contributions: first, it provides a coherent framework for analyzing industries; second, it emphasizes the importance of exit barriers as an influence on corporate behavior; and third, it focuses on the means of providing customer value. In later work, Porter has noted the need to adopt a more dynamic approach to competitive strategy formation (Porter, 1991).

Commentators such as Ohmae (1988) believe that the focus on "competitive strategy" can lead to an emphasis on competitors per se rather than on the changing values and requirements of customers, and that this may lead to tit-for-tat competitive rivalry, perhaps at the expense of providing adequately satisfactory offerings to customers, thereby opening up opportunities to those, including new entrants, which do.

**Bibliography**

Cronshaw, M., Davis, E. & Kay, J. (1994). On being stuck in the middle or Good Food Costs Less at Sainsbury. *British Journal of Management*, 5, 19–32.

Hall, W. K. (1980). Survival strategies in a hostile environment. *Harvard Business Review*, 58, (5), Sept.–Oct., 75–85.

Ohmae, K. (1988). Getting back to strategy. *Harvard Business Review*, 66, (6), Nov.–Dec., 149–156.

Porter, M. E. (1980). *Competitive strategy: Techniques for analyzing industries and competitors*. New York: Free Press.

Porter, M. E. (1991). Towards a dynamic theory of strategy. *Strategic Management Journal*, 12, special issue, "Fundamental Research Issues in Strategy and Economics", 95–117.

DALE LITTLER

**comprehension**   Comprehension is the second step in the DAGMAR MODEL OF COMMUNICATIONS. It is part of the COGNITIVE STAGE, i.e., when the target buyer or customer understands the product or service and what it is designed to achieve. Measurement of comprehension is far from easy because, despite care in the design of the communication, some individuals may interpret the message or illustration in different ways from others.

**Bibliography**

Colley, R. H. (1961). *Defining advertising goals for measured advertising results.* New York: Association of National Advertisers.

Kotler, P. (1994). *Marketing management: Analysis, planning, implementation and control* (8th edn). Englewood Cliffs, NJ: Prentice-Hall. Chapter 22.

DAVID YORKE

**computers in marketing**   Computers have had far-reaching effects on MARKETING RESEARCH and MARKETING and their use stretches to all aspects of marketing.

Computers are being utilized increasingly for the storage and retrieval of data using databases and MARKETING INFORMATION SYSTEMS. These data can form the basis of the monitoring of an organization's external and internal environments which permits the analysis of the OPPORTUNITIES and THREATS facing the organization. Again, such data are useful in the preliminary problem identification stages of the marketing research process.

In PRIMARY RESEARCH, software is available to help in the design of questionnaires (*see* QUESTIONNAIRE DESIGN). A satisfactory questionnaire can be printed and used in postal surveys or personal interviews but the use of the computer can be taken further in telephone interviewing when the questionnaire appears on a screen used by the interviewer as a prompt and as a means of recording the answers as given by the respondent to the interviewer. In computer interviewing, the respondent, using a keyboard or mouse or touch screen, directly communicates the answers to the questions as they appear on the screen without the use of an interviewer. Computers can be used in telephone interviewing to select members of the sample using random digit dialing. The computer will dial numbers, make recalls if needed, check on the productivity of the interviewers and generally help in the management of the interviewing stage of a survey.

Further examples of the use of computers to capture data occur in the use of electronic devices in observational research (*see* OBSERVATION). The use of scanners at the point of sale is revolutionizing marketing research by providing management with timely data on sales that help decisions on new products, new styles, new designs, new packaging, sales promotions, pricing, point of sale advertising, and on such routine decisions as inventory control and production planning for established products.

An important use of computers is in the analysis of PRIMARY DATA collected using both qualitative and quantitative methods, especially the latter. The statistical analysis of surveys is carried out using computer packages such as the STATISTICAL PACKAGE FOR THE SOCIAL SCIENCES (SPSS) and MINITAB. Large samples need computers for data analysis even to get simple summaries for each variable such as tabulations of frequencies or DESCRIPTIVE STATISTICS such as measures of average and dispersion. In BIVARIATE ANALYSIS, analyses such as CROSS-TABULATIONS or comparisons of means are readily specified and obtainable using these packages. MULTIVARIATE METHODS (ANALYSIS) is only possible using computers. Such methods as multiple regression (*see* REGRESSION AND CORRELATION), DISCRIMINANT ANALYSIS, FACTOR ANALYSIS, CLUSTER ANALYSIS, STRUCTURAL EQUATION METHODS, and MULTIDIMENSIONAL SCALING including CONJOINT ANALYSIS are carried out using either general packages such as those mentioned above or specialist software available for some of the methods.

Multiple regression (*see* REGRESSION AND CORRELATION) is useful in FORECASTING along with such time series methods as exponential smoothing and auto-regressive moving average methods. Computers are useful in the selection and development of a suitable forecasting procedure for a particular problem such as the demand for a specified product. Since organizations often require forecasts for many products, computers are also useful in the

application of the chosen procedures for the different products.

Marketing decision support systems involve databases, marketing models and, crucially, computer hardware and software and a communication interface so that the user can interact directly with the databases and marketing models. Marketing decision support systems have been devised to help marketing decision-makers with a variety of problems, especially those concerning the elements of the MARKETING MIX.

Marketing decision support systems have been created using spreadsheets. Spreadsheets have also been used in marketing for forecasting, budgeting, and controlling.

Computers are also useful in teaching marketing and marketing research. Obvious examples include business games centered around marketing topics, computer-based marketing case studies, exercises, and computer-aided learning modules.

**Bibliography**

Parkinson, L. K. & Parkinson, S. T. (1987). *Using the microcomputer in marketing*. Maidenhead: McGraw-Hill.

MICHAEL GREATOREX

**conative stage**  Consumer decision-making models (*see* CONSUMER DECISION-MAKING PROCESS) which suggest that a target buyer or customer moves from a state of ignorance or unawareness of an organization and/or its products or services to ultimately making a purchase comprise three main stages: COGNITIVE, AFFECTIVE, and conative. The conative or behavioral stage is that which elicits some ACTION on the part of the buyer or customer. Action is not necessarily a purchase, although this is, ultimately, what is desired by organizations; rather, it may be seeking further information about the product or service, or product TRIAL.

Of the MARKETING COMMUNICATIONS techniques available (*see* COMMUNICATIONS MIX), those which are more likely to initiate action in the conative stage are PERSONAL SELLING, SALES PROMOTION, and forms of DIRECT

MARKETING such as TELEMARKETING, DIRECT MAIL, and OFF THE PAGE selling.

**Bibliography**

Kotler, P. (1994). *Marketing management: Analysis, planning, implementation and control* (8th edn). Englewood Cliffs, NJ: Prentice-Hall. Chapter 22.

DAVID YORKE

**concept testing**   Concept testing is concerned with the evaluation of a new PRODUCT CONCEPT to: determine ways to improve the concept; ascertain the best target markets; and gauge potential customer acceptance to warrant further product development (*see* NEW PRODUCT DEVELOPMENT).

A product concept is "a printed or filmed representation of a product or service. It is simply a device to communicate the subject's benefits, strengths and reasons for being"(Schwartz, 1987). The concept is a description of the product that also includes the benefits it offers.

Concept tests identify: whether or not there is sufficient consumer appeal to warrant further development; the appropriate target market; and ways to improve the concept. They also provide an estimate of the percentage of people who may try the new product (Moore & Pressemier, 1993). Concept testing can also be used to help assess ADVERTISING or POSITIONING approaches by identifying which benefits should be offered.

A variety of techniques are available for concept testing, e.g., qualitative discussions with potential customers to assess their reaction to possible new product ideas, postal questionnaire surveys, telephone interviews, and personal interviews (*see* SURVEY RESEARCH). Monadic tests are where the respondents evaluate one concept. Competitive tests involve presenting the new concept alongside the old concept(s). Monadic tests have yielded successful applications; others argue that competitive tests are more realistic. Cooper (1993) argues that the most reliable results arise from a full-proposition concept test, i.e., a test designed to convey to the final customer what the final product will be and do, e.g., a simulated shopping triInformation objectives for the concept test include: a measure of the customer's interest in the proposed product, a measure of the liking of the product, a comparative measure with competing products/brands currently in use, and an indication of the intention to purchase.

It is important to note that concept tests are likely to overstate the market acceptance, so that a result of "30 percent of respondents would definitely buy" is not likely to translate into a MARKET SHARE of 30 percent. The respondent may well continue to buy competing products, the potential buyers may lack information on the product because they may not be reached by advertising and promotion, and people may tend to respond positively to concept tests where money and commitment is not involved. Typical problems with concept tests include asking the 'wrong' respondents and promising more than the product will actually deliver. Product adoption (*see* ADOPTION PROCESS) can be longer than could be predicted in a concept test, e.g., automotive bank teller machines took years to become fully accepted.

A single exposure may not be a good predictor of eventual reaction to a product. Concept tests can only estimate the number of people who will try the product. The concept can change between the test and the market introduction (*see* TEST MARKETING), CONSUMER ATTITUDES can change, and other new products may be introduced between the test and the market introduction. All of this can affect the accuracy of the predictions from concept tests.

**Bibliography**

Cooper, R. G. (1993). *Winning at new products: Accelerating the process from idea to launch* (2nd edn). Reading, MA: Addison Wesley. Chapter 6, pp. 153–161.
Moore, W. L. & Pressemier, E. A. (1993). *Product planning and management: Designing and delivering value.* New York: McGraw-Hill. Chapter 8, pp. 253–265.
Schwartz, D. (1987). *Concept testing: How to test new product ideas before you go to market.* New York: American Management Association.

MARGARET BRUCE

**confidence intervals**   Estimates of population parameters, e.g., the population mean, based upon data from a sample are often required.

When a probability sample (*see* SAMPLING) has been taken, relatively simple methods and formulae are available to provide best single point estimates. For instance, the best estimate of the population mean based upon data collected by a simple random sample is the sample mean.

However, by the very nature of sampling, a single point estimate is unlikely to give an exactly true estimate. Therefore, as well as providing single point estimates, interval estimates are also calculated. Confidence interval estimation is a way of computing two points between which the population parameter will lie with a given level of probability. Thus, in addition to reporting that the best point estimate of the population average is 200, it can more realistically be said that there is a 95 percent chance that the population mean lies in the range 190 and 210.

Confidence intervals, which are calculable for data from probability samples, depend upon the variability of the data in the sample, the size of the sample, the appropriate sampling distribution, and the specified level of probability. The greater the variability, the smaller the sample and the greater the specified level of probability, the larger will be the confidence interval. The relevant sampling distribution is often the t-distribution or the standard normal distribution.

Bibliography

Chisnall, P. M. (1992). *Marketing research* (4th edn). Maidenhead: McGraw-Hill, pp. 57–59.

MICHAEL GREATOREX

conjoint analysis  Conjoint analysis is a set of techniques that allows the researcher to derive indirectly the relative importance respondents place on different attributes and the utilities assigned to different values of each attribute when selecting from among several brands (*see* BRAND).

The several attributes (and the levels they can take) that are used to characterize a product are identified. Thus, the attributes for a car may be style, color, country of origin, running costs, price, performance, etc., and, as an example, the values that the attribute style may take could be saloon, hatchback, and estate car, and so on. Rather than ask the respondent to evaluate the attributes and their values directly, respondents are offered hypothetical combinations of levels of the attributes and asked to evaluate the overall offerings. If the numbers of attributes and levels are small, all possible combinations can be offered to the respondent for evaluation. In more typical circumstances a reduced set of combinations, chosen in a way similar to the way experiments (*see* EXPERIMENTATION) are designed, is offered so that sufficient information is efficiently collected. The implied utility attached to each possible level of an attribute is calculated by the computer and the relative importance of each attribute can be identified. Combinations not evaluated by respondents can then be analyzed, trade-offs involving different levels of different attributes can be evaluated, and the utilities of potential new brands can be compared to those of brands on the market. Simulations can be used to estimate MARKET SHARE. Specialized software for PCs is available to help the researcher conduct conjoint analysis.

Bibliography

Tull, D. S. & Hawkins, D. I. (1987). *Marketing research: Measurement and method* (4th edn). New York: Macmillan, pp. 301–304.

MICHAEL GREATOREX

consumer attitudes  Attitudes may be considered as a mental state of readiness, organized through experience, exerting a directive or dynamic influence upon an individual's response to all objects and situations with which he/she is related.

Attitudes structure the way consumers perceive their environment and guide the ways in which they respond to it, i.e., attitudes are characterized by a pre-disposition or state-of-readiness to act or re-act in a particular way to certain stimuli. They are relatively enduring and are useful guidelines as to what buyers may do in certain circumstances.

Attitudes have three components. The cognitive component refers to beliefs, i.e., the knowledge or descriptive thoughts one has, for example, about a product or brand, which is a function of available information. The affective component refers to the emotional content of attitudes and arouses either like or dislike; such feelings derive from personality, motives, social norms, and previous experience. The conative component, or action tendency, concerns the disposition to take action of some kind, e.g., a purchase; a consumer may have favorable attitudes without making purchases or even intending to purchase.

A number of sources of influence are important in the formation of attitudes. These include: information exposure – the cognitive content of attitudes is largely built up from information from other people and from the media; group membership – the attitudes and opinions of people one interacts with have an impact on the individual; environment, to include economic factors; and present levels of need satisfaction.

Attitudes are held toward many aspects of buying and consuming, e.g., toward products and services, brands, companies, stores, product appearance and packaging, promotion and price, and levels of service. Attitudes vary along various dimensions: direction, e.g., positive or negative, favorable or unfavorable; intensity, i.e., how positive or negative; complexity, i.e., toward one or more aspects of a product or brand; and fixity, i.e., will they change. With regard to complexity, one can refer to overall or general attitudes, e.g., toward a model of car; and to particular or specific attitudes, e.g., the individual features of a car such as its design, performance, or service provided. Further, one can consider "determinant" buying attitudes (*see* Alpert, 1971; Myers & Alpert, 1968) which refer to the features/aspects of a product that are critical in the decision to purchase a specific item or brand/model, e.g., cars and safety.

A major question for marketers is the extent to which attitudes predict subsequent purchase behavior. This has been considered by Fishbein (1967), and others (Sheth, 1974; Ajzen & Fishbein, 1980; Fishbein & Ajzen, 1975; Wells, 1985), who present a framework in which a consumer moves from beliefs to attitudes to purchase intention to purchase. Fishbein's suggestion is that purchase intention may be a better predictor of behavior than merely having favorable attitudes. Even so, one has to take account of "intervening" variables which may prevail between the stages of intention to buy and purchase: these include economic factors, availability, price, and promotional activities.

Attitude change also needs to be taken into account. This includes changes in direction, intensity, and complexity. Factors which affect attitude change are: the attitudes themselves, e.g., extreme attitudes are harder to change; individual factors, e.g., personality and product needs; marketing communications, both the MASS MEDIA and INTERPERSONAL COMMUNICATIONS; and the MARKETING ENVIRONMENT, in particular economic variables and financial considerations.

### Bibliography

Ajzen, J. & Fishbein, M. (1980). *Understanding attitudes and predicting social behavior.* Englewood Cliffs, NJ: Prentice-Hall.

Alpert, M. I. (1971). Identification of determinant attributes: A comparison of methods. *Journal of Marketing Research*, 8, May, 184–191.

Engel, J. F., Blackwell, R. D. & Miniard, P. W. (1990). *Consumer behavior* (6th edn). Orlando, FL: The Dryden Press. Chapter 11.

Fishbein, M. (1967). Attitudes and prediction of behavior. In M. Fishbein (Ed.), *Readings in attitude theory and measurement*, (pp. 477–492). New York: John Wiley.

Fishbein, M. & Ajzen, I. (1975). *Belief, attitude, intentions and behavior.* Reading, MA: Addison Wesley.

Foxall, G. R. & Goldsmith, R. E. (1994). *Consumer psychology for marketing.* London: Routledge. Chapter 5.

Hawkins, D. I., Best, R. J. & Coney, K. A. (1992). *Consumer behavior: Implications for marketing strategy* (5th edn). Homewood, IL: Irwin. Chapter 12.

Loudon, D. L. & Della Bitta, A. J. (1993). *Consumer behavior* (4th edn). McGraw-Hill Int. Chapters 12, 13.

Myers, J. H. & Alpert, M. I. (1968). Determinant buying attitudes: Meaning and measurement. *Journal of Marketing*, 32, Oct., 14.

Schiffman, L. G. & Kanuk, L. Z. (1991). *Consumer behavior* (4th edn). Prentice-Hall: Chapter 8.

Sheth, J. N. (1974). An investigation of relationships among evaluative beliefs, affect, behavioral intention and behavior. In J. U. Farley, J. A. Howard & L. W. Ring (Eds), *Consumer behavior, theory and application*, (pp. 89–114). Boston: Allyn & Bacon.

Solomon, M. R. (1992). *Consumer behavior.* Needham Heights, MA: Allyn & Bacon. Chapter 5.

Wells, W. D. (1985). Attitudes and behavior. *Journal of Advertising Research*, March, 40–44.

BARBARA LEWIS

**consumer buyer behavior** Consumer buyer behavior has developed, since the 1960s, as a separate discipline within marketing, for a number of reasons. The impact of the MARKETING CONCEPT throughout all industries, in both the public and private sectors, and on an international basis, has led to increasing consumer awareness and sophistication. Consumers are better educated and informed and thus more

provide the tools and techniques to facilitate research into consumer behavior and develop customer databases.

In consumer markets (*see* MARKETS), various market exchanges take place between companies and "consumers" who may be described as "consumers," "buyers," "customers," "purchasers," etc., as a function of their involvement in buying and consuming. This is better understood in terms of buying roles within a household or family. These roles are typically: *initiator* – someone who first suggests the idea of buying a particular good or service; *influencer(s)* – those who have implicit or explicit influence from within or outside the household;

**Consumer buyer behavior**

| Marketing Stimuli | Other Stimuli | | Buyer's Characteristics | Buyer's Decision Process | | Buyer's Decision |
|---|---|---|---|---|---|---|
| Product Price Place Promotion | Economic Technological Political Cultural | $\longrightarrow$ | Culture Social Personal Psychological | Problem recognition Information search Evaluation Decisions Post-purchase behavior | $\longrightarrow$ | Product choice Brand choice Dealer choice Purchase timing Purchase amount |

*Figure 1   Influences on Consumers*
*Source:* Kotler, 1994, p. 174

discriminating in their selection of goods and services. Hence, it behoves manufacturers and distributors to research and understand their needs and preferences and to respond accordingly. With the fast pace of product introductions, spurred by technological development, companies need to search for better information about what people are willing to buy. Product life cycles are shorter and so it is necessary to anticipate consumer lifestyles and to develop products to satisfy future needs. The growth of segmentation as a MARKETING STRATEGY enables companies to better cater for the needs of specific, homogeneous groups of consumers. Further, there is: increased interest in consumer protection and the growth of private consumer groups; the setting of public policy to protect the interests and well-being of consumers; and increasing environmental concerns. Additionally, computer and statistical developments

*decider(s)* – a person who decides on any component of a buying decision in relation to whether to buy, what to buy, where from, when, and how to pay; *purchaser* – to mean the purchasing agent who goes into a shop; and *user(s)* – those who use or consume the product/service. In addition, one can consider who pays for/funds the purchase. Also, the extent to which joint decision-making is evident, i.e., where two or more people fulfil buying role(s) (*see* e.g., Davis, 1976; Davis & Rigaux, 1974; Filiatrault & Brent–Ritchie, 1980); this in turn may depend on stages in the CONSUMER DECISION-MAKING PROCESS.

Consumer buyer behavior is concerned with the process of buying and consuming goods and services. One can also consider consumer shopping behavior, i.e., visiting the retail shopping environment, which is characterized by various personal and social motives (*see* Tauber, 1972). Personal motives include: role playing, diversion, self-gratification, learning about new trends, physical activity, and sensory stimulation. Social motives include social experience outside the home, communication with others having a similar interest, peer group attraction, status and authority, and pleasure of bargaining.

Consumer buyer behavior is partly explained and understood in terms of economic theory (*see* BUYER BEHAVIOR THEORIES). However, it is also necessary to consider social and psychological explanations, together with other influences on consumers (*see* figure 1), to include marketing and other stimuli and buyer characteristics.

Marketing stimuli relate to the activities and inputs of manufacturers and distributors, in particular the components of their MARKETING MIX, namely, product, price, place, and promotion. Other stimuli include economic, political, and technological elements in the MARKETING ENVIRONMENT. These impact on buyers whose social and cultural background (*see* CULTURE; SOCIAL CLASS), LIFESTYLES, and group memberships (*see* INTERPERSONAL COMMUNICATIONS) influence their buying behavior.

In addition, one needs to consider the make-up of consumer psychological characteristics (e.g., PERSONALITY; CONSUMER NEEDS AND MOTIVES; CONSUMER PERCEPTIONS; CONSUMER LEARNING), together with an understanding of the ways in which consumer attitudes are formed and developed (*see* CONSUMER ATTITUDES; COGNITIVE DISSONANCE), and the ways in which consumers perceive and handle risk in buying situations (*see* PERCEIVED RISK).

In most buying situations, consumers progress through a decision-making process (*see* CONSUMER DECISION-MAKING PROCESS), which results in various buying decisions in relation to product and brand choice, store/dealer choice, purchase time, methods of payment, etc. Buying decisions of special interest to researchers and practitioners include those which involve a time dimension, e.g., BRAND LOYALTY and the ADOPTION PROCESS for product innovations.

### Bibliography

Davis, H. L. (1976). Decision-making within the household. *Journal of Consumer Research*, 2, March, 241–260.

Davis, H. L. & Rigaux, B. P. (1974). Perceptions of marital roles in decision process. *Journal of Consumer Research*, 1, 51–62.

Filiatrault, P. & Brent-Ritchie, J. R. (1980). Joint purchase decisions: A comparison of influence structure in family and couple decision-making units. *Journal of Consumer Research*, 6, Sept., 131–140.

Katona, G. (1960). *The powerful consumer*. New York: McGraw-Hill.

Kotler, P. (1994). *Marketing management: Analysis, planning, implementation and control* (8th edn). Prentice-Hall Int., p. 174.

Tauber, E. M. (1972). Why do people shop? *Journal of Marketing*, 36, Oct., 46–49.

BARBARA LEWIS

**consumer decision-making process**   The consumer decision-making process is concerned with buying operations and the stages that a buyer (individual or household) may be involved in when making purchases. These are usually referred to as stages of: problem recognition, information search, information evaluation, purchase decisions, and post-purchase evaluations.

Problem recognition occurs when a consumer recognizes a buying problem or goal, an unsatisfied or unfilled need. Sources of problems are various and include: assortment deficiency (e.g., the coffee jar is empty), exposure to new information, expanded desires for more or better products and services, expanded means (i.e., finance available), and changing expectations and needs (*see* CONSUMER NEEDS AND MOTIVES). Buying needs may relate to products, brands, stores, service, etc., and a variety of needs will prevail at any one time which have to be prioritized (for an individual or household) as a function of time, money, urgency, role involvement, etc. A readiness to buy thus emerges.

Information search is the stage at which consumers attempt to match needs with market offerings, to identify purchase alternatives and find out more about them. Information may come from: personal sources, such as friends, family, neighbors; commercial sources, e.g., advertising and promotion, displays and salespeople; public sources, e.g., mass media and consumer organizations; and experience/use.

The amount of information sought will be a function of both product and individual factors. Product factors include frequency of purchase, price, social conspicuousness, essentiality of the product, and intensity of need. Individual factors, or search styles, include values and aspirations, degree of involvement with the purchase, risk perceptions and risk handling styles (*see* PERCEIVED RISK), availability of information without search, previous experience and knowledge of the product, time available, perceptions of the costs and value of information search, and satisfaction to be gained from searching.

*Information Evaluation (see* Bettman, 1979)

When considering consumers' evaluation of information with respect to product and brand alternatives, formal or informal organization of information may occur. Formal organization might include detailed financial analysis, e.g., with respect to house or car purchase. Further, alternatives are evaluated with respect to various decision criteria. These are related to: costs, e.g., price, operating costs, repairs, service, extras; performance, e.g., durability, economy, efficiency, dependability; suitability – of brand, style, store image, appearance, etc.; and convenience – of store location, atmosphere, service, etc.

Alternatives which are evaluated will be part of an awareness set as the consumer does not necessarily have information with respect to all the alternatives available. Those which meet initial buying criteria fall into a consideration set, which leads to a choice set.

At this point one can refer to consumer purchase intentions, i.e., those products/brands or other aspects of buying and consuming that a consumer (or household) is intending to carry out in the form of PURCHASE DECISIONS. However, one has to be aware that intervening variables may come into play between purchase intention and purchase decision. These include attitudes of other consumers, availability, and unexpected situational factors (e.g., with respect to income and employment), and may delay purchase decisions or cause them not to take place at all. For example, plans for a holiday may be cancelled due to unforeseen financial circumstances or ill health, and intention to purchase satellite television may be postponed

because a washing machine suddenly breaks down and has to be replaced.

Purchase decisions are made with respect to products and services, stores, and methods of payment. Product decisions include choice of brands (including distributors' *versus* manufacturers' brands), reaction to price deals, and impulse purchase decisions. Decisions also relate to choice of store (to include location, personnel, atmosphere, car parking, services, credit availability), home shopping, mail order, and frequency of shopping.

*Post-purchase Evaluation*

After purchasing, consumers experience some level of satisfaction or dissatisfaction with each of their decisions. With respect to product/brand choice, if perceived product performance meets consumer expectations then he/she is satisfied; if performance does not meet expectations (i.e., disconfirmed expectations) then dissatisfaction occurs. Dissatisfaction leads to one of several post-purchase activities to include: returning the product, seeking information to confirm the choice made (*see* COGNITIVE DISSONANCE), or complaining (*see* Gilly & Hansen, 1985).

Further, results of purchasing activities can be evaluated either informally, among family and friends, or more formally, e.g., with respect to car performance and costs, comparison with others. Post-purchase evaluations provide the consumer with an idea of how well he/she is doing in the market and add to his/her state of experience, knowledge, and information to be used in future purchasing decisions.

When considering models of the consumer decision-making process it is important to note that not all the stages may be relevant, timing between stages varies, and feedback loops exist. Further, the extent to which a formal process does happen will depend on the extent of consumer involvement. One can consider a continuum of low-high involvement consumer decision-making. Products which are expensive, risky, reflect self-image, or have positive reference group influence (*see* INTERPERSONAL COMMUNICATIONS) may be referred to as high involvement situations and subject to extensive problem solving, i.e., active information search and evaluation. At the other end of a continuum are routine, low involvement (often re-purchase) situations with no motivated search for information (the costs are likely to outweigh the benefits), and the consumer proceeds on the basis of what he/she already knows. This is further developed by Assael (1987) who identified four types of consumer buying behavior based on the degree of buyer involvement and the degree of difference among brands. These are: *complex buying behavior*, when consumers are highly involved and there are significant differences between brands (e.g., personal computers); *dissonance-reducing buying behavior*, when consumers are highly involved in a purchase but see little difference between brands (e.g., carpets); *habitual buying behavior*, characterized by low consumer involvement and little difference between brands (e.g., petrol and commodities); and *variety seeking buying behavior*, with low involvement but significant differences between brands (e.g., biscuits, soap powders).

### Bibliography

Assael, H. (1987). *Consumer behavior and marketing action*. Boston: Kent Publishing Co.

Bettman, J. R. (1979). *Information processing theory of consumer behavior*. Reading, MA: Addison Wesley.

Engel, J. F., Blackwell, R. D. & Miniard, P. W. (1990). *Consumer behavior* (6th edn). Orlando, FL: The Dryden Press. Chapters 17, 18, 19.

Gilly, M. C. & Hansen, R. W. (1985). Consumer complaint handling as a strategic marketing tool. *Journal of Consumer Marketing*, Fall, 5–16.

Hawkins, D. I., Best, R. J. & Coney, K. A. (1992).: Consumer behavior: Implications for marketing strategy (5th edn). Homewood, IL: Irwin. Chapters 14, 15, 16, 17, 18.

Kotler, P. (1994). *Marketing management: Analysis, planning, implementation and control* (8th edn). Prentice-Hall, pp. 193–201.

Loudon, D. L. & Della Bitta, A. J. (1993). *Consumer behavior* (4th edn). McGraw-Hill Int., Chapters 15, 16, 17, 18.

Solomon, M. R. (1992). *Consumer behavior*. Needham Heights, MA: Allyn & Bacon. Chapter 8.

Wilkie, W. L. (1994). *Consumer behavior* (3rd edn). New York: John Wiley. Chapters 17, 18, 19.

BARBARA LEWIS

**consumer learning**   Most behavior of consumers is learned from experience and consumer learning may be defined as a trend, change, or modification of perceptions, attitudes, and behavior resulting from previous experience and behavior in similar situations. Learning is to do with acquiring information and there are two major theories concerning learning and consumer behavior which are, together, relevant.

Stimulus-response theories postulate that learning is the development of behavior (response) as a result of exposure to a set of stimuli, and that consumer behavior is conditioned by association. The suggestion is that consumers respond to marketing cues or stimuli as a function of their drives/needs, that determine when, where, and how they respond. For example, a beer advertisement may stimulate a thirst drive but response also depends on other cues, such as time of day and availability of beer and other thirst quenchers. Satisfaction leads to reinforcement and a tendency for repetition when the same drives and cues reappear.

On the other hand, cognitive theories view learning as a process of restructuring individual cognitions with respect to specific problems. The suggestion here is that individuals acquire habits not only from stimulus-response repetition but also by using their insight, thinking, and problem-solving techniques, i.e., using intellectual activities. Problem solving becomes the focus of consumer behavior, and to solve problems consumers need information about products and services, acquisition of which may be planned or incidental. Given the range of information available, consumers are receptive to and retain some (*see* CONSUMER PERCEPTIONS) which in turn leads to knowledge about products/brands which may or may not lead to purchase or repurchase. Information will include that which is stored from previous experience to help form, change, or reinforce attitudes toward products/brands – which might encourage reinforcement of prevailing attitudes and stimulate repurchase, or lead to product/brand rejection.

### Bibliography

Engel, J. F., Blackwell, R. D. & Miniard, P. W. (1990). *Consumer behavior* (6th edn). Orlando, FL: The Dryden Press. Chapter 14.

Foxall, G. R. & Goldsmith, R. E (1994). *Consumer psychology for marketing*. London: Routledge. Chapter 4.

Hawkins, D. I., Best, R. J. & Coney, K. A. (1992). *Consumer behavior: Implications for marketing strategy* (5th edn). Homewood, IL: Irwin. Chapter 9.

Loudon, D. L. & Della Bitta, A. J. (1993). *Consumer behavior* (4th edn). McGraw-Hill Int. Chapter 12.

Schiffman, L. G. & Kanuk, L. Z. (1991). *Consumer behavior* (4th edn). Prentice-Hall. Chapter 7.

Solomon, M. R. (1992). *Consumer behavior.* Needham Heights, MA: Allyn & Bacon. Chapter 4.

Wilkie, W. L. (1994). *Consumer behavior* (3rd edn). New York: John Wiley. Chapter 10.

BARBARA LEWIS

**consumer marketing**    Consumer marketing refers to the buying of products and services for personal or household use, as opposed to buying by organizations. The implied alternative is BUSINESS-TO-BUSINESS MARKETING, although the distinction between the two areas is not entirely clear-cut (*see* BUSINESS-TO-BUSINESS MARKETING). The techniques of consumer marketing management dominate most standard marketing textbooks, with the result that specialized textbooks tend not to be exclusively devoted to consumer marketing in the same way as for business-to-business marketing. Indeed, the view of MARKETING MANAGEMENT presented in standard texts such as Kotler (1994) or McCarthy & Perreault (1993) is often seen as essentially synonymous with *consumer*, as opposed to business-to-business, marketing management (*see* MARKETING MANAGEMENT). More recently, however, consumer marketing, especially for services, has developed somewhat in nature and scope to include, in particular, some of the techniques more traditionally found in BUSINESS-TO-BUSINESS MARKETING, for example (*see* RELATIONSHIP MARKETING; SERVICES MARKETING).

Consumer purchase decision-making is also generally held to be subject to the influence of "non-task" or "irrational" factors to a far greater extent than business-to-business marketing. CONSUMER BUYER BEHAVIOR is a major area for research in marketing and has involved the investigation of such areas as: individual decision-making influences (such as personality, perceptions, and attitudes); group decision-making influences (such as opinion leadership, reference groups, or lifestyle influences); and cultural influences on consumer behavior (*see* CONSUMER BUYER BEHAVIOR).

**Bibliography**

Kotler, P. (1994). *Marketing management: Analysis, planning, implementation and control* (8th edn). Englewood Cliffs, NJ: Prentice-Hall.

McCarthy, E. J. & Perreault, R. (1993). *Basic marketing* (11th edn). Homewood, IL: Irwin.

FIONA LEVERICK

**consumer motivation**    *see* CONSUMER NEEDS AND MOTIVES

**consumer needs**    *see* CONSUMER NEEDS AND MOTIVES

**consumer needs and motives**    It may be argued that marketing rests on the premise that consumer needs are the starting point from which business activity should be planned. Consumer needs are biological, relating to primary or physiological elements; or psychological, i.e., emotional. Primary needs are often modified by psychological needs, i.e., they are subject to social and other influences. Consumers have a sophisticated structure of needs relating to social, cultural, emotional, and intellectual interests, all affecting buyer behavior.

Maslow (1970) offered a hierarchy of needs moving from the level of physiological needs, i.e., primary needs for food and shelter, to safety needs, e.g., for security, protection, education and training, assurance and insurance; belongingness and love needs, e.g., for affection, affiliation, sense of being part of a group; esteem needs, e.g., the desire for prestige, reputation, attention, recognition and appreciation, achievement and success, confidence; and the need for self-actualization, e.g., personal influence. The hierarchy suggests fulfilment at one level before progressing to the next; however, in reality, consumers may well be influenced by higher level needs when lower needs have not been satisfied.

Consumer motives actuate and direct action to be taken in satisfaction of identified needs, i.e., they are an internal driving force or stimulus to purchase. They organize, sustain, and direct activities toward diverse objects and needs. Two types of motives are relevant for the consumer: rational buying motives which take account of economic factors, price, product reliability, cash and credit facilities; and irrational buying motives, which relate to higher level consumer needs, to take account of the influence of other people.

## Bibliography

Dichter, E. (1964). *The handbook of consumer motivations.* New York: McGraw-Hill.

Foxall, G. R. & Goldsmith, R. E. (1994). *Consumer psychology for marketing.* London: Routledge. Chapter 7.

Hawkins, D. I., Best, R. J. & Coney, K. A. (1992). *Consumer behavior: Implications for marketing strategy* (5th edn). Homewood, IL: Irwin. Chapter 10.

Loudon, D. L. & Della Bitta, A. J. (1993). *Consumer behavior* (4th edn). McGraw-Hill Int. Chapter 10.

Maslow, A. H. (1970). *Motivation and personality* (2nd edn). New York: Harper & Row.

Schiffman, L. G. & Kanuk, L. Z. (1991). *Consumer behavior* (4th edn). Prentice-Hall. Chapter 3.

Solomon, M. R. (1992). *Consumer behavior.* Needham Heights, MA: Allyn & Bacon. Chapter 3.

Wilkie, W. L. (1994). *Consumer behavior* (3rd edn). New York: John Wiley. Chapter 5.

BARBARA LEWIS

**consumer panels**   In MARKETING RESEARCH, the same sample of individuals may be used over and over again, often asked questions on the same topic, indeed asked the same questions at different points in time. Studies of buying behavior often require respondents to keep diaries of their purchases, or, more recently, to use a scanner to record the bar-codes on all their purchases. Such a sample is called a panel and such continuous research is becoming more and more prevalent compared to 'one-off' research. The need for benchmarks, as in one-off research, is less important in continuous research as comparisons with previous results provided by the same panel are integral to this research process.

*Advantages of Panels*

Panels allow the study of trends over time, allow changes to be identified, and thus facilitate the search for causes of changes. They place less reliance on recall and more reliance on recording of behavior as it happens. The cost of recruiting the sample can be spread over several pieces of research.

*Disadvantages of Panels*

It is harder to recruit individuals to the sample if they know that they will be expected to cooperate again and again. Some members of the panel will drop out and equivalent replacements will have to be found. There may be a policy of rolling replacement of a given proportion of the panel each period, partly to forestall fatigue. Finally, respondents' behavior may be affected because they know that they are on the panel or because their behavior is conditioned by answering questions on a previous occasion.

## Bibliography

Aaker, D. A., Kumar, V. & Day, G. S. (1995). *Marketing research* (5th edn). New York: John Wiley, pp. 144–148.

MICHAEL GREATOREX

**consumer perceptions**   Consumers are continually exposed to a multitude of stimuli from companies, the environment, and other people, and they endeavor to make sense of visual stimuli through the perceptive process – which may be defined as the result of interaction between stimuli and individual/personal factors.

The perceptive process is subjective and individuals tend to select, organize, and interpret stimuli and information according to existing beliefs and attitudes, which in turn influence consumer reaction, attitudes, and behavior. Further, there are limits to the number of stimuli that consumers can pay attention to and comprehend at any one time and so the receptive process becomes selective. In fact, consumers have selective exposure to stimuli, selective perceptions (and sometimes distortion), and in turn selective retention and selective decision-making. In addition, perception changes as needs and motives change, as more stimuli become available, and as a function of increasing experience as consumers.

## Bibliography

Foxall, G. R. & Goldsmith, R. E. (1994). *Consumer psychology for marketing*. London: Routledge. Chapter 3.

Hawkins, D. I., Best, R. J. & Coney, K. A. (1992). *Consumer behavior: Implications for marketing strategy* (5th edn). Homewood, IL: Irwin. Chapter 8.

Schiffman, L. G. & Kanuk, L. Z. (1991). *Consumer behavior* (4th edn). Prentice-Hall. Chapter 6

Solomon, M. R. (1992). *Consumer behavior*. Needham Heights, MA: Allyn & Bacon. Chapter 2.

Wilkie, W. L. (1994). *Consumer behavior* (3rd edn). New York: John Wiley. Chapters 8, 9.

BARBARA LEWIS

**consumer protection** Despite the notion of *caveat emptor* (let the buyer beware), consumer protection is now a part of the legal framework of most developed countries. For example, modern laws concerned with food and drink go back to 1860 in the UK and modern weights and measures legislation began in the UK in 1878.

The UK Sale of Goods Act (1893) gave some protection to consumers but allowed sellers to contract out of their liability under the Act by inserting exclusion clauses into contracts. The UK Unfair Contract Terms Act (1977) significantly limited the rights of the seller to insert such clauses which purport to exclude or limit liability, thus increasing consumer protection. The UK Consumer Protection Act (1987) came into force as a result of the government's obligation to implement a European Community (EC) directive and provides a remedy in damages for any person who suffers personal injury or damage to property as a result of a defective product or service. It is the responsibility of the injured person to prove that the loss was caused by the defect and that general expectations were not satisfied. The Act supplements the existing civil law: a consumer may well have a remedy in contract or in the tort of negligence.

## Bibliography

Dibb, S., Simkin, L., Pride, W. M. & Ferrell, O. C. (1994). *Marketing, concepts and strategies* (European edn). Boston, MA: Houghton Mifflin Co. Chapter 2.

Harvey, B. W. & Parry, D. L. (1987). *Law of consumer protection and fair trading*. London: Butterworths.

Palmer, A. & Worthington, I. (1992). *The business and marketing environment*. Maidenhead: McGraw-Hill. Chapter 8.

DAVID YORKE

**consumerism** Consumerism involves those activities of government, business, independent organizations, and consumers themselves which help protect consumers against unfair or unethical business practices.

The main era of development for the consumerist movement was in the USA in the early 1960s when President John F. Kennedy presented his consumers' Bill of Rights to Congress in 1962. This Bill established the basic principles of consumerism, namely, the *right to safety*, to be protected against dangerous and unsafe products; the *right to be informed* and protected against fraudulent, deceitful, and misleading statements, advertisements, labels, etc. and to be educated on how to use financial resources wisely; the *right to choose* and be assured access to a variety of products and services at competitive prices – although when competition is not possible government regulation should be substituted; and the *right to be heard* by government and business regarding unsatisfactory or disappointing practices.

In addition, one of the most successful consumer groups was founded around this time. Ralph Nader's Public Citizen group lifted consumerism into a major social force, following publication of his book *Unsafe at Any Speed* (1965), which was a detailed examination of the automobile industry. Following similar investigations into meat processing and money lending, several laws were passed which established fairer practices. Consumer organizations have won battles for consumers in many other countries, e.g., in Scandinavia, Netherlands, France, Germany, Japan, and the UK, in a number of areas of business activity. For example, the practice of inertia selling which involved the sending of unsolicited goods to people was curbed in the UK by laws passed in 1971 and 1975; and organizations such as the Better Business Bureau in the USA and the

Consumers' Association in the UK have fought for truth in advertising, adequate food labeling of nutrition and ingredients, and the use of "sell-by" and "open-by" dates.

Consumerism can be seen as the ultimate expression of the MARKETING CONCEPT since it compels companies to think from the consumer's perspective. For example, environmental groups have raised consumer awareness of green issues and companies have responded to the opportunity by creating "green" products. One UK group, the Campaign for Real Ale (CAMRA), successfully ensured the existence of naturally-fermented beers which were in danger of being phased out by the major breweries. Several reasons have been given for the growth of consumerism in Western economies, such as a more impersonal market place, increased product complexity, more intrusive advertising, increasing two-earner families, mass media which are quick to publicize unethical questionable practices by marketers, and the emergence of less materialistic values in consumers (Hawkins & Best, 1995).

In one sense, there is a philosophical conflict between the existence of consumerism and the marketing concept, because if the marketing concept were operating properly, there should be no need for consumerism. However, the diversity of consumer needs means that it is virtually impossible to produce products which satisfy every individual's needs. Secondly, organizations must produce goods within certain cost parameters to ensure profit. Thirdly, not all organizations have embraced or implemented the marketing concept fully. In practice, these three considerations explain the existence of both consumerism and the marketing concept.

**Bibliography**

Bloom, P. N. & Greyser, G. A. (1981). The maturity of consumerism. *Harvard Business Review*, Nov.–Dec., **59**, 130–139.

Hawkins, D. I., Best, R. J. & Coney, K. A. (1995). *Consumer behavior, implications for marketing strategy* (6th edn). Boston, MA: Irwin. Chapter 21.

Nader, R. (1965). *Unsafe at any speed*. Public Citizen group.

VINCE MITCHELL

**contingency planning** In stable environments, organizations should be able to devise and implement plans based on their analysis of the important variables likely to affect demand and supply. However, in general organizations operate in environments where there is significant change and, therefore, some UNCERTAINTY about the possible future outcomes. Even in relatively stable environments there is always the probability of some unforeseen event which can affect the outcome. Organizations may, therefore, strive to forecast a possible range of future states or scenarios and to devise appropriate plans for each of these. This is contingency planning. As it becomes clearer which scenario is unfolding, the organization can draw on the appropriate contingency plan.

DALE LITTLER

**continuous innovation** It has been suggested that INNOVATIONS, and in particular technological innovations, can be viewed along a continuum, ranging from incremental or continuous innovations to the more radical or DISCONTINUOUS INNOVATIONS (Littler, 1988; Robertson, 1971). Continuous innovation involves relatively little change in such dimensions as technology, habits, motivations, and working practices.

**Bibliography**

Littler, D. A. (1988). *Technological development*. Oxford: Philip Allan. Chapter 1.

Robertson, T. S. (1971). *Innovative behavior and communication*. New York: Holt, Rinehart & Winston.

DALE LITTLER

**contribution** The contribution of a product or service is the residual sum (after deducting variable costs) which a product contributes toward PROFIT and toward the fixed costs of its production and distribution. Thus, contribution is an internal measure used to analyze the performance of a product in contributing to the productivity and profitability of an organization (Thomas, 1986). The concept of contribution is particularly useful where fixed costs may be difficult to assign to any specific offering, perhaps because they are shared by several product ranges and variants. Therefore, a predetermined contribution margin is sometimes assigned to a product for the purposes of calculating price because it is not possible (or practicable) to identify its contribution more precisely, making it difficult to calculate price on the basis of cost-plus methods (*see* PRICING METHODS). Thus, products with low contribution will generally be low priorities for investment purposes and in strategic MARKETING PLANNING. It is important to take into account interlinkages among products whereby, for example, a product may have a low (or even negative) contribution while being a necessary prerequisite for another more profitable offering (e.g., after-sales warranty services). Equally, a product or service may seem to be unproductive and unprofitable (e.g., a train with very few passengers) and yet still earn a worthwhile contribution because the variable costs involved (e.g., the fuel to run the train) are very low compared to the fixed costs (e.g., the cost of the railway network, stations, engine, and rolling stock) which have already been incurred.

### Bibliography

Thomas, M. J. (1986). Marketing productivity analysis: A research report. *Marketing Intelligence and Planning*, **4**, (2), 3–71 (entire issue).

DOMINIC WILSON

**conviction**    Conviction is the third step in the DAGMAR communication MODEL. It is part of the AFFECTIVE stage, i.e., the buyer or customer is convinced that the product or service will meet the need or specification. Although it is the penultimate step before ACTION, the link between conviction and a subsequent purchase is difficult to measure.

### Bibliography

Colley, R. H. (1961). *Defining advertising goals for measured advertising results*. New York: Association of National Advertisers.
Kotler, P. (1994). *Marketing management: Analysis, planning, implementation and control* (8th edn). Englewood Cliffs, NJ: Prentice-Hall. Chapter 22.

DAVID YORKE

**corporate strategy**    Corporate strategy is regarded as encompassing the aims and objectives of the organization together with the means of how these are to be achieved. It is, by definition, holistic, i.e., it embraces all of the company's different businesses and functions. Andrews (1971) defined corporate strategy as: "the pattern of major objectives, purposes or goals and essential policies or plans for achieving those goals, stated in such a way as to define what business the company is in or is to be in and the kind of company it is or is to be" (28). Chandler (1962) believed that it should also be concerned with "the allocation of resources necessary for carrying out these goals" (13).

In defining its corporate strategy, the firm has to satisfy the sometimes contradictory expectations of several differing constituencies including, obviously, customers as well as suppliers, shareholders, and employees. It has been suggested that in countries such as the UK the short-term requirements of institutional shareholders prevent longer term investments, often to the detriment of sustainable competitiveness (*see* COMPETITIVE STRATEGY).

It is widely believed that corporate strategy should address the essentials of the organization, namely, the "what," "why," "how," and "when," of the organization. It is concerned with "what businesses is the company in or would like to be in?" Secondly, it embraces "why the company is in business," i.e., the specific sales, profit, rate of return, and growth targets it has or should have. Thirdly, the company needs to define "how" it aims to achieve those targets, such as the technologies it will use, the markets it is or should be operating in, and the products it markets or should market in order to achieve those objectives. Finally, the company needs to decide "when" it aims to achieve those goals and the period over which it defines its strategy.

Often, companies engage in formal STRATEGIC PLANNING as a means of developing a coherent corporate strategy, and the corporate strategy may be embodied in written strategic plans. In recent years, there has been much emphasis on COMPETITIVE STRATEGY with the focus on identifying the various structural determinants of performance and positioning the company to exploit these advantageously. However, it has been convincingly argued that a sound corporate strategy will be informed by a close monitoring of the evolving requirements of the various constituencies that the organization has to satisfy, and in particular of its existing and potential customer targets.

### Bibliography

Andrews, K. (1971). *The concept of corporate strategy.* Homewood, IL: Irwin.
Chandler, A. D. (1962). *Strategy and structure.* Cambridge, MA: MIT Press.

DALE LITTLER

**correlation**   *see* REGRESSION AND CORRELATION

**cost**   The production and distribution of any good or service involves costs which will vary over the life cycle (*see* PRODUCT LIFE CYCLE) of the good/service. These costs can be divided into fixed costs and variable costs. Fixed costs are those which are incurred in order for production to take place and so are, broadly speaking, not directly related to the volume of actual production (e.g., costs of R&D, premises, production assets, basic workforce), whereas variable costs are those which vary directly in proportion to the level of actual production (e.g., costs of materials and energy). Investment in capital assets (and therefore the level of fixed costs) is generally higher at the start of a product's life cycle than toward the end. It can sometimes be very difficult to identify the costs of a product unambiguously, especially where fixed costs are shared by a wide range of products at different stages of their life cycles. Corporate accounting policies (e.g., in depreciation and asset valuation) can also affect cost calculations. However, assessing costs is obviously a crucial part of assessing price, despite the many problems involved.

### Bibliography

Shim, E. & Sudit, E. F. (1995). How manufacturers price products. *Management Accounting*, 76, (8), Feb., 37–39.

DOMINIC WILSON

**cost leadership strategy**   This is one of the GENERIC STRATEGIES proposed by Porter (1980) (*see* COMPETITIVE STRATEGY). Companies having the lowest costs should be in a strong position with regard to: *competitors*, because they will always be able to undercut them, while taking advantage of a higher margin to invest in increasing market share, new product development, and other corporate development policies; *suppliers*, because they can more easily absorb increases in costs; *customers*, because they are able to respond to demands for lower prices; and *substitutes*, because they will be better able to react to them in terms of cost. In order to be a cost leader, the company must have low overheads, be highly efficient, and generally not direct resources to activities which are seen as being extraneous to achieving continued lowest cost. Companies may follow a focused cost leadership strategy aimed at particular customers or market segments (*see* MARKET SEGMENTATION), or a broad market cost leadership strategy. There are risks to the emphasis on cost leadership, in particular the bases of customer choice may move toward NON-PRICE FACTORS and technological change may shift the COMPETITIVE ADVANTAGE to rivals, including late entrants.

### Bibliography

Porter M. E. (1980). *Competitive strategy: Techniques for analyzing industries and competitors.* New York: Free Press. Chapter 2.

DALE LITTLER

**cost per thousand**   Media efficiency is usually measured in terms of the cost per thousand exposures among members of the target audience (viewers, listeners, readers). However, this is often too simple. The target audience may use a variety of media and, thus, combinations of media must be considered in arriving at an efficient MEDIA SCHEDULE. Unfortunately, even with six media, any choice of three will involve 20 potential different combinations. Computer models assist in MEDIA PLANNING.

## Bibliography

Aaker, D. A. & Myers, J. G. (1987). *Advertising management* (3rd edn). Englewood Cliffs, NJ: Prentice-Hall. Chapter 15.
Kotler, P. (1994). *Marketing management: Analysis, planning, implementation and control* (8th edn). Englewood Cliffs, NJ: Prentice-Hall. Chapter 23.

DAVID YORKE

**coupons** Coupons are a SALES PROMOTION device which try to persuade buyers/customers to purchase. They may offer a discount on the first or subsequent purchase of a product/service or they may need to be collected in order to be redeemed against a future purchase or to receive gifts or cash. Such redemption is often difficult to control from the sponsor's point of view and retailers often do not favor them as they represent an administrative and time-consuming inconvenience.

## Bibliography

Dibb, S., Simikin, L., Pride, W. M. & Ferrell, O. C. (1994). *Marketing, concepts and strategies* (European edn). Boston, MA: Houghton Mifflin Co. Chapter 16.
Kotler, P. (1994). *Marketing management: Analysis planning, implementation and control* (8th edn). Englewood Cliffs, NJ: Prentice-Hall. Chapter 24.
Semenik, R. J. & Bamossy, G. J. (1993). *Principles of marketing*. Cincinnati, OH: South-Western Publishing Co. Chapter 11.

DAVID YORKE

**creative content** Creative content refers to the visuals and words or elements of the visual identity system of an organization. The creative content of these elements reinforces, for example, a hospital's IMAGE through the use of color, symbol, logotype, and typeface (Bruce & Greyser, 1995). The creative content of a brochure or an advertisement or a pack are tangible expressions of the organization and offer signals of its values which, in turn, influence the perceptions and opinions of its various publics. A corporate communications brochure of Caterpillar (1994) points out that the visual material cannot just show pictures of the products but "they have to show what we make possible for our customers, we have responsibility to show products being used by the types of people who actually use them." Similarly with the text, "we can't just say Caterpillar products and services are best. We have to demonstrate their superiority in terms people find meaningful and important ... to our many audiences, it's not what we make that counts; it's what we make possible." So, the creative content (e.g., the words and visuals) of an advertisement or brochure or other form of communication usually contains four elements: the principal benefit offered by the product or service; the characteristics of the product or service; the image of the product or service; and the uses of the product or service.

## Bibliography

Aaker, D. A. & Myers, J. G. (1987). *Advertising management* (3rd edn). Englewood Cliffs, NJ: Prentice-Hall. Chapter 15.
Bruce, M. & Greyser, S. (1995). *Changing corporate identity: The case of a regional hospital*. Teaching case. Boston, MA: Design Management Institute and Harvard Business School.
Caterpillar, Inc. (1994). *Communicating Caterpillar: One voice*. Peoria, IL.

MARGARET BRUCE

**cross-tabulations** Cross-tabulations are very popular in the analysis of survey data and they are concerned with the quantitative analysis of data where several variables are analyzed together, usually to see if there are any relationships between the variables.

If two of the variables are measured on nominal (categorical) scales, cross-tabulations (cross-tabs) can be used to summarize the sample data. A cross-tab is a table with the categories (or values) for the two variables set out on the two axes and the counts of the number of times each pair of values occurs recorded in the cells of the table. The row and column totals are usually calculated and percentages across the rows and/or down the columns are also computed to aid in the interpretation, description, and discussion of the results. Cross-tabs can be formed in more than two dimensions when data for more than two categorical variables are analyzed, but interpretation may become difficult as the increased number of cells often leaves empty cells or a number of cells with small counts.

The variables may be ordinal variables such as those measured on rating scales or interval variables where the data have been grouped into a few classes for each variable. Again, the cross-tab records the counts of the number of cases falling into each cell of the table.

HYPOTHESIS TESTING relating to cross-tabs often involves the chi-square test. Other tests and summary statistics are available depending on the type of data; for instance, if both variables are measured on ordinal scales then Spearman's rank correlation coefficient or Kendall's tau may be used.

As well as recording the number of cases in each cell, a cross-tab can be used to present summary statistics of other variables for the cases in each cell. For instance, while a basic cross-tab may count the sample numbers, broken down by gender and occupation, it is possible to present the average income (or the average of any similar variable) of the cases in each gender/occupation cell. Further analysis of such data may involve analysis of variance, but the cross-tab analysis described earlier in this paragraph is a convenient way to get a feel for these data and to present results in a convenient, descriptive manner.

### Bibliography

Tull, D. S. & Hawkins, D. I. (1987). *Marketing research: Measurement and method* (4th edn). New York: Macmillan. Chapter 13.

MICHAEL GREATOREX

**cue** A cue is a non-verbal signal communicated by a person, product, or service. People draw inferences from visual interpersonal contact which gives access to the face, the hands, the posture, or the physical environment in which the interaction is taking place. Information is communicated via the aggregate of social cues provided by visual and physical presence. Products and services also communicate evaluative information via intrinsic and extrinsic stimuli such as physical attributes, or ADVERTISING messages. Thus, desired impressions, feelings, and attitudes may be subtly encouraged by MARKETING COMMUNICATIONS techniques (e.g., PERSONAL SELLING, PACKAGING, TELEMARKETING).

### Bibliography

Loudon, D. L. & Della Bitta, A. J. (1993). *Consumer behavior* (4th edn). McGraw-Hill Int.
Rutter, D. R. (1994). *Looking and seeing. The role of visual communication in social interaction.* Chichester: Wiley.

DAVID YORKE

**cultural environment** This is one of the elements of the MARKETING ENVIRONMENT. It concerns cultural and ethnic variation between and among markets, as well as changes in cultural or ethnic perspective. It is of course particularly important in INTERNATIONAL MARKETING, but is also increasingly important as national markets are segmented into smaller niches, often based on cultural and ethnic criteria (e.g., in the fast food and fashion clothing markets).

*See also* **Environmental analysis; Culture**

DOMINIC WILSON

**culture** Individuals may be described as conforming to the norms of cultures and subcultures in their lives. Culture refers to the total way of life of a society and a national culture reflects its population, government, and economy. Culture is a determinant and regulator of behavior, including CONSUMER BUYER BEHAVIOR. Members of a culture share beliefs, values, customs, traditions, and norms which shape their attitudes and behavior as consumers. Cultural beliefs and values intervene in economic decisions made by consumers.

There are a number of distinguishing characteristics of culture, namely, *learned behavior* – patterns of behavior may be learned; *sharing of values*; a *transmissive quality* as families shape the values and perceptions of children and pass them on to be reflected in attitudes and behavior; a *social quality*, i.e., the rules of social behavior; an *ideational quality*, as groups have ideals with respect to behavior; a *gratifying quality* as a culture satisfies biological and social needs; *an adaptive quality* as cultures adapt to changing needs and environment; and an *integrative quality* – a culture will embrace a number of subgroups and subcultures.

The fundamental orientation of culture in modern industrial society is toward achievement and attainment and increasing levels of satisfaction. Further, Western culture is characterized by various trends: increasing affluence and a leisure orientation; increasing education and more questioning of traditional values; increasing communications/mobility, leading to increased awareness and purchase of alternatives/variety; and decreasing influence of the family.

Cultural change is the process by which a society improves or revises its responses to the environment, and cultural patterns change as new values emerge and subcultures develoSubcultures within a national culture have their own distinctive ideas, values, and characteristics which may be very different from the total pattern of culture. These are based on cultural traditions emanating from various sources, and examples of subcultures are: *ethnic and racial –* in particular immigrant groups – which provide a two-way cultural influence with an indigenous population, stimulated by mass media communications and opportunity for travel; *youth –* i.e., teenage markets which are exemplified by relatively high spending power and little BRAND LOYALTY; *regional*; and *religious*. In modern society subcultures are of significance to marketers because of their influence on products and services demanded, i.e., market segments may derive from subcultural needs.

Further, cultural variations on an international basis have implications for organizations which export their products and services. For example, products, packages, tastes, colors, promotions, and distribution may not be acceptable across national boundaries – e.g., relating to the status of women in the Middle East, cultural taboos, communications deficiencies, the state of economic development. So, marketing strategies need to be moderated accordingly.

### Bibliography

Engel, J. D., Blackwell, R. D. & Miniard, P. W. (1990). *Consumer behavior* (6th edn). Orlando, FL: The Dryden Press. Chapter 3.

Hawkins, D. I., Best, R. J. & Coney, K. A. (1992). *Consumer behavior: Implications for marketing strategy* (5th edn). Homewood, IL: Irwin. Chapter 2.

Krech, D., Crutchfield, R. S. & Ballachey, E. L. (1962). *Individual in society*. New York: McGraw-Hill.

Loudon, D. L. & Della Bitta, A. J. (1993). *Consumer behavior* (4th edn). McGraw-Hill Int. Chapters 3, 4.

Moschis, G. P. (1987). *Consumer socialization.* Lexington, MA: Lexington Books.

Schiffman, L. G. & Kanuk, L. Z. (1991). *Consumer behavio* (4th edn). Prentice-Hall. Chapters 14, 15, 16.

Solomon, M. R. (1992). *Consumer behavior.* Needham Heights, MA: Allyn & Bacon. Chapters 13, 15.

BARBARA LEWIS

**customer satisfaction**   *see* SERVICE QUALITY

**customer service**   *see* SERVICE QUALITY

**customers**   Traditionally, customers might be defined as the actual or intended purchasers of products or services. Recent developments in the scope of marketing might also see other parties in the organization's MARKETING ENVIRONMENT as customers. For example, INTERNAL MARKETING theory suggests that an organization view its employees as customers, or that the marketing function might regard other parts of the organization as customers.

*See also* **Suppliers**

FIONA LEVERICK

# ——— D ———

**DAGMAR model** The DAGMAR model (Defining Advertising Goals for Measured Advertising Results) is a model of MARKETING COMMUNICATIONS and was developed by Colley (1961) specifically for the measurement of ADVERTISING effectiveness. It postulates that the customer/buyer moves from a state of unawareness through AWARENESS of the product or service, COMPREHENSION (an understanding of what the product or service will do), CONVICTION that it will meet requirements, to ACTION (a purchase). A benchmark measure is first taken of the position along the spectrum to which members of the target group(s) have progressed. Objectives are then established, advertising is produced, and a further measure is taken to discover whether or not any effective shift has occurred (i.e., whether or not the objectives have been met). Precise measurement is impossible as so many other variables are present. Furthermore, such variables become more numerous the further one moves toward action.

*See also* **Communications objectives**

**Bibliography**

Colley, R. H. (1961). *Defining advertising goals for measured advertising results.* New York: Association of National Advertisers.
Kotler, P. (1994). *Marketing management: Analysis, planning, implementation and control* (8th edn). Englewood Cliffs, NJ: Prentice-Hall. Chapter 22.

DAVID YORKE

**database** A database is a collection of related information which is capable of being organized and accessed by a computer. Depending on the software being used, information can be entered in numeric or word form. Common numerical database systems such as spreadsheets allow a high degree of querying, analysis, sorting, and extraction of information. The most common usage of databases in marketing is to develop a customer database. Typically, customer information such as purchase history, value and timing of orders, responses to previous offers, name, address, and demographic characteristics will be gathered as well as additional information from salespersons' reports and external sources such as geodemographic profiles (*see* GEODEMOGRAPHICS). Database marketing allows closer monitoring of a company's customers and can be used to: identify the most profitable/least profitable customers, allow cross-selling of goods, identify possible customer segments, and help in communicating individually with customers. Database marketing has developed hand in hand with a more tailored approach to marketing goods and services, since more is known about customers as individuals and they can be reached through DIRECT MAIL campaigns.

Database can also be useful for bibliographic searches, site location, MEDIA PLANNING, market FORECASTING, market potential studies, and MARKET SEGMENTATION studies. Many commercial numeric databases exist which contain information on sales, population characteristics, the business environment, economic forecasts, specialized bibliographies, and other material. For example, ABI/Inform contains abstracts of articles in approximately 1,300 business publications worldwide. Predicasts (PTS) provides numerous on-line databases on products, markets, competitors, demand forecasts, annual reports, etc. *see* PROFIT IMPACT OF MARKETING STRATEGIES (PIMS) is an ongoing program of research conducted by the Strategic Planning Institute (Cambridge, MA, USA) into the impact of MARKETING STRATE- GIES: over 250 companies provide data on over 2,000 businesses for at least four years' trading. Given the huge diversity of databases available, several networks have been established to allow users easier access to each. One of the largest of these host networks is DIALOG which contains over 200 different databases. NEXIS is another large system.

### Bibliography

Fletcher, K. (1994). The evolution and use of information technology in marketing. In M. J. Baker (Ed.), *The marketing book* (3rd edn) (pp. 333–357). Oxford: Butterworth Heinemann.
Rapp, S. & Collins, T. L. (1987). *Maximarketing.* New York: McGraw-Hill.

VINCE MITCHELL

**deciders**   Deciders are those members of the DECISION-MAKING UNIT (DMU) who are responsible for the final purchase decision (though they do not always sign the purchase contract). For major purchase decisions the decider may be the chief executive, a director, or the chief procurement officer but for relatively insignificant purchase decisions the decider may be a junior member of the purchasing staff (*see* ORGANIZATIONAL BUYING BEHAVIOR; PUR- CHASING PROCESS)

DOMINIC WILSON

**decision-making unit**   *see* BUYING CENTER

**demand**   The assessment of demand is crucial to responsible pricing analysis and decision- making, yet demand can often be an unknowable and even a mercurial factor. At one extreme, analysis of demand can be little more than a statistical extrapolation of historic demand data, regardless of the validity of the data, the methodology used for their collection, or the assumptions underlying their use (as with the Ford Edsell motor-car). At another extreme,

assessment of demand can be no more than intuitive guesswork propped up by selective data (as with the Sinclair C5 electric mini-car).

The demand for a product or service can be seen as historic, existing, latent, or potential. Historic demand describes customers (indivi- duals and organizations) who have purchased a particular product or service in the past, whereas existing demand describes customers who are currently purchasing the product or service, and potential demand describes those customers who might purchase the product or service in the foreseeable future given various changes in marketing strategy or environmental circumstances (e.g., protectionism). Some authorities also use the term latent demand to refer, in effect, to demand which could be developed reasonably quickly (so distinguishing latent demand from potential demand) with appropriate marketing strategies but which meanwhile remains dormant. The most easily adapted aspect of marketing strategies is PRI- CING and this is usually the quickest way to translate latent demand or potential demand into existing demand. Yet too much demand can be just as problematic for a supplier as too little demand and a responsible pricing policy will therefore depend crucially on careful assessment of demand.

Clearly there will often be similarities between these forms of demand but there can also be important differences. For example, the product or service in question may well have changed significantly over time to the extent that historic demand is no longer a useful indication of potential demand. The character- istics of demand can also change over time (e.g., in disposable income, customer sophistication, sensitivity to particular product aspects). And there is usually sufficient environmental change and uncertainty about the data to mean that demand should generally be assessed cautiously. Demand is even more difficult to assess where a product or service is innovative, making historic reference points even more problematic. This caution is captured in the concept of realizable demand which refers to that fraction of potential demand which an organization considers it can realistically achieve with its MARKETING STRATEGY and PRICING decisions.

DOMINIC WILSON

**demographic environment** The demographic environment is one of the elements of the MARKETING ENVIRONMENT (*see also* ENVIRONMENTAL ANALYSIS).

*See also* **Demographics**

DOMINIC WILSON

**demographics** Demographics comprise probably the most important variable in the MARKETING ENVIRONMENT of any organization. Demographics describe, and provide a statistical study of, a human population in terms of its size, structure, and distribution. Size is the number of individuals in a population, and is determined by: fertility and birth rates; life expectancy and death rates; and migration between and within countries. Structure describes the population in terms of age, gender, education, and occupation, and distribution refers to the location of individuals in terms of geographic region or rural, urban, or suburban location.

Demographic data are developed, primarily, from population censuses and the study of demographics is concerned with understanding trends to include forecasts of future demographic size, structure, and distribution.

Demographics impact on the behavior of consumers and contribute to the overall demand for goods and services. They are changing in an number of ways, influenced by social and cultural variables (*see also* CULTURE). Such trends, in developed economies, include:

- increased life expectancy and an aging population

- a slowing down of the birth rate and population growth

- growing per capita income and discretionary income

- changing mix of household expenditure

- increasing participation of women in the work force and their changing roles at home and at work

- increasing proportion of white collar workers

- trends in literacy and education

- geographical shifts in population, e.g., urban to rural and city to suburbs and new towns

- changing ethnic and racial mixes

- changing family and household structure, to take account of age profiles, later marriage and age of child-bearing, fewer children in a family, divorce and single-parent families, increasing numbers of single-person households, and total number of households

- increased home ownership and increased ownership of consumer durables

- widespread availability of credit

- fewer traditional shoppers and more home shopping

- increased leisure time and participation in leisure activities

- changing media habits

- increases in crime and social problems.

These changes/trends are of key interest to marketing organizations. For example, they may see opportunities arising as particular age groups increase, or threats occurring as some age groups decline. Demographic trends have implications for: product and service development; identification of target MARKETS and market segments (*see* MARKET SEGMENTATION) and other elements in the MARKETING MIX. These impact not only on manufacturers and distributors but also on those organizations which supply consumer good manufacturers, e.g., producers of commodities and capital equipment.

*See also* **lifestyles**

**Bibliography**

Central Statistical Office. *Annual abstract of statistics.* London: HMSO.

Hawkins, D. I., Best, R. J. & Coney, K. A. (1995). *Consumer behavior: Implications for marketing strategy* (6th edn). International student edition. Chicago: Irwin. Chapter 3, pp. 78–88.

Kotler, P. (1994). *Marketing management: Analysis, planning, implementation and control* (8th edn). Englewood Cliffs, NJ: Prentice-Hall. Chapter 6.

McCarthy, E. J. & Perreault, W. D. Jr (1993). *Basic marketing.* Homewood, IL: Irwin. Chapter 6.

Palmer, A. & Worthington, I. (1992). *The business and marketing environment.* Maidenhead: McGraw-Hill. Chapters 9 & 10.

Pol, L. G. (1986). Marketing and demographic perspective. *Journal of Consumer Marketing*, Winter, 56–64.

United States Bureau of the Census. *Statistical abstract of the United States.* Austin: Reference Press.

Wilkie, W. L. (1994). *Consumer behavior* (3rd edn). New York: John Wiley, pp. 54–83.

BARBARA LEWIS

**depth interviews** Depth interviewing is a qualitative marketing research technique (*see* QUALITATIVE RESEARCH) in which a highly skilled interviewer conducts an unstructured, direct, personal interview with a single respondent to probe underlying feelings, motives, opinions, beliefs, and attitudes. The interviewer asks questions and probes relevant responses. Respondents answer questions as they feel appropriate.

Depth interviews are used (1) when the subject under discussion is highly confidential or embarrassing, (2) when studying complicated behavior such as that of professional people in their jobs or discretionary purchases by households, and (3) in situations where focus group (*see* FOCUS GROUPS) interviews are likely to bias the responses of individuals who have a tendency to conform to group pressures.

As with other kinds of depth interviews (*see* FOCUS GROUPS), the advantages of individual depth interviews center around the ability of the interviewer to probe underlying feelings to a greater depth than is possible with questionnaire techniques. The disadvantages include the greater possibility of interviewer bias and the subjective nature of the analysis and interpretation of the data. The shortage of skilled interviewers and the limited number of interviews that each can accomplish usually means that samples are small and possibly unrepresentative.

**Bibliography**

Malhotra, N. K. (1993). *Marketing research: An applied orientation.* Englewood Cliffs, NJ: Prentice-Hall. Chapter 6.

MICHAEL GREATOREX

**descriptive statistics** Unless the sample in a market research project is very small the data will be tabulated and analyzed using a computer. The simplest kind of statistical analysis of data involves descriptive statistics where the object is to summarize the data and describe the results for the sample. The alternative kind of analysis involves statistical inference, and such topics as CONFIDENCE INTERVALS and HYPOTHESIS TESTING. Descriptive statistical analysis can be carried out on a univariate or bivariate or multivariate basis (*see* UNIVARIATE ANALYSIS, BIVARIATE ANALYSIS, MULTIVARIATE METHODS ANALYSIS).

UNIVARIATE ANALYSIS involves the quantitative analysis of data where each variable is analyzed in isolation and is often the first stage in the analysis of a survey. If the original data are presented, then there are usually too many numbers for the analyst to make any sense of the data. This is true even when the data for a single variable are considered. The first step in the summarization process is for the data for each variable taken one at a time for the whole of a sample to be tabulated into a frequency distribution, having grouped the data, if necessary, into a convenient number of classes. A frequency distribution may be in actual counts or in percentages, in cumulative or non-cumulative form. The next stage may be to present the data in a graphical form, using a pie diagram, bar chart, histogram, ogive, etc., as required. A final stage in the summarization process is to calculate and present descriptive statistics such as measures of average, variation, skewness, and kurtosis for each variable. In this way, surveys yielding thousands of numbers on each variable can be summarized into one or two numbers (e.g., an average and a measure of variation) for each variable. This enables comparisons to be made more easily with other surveys and allows the researcher to report his/her results in a condensed form and to incorporate the results using the summary descriptive statistics into the text of the report.

BIVARIATE ANALYSIS is concerned with the quantitative analysis of data where pairs of variables are analyzed together, usually to see if there is any relationship between the variables. The analysis depends upon the types of measurements. CROSS-TABULATIONS can be used to compare variables measured on nominal scales or even variables measured on interval scales where the cases are grouped into classes. At the other extreme, simple correlation and regression (*see* REGRESSION AND CORRELATION) is useful for data measured on interval scales. If one variable is measured on a nominal scale and the other on an interval scale, the nominal variable can be used to split the sample into subsamples, and arithmetic means for the other variable can be calculated to enable the subsamples to be compared. GRAPHICAL REPRESENTATIONS such as scatter diagrams, bar charts, etc. are useful aids in bivariate statistical description.

The methods of MULTIVARIATE METHODS ANALYSIS, including those methods which require an understanding of statistical inference for maximum appreciation, can be used in a descriptive, explorative way. Methods such as multiple regression (*see* REGRESSION AND CORRELATION), DISCRIMINANT ANALYSIS, FACTOR ANALYSIS, CLUSTER ANALYSIS, CONJOINT ANALYSIS, and MULTIDIMENSIONAL SCALING are available in computer analysis packages to help the researcher analyze the quantitative data on many variables obtained in surveys.

### Bibliography

Tull, D. S. & Hawkins, D. I. (1987). *Marketing research: Measurement and method* (4th edn). New York: Macmillan. Chapters 12 & 13.

MICHAEL GREATOREX

**design**    The term "design" covers a wide range of activities – architecture, interior design, graphic design, industrial design, and engineering design. Designers usually specialize in one of these disciplines. All design terms involve the creative visualization of concepts, plans, ideas, and the representation of those ideas (as sketches, blueprints, models, or prototypes) so as to enable the making of something that did not exist before, or not quite in that form. Marketing managers tend to regard design as a tool to differentiate products, to entice consumers to buy; and consumers want the design to satisfy a given need – fun, function, price, etc.

Also, design is referred to as "the process of seeking to optimise customer satisfaction and company profitability through the creative use of major design elements (performance, quality, durability, appearance and costs) in connection with products, environments, information and corporate identities" (Kotler & Rath, 1984). Design activities lead to the creation of new products or services, new packs, corporate identities, and advertisements. It is design that takes the values of the organization and the ideas about the product or service and transforms these into the desired artifacts. To communicate the Body Shop's mission statement, "We will be the most honest cosmetic company," this has to be translated into a strategy for design in terms of: a corporate identity program, the product presentation, the labeling and container design, and the retail outlets.

Mounting evidence supports the case that investment in design expertise contributes to commercial performance (Lorenz, 1986; Walsh et al., 1992). Walsh et al. (1992) carried out an international study of different industries, ranging from electronics to furniture, to assess systematically the economic effect of design investment on business performance. The results of the study showed that design investment made a positive contribution to business performance, but only if the design resource was well managed and integrated with other corporate activities, notably marketing and production. Another study of over 200 British firms found that investment in design positively influenced project performance. Over 90 percent of products launched into the market achieved profitability and a return on investment within a short time frame (average 15 months). Critical factors affecting project outcome were top-level commitment to design investment and the ability of managers, particularly marketing, to liaise effectively with the design resource (Potter et al., 1991).

### Bibliography

Kotler, P. & Rath, G. A. (1984). A powerful but neglected strategic tool. *Journal of Business Studies*, 5, (2), 16–21.

Lorenz, C. (1986). *The design dimension*. Oxford: Basil Blackwell.

Potter, S., Roy, R., Capon, C., Bruce, M., Walsh, V. & Lewis, J. (1991). *The benefits and costs of investment in design expertise in product and graphics projects.* Milton Keynes, UK: Design Innovation Group, The Open University.

Walsh, V., Roy, R., Bruce, M. & Potter, S. (1992). *Winning by design: Technology, product design and international competitiveness.* Oxford: Basil Blackwell. Chapter 1.

MARGARET BRUCE

**design management** Design management refers to the process entailed in the generation, integration, coordination, and evaluation of corporate communication strategies. Design management has the responsibilities of defining, in a visual way, the nature of the organization and ensuring that this visual expression is reinforced throughout the organization. The physical manifestations of a service organization, for example, are planned to convey the nature and quality of the organization, such as the environment, company logo, and packaging. British Airways, for instance, has a distinctive identity which is conveyed throughout the organization from its logo, staff uniforms, and brochures, etc. For product companies, the functional and aesthetic elements of the product are supported by the presentation of the product, its packaging, and advertising. For example, Volvo communicates its attention to safety in car design in its promotion and advertising; Citroen focuses on price and fun for a "youth" market.

Three main activities are undertaken by design managers: conducting design audits; preparation of design briefs; and sourcing of design expertise from within the organization and from external suppliers.

*Design Audits*

This involves examining, periodically, the corporate use of design, through every aspect of product, environment, and communication. Oakley (1990) regards design audits as serving much the same function as financial audits – "basically to review the return (or potential return) being achieved on the resources employed, to check whether the level of resources is adequate for the tasks involved and to highlight the relative successes and failures." Cooper & Press (1995) suggest that a design audit covers a number of issues: firstly,

environmental issues (such as legislation and market trends); secondly, corporate culture (e.g., an organization's values and vision); thirdly, "tactical" management of design projects and processes; and, finally, the physical manifestation of design (i.e., the offering and its communication by the organization).

*Design Brief*

For the design function to have a good grasp of the project, objectives, and the work entailed, a design brief is prepared. The brief needs to indicate the target market, the intended price, and timescales and should include inputs from the functions involved in developing and implementing the end product, including marketing and production. If the brief is not fully prepared, then critical technical and other information may be missing that can delay project completion, or the design may be developed to a higher price than intended, e.g., more expensive materials may be used by the design function (Walsh et al., 1992).

*Design Sourcing*

Organizations use a range of different skills from graphic, interior, engineering, and industrial design. These may have to be outsourced and if so design managers have to identify and liaise with external design professionals. Choice of external design suppliers is based on the competence of the designer to accomplish the objectives for a set fee, as well as more intangible considerations of the design–client relationship, such as trust and loyalty. Regular contact between design and other functions, notably marketing, during the project is critical to ensure that the concepts and prototypes are meeting their requirements and that the project is on time and to the appropriate cost (Bruce & Morris, 1994).

**Bibliography**

Bruce, M. & Davies-Cooper, R. (1993). Design: Making marketing strategy visible. UMIST, UK: Manchester School of Management Working Paper.

Bruce, M. & Morris, B. (1994). Managing external design professionals in the product development. *TechnoVation*, **14**, (9), 585–599.

Cooper, R. & Press, M. (1995). *The design agenda: A guide to succesful design management.* Chichester: John Wiley. Chapter 6.

Oakley, M. (1990). Assembling and managing a design team. In M. Oakley (Ed.), *Design management: A handbook of issues and methods,* Oxford: Basil Blackwell. Chapter 34, p. 325.

Potter, S., Roy, R., Capon, C., Bruce, M., Walsh, V. & Lewis, J. (1991). *The benefits and costs of investment in design expertise in product and graphics projects.* Milton Keynes, UK: Design Innovation Group, The Open University.

Walsh, V., Roy, R., Bruce, M. & Potter, S. (1992). *Winning by design.* Oxford: Basil Blackwell. Chapter 7.

MARGARET BRUCE

**differentiation strategy** This is the alternative generic strategy to the COST LEADERSHIP STRATEGY, as suggested by Porter (1980). Organizations strive to secure a sustainable COMPETITIVE ADVANTAGE by distinguishing themselves from their competitors using such means as design, customer service, image, packaging, and additional functionality in ways which are perceived by customers as adding value. The differentiation strategy can be focused on particular customers or market segment(s) or devised for the general market.

*See also* **Competitive strategy**

**Bibliography**

Porter, M. E. (1980). *Competitive strategy: Techniques for analyzing industries and competitors.* New York: Free Press. Chapter 2.

DALE LITTLER

**diffusion of innovation** *see* DIFFUSION PROCESS

**diffusion process** The diffusion process is concerned with how product innovations are spread or assimilated within a market or industry. It is a macro process and may be defined as the process by which the acceptance of an innovation (product, service, or idea) is spread by communications (impersonal and interpersonal) to members of a social system (e.g., market or target segment) over a period of time. In other words, it is the spread of a new idea from its source of invention or creation to its ultimate users or adopters.

A number of product characteristics influence the diffusion of innovation and the rate of adoption by users (*see* ADOPTION PROCESS), i.e., some products may be an overnight success (e.g., video recorder), and some may be very slow to diffuse (e.g., dishwasher). These characteristics are:

- relative advantage with respect to ease of operations and reliability, i.e., the degree to which a new product appears superior to the buyer than previous products, and existing substitutes;

- compatibility: i.e., the degree to which a potential customer feels that a new product is consistent with present needs, values, and behavior, i.e., with experiences in the social system, or complementary processes in the case of industrial innovations;

- complexity: the degree to which a new product is difficult to comprehend and use – more complex innovations take longer to diffuse;

- divisibility: the degree to which a new product may be tried on a limited basis – the more opportunity to try, the easier it is for a consumer or user to evaluate; and

- communicability: the degree to which results from product use and ownership are observable and describable to others, i.e., the ease of seeing a product's benefits and attributes – so that products with a high degree of social visibility (e.g., fashion) are more easily diffused.

*See also* **Adoption process**

**Bibliography**

Robertson, T. S. (1967). The process of innovation and the diffusion of innovation. *Journal of Marketing,* Jan., 14–19.

Rogers, E. M. (1962). *Diffusion of innovations.* New York: Free Press.

Schiffman, L. G. & Kanuk, L. Z. (1991). *Consumer behavior* (4th edn). Prentice-Hall. Chapter 18.

BARBARA LEWIS

**direct mail**   Direct mail is a part of DIRECT MARKETING and, specifically, is ADVERTISING that is sent directly to the mailing address of a target customer. Thus, it offers the advertiser the opportunity for high audience selectivity and TARGETING, and wide-ranging geographic flexibility. It can be personalized (via individual letters) but much direct marketing is either lacking in personalization or is personalized with computer fill-ins, leading to a "junk mail" appearance.

Evidence of the growth of direct mail is seen in the: generation and sale/purchase of computer-based mailing lists, i.e., databases (*see* DATABASE), so that direct mail messages (*see* MESSAGE) may be carefully targeted to create consumer AWARENESS and/or to generate ACTION; the growth of specialized direct mail agencies (*see* AGENCY); and the increasing marketing orientation of the postal services with various incentive discounts.

### Bibliography

Dibb, S., Simkin, L., Pride, W. M. & Ferrell, O. C. (1994). *Marketing: Concepts and strategies* (European edn). Boston, MA: Houghton Mifflin Co. Chapter 16.

DAVID YORKE

**direct marketing**   Direct marketing is sometimes confused with DIRECT MAIL. It is not a medium but a marketing technique, comprising an interactive system of marketing, which uses one or more communications media (direct mail, print, telephone, i.e., TELEMARKETING, broadcast) for the purpose of soliciting a direct and measurable consumer response. Its objective is to make a sale or obtain a sales lead enquiry.

Computers are an indispensable tool in direct marketing, in particular in generating personalized direct mail sources. Indeed, the success of direct marketing depends on the acquisition and maintenance of a DATABASE of customers or potential customers.

The growth of direct marketing has been stimulated by socio-economic changes (e.g., an aging population, single-person or single-parent households, and working women with less shopping time), the increasing use of credit, a consumer convenience orientation, rising DISCRETIONARY INCOME, and developing computer technology and communications media.

### Bibliography

Dibb, S., Simkin, L., Pride, W. M. & Ferrell, O. C. (1994). *Marketing: Concepts and strategies* (European edn). Boston, MA: Houghton Mifflin Co. Chapter 16.
Kotler, P. (1994). *Marketing management: Analysis, planning, implementation and control* (8th edn). Englewood Cliffs, NJ: Prentice-Hall. Chapter 24, pp. 653–683.
Roberts, M. L. & Berger, P. D. (1989). *Direct marketing management*. Englewood Cliffs, NJ: Prentice-Hall.
Schiffman, L. G. & Kanuk, L. L. (1991). *Consumer behavior* (4th edn) pp. 292–294. Prentice-Hall.

DAVID YORKE

**directional matrix**   This summarizes the major growth strategies. As defined by Ansoff (1965), it consists of two parameters: markets and technologies, subdivided according to whether or not they are "new" or "existing." The quadrants are: *market penetration (existing markets and technologies)* with the aim being to increase volume sales through, for instance, higher market share or greater per capita consumption from, for example, new uses for the product; NEW PRODUCT DEVELOPMENT, involving the introduction of products based on new technologies into existing markets; *market development*, which involves extending the geographical reach of existing products; and DIVERSIFICATION, the introduction of products based on new technology into new markets. It is obvious that the last strategy is the most risky option. Although overly simplistic and general, the framework may be useful for practitioners when formulating specific development strategies. It does not draw the distinction between organic, or internal, development, and external development through mergers and acquisitions.

*See also* **Corporate strategy**

**Bibliography**

Ansoff, H. I. (1965). *Corporate strategy: An analytic approach to business policy for growth and expansion*. New York: McGraw-Hill. Chapter 6.

DALE LITTLER

**discontinuous innovation** This can be viewed as being at the polar extreme of a continuum with CONTINUOUS INNOVATION at the other extreme. It is generally used with reference to technological innovation. It can be seen as involving radical changes in technologies and, consequently, it may result in the development of new demand schedules.

*See also* **Continuous innovation; Innovation**

DALE LITTLER

**discount** Discount is the term used to refer to any reduction in price offered to a customer. Discounts are offered to encourage customers to purchase where it is thought they may not otherwise do so. Discounting is widely practiced in organizational markets where price is more often a matter of negotiation than in consumer markets (Blois, 1994). The usual reasons for offering discounts include: to encourage purchase in greater quantity than normal (discount for volume); to respond to competitive developments (e.g., price wars, tendering); to accelerate sales of outdated stock (e.g., discontinued lines); to encourage purchase at "unpopular" times (e.g., end-of-season sales, off-peak electricity tariffs); to reduce a customer's PERCEIVED RISK (e.g., introductory discounts for new products); to provide incentives for another product (e.g., membership discounts); and, illegally, to drive out competition with a view to achieving a monopoly (*see* PREDATORY PRICING).

**Bibliography**

Blois, K. J. (1994). Discounts in business marketing management. *Industrial Marketing Management*, **23** (2), April, 93–100.

DOMINIC WILSON

**discretionary income** An element in the ECONOMIC ENVIRONMENT, discretionary income, i.e. that part of household net income which remains after fixed commitments, such as mortgage and loan repayments, have been made, is likely to vary from one market segment to another. It represents a challenge for all organizations to be able to persuade buyers and customers to spend a greater proportion of their discretionary income than hitherto on a particular product or service. Changes in discretionary income not only affect those organizations selling directly to households, but also, ultimately, have repercussions on suppliers of capital equipment.

**Bibliography**

Dickson, P. R. (1994). *Marketing management* (international edn). Fort Worth: The Dryden Press. Chapter 12.
McCarthy, E. J. & Perreault, W. D. (1993). *Basic marketing*. Homewood, IL: Irwin. Chapter 6.
Palmer, A. & Worthington, I. (1992). *The business and marketing environment*. Maidenhead: McGraw-Hill. Chapter 6.

DAVID YORKE

**discriminant analysis** Discriminant analysis is used when there are observations from a sample of a population on many variables for cases which belong to two or more known groups. The groups may be owners and non-owners of a particular consumer durable, or good or bad credit risks, or buyers of three different brands of coffee, and the variables could be typical marketing research variables, e.g., socioeconomic, demographic, psychographic, etc. variables for each respondent, or the respondent's opinions, perceptions, evaluations, etc. measured on a range of RATING SCALES. The purpose of discriminant analysis is to use these data about individuals whose group membership is known to facilitate the classification of individuals whose group membership is unknown, to one or to other of the groups.

In the situation where there are just two groups, a linear discriminant function of the variables is formed, the coefficients of the variables being chosen to best separate the two groups.

Discriminant scores can be calculated for each individual in the groups and a plot of these scores, indicating to which group each case belongs, will show, it is hoped, two non-intersecting histograms. Usually, however, the plots will overlaA critical value will be chosen so that cases will be classified by the discriminant function according to whether they are above or below the critical value. If there is overlap, some cases will be misclassified, even by the discriminant function whose fitting they contributed to. A classification table of "hits and misses" is one way of judging the usefulness of the discriminant analysis. Also used to judge the adequacy of a discriminant function are measures such as Wilks' Lambda and the canonical correlation coefficient.

A satisfactory discriminant function can then use measurements on the variables for a previously unclassified case to predict to which of the groups the case belongs. For example, based on the data for an individual on the variables in a discriminant function on good and bad credit risks, the discriminant function should indicate whether or not the individual is a good credit risk.

Significance tests for coefficients are available. The discriminant function can be built up in a step-wise fashion. The method can be used in an analytical way. Thus, large coefficients identify variables that are important for discriminating between and describing the groups and therefore worthy of further attention by management.

The method can be extended to more than two groups when several discriminant functions will be estimated. Statistical packages, e.g. the STATISTICAL PACKAGE FOR THE SOCIAL SCIENCES or SPSS, that have discriminant analysis routines are essential.

## Bibliography

Hair, J. F., Anderson, R. E. & Tatham, R. L. (1987). *Multivariate data analysis* (2nd edn). New York: Macmillan. Chapter 3.

MICHAEL GREATOREX

**disposable income** Unlike DISCRETIONARY INCOME, total disposable income (household income after deduction of direct taxation and national insurance contributions) is not available for competition among all suppliers. Local taxes have to be paid and "essential" purchases (e.g., fuel for heating and energy) are likely to reduce the amount of total disposable income available for spending/saving.

## Bibliography

McCarthy, E. J. & Perreault, W. D. (1993). *Basic marketing*. Homewood, IL: Irwin. Chapter 6.
Palmer, A. & Worthington, I. (1992). *The business and marketing environment*. Maidenhead: McGraw-Hill. Chapter 6.

DAVID YORKE

**distribution**    *see* RETAIL DISTRIBUTION CHANNELS

**distributors**    *see* RETAIL DISTRIBUTION CHANNELS

**diversification** This is regarded as the option involving the greatest risk in Ansoff's (1965) DIRECTIONAL MATRIX. It involves the organization introducing products based on new technologies into new markets. However, there are gradations in the degree of risk involved, depending on whether or not the diversification is related or unrelated (also referred to as concentric diversification). Related diversification involves commonalities with the firm's existing business, so that there is potential synergy between the new and the existing businesses based on a common facility, asset, channel, skill, or opportunity (Mintzberg, 1988). These commonalities may be either tangible or intangible (Porter, 1985), the latter involving tacit management skills. Unrelated, or conglomerate, diversification involves the extension into new business areas which have no relationship with the company's existing technologies, markets, or products. Kotler (1994) also refers to horizontal diversification whereby the company may develop new products aimed at its existing customers but which are unrelated to its existing technologies, although this does not accord with Ansoff's definition of diversification.

## Bibliography

Ansoff, H. I. (1965). *Corporate strategy: An analytic approach to business policy for growth and expansion.* New York: McGraw-Hill. Chapter 6.

Kotler, P. (1994). *Marketing management: Analysis, planning implementation and control* (8th edn). Englewood Cliffs, NJ: Prentice-Hall. Chapter 3.

Mintzberg, H. (1988). Generic strategies: Toward a comprehensive framework. In *Advances in strategic management*, Greenwich, CT: JAI Press, vol. 5 pp. 1–67.

Porter, M. E. (1985). *Competitive advantage: Creating and sustaining superior performance.* New York: Free Press.

DALE LITTLER

# E

**economic environment** The economic environment is one of the elements in the MARKETING ENVIRONMENT in which a supplier organization is operating. A national government, after taking account of international factors such as capital and currency movements, is responsible for creating and maintaining a favorable macroeconomic environment (*see* MACRO ENVIRONMENT). It achieves this by the use of monetary and fiscal policies aimed at manipulating the levels of inflation and employment and, hence, the levels of DISPOSABLE and DISCRETIONARY INCOME among various segments of the population. Thus, the level of economic activity will govern the possible success of all organizations. At any one time, the economic environment for different countries will vary widely. Thus, the ability to forecast changes from current base levels will be a major factor in the decision to invest or not.

## Bibliography

Dibb, S., Simkin, L., Pride, W. M. & Ferrell, O. C. (1994). *Marketing, concepts and strategies* (European edn). Boston, MA: Houghton Mifflin Co. Chapter 2.

Palmer, A. & Worthington, I. (1992). *The business and marketing environment*. Maidenhead: McGraw-Hill. Chapter 6.

Semenik, R. M. & Bamossy, G. J. (1993). *Principles of marketing*. Cincinnati, OH: South-Western Publishing Co. Chapter 2.

DAVID YORKE

**EFTPOS** EFTPOS or electronic funds transfer at point of sale, refers to debit or "plastic" card payment at the point of sale by direct funds transfer from the customer's account to the retailer's account. It evolved in the early to mid 1980s. It is an area of continuing development and is fast becoming a leading payment system for retailers.

## Bibliography

McGoldrick, P. J. (1990). *Retail marketing*. Maidenhead: McGraw-Hill.

Penn, V. (1990). Retail EFTPOS 90: Paper holds out against plastic. *International Journal of Retail and Distribution*, **19**, (1), 10–12.

STEVE GREENLAND

**electronic data interchange (EDI)** Electronic data interchange (EDI) refers to computer-to-computer exchange of standard business documentation in machine processable form. EDI messages are highly structured so that information generated by one organization on one computer can be read by that of another computer in the same or a different organization. The prime applications for EDI have been for transactions, e.g., orders and invoices. The benefits of this have been found in speeding up trade communications and reducing labor costs. In the automotive industry, EDI is used by component suppliers, manufacturers and dealers to facilitate the trading processes involved in buying and selling components and cars.

## Bibliography

Holland, C., Lockett, G. & Blackman, I. (1992). Planning for electronic interchange. *Strategic Management Journal*, 13, 359–550.

MARGARET BRUCE

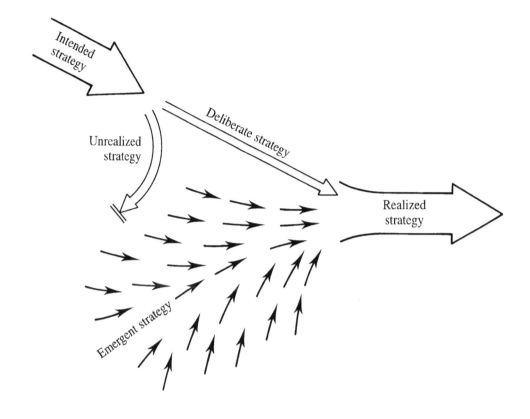

*Figure 1   Emergent Strategy*
*Source:* Mintzberg, 1987.

**emergent strategy**   Emergent strategy, as termed by Mintzberg (1987), is a strategy that is not carefully pre-planned; it is realized in the absence of intentions, or despite unrealized intentions. As Mintzberg notes: "strategies can form as well as be *formulated*. A realized strategy can emerge in response to an evolving situation, or it can be brought about deliberately, through a process of formulation followed by implementation." Such a view is in contrast to traditional STRATEGIC PLANNING which is founded on the premise that it is possible to analyze the MARKETING ENVIRONMENT, forecast possible outcomes, select strategic alternatives based on an evaluation of the returns each is likely to yield, and devise plans to implement the chosen strategic options in order to ensure that they come about. However, it is increasingly recognized that UNCERTAINTY considerably clouds

the ability to predict all the possible influences and therefore possibilities that might arise. Consequently, there may be unforeseen opportunities and difficulties. Even carefully planned strategies might lead to different outcomes to those sought. (See figure 1.)

**Bibliography**

Mintzberg, H. (1987). Five Ps for strategy. *California Management Review*, **30**, (1), Fall.

DALE LITTLER

**end users**   End users may or may not be the purchasers of products. They can have a significant influence on the purchasing decision (e.g., children in connection with certain household purchasing decisions).

DALE LITTLER

**entrepreneurial strategy**    Entrepreneurial strategy is one of Mintzberg's (1973) three strategic styles (*see* STRATEGIC STYLES; ADAPTIVE STRATEGY; PLANNING STYLE). The features of this strategic style are likely to be bold decision-making by single visionary individuals who are risk takers. Mintzberg suggests that it is likely to occur most in organizations which are under the personal control of one individual and which are "located in a protected niche in the environment."

Such risk-taking behavior is not restricted to small organizations, as, for example, Littler & Leverick (1994) identified in their study of entrants into mobile communications markets. Indeed, many decisions to enter new markets and especially, but not exclusively, those founded on advances in technology, are likely to have a degree of entrepreneurial behavior if only because the uncertainties (*see* UNCERTAINTY) make calculation of the costs and benefits extremely problematic.

**Bibliography**

Littler, D. A. & Leverick, F. (1994). Market planning in new technology sectors. In J. Saunders (Ed.), *The marketing initiative*. Prentice-Hall.

Mintzberg, H. (1973). Strategy making in three modes. *California Management Review*, **16**, (2), Winter, 44–53.

DALE LITTLER

**environmental analysis**    Organizations exist within a complex and dynamic environment which can be described as the MARKETING ENVIRONMENT. Understanding this environment is one of the most important and difficult aspects of management and has traditionally been regarded as a marketing responsibility (*see* MARKETING AUDIT). Obviously, the number of variables influencing this marketing environment are many, so environmental analysis attempts to identify the most influential factors and trends affecting the organization and its offerings.

Kotler (1994) has suggested that it may be helpful to group these variables into two interdependent but distinguishable categories: the MICRO ENVIRONMENT and the MACRO ENVIRONMENT, together comprising the MARKETING ENVIRONMENT. Analysis of the macro environment – sometimes referred to as the external marketing audit (*see* EXTERNAL AUDIT) – can usefully be considered under six headings: the DEMOGRAPHIC ENVIRONMENT; the ECONOMIC ENVIRONMENT; the NATURAL ENVIRONMENT; the TECHNOLOGICAL ENVIRONMENT; the POLITICAL ENVIRONMENT; and the CULTURAL ENVIRONMENT. Whereas all six of these aspects of the environment will be relevant to all markets, some aspects will, of course, be more applicable than others in specific markets. There can also be a danger of compartmentalization using this approach – for example, important issues of ecology or consumerism might seem less significant when split up between six headings. Perhaps the most notable limitation of this approach to environmental analysis is that it seems to give little priority to competitors *per se* and it may therefore be appropriate to add a "competitive environment" to Kotler's six categories.

The level of effort and resources which any organization will invest in environmental analysis will depend on many factors including: the availability and reliability of SECONDARY DATA (e.g., census data, government statistics, published market analyses); the cost of PRIMARY DATA (e.g., commissioned market research, in-house surveys); the volatility of the environment (where analysis can be out of date even before it is finished); the competitiveness of markets (why should organizations invest in analysis when there is little threat of losing customers?); and what priority managers give to environmental analysis, in the context of other demands on their time.

It is often suggested that the environment is becoming increasingly complex and fast-moving. This observation has, of course, been made of many earlier centuries also, but it does seem particularly true of the late 20th century and this emphasizes the importance of environmental analysis, while also highlighting the problems of analyzing such volatile dynamics. These problems have encouraged the development of different analytical techniques, such as scenario development (Schoemaker, 1993), delphi methods (Linstone & Turoff, 1975), and even the use of chaos theory (Stacey, 1975), in order to understand the marketing environment surrounding an organization.

*See also* **Marketing environment**

**Bibliography**

Day, G. S. & Wensley, R. (1988). Assessing advantage: A framework for diagnosing competitive superiority. *Journal of Marketing*, **52**, April, 1–20.

Kotler, P. (1994). *Marketing management: Analysis, planning, implementation and control* (8th edn). Englewood Cliffs, NJ: Prentice-Hall. Chapter 6, pp. 150–171.

Linstone, H. A. & Turoff, M. (1975). *The delphi method: Techniques and application*. Reading, MA: Addison Wesley.

Porter, M. E. (1979). How competitive forces shape strategy. *Harvard Business Review*, **57**, Mar.–Apr., 137–145.

Sanderson, S. M. & Luffman, G. A. (1988). Strategic planning and environmental analysis. *European Journal of Marketing*, **22**, (2), 14–27.

Schoemaker, P. J. H. (1993). Multiple scenario development: Its conceptual and behavioral foundation. *Strategic Management Journal*, **14**, 193–213.

Shapiro, B. P. (1988). What the hell is market oriented. *Harvard Business Review*, **66**, (6), 119–25.

Stacey, R. D. (1995). The science of complexity: An alternative perspective for strategic change processes. *Strategic Management Journal*, **16**, (6), 477–495.

DOMINIC WILSON

**environmental scanning**    Environmental scanning is the process of examining the MARKETING ENVIRONMENT, usually with the intention of identifying trends and developments in the environment which may require MARKETING STRATEGIES or tactics to be adjusted. The complexity, volatility, and potential strategic significance of environmental developments are becoming more apparent to many organizations and there is increasing attention to using information and communication technologies to cope with the rapidly growing volume of data concerning environmental developments. For example, there are now many commercially available MARKETING INFORMATION SYSTEMS (MkIS) and executive information systems (EIS) which claim to offer environmental scanning services. On closer examination, however, these systems often only scan those aspects of the environment at which they are "directed" (through programming) by the systems designers and managers involved and so they risk perpetuating and legitimizing the very perceptual prejudices which they are meant to correct. Computer systems do, of course, provide a valuable aid to coping with the sheer diversity and volume of environmental data, both in terms of scanning and in terms of analysis and manipulation, but there is no substitute for the human characteristics of alertness, curiosity, and openness-to-innovation which are essential in turning environmental "scanning" into environmental "understanding."

**Bibliography**

Brownlie, D. (1994). Environmental scanning. In M. J. Baker (Ed.), *The marketing book* (3rd edn). London: Heinemann, pp. 139–192.

Calori, R. (1989). Designing a business scanning system. *Long Range Planning*, **22**, (113), Feb., 69–82.

DOMINIC WILSON

**EPOS**    EPOS or electronic point of sale systems record data, concerning goods sold, via highly efficient electronic scanning equipment reading product bar-codes at the retailer checkout. Their introduction has radically improved distribution and merchandise management in the retail sector by providing detailed and accessible information concerning product movement through stores and purchasing behavior, dramatically reducing the paperwork associated with inventory control.

**Bibliography**

Harris, D. & Walters, E. (1992). *Retail operations management*. Prentice-Hall.

McGoldrick, P. J. (1990). *Retail marketing*. Maidenhead: McGraw-Hill.

Rosenbloom, B. (1991). *Marketing channels*. Chicago: The Dryden Press.

STEVE GREENLAND

**ethical issues**    *see* MARKETING ETHICS

**exchange**    While it is often seen as the central concept underpinning marketing, there is some debate over exactly what constitutes exchange. At the simplest level, exchange might be seen as the action of voluntarily transferring ownership of a product or service to another in return for another object deemed to be equivalent in value. Wider definitions of the scope of exchange might not see payment as a necessary condition or indeed might not restrict the scope of exchange to two parties or to products and services. The debate is paralleled by that on the nature and scope of marketing itself and is well summarized in Bagozzi (1975).

### Bibliography

Bagozzi, R. P. (1975). Marketing as exchange. *Journal of Marketing*, **39**, (4), Oct., 32–39.

FIONA LEVERICK

**exhibitions** Exhibitions or trade shows are an element in the marketing COMMUNICATIONS MIX and are used, primarily, for ORGANIZATIONAL MARKETING and are usually industry-specific. They are designed to promote supplier organizations and their products/services, identify prospective customers, and are integral to building relationships (*see* RELATIONSHIP MARKETING) with existing customers.

Their success is often evaluated in terms of "number of enquiries received" at the event, as other measures such as "orders placed" may take place after the exhibition or trade show, and in any case may be a reflection of other communication activities.

### Bibliography

Bonoma, T. V. (1983). Get more out of your trade shows. *Harvard Business Review*, **61**, 75–83.
Dickson, P. R. (1994). *Marketing management* (international edn). Fort Worth: The Dryden Press. Chapter 11.

DAVID YORKE

**existing demand** *see* DEMAND

**experience curve** The experience curve is a composite of several factors including: the learning curve, first observed in the US aircraft industry in the 1930s, by which workers become more efficient with the number of times they repeat a task; economies of scale; the substitution of more efficient factors of production; and the general use of technological advances. By plotting unit costs against cumulative production, a downward sloping experience curve is produced. It is suggested (Hedley, 1976) that unit costs decline by 20 to 30 percent for each doubling of cumulative production, but only through organizations actively seeking to capitalize on experience curve effects by, for example, investing in labor-substituting technologies.

The experience curve underpins the BCG methodology for business PORTFOLIO ANALYSIS (*see* BCG MATRIX) and results in an emphasis on striving to achieve maximum MARKET SHARE (since this suggests greater cumulative experience). However, the strategic implications of the experience curve can be questioned (*see* Porter, 1979). For instance, a firm's market share dominance, and therefore its alleged greater experience, can be undermined by superior innovative technology, while later entrants to an industry can purchase plant and equipment which embodies accumulated experience in the form of, for example, latest versions of the technology.

### Bibliography

Hedley, B. (1976). A fundamental approach to strategy development. *Long Range Planning*, **9**, (6), 2–11.
Porter, M. E. (1979). How competitive forces shape strategy. *Harvard Business Review*, **57**, 135–145.

DALE LITTLER

**experimentation** Experimentation is a type of primary marketing research (*see* PRIMARY RESEARCH) in which the experimenter systematically manipulates the values of one or more variables (the independent variables), while controlling the values of other variables, to measure the effect of the changes in the independent variables on one or more other variables (the dependent variables).

Experimentation is often used to infer causal relationships. Causation cannot be inferred unless there is evidence that (1) the change in the independent variable(s) occurs before or simultaneously with the change in the dependent variable(s), (2) the effects of other extraneous variables are measured or controlled, and (3) there is a strong association between the changes in independent and dependent variables in the way predicted by hypotheses. Unfortunately, the scientific process is such that, even if these conditions are satisfied, one can never prove causation, only infer that a causal relationship may exist.

The need to rule out other causal factors in order to infer that the changes in the experimental variables cause the changes in the dependent variables is the reason behind the control of other possible causal factors. Control is obtained by devices such as (1) use of a control group which receives no treatment, (2) randomization, where test units are assigned to different experimental and control groups at random, (3) matching, where test units are matched on background variables before being assigned to groups, (4) use of a laboratory where conditions are controllable, (5) use of specific experimental designs that control extraneous variables, and (6) measuring and accounting for the effect of extraneous variables using statistical techniques such as multiple regression or analysis of covariance.

There are many types of experimental design. The simplest, the "after-only" design, involves changing the independent variable (the treatment) and following this with measurement of the dependent variable. Obvious weaknesses include the lack of a benchmark for comparison purposes and failure to control for the effect of extraneous variables. The "before-after" design which takes measurements of the dependent variable both before and after the treatment does allow effect of the treatment to be measured by the difference between the before and after measurement. This design suffers from a lack of control of intervening variables.

The "before-after with control group" design (with cases assigned to groups at random) can help to overcome the problem of intervening variables in that changes to many intervening variables will affect both groups and so the effect of the treatment can be measured when the before-after differences for the treatment group and the control group are compared.

Statistical designs permit the effect of changes to more than one independent variable to be measured. They allow the researcher to control for specific extraneous variables and an efficient design will allow several effects to be measured using as small a number of observations as possible. A randomized block design is useful when there is one major extraneous variable in addition to the dependent variable and treatment variable. The units being tested are assigned to groups or blocks defined by the extraneous variable, the experiment is carried out on the test units and the results analyzed to see if the treatment has an effect and to see if the effect is different in the various blocks. A Latin square design is similar to a randomized block design except that it allows the experimenter to specify blocks using two non-interacting external variables thus allowing the experimenter to control for two extraneous variables. A Graeco-Latin square allows the experimenter to control for a third non-interacting extraneous variable.

A factorial design is used to measure the effects of two or more independent variables. Factorial designs allow interaction effects to be measured.

Data obtained from such experimental designs are analyzed using statistical methods such as analysis of variance (see STATISTICAL TESTS).

Experiments can take place in the field or in the laboratory. The advantage of field experiments is the high degree of realism that can be generated. Unfortunately, there is a lack of control, especially over intervening variables such as the weather, competitors, and the economy at large. What is worse is that the researcher may not be aware of changes to these variables. Field research is harder to conceal from competitors who have an opportunity of early discovery of possible new developments. Field research often turns out to be time-consuming and costly. However, for TEST MARKETING of new products or for measuring the effects of advertising, field experiments in actual market conditions may be necessary.

Laboratory experiments allow the researcher more control over not only the possible extraneous variables but also the measurement of the dependent variables and the changes to the independent variables. It is easier to use electronic/mechanical devices to measure dependent variables in the laboratory and the changes to the independent variables can be speeded up to reduce the time needed to conduct the experiment. However, because the experiment is conducted in an artificial environment, the generalizability of the results of laboratory experiments to the real world is reduced. Copy testing of TV (or press) commercials is an example of experimentation often carried out in the laboratory.

**Bibliography**

Aaker, D. A., Kumar, V. & Day, G. S. (1995). *Marketing research* (5th edn). New York: John Wiley. Chapter 12.

MICHAEL GREATOREX

**expert opinion**   *see* INTERPERSONAL COMMUNICATIONS

**expert systems**   A computer program that uses knowledge and inferencing to solve problems can be regarded as a knowledge-based system. When knowledge and inference procedures are modeled after human experts, then such a knowledge-based system is an expert system. In other words, an expert system is a computer program that uses expert knowledge to solve problems in a specific domain. Expert systems technology incorporates some "expertise," some knowledge in a program to enable a relatively inexperienced individual to make accurate decisions, or to provide a backup decision-support system perhaps to facilitate or check the stages in a decision-making process. Thus, an "expert's" knowledge can be decentralized and made more widely available. Expert systems are advisory systems and can provide advice directly to the consumer, so generating a new product. Main applications include fire-risk underwriting in financial services, flight scheduling in the travel industry, and generic marketing uses, e.g., the creation of customer profiles for database marketing and staff training. More "radical" potential uses, such as self-service holiday booking systems, may come into everyday use at some future stage.

**Bibliography**

Moutinho, L. & Rita, P. (1994). Expert systems. In S. Witt & L. Moutinho (Eds), *Tourism marketing and management handbook* (2nd edn). (pp. 554–558). Hemel Hempstead, UK: Prentice Hall.

MARGARET BRUCE

**exporting**   It is not easy to make a clear-cut distinction between exporting and INTERNATIONAL MARKETING, either for conceptual purposes or in terms of operational practices. However, it could be argued that, whereas exporting entails some elements of international marketing, international marketing can be understood as a business function quite independent of exporting. In international marketing, the emphasis is on: firms' strategy development; the management of marketing functions pertaining to firms' overall international position; and the degree and complexity of their involvements in foreign markets. Exporting may be seen, therefore, as one of the minimal stages of firms' involvements with foreign markets. The characterization of exporting as "selling in foreign markets" is only of limited value, implying that exporting is somewhat hit-and-miss or unfocused.

The point not to be overlooked is that a majority of all international firms, no matter how globally known and dominant today, were at one time small or at least substantially smaller international players. Exporting can then be seen to be a element of the growth path or learning curve of international business operations. In the 1970s and 1980s a substantial number of academic studies examined exporting firms with the center of interest being how they became exporters. There were two dimensions of interest. The first dimension was concerned with the motives that stimulated non-exporters to become exporters: the second with the stages of internationalization, in other words forms or degrees of dependence on foreign business. With respect to the first dimension, the motives would be classified in terms of internal and external impulses, on the one hand, and proactive and reactive factors, on the other, as exemplified in table 1.

The second dimension, which attracted considerable scholarly attention, posited stages of internationalization of the firm through the increasing extension of its exporting activities and their sophistication. The 1970s and 1980s produced a number of models in Europe and the USA, based on industry samples. The

**Table 1**   Motives for non-exporters to become exporters

|                   | *Internal stimuli*                                                                                                                          | *External stimuli*                                                                                            |
| ----------------- | ----------------------------------------------------------------------------------------------------------------------------------------- | ----------------------------------------------------------------------------------------------------------- |
| Proactive factors | • management decision<br>• economies of scale<br>• unique product or competence<br>• perceived profitability<br>• marketing competence      | • identified foreign business opportunities<br>• stimulation/incentives from government, chambers of commerce |
| Reactive factors  | • risk diversification<br>• excess capacity<br>• retrenchment                                                                               | • unsolicited foreign orders<br>• small or shrinking home market                                             |

Swedish scholars Johanson & Vahlne (1977) proposed a four-stage model, according to which firms: export sporadically; export using an agent; export via a sales subsidiary; and manufacture in a foreign subsidiary. Other models have attempted to demonstrate a "natural" progression from passive or occasional exporting to a stage of making no distinction between home and foreign markets. But these characterizations have been criticized by subsequent scholars who, with some justification, find them "too logical" and therefore not consistent with actual experience. This has developed, in the USA, to a keen interest in the managerial influences, including competencies, on export development; in Europe, studies of internationalization have led to extensive investigations of firms' international networking (*see* NETWORK) behavior.

The problem with these preoccupations with export motivations and stages of internationalization is that they deflect attention from exporting as an everyday business activity. It is in the exporters' task that we find a clear distinction between exporting and international marketing. First of all, exporting is a form of foreign market entry (*see* INTERNATIONAL MARKET ENTRY AND DEVELOPMENT STRATEGIES), the essential characteristic of which is that it involves direct selling to foreign customers. The selling can be completely direct in the sense that, even if the firm makes use of the services of an export house or a locally appointed agent or sets up an export department, the direct investment in the foreign market is small. In other words, exporting is selling into foreign markets with a permanent and (more or less)

exclusive representation by a *stock-holding* market intermediary such as a distributor.

With respect to export departments, it should be emphasized that their prime purpose, generally, is not to support the foreign sales effort through undertaking market studies or assisting with export development plans, but to process the paperwork associated with the physical transfer of products into foreign markets. Such activity can include: the issuing and processing of invoices; the arranging of payments inward and outward in foreign currencies; the preparation of company brochures in foreign languages; and the supervision of transportation arrangements taking account of special requirements concerning customs procedures and goods certification in the target market.

As for the job of export managers, one of their main tasks is to forecast demand in given foreign markets and to prepare the company accordingly to meet it. Evidence suggests that forecasts of demand are based on personal relationships (*see* RELATIONSHIP MARKETING) with customers which are particularly close. The export manager is unlikely to engage in the more sophisticated and expensive forms of international MARKETING RESEARCH, which seek to create coherent and systematic methodologies for identifying foreign customers and developing specific, culture-sensitive, business approaches. It would, however, be mistaken to assume that the export manager is perforce less adroit than the international marketing manager. The point to emphasize is that they represent different approaches to business development in foreign markets, the crucial difference residing in the scale of investment that the firm is willing to commit to foreign markets. In relative terms, selling industrial refrigerators to Saudi Arabia may be equally demanding as developing a marketing strategy for the same products in China.

## Bibliography

Johanson, J. & Vahlne, J.-E. (1977). The internationalisation process of the firm – a model of knowledge development and increasing foreign market commitments. *Journal of International Business Studies*, 8, (1), Spring/Summer 23–32.

NIGEL HOLDEN

**external audit** This is one part of a MARKETING AUDIT (the other being INTERNAL AUDIT), and it involves examination of the external environment, threats, and opportunities surrounding an organization. The external audit is synonymous, in effect, with ENVIRONMENTAL ANALYSIS.

*See also* **SWOT analysis**

## Bibliography

Kotler, P. (1994). *Marketing management: Analysis, planning, implementation and control* (8th edn). Englewood Cliffs, NJ: Prentice-Hall. Chapter 27.

DAVID YORKE

# F

**factor analysis** Factor analysis, a type of MULTIVARIATE ANALYSIS, is concerned with the interrelationships within a set of variables and with reducing the variables required to represent a set of observations. The procedure involves the construction of a number of factors to explain the variation in the measured variables. The data reduction arises because the number of factors created is less than the number of variables. One example has 17 variables concerned with the usefulness of 17 risk relievers explained by three factors identified as clarifying, simplifying, and risk-sharing factors.

Factor analysis is empirical in that the computations are carried out on the data set, the number of factors being determined by a stopping rule. The factors may or may not be meaningfully interpreted to fit in with any theoretical ideas. If meaningful factors are obtained, factor scores for each case are computed for further use, e.g., to describe individuals or as variables in multiple regression (*see* REGRESSION AND CORRELATION) or in CLUSTER ANALYSIS.

Factor analysis is best carried out using a computer package such as the STATISTICAL PACKAGE FOR THE SOCIAL SCIENCES, or SPSS. STRUCTURAL EQUATION MODELS have extended the ideas of factor analysis.

### Bibliography

Hair, J. F., Anderson, R. E. & Tatham, R. L. (1987). *Multivariate data analysis* (2nd edn). New York: Macmillan. Chapter 6.

MICHAEL GREATOREX

**feel-buy-learn model** The feel-buy-learn model in MARKETING COMMUNICATIONS (*see also* AIDA MODEL, HIERARCHY OF EFFECTS MODEL and INNOVATION-ADOPTION MODEL) suggests that in particular situations buyers/customers do not follow the logical LEARN-FEEL-BUY sequence. In the FBL situation, buyers/customers have images of and feelings toward products and services prior to purchase but learning about the product (service) attributes does not occur until after purchase. This happens, for example, when it is not easy or possible to describe a product or service using words; instead pictures or images are used to invoke feelings in the potential buyers'/customers' minds in the hope that such feelings will lead to a purchase. Examples include perfume, travel, aspects of entertainment, and leisure activities.

*See also* **Learn-feel-buy model** and **Buy-feel-learn model**

### Bibliography

Dickson, P. R. (1994). *Marketing management* (international edn). Fort Worth: The Dryden Press. Chapter 12.
Kotler, P. (1994). *Marketing management: Analysis, planning, implementation and control* (8th edn). Englewood Cliffs, NJ: Prentice-Hall, p. 602.

DAVID YORKE

**financial planning for marketing communications** Expenditure on MARKETING COMMUNICATIONS activities must be monitored, evaluated, and controlled. Such control can only be undertaken against a plan, using one of the communication models. The plan should contain (both in total, and for each target segment of buyers/customers (*see* MARKET SEGMENTATION)): an analysis of the current situation, e.g., level of AWARENESS, number of product TRIALS; an objective, e.g., to increase the level of trial from X percent to Y percent in six months; and an allocation of financial resources over the chosen elements in the COMMUNICATIONS MIX, e.g., SALES PROMOTION, PERSONAL SELLING, EXHIBITIONS. Both during and after the period of time of the plan, performance can be monitored against objectives.

**Bibliography**

Kotler, P. (1994). *Marketing management: Analysis, planning, implementation and control* (8th edn). Englewood Cliffs, NJ: Prentice-Hall. Chapter 27.
McCarthy, E. J. & Perreault, W. D. (1993). *Basic marketing.* Homewood, IL: Irwin. Chapter 21.

DAVID YORKE

**financial services retailing** Financial services retailing refers to the distribution of financial services via branch distribution networks. Within this sector the services offered are increasingly being viewed as products and the branches are being viewed as retail environments in which the staff members are salespersons, rather than "bankers," practicing selling skills (Riley & Knott, 1992). Concepts and techniques of retail marketing have been readily adopted by most types of financial institution that have direct interface with the consumer market. Since the late 1980s the major UK institutions, some with network sizes in excess of 2,000 branches, have without exception been conducting nationwide rationalization and refurbishment programs (Greenland, 1994).

Unable to differentiate by product, financial institutions see retail image as a key to achieving competitive advantage. The branch, the front line physical presence on the high street, is an important medium for image communication. Outlets have become far more customer orientated with key retail merchandising concepts and principles being incorporated into modern branch designs. The modern financial service outlet is far more open plan, with reduced use of bandit screens and with placement of staff out in

the banking hall area, large glass frontages and much more of a shop-like appearance than traditional branches.

*See also* **Retail image; Retail merchandising; Store design**

**Bibliography**

Greenland, S. J. (1994). Rationalization and restructuring in the financial services sector. *International Journal of Retail and Distribution Management*, **22**, (6), 21–28.
McGoldrick P. J. & Greenland S. J. (1994). *Retailing of financial services.* Maidenhead: McGraw-Hill.
Riley, D. & Knott, P. A. (1992). Through the eyes of the customer: Research into the new look and functioning of bank and building society branches. 155th ESOMAR Seminar on Banking and Insurance.

STEVE GREENLAND

**focus groups** A focus group interview, a form of depth interview (*see* DEPTH INTERVIEWS), is conducted by a trained moderator with a small group of respondents. Focus group interviews are often referred to as a type of qualitative marketing research (*see* QUALITATIVE RESEARCH). They are used mainly as alternatives to structured interviews using questionnaires, in complex situations where direct questioning may not provide satisfactory information due to respondents being unwilling or unable to give answers to questions that they find embarrassing or feel are invasions of privacy. Also, focus groups are used in preliminary research to help in clarifying the research issues, in new product research and concept testing, in advertising and communications research, in studying attitudes and behavior, and in designing questionnaires for use in subsequent research.

Groups of about ten individuals are selected and often each group is chosen to represent a particular market segment (*see* MARKET SEGMENTATION). The discussion is usually taped or videoed. Although the interview is relatively unstructured, the moderator leads the group to provoke an in-depth and interactive discussion of the relevant topics.

The advantages of focus groups include the stimulation from interaction within the group which allows each individual to refine and expand his/her views in the light of contributions from other members of the grouFurthermore, the ability to show the video tape of the discussion to executives provides them with almost direct contact with customers. The disadvantages include the possibility of respondents "lying" in order to conform to group pressures or, conversely, disagreeing with fellow participants to whom they take a dislike. The moderator can introduce biases. Interpreting and reporting the results of the discussions is subjective. Because the number of groups is usually small and the selected samples not random, generalizing the results to the population is hazardous.

**Bibliography**

Malhotra, N. K. (1993). *Marketing research: An applied orientation.* Englewood Cliffs, NJ: Prentice-Hall. Chapter 6.

MICHAEL GREATOREX

**focus strategy**   The focus strategy is one of Porter's (1980) generic strategies (*see* GENERIC STRATEGIES) and involves concentrating on one or more niches or segments (*see* MARKET SEGMENTATION), as against aiming at broad market appeal. Companies adopting a focus strategy aim to secure a sustainable COMPETITIVE ADVANTAGE by being able to differentiate more effectively, or have lower costs, than their rivals for the particular customer clusters which they have targeted. However, there is the risk that competitors may adopt a narrower focus or that the costs of the focus strategy make those adopting it uncompetitive compared to those firms aiming at the broad market. Moreover, if such a niche strategy is highly profitable it will attract rivals which, in turn, will diminish profits.

*See also* **Competitive strategy; Cost leadership strategy; Differentiation strategy**

**Bibliography**

Porter, M. E. (1980). *Competitive strategy: Techniques for analyzing industries and competitors.* New York: Free Press. Chapter 2.

DALE LITTLER

**forecasting**

*Uses of Forecasting*

Forecasts, implicit or explicit, are used every time a marketing decision is made. Strategists need long-term forecasts of changes in the environment and of demand for both current and potential products in different markets and segments. Marketing managers use medium-term forecasts to aid decision-making concerning pricing and the allocation of resources such as advertising budgets and salesforce personnel to different products and markets. In addition, marketers are often called upon to provide short-term forecasts of sales to enable the production and distribution departments to plan production, inventories, and distribution. Further, marketers are required to provide forecasts of sales and revenues for the budgets which are the basis of management and control in every organization.

*Forecasting Methods*

Forecasting techniques divide into qualitative and quantitative methods and the quantitative methods further subdivide into causal and non-causal approaches.

*Non-causal forecasting methods.* Non-causal methods take a time series of past observations of the variable to be forecast and extrapolate the series into the future using graphical or, more usually, numerical methods.

The naive method uses a single observation, usually the latest, as the forecast of future values.

A well-known method decomposes the series into its constituent parts, namely: trend, cycle, seasonality, and error. The constituent parts may be combined in additive or multiplicative fashions. Forecasts are prepared by extrapolating separately each component of the time series and recomposing the extrapolations to form forecasts of the whole variable. The classical decomposition method has been extended into an iterative form, together with an ability to take account of special events, in the Census II software currently available and in use today.

However, forecasting methods based on exponential smoothing are more popular than the classical decomposition and the Census II methods. Simple exponential smoothing uses a weighted average of past observations; the fact that the weights decline exponentially gives a simple formula that enables the computations to be made every time a new observation becomes available thus making timely use of up–to–date data. Simple exponential smoothing is used for data that fluctuate about a level. Data with a trend require a slightly more complicated procedure, such as Holt's method, while data that also contain a seasonal cycle can be handled by Winters' method (*see* Bails & Pepper, 1993, Chapter 8). It is essential that a control procedure is used with exponential smoothing. Typical control procedures are based on cumulative sums of the errors in one–period–ahead forecasts or a tracking procedure such as Trigg's tracking signal. The main advantage of exponential smoothing methods is the simplicity of the computations and the potential flexibility and responsiveness of the methods.

Box & Jenkins (1976) developed a technique that explained the data series in terms of autoregressive and moving average processes. Potential models are identified by examining the autocorrelation and partial autocorrelation functions. The model is then estimated and a series of diagnostic checks test the adequacy of the model. Forecasts are then obtained from an acceptable model.

Trend curve analysis attempts to fashion a relationship between the data series and time as the single explanatory variable. Various forms of relationship such as linear, quadratic, logarithmic, (negative) exponential, Gompertz, etc. are fitted using least squares regression where possible, otherwise by using ad hoc numerical methods.

*Causal forecasting methods.* Causal modeling attempts to identify the underlying determinants of demand. The relationship of these variables with demand is investigated with a view to using the relationship to obtain forecasts. Thus, as well as providing forecasts, causal methods can provide insights into underlying processes, in particular into identifying the variables that affect the variable being forecast. The methods include leading indicators, multiple regression, econometrics, and input–output methods.

A leading indicator is a time series of data for another variable whose changes tend to lead changes in the variable of interest by a fixed period. There may be a reason for the relationship, e.g., sales of drainage pipes may precede sales of roofing tiles by a period equivalent to the difference between the laying of the foundations in a housing development and the building of the roofs. The main use of leading indicators (or diffusion indices) is to predict the overall level of the economy.

In multiple regression, variations in a dependent variable are explained by several independent variables. Time series data or, sometimes, cross-sectional data are used with the least squares method to estimate the relationship. A number of checks are carried out to test the applicability of the least squares method. If a suitable regression equation is found, forecasts of the dependent variable are forthcoming but are based on values of the independent variables which themselves may need forecasting. Although this may be a disadvantage of the regression method as far as forecasting is concerned, the insight into the underlying influences may be invaluable.

Econometric models build upon multiple regression methods and usually involve specifying several (sometimes many depending on the problem) simultaneous relationships between the variables of interest. Special estimation techniques for econometric models are available. While econometric models are used at the company level, they are best known for their use in modeling and forecasting at the national macroeconomic level.

Input-output methods are based mainly upon the transactions between industries as measured by government statisticians in input-output matrices. The focus is on inter-industry flows. Potentially, this should be a good basis for forecasting, especially for industrial markets. However, the collection of data upon which input-output matrices are built is so slow that by the time the tables are published the information is out of date for most practical forecasting purposes.

*Qualitative forecasting methods.* Qualitative methods rely on "soft" data based on the perceptions and subjective judgement of individuals. These may involve the subjective opinions of sales people, sales managers, marketing managers, or subjective forecasters providing forecasts on sales for budgets, production, inventory control, and marketing mix decisions. Aggregating the forecasts of individual sales representatives of sales of each product to each customer and potential customer (after adjustment for biases in previous forecasts) is a common procedure.

Forecasts can be point forecasts or interval forecasts or probability forecasts. A point forecast is a specific amount and is almost bound to be wrong. An interval forecast provides a range of values in which the actual value may fall with a given level of probability. Sometimes minimum, most likely, and maximum values are estimated; other assessors are asked to provide pessimistic, most likely, and optimistic forecasts. A probability forecast attaches probabilities to given outcomes, e.g., that the variable being forecast will lie in several possible intervals, or uses a probability distribution to describe the subjective assessment.

Long-range forecasts concerning technical innovations may be obtained from "experts" in the relevant field using, for instance, the delphi method. Surveys of buyers' intentions and consumer confidence are considered to provide soft data that may be useful for predicting discretionary purchases such as consumer durables.

*Combining Forecasts*

Forecasts of the same variable obtained by different methods are often combined. In addition, forecasts obtained by exponential smoothing may be adjusted using the subjective estimates of a forecaster.

*Selection of Forecasting Method*

The selection of an appropriate forecasting technique is fraught with difficulty, depending as it does on forecasting horizon, the nature of the data, the accuracy required, the ease and cost of use of different methods. Practitioners need to employ an appropriate technique for the specific situation. For instance, non-causal time series methods such as exponential smoothing are particularly suitable for use by multi-product organizations that need detailed and frequent short-term forecasts for the planning of production and inventories.

**Bibliography**

Bails, D. G. & Pepper, L. C. (1993). *Business fluctuations: Forecasting technique and applications* (2nd edn). Englewood Cliffs, NJ: Prentice-Hall.

Box, G. E. P. & Jenkins, G. M. (Eds) (1976). *Time series analysis: Forecasting and control.* San Francisco: Holden Day.

MICHAEL GREATOREX

**franchises**  *see* RETAIL FRANCHISES

**franchising**  Franchising has become, increasingly, a significant business format in recent years. For example, about one third of retail sales in the USA are now estimated to come from franchise arrangements, and more than a quarter of all British foreign retail investments are in the form of franchises. Burger-King, the major hamburger restaurant chain, has 7,500 outlets in 56 countries. Benetton, the Italian retailer, has some 6,000 outlets in over 80 countries. The popularity of franchising as a form of market entry (*see* INTERNATIONAL MARKET ENTRY AND DEVELOPMENT STRATEGIES) is due to the fact that it entails less risk and makes less demands on capital than other options such as INTERNATIONAL JOINT VENTURES or acquisitions. Advantages to the franchisee also include a rapid international awareness of brands and trademarks and sales growth, witness McDonalds, Benetton, and Body Shop who have been particularly successful at "exporting" their business concepts to franchisees worldwide.

There is evidence to suggest that franchises which are set up to test a business idea without prior MARKETING RESEARCH are prone to failure, and that successful franchises are those in which a close relationship exists between franchisor and franchisee to the extent that their complementary companies become vertically integrated business organizations.

**Bibliography**

Daniels, J. D. & Radebaugh, L. H. (1994). *International business: Environments and operations.* Reading, MA: Addison Wesley.

McGoldrick, P. & Davies, G. (1995). *International retailing: Trends and strategies*. London: Pitman Publishing.

NIGEL HOLDEN

**free sample**   The provision of a free sample, particularly of a new product, is a means of encouraging TRIAL. Free samples may be distributed to households; provided with magazines or newspapers; or given with existing products which are purchased. Free samples are obviously a means of reducing PERCEIVED RISK and (generally) apply to fast-moving consumer goods.

DALE LITTLER

**frequency**   As part of their ADVERTISING programs, organizations have to decide which media (*see* MASS MEDIA) to use, and a major consideration here is the desired frequency, i.e., the number of times within a specified period that an average person, household, or organization is exposed to the advertising MESSAGE.

*See also* **Advertising**

DAVID YORKE

# G

**gatekeepers** Gatekeepers can have an important (if often unnoticed) informal influence on organizational purchasing (*see* ORGANIZATIONAL BUYING BEHAVIOR; PURCHASING PROCESS), although they are not members of the DECISION-MAKING UNIT (DMU) in a formal sense. The term refers to those individuals who control access to an organization (such as receptionists, telephone operators, security staff, personal assistants, secretaries, and aides) and so may influence the flow of information into an organization. As information is a crucial aspect of the process of marketing between organizations, the influence of gatekeepers can be appreciated.

DOMINIC WILSON

**generic strategies** These are a menu of broad or general strategies which can be applied by different organizations in different contexts. Writers on strategy tend to have their own lists. For example, Igor Ansoff (1965) presented the matrix of four "directional" strategies (*see* DIRECTIONAL MATRIX). Michael Porter (1980) defined the widely known group of generic strategies: COST LEADERSHIP STRATEGY, DIFFERENTIATION STRATEGY and FOCUS STRATEGY (*see also* COMPETITIVE STRATEGY). Others have produced more extensive lists. Mintzberg (1988) developed what he argued is a comprehensive set of generic strategies, grouped into five clusters. There are those which are concerned with: locating the core business, i.e., defining what are the boundaries of the business, its essential processes, etc.; distinguishing the core business, i.e., identifying what is different about the business which can provide a competitive advantage, including how

value is added and the core competitive strategies it has adopted; elaborating the core business, such as developing its product offering within the business and other strategies defined within the Ansoff matrix; extending the core business, such as through diversification, vertical integration; and reconceiving the core business, such as through redefining the business in terms of broader needs, rather than from a narrow product or technology perspective, as Levitt (1960) argued.

The notion of generic strategies can be criticized along two fronts. First, they can only be presented in broad outline form since the specific features of the business, and the context within which the organization operates, will define the content and influence the process of implementation. Second, the competitive process involves rivalry between businesses seeking to secure some advantage from being different, so that the most appropriate competitive strategies are likely to be those which are innovative or at least different in some way from those of other firms, and do not follow some accepted strategic recipe.

## Bibliography

Ansoff, H. I. (1965). *Corporate strategy: An analytic approach to business policy for growth and expansion.* New York: McGraw-Hill.

Levitt, T. (1960). Marketing myopia. *Harvard Business Review*, **38**, (4), July–Aug., 45–56.

Mintzberg, H. (1988). Generic strategies: Toward a comprehensive framework. In *Advances in strategic management*, Greenwich, CT: JAI Press, **vol. 5**, pp. 1–67.

Porter, M. (1980). *Competitive strategy: Techniques for analyzing industries and competitors.* New York: Free Press. Chapter 2.

Rumelt, R. (1980). The evaluation of business strategy. In William F. Glueck (Ed.), *Business policy and strategic management* (3rd edn). Maidenhead: McGraw-Hill.

DALE LITTLER

**geodemographics** Geodemographic groups of consumers (i.e., identified by geographic and demographic variables), referred to as geodemographic classifications, are built on the premise that people who live in similar neighborhoods are likely to have similar purchasing and lifestyle habits (*see also* LIFESTYLES). Most classifications are built by using data from the

Census of Population such as employment type, age, marital status, family size, property type, etc. Other variables can be used and some classifications have adopted this approach, e.g., Mosaic, Finpin. Sometimes, a preliminary process called PRINCIPAL COMPONENT ANALYSIS is used on the raw variables to identify commonalities in the data. Either the raw variables or the principal components are then subject to CLUSTER ANALYSIS to identify similar types of geographical areas. (For details of the classifications and methods, *see* Journal of the Market Research Society, 1989.)

**Table 1**   The Main 1991 Census-based geodemographic classifications in the UK

| Classification system | No. of input variables | No. of clusters | Non-census data used? |
|---|---|---|---|
| ACORN | 79 | (a) 6<br>(b) 17<br>(c) 54 | No |
| PIN | 49 | (a) 4<br>(b) 16<br>(c) 42 | No |
| FINPIN | 58 | (a) 4<br>(b) 10<br>(c) 40 | FRS data |
| MOSAIC | 87 | (a) 11<br>(b) 52 | Credit data; Electoral Roll; PAF data; CCJs; Retail access; Age model; prop'n. director |
| SuperProfiles | 120 | (a) 10<br>(b) 40<br>(c) 160 | TGI; electoral roll; credit data; CCJs |
| DEFINE | 146 | (a) 10<br>(b) 50<br>(c) 1050 | Credit data; Electoral Roll; Unemployment statistics; Insurance rating |
| Neighbors & Prospects | 48 | (a) 9<br>(b) 44 | No |

*Source*: Sleight, 1995.
(a) (b) and (c) identify different levels of aggregation.
FRS = Financial Research Survey; CCJ = County Court Judgement; PAF = Postal Address File; TGI = Target Group Index.

Some of the major classifications in the UK are: ACORN (A Classification Of Residential Neighbourhoods); PIN (Pinpoint Identification Neighbourhoods); Mosaic; and Superprofiles (see Table 1 for details). As an example, ACORN classifications have been divided into six major categories, i.e., Thriving, Expanding, Rising, Settling, Aspiring, and Striving. These are further desegregated into 17 groups and 54 types. For example, the ACORN category Thriving includes groups of Wealthy Achievers in Suburban Areas, Affluent Greys in Rural Communities, and Prosperous Pensioners in Retirement Areas, and thus provides a means of locating where these types of individuals are likely to reside.

One question which has been raised in the literature is: does it really make sense to use one standard segmentation tool across all sorts of industry sectors, markets, products, and organizations? The answer appears to be that each general classification product does discriminate, but the degree of discrimination varies according to market sector and there is no single best standard geodemographic product for all situations from those available. Two of the first market-specific applications to be devised were Financial Mosaic and Finpin, which were designed specifically to segment the market for financial services. Sources of data used for Financial Mosaic include: the number of company directors, the level and value of share ownership, the level of application for various financial services, the proportion of mortgages and outright home owners, and the frequency and value of County Court Judgements. This has resulted in a classification of 36 Financial Mosaic types; for example, Young Entrepreneurs, Wealthy Businessmen, and Captains of Industry are three types which are grouped under Capital Accumulators. The demand for, and supply of, tailored or bespoke segmentation classifications has risen recently, e.g., Investor ACORN incorporates data from the Investor's Register, a database of over 1 million investors, and Art ACORN combines demographic data with information from the box offices of arts venues throughout Great Britain. The extension of these more targeted classifications is to have a bespoke classification for each particular market. If organizations have sufficient information on their customers, this can be used to create bespoke classifications for any product market, e.g., cars, food, hi-fis, etc.

CCN has made major inroads into building classifications within many European countries. Euromosaic identifies ten major pan-European types which are consistent across the European countries of: Great Britain; the Netherlands; Germany; Spain; Ireland; Sweden; and Belgium. An example of a Euromosaic type is Elite suburbs. These are well-established suburban neighborhoods in large and medium-sized cities, consisting of residential properties in large grounds. These people are wealthy, but live in restrained luxury.

The major advantages of geodemographics are: their multi-faceted nature, i.e., they do not rely on unidimensional classification variables; their ease of use and actionability, being linked to the postcode system and covering all consumer addresses within the UK; their ability to link with different data sets which have been geodemographically coded for above-the-line and below-the-line marketing activities, e.g., TV audience rating data and regional press; and their ability to describe the types of houses people live in which can help the marketer to understand his/her target segment. They are now an essential part of retail site analysis and branch/store assessment. For example, by knowing how many of a certain type of customer are within a branch/store catchment area, a more accurate assessment of alternative branch locations and of market and sales targets can be undertaken. They are useful in media planning, since media data sources such as the National Readership Survey and Target Group Index are geodemographically coded. Advertising and promotional messages can also be communicated to the target audience using DIRECT MAIL and door-to-door leaflet campaigns which can be geodemographically targeted. Finally, they are extensively used in customer profiling which involves geodemographically analyzing existing customers.

Geodemographic systems do have several weaknesses. First, because the Census information is released at an aggregated level of about 150 households (Enumeration District), classifications are not particularly good at targeting certain differences, e.g., age, at the household or postcode level. However, several products have been designed to overcome this problem.

'Monica' from CACI attempts to use the Christian names of household dwellers to indicate their likely age band, e.g., Ethel and Arthur are names which have an older age profile than Simon and Amanda.

A second problem, known as the "ecological fallacy," refers to the assumption that the behavior of all individuals will be the same within a given geodemographic type. Since geodemographic classifications describe neighborhoods rather than people, it is fallacious to assume that all the people within a given neighborhood will purchase in the same way. Mosaic is one system which has attempted to address both the age and the aggregated data problem by incorporating many variables which are measured at the postcode, rather than at the Enumeration District, level. This allows more precise targeting, since there are typically only 15 households per postcode. In addition, Persona from CCN, is one of the first behavioral targeting systems. If in geodemographic terms "you are where you live," with Persona, "you are what you do." Developed from the National Shopping Survey, it divides UK households into distinctive behavioral types. These types range from so-called "Bonviveurs" to "New Teachers" and "Craftsmen" and "Home Makers." Such data counter another of the weaknesses of traditional Census-based classifications in that they give more information about people's income, assets, leisure activities, and purchasing behavior, which is not available from the Census.

A final problem with Census-based classifications is the age of the data on which they are based – resulting from the fact that the Census is conducted only once every ten years in most countries including the UK. Fifty-six percent of the data contained within Mosaic is non-Census information and is updated regularly; although the Mosaic types themselves are only updated every two years. These non-Census data sources allow the classification to be applied to newly built areas.

*See also* **Market segmentation; Segmentation variables**

**Bibliography**

*Journal of Market Research Society*. (1989). 31, (N4), January, Special issue on geodemographics.

Sleight, P. (1995). Explaining geodemographics. *APMAP*, January, No. 347, 48.

VINCE MITCHELL

**global strategy**  A global strategy can be considered as a coherent overarching strategy for the parts of the world in which an organization operates. Yip (1989) suggests that it emerges as part of a three-stage process. First, the development of a core strategy or a distinct COMPETITIVE ADVANTAGE, generally in the firm's domestic market. Second, the extension of the firm's geographical reach of the core strategy, which will be adapted to match local features. Third, globalization, viewed as the international marketing of standard offerings (*see* OFFERING) (Levitt, 1983), through the integration of these adapted strategies into a global strategy. This is an obvious simplification of the international development of organizations which may not involve this sequence of stages.

A global strategy tends to be seen as synonymous with a standard strategy across international markets. Such a strategic approach can be regarded as yielding distinct advantages through, in particular, economies of scale. However, as several commentators have noted, there are many barriers toward such a standard global strategy, including differences in the physical environment and CULTURE, and they question the feasibility of a global standardized BRANDING strategy, arguing that the differences, from language alone, far outweigh any similarities. Adaptability and variation in MARKETING STRATEGIES across geographical markets are likely to be the norm. As Bradley (1991) notes, it may be an essential requirement to acknowledge dissimilarities between countries and adjust marketing strategies to suit specific regional requirements. Quelch & Hoff (1986) suggest that there is a spectrum of strategic possibilities with different elements (such as product features, advertising message content) having greater or smaller degrees of homogeneity across markets.

It has been suggested (e.g., Littler & Schlieper, 1995) that many markets may be converging under the influences of more widespread communications, the market DIVERSIFICATION strategies of manufacturers and retailers and the development of free trade areas, such as the European Union, leading to more standardization across markets.

## Bibliography

Bradley, F. (1991). *International marketing strategy*. Prentice-Hall.

Levitt, T. (1983). The globalization of markets. *Harvard Business Review*, **61**, (3), May–June, 92–102.

Littler, D. & Schlieper, K. (1995). The development of the Eurobrand. *International Marketing Review*, **12**, (2), 22–37.

Quelch, J. A. & Hoff, E. J. (1986). Customizing global markets. *Harvard Business Review*, **64**, May–June, 59–68.

Yip, G. S. (1989). Global strategy in a world of nations? *Sloan Management Review*, **30**, Fall, 29–41.

DALE LITTLER

**globalization**   Globalization is best described as a process of deepening internationalization. The major actors in the global economy, firms and governments, are both impacted by this process and also have helped to shape its development. So far as firms are concerned, internationalization has been an uninterrupted process of increasing significance and intensity since the 1950s. Three aspects of this process are particularly noteworthy.

First, an increasing number of firms have been involved in international production. Leading firms from all major capitalist countries have followed the earlier example of their US and UK rivals and have become more and more international in their scope, utilizing not only international trade but also direct foreign investment, and other forms of international production such as LICENSING, INTERNATIONAL JOINT VENTURES, and subcontracting.

Second, there has been a sectoral widening of international production. Thus, while, during the 1960s, the most rapid growth of international production took place in manufacturing, since then it has been the service sector that has experienced the most rapid growth in internationalization. This tendency has been most prominent in banking and financial services. Other business-related services such as advertising and accountancy have also experienced growing internationalization.

Finally, it is important to note that international business activities have experienced qualitative as well as quantitative expansion. These qualitative changes relate to the increasing process of intra-firm integration of international business activities. Most firms have changed from being international to being more multinational or even global in their internal organization (Leong & Tan, 1993). An international firm is one for whom its domestic market is of predominant importance and which views international business as a way of further exploiting assets and capabilities developed for the domestic market. A multinational firm treats foreign markets as being equally important to the home market. A global firm makes little distinction between foreign and domestic markets.

Although direct participation in international production is still confined to a relatively small number of firms, all firms are nevertheless impacted by the process of internationalization. For one thing, firms in almost all industries face direct competition from international rivals. As an example, the majority of firms in the fast food industry are very small with only local marketing horizons; however, the most fierce competition faced by such firms comes from global firms such as McDonalds or Pizza Hut. Further, technological change is breaking down industry boundaries and, as a consequence, firms experience (unexpected) competition whose origin is often from outside their domestic market. For example, traditional postal businesses are increasingly being impacted by electronic mail and other computer network services.

## Bibliography

Leong, S. & Tan, C. (1993). Managing across borders: an empirical test of the Bartlett and Ghoshal organisational typology. *Journal of International Business*, **24**, (3), 449–464.

MO YAMIN

**graphical representation**   The results of MARKETING RESEARCH can be presented in graphical form as part of the reporting procedure. Quantitative analysis, starting with the summarization procedures of the construction of frequency distributions or calculation of measures such as totals or measures of average and variation, is taken a stage further with the presentation of the results of quantitative research in the form of pie diagrams, line charts often showing graphs over time, bar charts, histograms, ogives, and scatter diagrams.

A pie diagram is simply a circle divided into sections with each section representing portions of a total. For instance, the total sales in a market can be represented by the area of the circle with sections representing competitors' sales, thus permitting market shares to be presented. Pie diagrams allow relative sizes at any moment to be presented. It is possible to present a few pie diagrams side by side to show shares in different situations, e.g., at two different times or in two different markets. In this case the total area of the circles would vary to represent the totals in the different situations.

The line chart is useful for depicting results over many periods. It is the common time series graph with time measured on the horizontal axis and the variable(s) of interest measured on the vertical axis. When more than one variable is presented, different colored lines or dashed and dotted lines can be used to identify the particular variables. A stacked line chart showing a total and its components stacked on each other shows how relative sizes or shares change over time and is similar, yet preferable, to a series of pie diagrams.

A bar chart has many variations. The magnitude of a variable is represented by a bar on a graph. The sales of each of several brands in a period can be represented in a bar chart by horizontal (or vertical) bars. Another simple version of a bar chart shows measures of a variable over time as a series of vertical bars as an alternative to a line chart as a means of depicting a time series. In pictograms, the bars are converted to pictorial representations of the variable. Thus, if the variable is sales of wine, a horizontal bar could be replaced by a number of bottles in a row. If several variables are to be represented over time, a simple bar chart can be replaced by a grouped bar chart in which the values of the variables for each period are represented by groups of bars placed next to each other, one group for each period. Alternatively, if the several variables are components of a total, a stacked bar chart can be used.

One use of a bar chart is to depict the numbers of times each value occurs for a variable measured on a nominal scale, e.g., the numbers of males and females in a sample. If the variable is measured on an interval scale that is split into a number of contiguous classes, the numbers in the classes can be represented in a histogram by a series of adjacent vertical rectangles, the areas of which are proportional to the frequencies, and the bases of the rectangles are determined by the width of each class. This is the standard way of representing frequency distributions, e.g., the distribution of heights in a sample of first-year male college students. When the data are based on a sample, the histogram may be a series of rectangles that give a very rough approximation to the population distribution which for some variables is the smooth bell-shaped curve known as the normal distribution.

If the frequencies are cumulated to show the numbers of cases below (or greater than) a series of values of the variable, then a cumulative frequency curve or ogive can be plotted. When the variable is normally distributed the less-than cumulative frequency curve will be S-shaped.

The relationship between two variables can also be represented on a scatter diagram. If one variable can be identified as the dependent variable it will be represented on the vertical (or Y) axis with the independent variable on the horizontal (or X) axis. Each pair of values is represented on the graph and a scatter of points builds uIf the points are scattered all over the graph then prima facie there is little or no relationship between the variables (a low correlation coefficient will confirm this). On the other hand, if there is a pattern to the points, then the analyst will be able to spot a possible relationship for further investigation using perhaps regression methods (see REGRESSION AND CORRELATION).

*See also* **Types of measure**

### Bibliography

Churchill, G. A. (1991). *Marketing research: Methodological foundations* (5th edn). Chicago: The Dryden Press. Chapter 18.

MICHAEL GREATOREX

**green issues**    *see* CONSUMERISM

**gross margin**    Gross margin (usually expressed as a percentage of sales) is sales revenues minus the costs of production (e.g., raw materials, components, labor, energy). Calculating the gross margin of a product or service is an important stage in assessing its unique CONTRIBUTION and profitability since gross margin should include the variable costs incurred in production. The allocation of subsequent costs (mostly fixed costs) is often heavily influenced by corporate accounting policy and so may not provide as good an indication of a product's individual profitability.

*See also* **Margin**

DOMINIC WILSON

**group influence**    *see* INTERPERSONAL COMMUNICATIONS

# H

**hierarchy of effects model**   This is a model of MARKETING COMMUNICATIONS developed by Lavidge & Steiner (1961) which has a number of stages through which the buyer/customer passes from unawareness of a product or service to purchase. The COGNITIVE STAGE is denoted by AWARENESS and knowledge, the AFFECTIVE STAGE by liking, preference, and CONVICTION, and the CONATIVE (or behavioral) STAGE by a purchase. Measures taken before and after a form of communication is used will enable objective(s) to be set and the success of it to be analyzed. Logical progression through the stages is not always possible – indeed, much depends on the product or service being offered and the target group of receivers.

*See also* **Communications objectives**

### Bibliography

Kotler, P. (1994). *Marketing management: Analysis, planning, implementation and control* (8th edn). Englewood Cliffs, NJ: Prentice-Hall. Chapter 22.
Lavidge, R. J. & Steiner, G. A. (1961). A model for predictive measurements of advertising effectiveness. *Journal of Marketing*, Oct., 61.

DAVID YORKE

**high street retailing**   High street retailing refers to retail activity in the traditional shopping areas of town, city, urban, and suburban locations. (Traditional shopping areas are described by Guy, 1994.) This type of shopping is frequently termed strip or ribbon centers by some US retailers, e.g., *see* Levy & Weitz (1995). Continued movement of major retailers to newly developed out-of-town, suburban locations and the growth of shopping malls and planned shopping centers has fueled debate concerning the future vitality and viability of high street retailing (e.g., Schiller, 1994).

*See also* **Shopping centers**

### Bibliography

Guy, C. (1994). *The retail development process* (2nd edn). London: Routledge.
Levy, M. & Weitz B. A. (1995). *Retail management* (2nd edn). Homewood, IL: Irwin.
Schiller, R. (1994). Vitality and viability: challenge to the town centre. *International Journal of Retail and Distribution Management*, **22**, (6), 46–50.

STEVE GREENLAND

**historic demand**   *see* DEMAND

**horizontal integration**   This is regarded as an integrative growth strategy and involves acquiring competitors within the same industry, as opposed to a vertically integrative strategy which might involve the acquisition of suppliers (backward integration) or customers (forward integration).

Horizontal integration may not necessarily be undertaken as a means of growth; it might also be employed to rationalize an industry, which is maturing or declining, by removing capacity.

*See also* **Competitive strategy; Vertical integration**

DALE LITTLER

**hypothesis testing** Hypothesis testing or statistical significance testing is important in MARKETING RESEARCH. A battery of significance tests is available to test hypotheses concerning population means, proportions, differences between means and proportions, correlation coefficients, etc. based on data from a probability sample (*see* SAMPLING and STATISTICAL TESTS).

Although there are many different tests depending upon the circumstances, the philosophy underlying the tests is the same. A null hypothesis is set up concerning a characteristic or parameter of the population. The null hypothesis is that the population parameter, e.g., a mean, a proportion, the difference between two means or two proportions, is equal to a particular specified value. This is the hypothesis that is tested and is assumed to be true for the purpose of the test. An alternative hypothesis is set up. The alternative hypothesis can be a simple hypothesis, e.g., that the parameter is equal to a different specific value, or more usually that the parameter is not equal to (or sometimes either greater than or less than) the value specified in the null hypothesis. The null and alternative hypotheses are specified before sample data are examined.

The test chooses between the two hypotheses using a test statistic whose sampling distribution is known, assuming the null hypothesis to be true. In practice, the null hypothesis is not rejected when the chances of obtaining a particular value or a more extreme value of the test statistic are high; it is rejected if those chances are low. The question is what is a high and what is a low chance? A probability level, the level of significance, say 5 percent or 1 percent or 10 percent, is fixed before the test statistic is calculated. This enables ranges of values for the test statistic to be worked out. If the test statistic, when calculated, falls in one range it is not rejected, if it falls in other ranges, usually extreme ranges, it is rejected. Alternatively, when the calculations are being done using computer packages, the computer works out the probability (often called the p value) of obtaining a more extreme value of the test statistic than the one obtained and if this is less than the previously specified significance level the null hypothesis is rejected, otherwise the null hypothesis is accepted.

Thus, when a null hypothesis is rejected, there is a small chance of rejecting a hypothesis that is true. It would, on the face of it, make sense to make the chances of this error, called a Type I error, as small as possible by using very low significance levels. However, there is another kind of error, Type II error, which is the chance of not rejecting a false hypothesis, which, for a given sample size and test statistic, increases when the chance of a Type I error is reduced. Increasing the size of the sample is one way of improving the sensitivity of a test.

It is important to note that a statistically significant difference between the means of two groups may or may not say something about the practical or commercial difference between the two groups. For instance, the difference between the means of two groups may be statistically significant (because of large samples) but the actual difference between the sample means may be very small and of no practical significance whatever.

### Bibliography

Chisnall, P. M. (1992). *Marketing research* (4th edn). Maidenhead: McGraw-Hill. Chapter 15.

MICHAEL GREATOREX

# I

**image**  Image is the perception of a service, brand, product, or organization by its publics. For example, a Ford Escort may be perceived in different ways by Ford dealers, by the corporate buyer of a fleet of cars, by a family man, and by a single female buyer. A hospital's image includes all aspects of patient care, customer service, and the overall impression of the hospital by those who encounter the organization in a variety of forms as patient, employee, and local resident. The image (or identity) of an organization is the sum of all the ways the organization chooses to present or define itself to the various publics. This includes the physical environment, stationery, publications, names, language style, signs, advertisements, uniforms, and so on.

### Bibliography

Aaker, D. A. & Myers, J. G. (1987). *Advertising management* (3rd edn). Englewood Cliffs, NJ: Prentice-Hall. Chapter 5.

MARGARET BRUCE

**impact**  In the context of ADVERTISING, and decisions relating to choice of media (*see* MASS MEDIA), organizations take account of the potential impact of advertisements. Impact is the qualitative value of an exposure through a given medium, e.g. an advertisement for kitchen appliances would have a higher impact in *Good Housekeeping* than in *Sports Illustrated*.

*See also* **Advertising**

DAVID YORKE

**implementation**  The implementation of strategy is regarded as the third part of a four-stage process of STRATEGIC PLANNING involving the stages of analysis, planning, implementation, and control. The process assumes that after analysis, plans are devised which act as blueprints for action. Appropriate feedback mechanisms should be in place to detect deviations from plans so that, where possible, actions can be taken to put the business back on course.

This perspective depicts the devisers of plans as separate from those who implement them. Action, then, is somehow depicted as divorced from the formulation of strategy which, according to Bonoma & Crittenden (1988), has tended to receive the greater academic emphasis.

However, it might be expected that the implementation of strategy might itself be significant in shaping the way in which it emerges. Those at the interface with the market, for example, will be faced with issues on a day-to-day basis that the planners remote from customers and the ebb and flow of the market will not have a detailed grasp of; while, of course, the plan formulators cannot possibly anticipate all of the issues and changes which arise. These may demand pragmatic responses which, in turn, can affect the emerging strategy. Mintzberg (1990) criticized the view of what he termed the "design school" which portrays formulation and application as separate stages: "Our critique of the Design School revolves around one central theme: its promotion of thought independent of action, strategy formation above all as a process of *conception*, rather than as one of *learning*" (182).

Because of the uncertainties (*see* UNCERTAINTY), it would be realistic to assume that organizations need to have the flexibility to adapt, adjust, and augment what may have been proposed in any original plans in response to newly emergent information, the consequences of past actions, competitors' reactions, and other developments. Effective implementation may, as Piercy (1990) argues, be an iterative process which involves the major protagonists and which takes cognizance of the different power relationships in the organization.

Strategy in some cases may be seen as emerging (Mintzberg, 1973; Hutt et al., 1988) (*see* EMERGENT STRATEGY) and the process of developing strategy may be intimately interwoven with the action of implementation.

### Bibliography

Bonoma, T. V. & Crittenden, V. L. (1988). Managing marketing implementation. *Sloan Management Review*, **29**, Winter, 7–14.

Hutt, M. D., Reingen, P. H. & Ronchetto, J. R. (1988). Tracing emergent processes in marketing strategy formation. *Journal of Marketing*, **52**, Jan., 4–19.

Mintzberg, H. (1973). Strategy making in three modes. *California Management Review*, **16**, (2), Winter, 44–53.

Mintzberg, H. (1990). The design school: Reconsidering the basic premises of strategic management. *Strategic Management Journal*, **11**, (3), Mar.–Apr., 171–195.

Piercy, N. (1990). Marketing concepts and actions: Implementing marketing-led strategic change. *European Journal of Marketing*, **24**, (2), 24–42.

DALE LITTLER

**impulse purchasing**   Impulse purchasing is a purchase resulting from an unplanned or spur-of-the-moment buying decision, where no prior intention existed. It is usually thought of as an in-store process, although it can occur in response to external or non-store promotional activities. Stimulating the impulse purchase has become a key objective of retailers and can account for significant proportions of sales volume. Store designs with visual merchandising principles, displaying expensive product ranges, have been developed to actively encourage impulse purchases.

*See also* **Store design**

### Bibliography

McGoldrick, P. J. (1990). *Retail marketing*. Maidenhead: McGraw-Hill.

Walters, D. (1994). *Retailing management*. London: Macmillan.

STEVE GREENLAND

**inbound communications**   Communications in DIRECT MARKETING may be either inbound or outbound (*see* OUTBOUND COMMUNICATIONS). The latter are initiated by the supplier organization directly to the buyer or customer, e.g. DIRECT MAIL and TELEMARKETING. Inbound communication occurs when a potential buyer or customer is stimulated to reply to a form of indirect communication which appears in the media, e.g., TELEVISION or RADIO advertisements or advertisements in NEWSPAPERS, MAGAZINES, or TRADE JOURNALS which may invite a response from the receiver either in person, in writing, by telephone, or through electronic mail. Evaluation of the cost-effectiveness of the stimulus is relatively easy either in terms of the number of positive responses, e.g. requests for information or, if possible, the value of sales generated.

### Bibliography

Roberts, M. L. & Berger, P. D. (1989). *Direct marketing management*. Englewood Cliffs, NJ: Prentice-Hall.

DAVID YORKE

**indirect communications**   MARKETING COMMUNICATIONS may be either direct, e.g. personal face-to-face, verbal, or in writing with the targeted buyer, customer, or consumer; or indirect where it is intended that the target will receive a communications MESSAGE through an appropriate, impersonal, channel. Indirect communication channels comprise the MASS MEDIA (e.g. TELEVISION, RADIO, NEWSPAPERS, MAGAZINES, TRADE JOURNALS), PUBLICITY, and the RETAIL ENVIRONMENT (e.g., SALES PROMOTION or PACKAGING).

Bibliography

Dibb, S., Simkin, L., Pride, W. M. & Ferrell, O. C. (1994). *Marketing: Concepts and strategies* (European edn). Boston, MA: Houghton Mifflin Co. Chapter 14.

Kotler, P. (1994). *Marketing management: Analysis, planning, implementation and control* (8th edn). Englewood Cliffs, NJ: Prentice-Hall. Chapters 22, 23, 24.

McCarthy, E. J. & Perreault, W. D. (1993). *Basic marketing*. Homewood, IL: Irwin. Chapter 15.

DAVID YORKE

**industrial marketing**    This is the term originally coined in the 1960s to describe the process of marketing between organizations. The term referred implicitly to organizations engaged in industry (especially "smokestack" industries). During the 1980s it became accepted that the term industrial marketing was inadequate because it failed to reflect the full diversity of marketing activities between organizations, especially between commercial organizations such as banks, publishers, distributors, and retailers. The term BUSINESS-TO-BUSINESS MARKETING was then coined as an alternative, though nowadays the term ORGANIZATIONAL MARKETING is preferred by many authorities because it recognizes that the principles and practice of marketing between organizations is not confined to "businesses" but also extends to a vast range of organizations such as hospitals, orchestras, prisons, armed forces, schools, charities, governments, and unions.

DOMINIC WILSON

**influencers**    Influencers are actual or potential members of the DECISION-MAKING UNIT (DMU) and are those individuals who may be influential in the PURCHASING PROCESS without necessarily being USERS or DECIDERS or SPECIFIERS. This is an imprecise categorization but might include individuals who are affected by a purchasing decision without being directly involved. For example, security staff might suggest additional features (such as temporary electronic tagging) which would make it more

difficult for personnel to steal components from a factory (e.g., theft of car radios from car factories).

*See also* **Organizational buying behavior**

DOMINIC WILSON

**information systems**    *see*    MARKETING INFORMATION SYSTEMS

**innovation**    Innovation involves the introduction of something new, such as products, processes, techniques, and organizational forms. Schumpeter (1939) highlighted what he regarded as its central role in economic development, which he depicted as a process of "creative destruction" caused by the introduction of innovations, which undermined existing forms and modes of doing things, and the responses of entrepreneurs to them. The upswing of a major economic cycle (the Kondratieff fifty-to-sixty-year cycle) has been associated with investment in a major innovation by pioneering entrepreneurs. These are later followed by a host of imitators who temporarily glut the market such that price declines and profits collapse. Some firms are bankrupted and business confidence lost, only to be revived by the next innovation.

However, such innovations are likely to be radical or discontinuous (*see* DISCONTINUOUS INNOVATION), whereas the majority of innovations are continuous or incremental adjustments to existing procedures, products, structures, and processes (*see* CONTINUOUS INNOVATION).

Given the significant changes that can occur in the environment (*see* ENVIRONMENTAL ANALYSIS) of an organization during any period, the need to be alert to external innovations has been emphasized in the strategic management literature, as well as the necessity for companies themselves to change and be innovative not only to respond to and preempt such changes, but also to establish a strategic agenda of their own. In their famous study of excellent companies, Peters & Waterman (1982) argued that:

> . . . *innovative companies are especially adroit at continually responding to change*

*of any sort in their environment* . . . . when the environment changes, these companies change too. As the needs of their customers shift, the skills of their competitors improve, the mood of the public perturbates, the forces of international trade realign, and government regulations shift, these companies tack, revamp, adjust, transform, and adapt. In short, as a whole culture, they innovate. (12)

**Bibliography**

Peters, T. J. & Waterman, R. H. Jr (1982). *In search of excellence*. New York: Harper & Row.
Schumpeter, J. A. (1939). *Business cycles*. New York: McGraw-Hill.

DALE LITTLER

**innovation-adoption model** The innovation-adoption model was developed by Rogers (1962) who postulated a number of stages through which a targeted buyer or customer passes, from a state of unawareness, through AWARENESS, INTEREST, evaluation, TRIAL, to purchase/adoption. Awareness relates to the COGNITIVE STAGE of the process, interest and evaluation to the AFFECTIVE STAGE, and trial and adoption to the CONATIVE or behavioral STAGE.

Progression through the stages may or may not be logical and will depend on factors such as: the product or service being offered; stage in the product life cycle; and the buyers – their needs, socioeconomic position, present product ownership, personality and perceptions of risk, media habits, etc.

*See also* **Adoption process; Diffusion process; Marketing communications**

**Bibliography**

McCarthy, E. J. & Perreault, W. D. Jr (1993). *Basic marketing* (11th International student edn). Homewood, IL: Irwin. Chapter 7 & 15.
Rogers, E. M. (1962). *Diffusion of innovations*. New York: Free Press, pp. 79–86.

DAVID YORKE

**interaction approach** Extensive research by the IMP (Industrial Marketing and Purchasing) Group of researchers into European buyer–seller purchasing relationships has generated significant insights into how such relationships develop (Håkansson, 1982; Turnbull & Valla, 1986; Ford, 1990). The Group describes these relationships in what has become known as the interaction approach to ORGANIZATIONAL MARKETING. In essence, the interaction approach regards purchasing in organizational markets as a multi-faceted and dynamic phenomenon where specific purchases are understood as "exchange episodes" in the evolving relationship between buyer and seller organizations, and between individuals in these organizations. These bilateral exchanges are also seen as part of a much wider and more complex NETWORK of multilateral interactions which bind organizations of suppliers and customers together in seamless "markets."

The interaction approach emphasizes stability and continuity of organizational markets which are evolving through many interrelated buyer–seller relationships, even where a superficial analysis may suggest greater volatility. It is also implied that the textbook dichotomy between "marketing" (by suppliers) and "purchasing" (by customers) may not be the most appropriate way to describe what is essentially a seamless and iterative process (*see* PURCHASING PROCESS). The interaction approach prefers a view of organizational marketing as, in effect, the management of buyer–seller relationships where it is more appropriate to differentiate participants in terms of power, expertise, experience, and cultural affiliation rather than broad organizational membership. This approach also emphasizes the importance of "ATMOSPHERICS" such as personal objectives and expectations, interpersonal familiarity, and levels of cooperation and dependence in understanding specific "exchange episodes." The elements of the interaction approach are summarized in the interaction model which is discussed elsewhere (*see* ORGANIZATIONAL BUYER BEHAVIOR). Acceptance of the interaction approach has significant implications for the management of organizational marketing. Four of these implications are listed here to illustrate the practical significance of the interaction approach:

- marketing planning should be focused on key customers in target markets (including foreign markets) rather than just on products/services;

- investment in product design and technology should only be made where this is based on an understanding of customer requirements;

- integrated team selling should be developed and managers should be appointed to coordinate all aspects of key customer relationships;

- the supplier's marketing function should be more closely integrated with the customer's purchasing function.

*See also* **Relationship marketing**

**Bibliography**

Ford, D. (Ed.) (1990). *Understanding business markets: Interaction, relationships and networks*. London: Academic Press.

Håkansson, H. (Ed.) (1982). *International marketing and purchasing of industrial goods – an interaction approach*. New York: John Wiley.

Turnbull, P. W. & Valla, J-P. (Eds) (1986). *Strategies for international industrial marketing*. Beckenham: Croom Helm.

DOMINIC WILSON

**interaction model** *see* INTERACTION APPROACH

**interest** Interest is a measure of a buyer's/customer's/consumer's state of mind *vis-à-vis* a product or service. It is a part of the AFFECTIVE STAGE in a number of models of MARKETING COMMUNICATIONS – i.e., the development of a positive attitude as a prerequisite of purchasing the product or service (*see* AIDA MODEL and INNOVATION-ADOPTION MODEL). Measures of evaluation are, as with most elements at the affective stage, difficult.

**Bibliography**

Kotler, P. (1994). *Marketing management: Analysis, planning, implementation and control* (8th edn). Englewood Cliffs, NJ: Prentice-Hall. Chapter 22.

DAVID YORKE

**internal audit** An internal audit is one part of the MARKETING AUDIT (the other being EXTERNAL AUDIT) and involves examination of the internal operations, strengths, and weaknesses of an organization. There are many ways to approach this audit but all methods involve, in essence, the allocation of all internal operations and assets into various categories labeled judgementally according to whether they are perceived as "good" or "bad" for the organization. Thus, one method recommends the identification of "strengths" and "weaknesses" while another method would be to identify "core" activities and "peripheral" activities (Prahalad & Hamel, 1990). Porter (1980) suggests that internal activities can be analyzed in terms of "value added" (*see* VALUE CHAIN) with the implication that operations which add little "value" to the organization's output should be improved, or minimized (if they are unnecessary), or subcontracted (if they lie outside the organization's core competence). All these methods of identifying internal strengths and problems risk, through disaggregation, losing sight of the collective synergies arising from the operations of the organization as a whole. Thus, an activity such as an annual Christmas Party or a weekly newsletter to customers may not seem to add significant value to the organization's offerings but cancellation could have important implications for the perception of an organization's commitment to its stakeholders.

**Bibliography**

Porter, M. E. (1980). *Competitive strategy: Techniques for analyzing industries and competitors*. New York: Free Press.

Prahalad, C. K. & Hamel, G. (1990). The core competence of the corporation. *Harvard Business Review*, **68**, (3), May–June, 79–91.

DOMINIC WILSON

**internal marketing** The role of an organization's personnel in service quality has come increasingly to the forefront, and investment in people becomes integral to the service-profit chain (*see* Schlesinger & Heskett, 1991b):

internal service quality → employee satisfaction → employee retention → external service quality → customer satisfaction → customer retention → profit

Much of the attention given to personnel relates to the concept of internal marketing which views employees as internal customers and jobs as internal products (Berry, 1980); and a company needs to sell the jobs to employees before selling its service(s) to external customers (Sasser & Arbeit, 1976). In other words, satisfying the needs of internal customers upgrades the capability to satisfy the needs of external customers. Gronroos (1981 & 1985) referred to three objectives of internal marketing:

(1) overall – to achieve motivated, customer-conscious and care-oriented personnel
(2) strategic – to create an internal environment which supports customer-consciousness and sales-mindedness among personnel
(3) tactical – to sell service campaigns and marketing efforts to employees – the first market place of the company – via staff training programs.

Internal marketing is primarily the province of human resources managers who have responsibility for developing enlightened personnel policies to include recruitment, selection, and training, and also appraisal, rewards, and recognition.

Successful personnel policies include recruitment and selection of the "right" people. Key characteristics for employees to perform effectively may relate to: process and technical skills, interpersonal and communication skills, teamwork skills, flexibility and adaptability, and empathy with the external customers. In general, employees must be willing and able to deliver desired levels of service and so avoid Gap 3, referred to as the service performance gap (Zeithaml et al., 1988 – see SERVICE QUALITY GAPS).

Training needs will, however, vary as a function of the amount of contact (visible and non-visible) with customers, the skills and equipment/technology required, and the extent of relationships with customers and with other employees (Gronroos, 1990; Schlesinger & Heskett, 1991a). Training programs cover: product, company and systems knowledge; awareness of employees' role in assessing and

meeting customer needs; and the economic impact of everyone working together to support company goals. Critical to this are service encounters (see SERVICE ENCOUNTERS) within organizations, at all levels and between levels (Lewis & Entwistle, 1990) which contribute to the service delivered to external customers – to include relationships between customer contact and backroom staff, between operations and non-operations staff, and between staff and management at all levels and locations.

In addition to product/technical knowledge and relationships management, personal skills and interpersonal communication skill development allows organizations to empower employees to respond to customers' needs and problems (see Schlesinger & Heskett, 1991a; Bowen & Lawler, 1992 – SERVICE RECOVERY). Empowerment should lead to better job performance and improved morale. It is a form of job enrichment, evidenced by increased commitment to jobs and reflected in attitudes toward customers. Knowing that management has confidence in employees helps create positive attitudes in the work place and good relationships between employees, and between employees and customers.

Zeithaml et al. (1988) indicate that successful training programs lead to:

● Teamwork: evidenced by a caring management and employees who are involved and committed to the organization and its objectives.

● Employee-job fit: the ability of employees to perform a job.

● Technology-job fit: are the "tools" appropriate for the employee and the job?

● Perceived control: e.g., do employees have flexibility in dealing with customers? If not stress levels may rise and performance decrease.

● Supervisory control systems: based on behaviors rather than output quality.

● Avoidance of role conflict: for employees in satisfying their expectations of the company and expectations of customers.

- Avoidance of role ambiguity: employees should know what is expected of them and how performance will be evaluated.

*Rewards*

Employee rewards, typically motivating factors, are subject to market research and segmentation (Berry, 1981). Organizations can carry out research among employees to identify their needs, wants, and attitudes with respect to working conditions, benefits, and company policies. People are as different as employees as they are as customers and may be segmented in a number of ways – e.g., with respect to flexible working hours which lead to increased job satisfaction, increased productivity, and decreased absenteeism. In addition, "cafeteria benefits" could be appropriate – e.g., health insurance, pensions, holidays, creche and nursery facilities, share options, profit-sharing schemes, etc. – the notion being that employees use "credits" (as a function of salary, service, age, etc.) to choose their benefits – i.e. fringe benefits to embrace the heterogeneity of the labor force. Recent attention of service companies is focused on issues of supervision, appraisal, and performance evaluation together with performance-related pay, recognition, and rewards schemes for excellent employees. Customer service awards may be financial or not, and may involve career development.

Successful internal marketing requires human resource managers to develop relationships not only with employees but also with marketing managers and operations management. Collins & Payne (1991) highlight some of the challenges and opportunities confronting interdepartmental organizational relationships. Success also leads to an appropriate service culture to support relationships with external customers.

## Bibliography

Berry, L. L. (1980). Services marketing is different. *Business*, **30**, (3), May–June, 24–29.
Berry, L. L. (1981). The employee as customer. *Journal of Retail Banking*, **3**, (1), 33–40.
Bowen, D. E. & Lawler, L. L. (1992). Empowerment: Why, what, how and when. *Sloan Management Review*, Spring, 31–39.
Collins, B. & Payne, A. (1991). Internal marketing: A new perspective for HRM. *European Management Journal*, **9** (3), 261–270.
George, W. (1990). Internal marketing and organizational behavior: A partnership in developing customer-conscious employees at every level. *Journal of Business Research*, **20** (1), 63–70.
Gronroos, C. (1981). Internal marketing: An integral part of marketing theory. In J. H. Donnelly & W. E. George (Eds), *Marketing of services* (pp. 236–238). Chicago: American Marketing Association.
Gronroos, C. (1985). Intenal marketing: Theory and practice. In T. M. Bloch, G. D. Upah & V. A. Zeithaml (Eds), *Services marketing in a changing environment* (pp. 41–47). Chicago: American Marketing Association.
Gronroos, C. (1990). *Service management and marketing*. Lexington, MA: Lexington Books.
Lewis, B. R. & Entwistle, T. W. (1990). Managing the service encounter: Focus on the employee. *International Journal of Service Industry Management*, **1**, (3), 41–52.
Mudie, P. & Cottam, A. (1993). *The management and marketing of services*. Oxford: Butterworth-Heinemann. Chapter 7.
Palmer, A. (1994). *Principles of services marketing*. Maidenhead: McGraw-Hill. Chapter 9.
Sasser, W. E. Jr & Arbeit, S. P. (1976). Selling jobs in the service sector. *Business Horizons*, **19**, 61–65.
Schlesinger, L. A. & Heskett, J. L. (1991a). The service-driven company. *Harvard Business Review*, **69** (5), Sept.–Oct., 71–81.
Schlesinger, L. A. & Heskett, J. L. (1991b). Breaking the cycle of failures in services management. *Sloan Management Review*, **32** (3), Spring, 17–28.
Zeithaml, V. A., Berry, L. L. & Parasuraman, A. (1988). Communication and control processes in the delivery of service quality. *Journal of Marketing*, **52**, Apr., 35–48.

BARBARA LEWIS

**international channel management** In marketing, the term distribution has two distinct, yet interconnected, meanings. The first refers to the physical movement of goods from the place of manufacture to a location in or close to points of purchase. A location in a point of purchase might be a supermarket; a location near a point of purchase might be a storage facility supplying, say, spare parts to industry in a given region. Distribution in this sense is called logistics or physical distribution management (*see also* DISTRIBUTION). The second meaning refers to channel management. This contribution is concerned with international channel management.

A marketing channel should not be seen narrowly as a pathway from the point of production to points of purchase by customers. Rather it should be seen as a concatenation of individuals and organizations involved in the process of making goods or services available for use or consumption. Distribution arrangements for making goods and services available for use and consumption in foreign markets are extremely varied. The persons or organizations involved in the distribution process include agents, distributors, other representatives who may be externally appointed (e.g., an export house), locally established sales offices, or franchisees.

The precise choice of these persons and organizations is influenced by factors such as the nature of the product or service, the degree of day-to-day control that the marketing firm wishes to exercise from the outside, its knowledge and experience of given markets, its strategic remit and INTERNATIONAL MARKETING policy. For example, a company supplying mass consumer goods, such as Coca Cola, needs as many outlets as possible supported by an intensive distribution system. By contrast, a selective or exclusive distribution system is required by products such as PCs or Chanel No. 5 respectively.

Consistent with these factors, internationally-operating firms address five specific challenges in the selection and implementation of schemes, which have been highlighted by Terpstra & Sarathy (1994) as follows:

(1) Should the firm extend its domestic distribution approach uniformly to foreign markets or adapt its distribution strategy to each national market?
(2) Should the firm use direct or indirect channels in foreign markets?
(3) Should the firm use selective or widespread distribution?
(4) How can the firm manage the channel?
(5) How can the firm keep its distribution strategy up to date?

This list needs to be qualified in two important ways. First, it needs to be emphasized that, the more sophisticated the operation, the more likely it is that a firm will use a combination of distribution approaches and underpin these approaches through PROMOTIONAL and ADVERTISING support. This latter activity can involve a locally appointed intermediary, such as an advertising agency or a public relations company, which it is not normal to view as a channel member on the grounds that these organizations are only indirectly involved in selling the goods or delivering the service. Second, advances in information technology and modern instant forms of electronic communication now mean that distribution in foreign markets, where IT is well established, is increasingly becoming an information management activity.

It has been argued by Dahringer & Mühlbacher (1991) that small and medium-sized enterprises, on the one hand, and multinational corporations (MNCs), on the other, show a marked tendency to leave matters of distribution to their local representatives or local offices. As a result, too many firms lack a coherent international or global distribution policy, which underpins company guidelines for setting "MARKET SHARE, sales volume, and profit margins for each market, taking account of market-entry alternatives, the desired level of company involvement in the distribution system, and the desirability of ownership of intermediaries." Market control becomes uncertain and the quality of marketing impaired. These arguments tend to reinforce Drucker's famous dictum that distribution, for all its hallowed status in the 4 P's, is still very much marketing's "dark continent."

Whatever the distribution system in given markets, the key factor for firms is to select arrangements that ensure profitability and are suited to the nature of the market in terms of its customer characteristics, structure, and distribution support facilities (e.g., transportation systems, warehousing, and storage). As for channel management, which means in practice the management of RELATIONSHIPS with channel intermediaries, specific challenges face international marketers relating to operationally interconnected areas of organization, communication, control, and motivation.

An appropriate organizational form must be developed, which links the supplier with key market intermediaries. This could be an extension of the firm's domestic organizational structure. Its organizational arrangements need to facilitate smooth and prompt exchanges of information with channel intermediaries to maintain a high level of cooperation, secure reliable feedback about the market, and encourage their ideas on all aspects of MARKETING, promotion, and selling in their territories. Apocryphal stories of channel intermediaries being the last people to hear about a price change affecting their market serve as a warning about the difficulties of handling these most important of international business relationships.

## Bibliography

Dahringer, L. D. & Mühlbacher, H. (1991). *International marketing: A global perspective*. Reading, MA: Addison Wesley.

Terpstra, V. & Sarathy, R. (1994). *International marketing*. Chicago: The Dryden Press.

NIGEL HOLDEN

**international joint ventures**    The term joint venture is a portmanteau term covering a wide range of collaborative, resource-sharing, arrangements between commercial organizations. Joint ventures are, in effect, companies that are owned by more than one organization (a joint venture owned by more than two organizations is a consortium). As a business type, joint ventures are exceptionally old; collaborative forms of trade involving joint risk-taking and profit-sharing are clearly identifiable in Ancient Egypt and other pre-Christian civilizations.

One can identify the key characteristics of a joint venture. The partners, who are independent organizations, pool resources to engage in a business activity held to be mutually advantageous; they share profits as well as losses and risks; and the period of cooperation is "long term." Joint ventures are extremely complicated to negotiate, each partner having to agree on the relative balances of financial stake-holding, risk-sharing, and management responsibility. Straight 50/50 ownership is relatively rare. In international business, the term joint venture "classically" used to imply that one partner, frequently a multinational corporation, was

stronger with respect to resource commitment and the other, frequently an organization in a lesser developed country (such as a government agency), was providing the multinational corporation (MNC) with a mechanism for securing a major foothold in that MARKET.

Joint ventures of this type, in which the host country partner was conspicuously weaker than the MNC in terms of financial allocation, production know-how, management know-how, and marketing competence, became a major feature of global economic life in the 1960s and 1970s. In that era, joint ventures, often with buy-back arrangements, became increasingly familiar in the communist world: the communist states secured some form of technical know-how and made use of the marketing skills and international distribution arrangements of MNCs, which in turn gained access to centralized economies. It is an irony of the times that joint ventures with buy-back arrangements are becoming very prominent business formats between MNCs and the reforming economies of the former USSR and socialist countries. Another example relates to the exploitation of the vast Russian gas and oil resources that is taking place in the form of joint ventures, whereby the price that the Western partners pay is in supplying major infrastructure projects such as the total redevelopment of a regional airport.

In modern international business operations, various combinations of partners may exist in joint venture arrangements. For example:

- Two companies from the same country forming a joint venture in a foreign market, such as Exxon and Mobil in Russia.

- A foreign company joining with a local company, such as Sears Roebuck in the USA and Simpsons in Canada.

- Companies from two or more countries establishing a joint venture in a third country, such as that of Diamond Shamrock (USA) and Sol Petroleo (Argentina) in Bolivia.

- A private company and a local government forming a joint venture, such as that whichexists between Philips and the Indonesian government.

- A non-profit organization and a commercial company forming a joint venture for delivery of management training, such as exists between UMIST (the University of Manchester Institute of Science and Technology) and European Construction Ventures (a UK management training organization) for implementing EU-funded management training projects in Russia.

In joint ventures involving the participation of major high-tech corporations, arrangements involve both market development and the pooling and transfer of technology. A notable example concerns the joint venture between Toshiba and Motorola, whereby the US firm was enabled to gain access to Japan's semiconductor market. In an analogous case, Sony has formed a joint venture with Intel so that the Japanese electronics giant can become a major player in the US home-computer market. In these cases, a major challenge to both partners is to overcome cultural prejudices about each other's management style.

An interesting aspect of joint ventures is that they raise ethical issues for corporations and their managers. For instance, a joint venture established in a particular country may be seen as the external partner's acquiescence in the doings of an unsavoury regime; or the path to completion of the joint venture status may have involved a partner in making "additional payments" to certain individuals to obtain a vitally important signature. In those joint ventures in which technology transfer is a major component, research and development managers may face ethical issues about making available "to the other side" valuable technological insights which fall outside the boundaries of the basic collaborative agreement.

**Bibliography**

Daniels, J. D. & Radebaugh, L. H. (1994). *International business: Environments and operations.* Reading, MA: Addison Wesley.

Hoecklin, L. (1995). *Managing cultural differences: Strategies for competitive advantage.* Wokingham, UK: Addison Wesley.

NIGEL HOLDEN

**international market entry and development strategies** The term "market entry and development strategies" has advantages over the term "market entry" in that the shorter expression focuses attention only on methods of entry, whereas the reality of INTERNATIONAL MARKETING is that the method of entry is a prelude to market penetration, the process of business development and consolidation within a foreign market over time. In other words, the selection of method of market entry or combination of methods is directly connected to both the overall business strategy for the market in question and the scale of investment allocated to achieve the STRATEGIC OBJECTIVES.

For convenience, market entry and development strategies can be classified into direct and indirect methods. It is also possible to make a distinction between strategies which involve marketing only and those which involve marketing and production. Each strategy involves trade-offs between market control and degree

**Table 1** Market entry and development strategies

| Indirect entry | Direct entry |
| --- | --- |
| • exporting<br>• direct mail (from outside)<br>• export management companies<br>• export trading companies | • import houses<br>• wholesale or retail purchasing groups<br>• public trading agencies<br>• export departments<br>• foreign sales representatives or branch offices |
| • licensing<br>• franchising<br>• production or management contracts | • joint ventures<br>• direct foreign investment<br>• acquisitions |

of risk. Table 1 neatly captures these distinctions.

The principal methods of market entry and development include EXPORTING, LICENSING, FRANCHISING, management contracts, turnkey contracts, INTERNATIONAL JOINT VENTURES, and cooperation agreements of which so-called strategic alliances (*see* INTERNATIONAL STRATEGIC ALLIANCES) are a prime example.

Market entry decisions are among the most important that internationally operating firms must make. A first consideration is that they depend on the quality and accuracy of information inputs obtained through international MARKETING RESEARCH. A second is that the decisions made have a direct bearing on the evolution of the main MARKETING STRATEGY for the selected foreign market. The point to emphasize is not only that one particular method or combination of methods entails a specific investment, but that every method comes with operational implications. Broadly speaking, market entry and development decisions cover four key areas: control issues (Are key decisions affecting operations in the market taken by a firm's local representatives or by an independent center such as a firm's international headquarters?); initial resource commitment; subsequent resource commitments; and definition of objectives.

In the case of consumer products, decisions on market entry and development involve decisions on, say, channel management (*see* INTERNATIONAL CHANNEL MANAGEMENT) or ADVERTISING campaigns. Miscalculations arising from wrong advertising or channel management decisions can result in unforeseen and therefore unwelcome costs in the form of product modifications, redeployment or reselection of market intermediaries. Nor can price rises be excluded. For firms supplying technical goods and operating primarily (though not necessarily exclusively) in industrial markets, strategy will be determined by the degree to which it is the firm's intention to enter the market and take up a position there by means of either some kind of collaboration (as through a technology transfer activity) or a more direct ("aggressive") penetration strategy.

NIGEL HOLDEN

**international marketing** Over recent years the theoretical underpinnings and definitional scope of international marketing have been both challenged and augmented by scholars. The impulses for this reappraisal of international marketing reflect changes in the international business environment, which have given rise to new market structures and forms of inter-firm cooperation. For example: the "classic" distinction between domestic and international marketing has become increasingly problematical; the emphasis on global products for global markets, so attractive in the 1980s, is now generally seen to be naive, if not out of place; similarly, a long-standing tendency to associate international marketing with nations' overall international competitiveness no longer reflects the nature and trends of modern business; the glib formulation that international marketing is the application of the domestic MARKETING CONCEPT to international scenarios does not always stand up to scrutiny; and pan-European marketing, itself a slippery concept, is becoming notionally distinct from international marketing.

These points then suggest a shift in the definitional scope of international marketing, particularly over the last ten years or so, even if the basic operational tasks associated with the management of international marketing activities have remained constant: the task of marketing of goods and services across national or other boundaries (such as linguistic and cultural ones within the European Union); the task of marketing within foreign markets; and the task of coordinating the marketing effort in multiple markets (*see* Terpstra & Sarathy, 1991).

The key challenge facing practitioners is all about understanding how the interplay of global, regional, and local processes affects their decisions about what to offer to their international customers and how to implement a well-planned business approach that is responsive to local conditions. The point to emphasize is that these decisions span an exceptionally broad range of issues of a strategic and tactical nature, ranging from major decisions about the scale of investment in particular markets to minor decisions, which nevertheless require detailed market knowledge, such as the wording and format of labels.

It is then not surprising that authors of international marketing texts show a wide divergence in their definitions of international marketing. Paliwoda (1993) emphasizes the relationship between international marketing and national competitiveness. Dahringer & Mühlbacher (1991) find limitations with the long-standing approach which emphasizes the need for a distinct MARKETING MIX for each MARKET. For them, the task lies in concentrating on "product markets (groups of customers with shared needs), emphasizing their similarities regardless of the geographic areas in which they are located." They call this approach "global marketing," but emphasize that it does not ignore differences among markets. Many leading corporations, e.g., Texas Instruments, General Electric, Sony, and Toyota, practice this kind of global marketing as opposed to producing and selling so-called global products for global markets, now an increasingly discredited concept.

Perhaps the most enduring concept of international marketing is the one which links international marketing to internationalization – the international extension of a firm's activities into and within foreign markets. A seminal paper in this regard was by Johanson & Wiedersheim-Paul in 1975. Advocates of what might be termed "the internationalization approach" have generated various models suggesting the processes whereby firms take up positions in markets by stages.

This approach has led to a preoccupation of European marketing scholars with firms' internationalizing activities as networking behavior. Supported by extensive empirical studies of predominantly industrial suppliers and buyers, this approach in effect views international marketing as a form of management of RELATIONSHIPS within NETWORKS (see Ford, 1990). American marketing scholars are less inclined to accept this behavioral interpretation and prefer to see and study international marketing as a global strategic function. American marketers tend to see internationalization in terms of the globalization of business – by which they frequently mean *American* business.

On the other hand, there is close agreement between European and American scholars that international marketing is a potentially incremental activity in the sense that firms select the degree of involvement with foreign markets. The degree of commitment begins, as it were,

with direct selling overseas (i.e., EXPORTING), and ends with a complex business investment in foreign markets such as a production facility or INTERNATIONAL JOINT VENTURE. Firms which engage heavily in international business operations tend not to make a distinction between home and overseas business. For example, Zeneca, the major UK pharmaceuticals producer, makes this a plank of its MISSION STATEMENT.

The creation of the Single European Market in 1993 has stimulated interest, on both sides of the Atlantic, in so-called "Euro-marketing" and there is a perennial debate about the mythic or actual status of the "Euro-consumer." But, perhaps the most significant feature of the Single European Market in terms of international marketing thinking is that this *planned* market of 340 million consumers can be seen to be a new and empirically significant battleground for arguably the most important operational issue in international marketing: namely, whether products can be marketed in more or less standardized formats or whether they should be adapted to suit local tastes and needs.

All in all, the subject-matter of international marketing is diffuse and certainly difficult to crystallize into an adequate definition which captures the essence of all marketing activity, namely that it is a management function in its own right *and* a business philosophy about the centrality of customer satisfaction to a firm's success. Also, a serviceable definition must somehow reflect the variety of locales of business and emphasize that international marketing is a learning activity. The definition we propose is that international marketing is the systematic internationally-based quest for CUSTOMERS in MARKET environments (*see also* MARKETING ENVIRONMENT involving a business approach that interprets customer requirements in terms of local behavior, tastes, and modes of thought.

These market environments themselves form what is traditionally known as the INTERNATIONAL MARKETING ENVIRONMENT, the wide arena in which marketers plan and execute their marketing programs. This international marketing environment is traditionally divided into sets of macro- and micro-level factors and influences, which in their totality act as a constraint, or even an impetus, on firms for developing and maintaining their international business commitments (*see also* MACRO ENVIRONMENT and MICRO ENVIRONMENT). These factors are variously classified under headings such as economic, cultural, social, legal, political, and technological. The macro-environmental factors can be global in their reach and impact, whereas the micro-level factors are associated with a distinct foreign market and are therefore "culture-specific." The more the environmental factors become culture-specific, the more they are likely to be bound up with local attitudes, values, and nuances of buyer behavior (*see also* CONSUMER BUYER BEHAVIOR). Experience suggests that marketers have most difficulty handling and apprehending attitudes and values, especially where there exists a major cultural gap.

Information from and about foreign markets stemming from international MARKETING RESEARCH activity is the key input for strategic and tactical decisions regarding policies and practices concerning product development, pricing, promotion, the establishment of market positions after the initial entry, and responses to competitive pressures. The information gathered by means of marketing research supplies input for decisions about three key questions of strategic significance: which markets to target for special attention; which markets to earmark for specific development; which method of market entry (*see also* INTERNATIONAL MARKET ENTRY AND DEVELOPMENT STRATEGIES) and market maintenance to adopt. In everyday business practice the processing of information is a slow and exacting task, for the decision-making process must take into account the risks associated with each possible line of action.

Sometimes firms' activities, especially where PROMOTION and ADVERTISING are concerned, go against the grain of local culture or sensitivities or simply bemuse the target market. For example, there is increasing evidence that consumers in former socialist countries of Eastern Europe find Western advertisements uninformative and unappealing intellectually. But, perhaps the most important transformation in the practice of international marketing is that as a business activity its operations are shifting from a competitive stance to a cooperative one. Super-regional environments such as the EU and ASEAN and even the Triad, which is a

purely notional structure linking the USA, the EU, and Japan, are creating business conditions in which even very big (often technologically leading) firms must combine resources with partner businesses, who may otherwise be direct competitors in many product areas.

Such INTERNATIONAL STRATEGIC ALLIANCES and other inter-firm and cross-border business formats suggest that in future a major task of international MARKETING MANAGEMENT will be to handle relationships involving sets of (occasionally competitive) partners in cooperative ventures. These relationships are going to become increasingly international with inter-firm cooperation spanning a multiplicity of cultures, languages, and outlooks. Thus, the international marketing manager of the future will almost need more competencies in communication and relationship management than even in the immediate past. Slowly, international marketing textbooks and curricula at business schools and management courses both for students and practitioners are reflecting this important change.

**Bibliography**

Dahringer, L. D. & Mühlbacher, H. (1991). *International marketing: a global perspective*. Reading, MA: Addison-Wesley.

Ford, D. (Ed.) (1990). *Understanding business markets*. London: Academic Press.

Johanson, J. & Wiedersheim-Paul, F. (1975). The internationalization process of the firm: Four Swedish case studies. *Journal of Management Studies*, **12**, October 305–322.

Paliwoda, S. J. (1993). *International marketing*. Oxford: Butterworth-Heinemann.

Terpstra, V. & Sarathy, R. (1991). *International marketing*. Chicago: The Dryden Press.

NIGEL HOLDEN

**international marketing culture**   The literatures of management, anthropology, and sociology are replete with definitions of "culture." In a significant study of the impact of cultural difference on management performance and behavior, Hofstede (1984) defined culture as "the collective programming of the mind which distinguishes one human group from another ... Culture, in this sense, includes systems of values; and values are the building blocks of culture." This definition implies that culture underpins values and by extension beliefs and attitudes which are particular to one group and not to others; that culture is learned and not innate; and that culture influences group behavior and attitudes in distinctive ways which are, within reason, predictable. Culture, looked at this way, is an implicit form of social life. However, culture can also be an explicit phenomenon, manifesting itself in material culture, aesthetic codes, belief systems such as religions, and conviction systems such as ideologies. Language is both an implicit and explicit manifestation: both a personal possession and a social influence.

In operational terms the key distinction between domestic marketing and INTERNA-TIONAL MARKETING is that the latter deals with the diversity of cultural differences and the impact of these differences on company planning and performance. In international marketing studies, the treatment of culture both as an internationally variegated phenomenon and in relation to specific economic-cultural constructs (i.e., markets) has frequently been found wanting. Virtually all writers of international marketing texts will devote a chapter to cultural elements of the international environment (*see* INTERNATIONAL MARKETING ENVIRONMENT), emphasizing how these elements act as a constraint on international marketing activity in a general way (e.g., language barriers) or on understanding the business mentality and associated behaviors in particular markets. Such insights enable marketers to acquire so-called cultural awareness, avoid gaffes, and present their product offerings to markets in culture-sensitive ways.

In recent years, however, there has been a noticeable trend to treat cultural issues more systematically in relation to MARKETING MIX factors and to embrace factors which are strongly influenced by cultural background and which exert a powerful influence over the quality and outcome of international business encounters. Such factors include business ethics and negotiation behavior (extending into conflict resolution). This broadening of the treatment of culture is welcome, even though it adds to existing confusions about the definitional bounds and operational relevance of culture to international marketing. A useful model has

been developed by Daniels & Radebaugh (1994), indicating that the need for greater cultural awareness can be associated with four key factors: the extent of foreign operations (i.e., the degree to which there is functional integration across various markets serviced by the company); the degree to which foreign-market activities are planned and managed at the local level; the degree of similarity (or otherwise) between the company's domestic culture and the local cultures; and the number of countries in which the company does business.

It is fairly certain that the rise of Japan to economic superpower status was one of the major impulses from the mid-1970s onward behind the quest to account for the impact of cultural differences on management and corporate behavior. But there was an additional imperative: how to understand Japanese culture to do business in that market of legendary difficulty. The search for the so-called secrets of Japanese success was more an act of desperation: Western business was not only being confronted, but also being outmanoeuvred by an Oriental culture that was at the leading edge of management and technology and taking business in markets which Western firms had long regarded as their cherished pastures. Japan then can take no small credit for introducing culture into international marketing scholarship – as well as into other branches of management studies.

However, it can be fairly said that in the 1990s Japan is no longer the magnet for culture-and-marketing analysis that it was in the past. The focus in the 1990s is squarely on the evolution of the Single European Market, which was developed as a unitary creation to facilitate business transactions among member states, while in no way diluting cultural and linguistic peculiarities of the members. The emergence of the Single European Market has given rise to a European variation of the "classic" debate over theories of customization versus standardization. In this case the issue is whether or not these cultural and linguistic traditions can, as it were, be overridden so that we witness a new kind of customer, whose counterpart can be clearly found in all the member states of the European Union, a customer who is susceptible to a general business approach and who responds to general appeals to his or her outlook on life – and pocket. This is the so-called "Euro-consumer," who is the target of so-called "Euro-marketing."

One of the limitations of writing on the impact of culture on international marketing practices is that there is considerable uncertainty as to how to assess the impact of cultural differences on the strategy formulation and business approach developed for a given market. The firm that plays down cultural differences might argue that it is not falling into the trap of using cultural stereotypes; the firm that claims to act in a culturally-sensitive way may be merely modifying its normal behavior using commonsense as a logical catalyst of adaptation. Although there is a sizeable literature on international marketing blunders, it cannot always be said that intercultural ignorance or incompetence is necessarily the cause. What is detectable is that firms who commit these blunders have either let themselves down by inadequate international MARKETING RESEARCH or have not developed a business style to suit the cultural impulses and values of foreign markets. It is international marketing activity which should forewarn a company that an advertising message or a brand name may prove comical, meaningless, or even obscene in a foreign language; that toys which appear to glorify war may be banned in Germany; and that doing business in many Asian and African countries means respecting the bonds of kinship that tie businessmen together in relationships that are baffling to outsiders.

### Bibliography

Daniels, J. D. & Radebaugh, L. H. (1994). *International business: Environments and operations.* Reading, MA: Addison-Wesley.
Hofstede, G. (1984). *Culture's consequences.* Beverly Hills, CA: Sage Publications.

NIGEL HOLDEN

**international marketing environment** The marketing environment is commonly defined as the set of actors and forces that influence the success of a company's marketing program. The important observation to be made regarding the marketing environment is that it is simultaneously complex, competitive, and dynamic. This observation is particularly pertinent so far as INTERNATIONAL MARKETING is concerned; it is unlikely that anyone can fully comprehend or understand the environment and beyond identifying broad and usually ill-defined forces or currents there can be little in the way of a common environmental diagnosis. In fact it is misleading to talk of "the" environment as the environment of a firm is partially defined or even created by itself. The success of Body Shop, for example, is presumably in part a reflection of the founder's early appreciation of the growing influence of "green" issues. The "same" environment was clearly perceived differently by established firms in the cosmetics industry.

What meaning can we attach to the notion of an international marketing environment? It is clearly not a seamless whole spanning many or all countries. On the other hand, it is not just a collection of different national environments as this would make international marketing almost redundant as a separate field of study. International marketing belongs somewhere between these two poles and international marketing environments can be viewed in some sense as the linkages between different national environments. This linkage can, in principle, be viewed in two quite different ways: interdependence or integration. Traditional trade theories, for example, implicitly adopt the interdependence view, whereas the notion of "GLOBALIZATION" that is popular within international business and management studies (including marketing) implies an integration view. Globalization is held to be a force that is either dissolving national differences or is transcending these differences. Levitt's (1983) view of the globalization of markets is one good example. Another is Badarocco's view regarding the globalization of knowledge and technology (1991). One can also meaningfully talk of the globalization of competition (Prahalad & Hamel, 1988) or the globalization of business, where this refers to growing integration of business activities in different countries within the multinational corporation.

Globalization is driven, essentially, by economic and particularly technological forces reducing the costs of and barriers to resource mobility including the mobility of people, money, and (of course) knowledge of all sorts. The same forces have also reduced radically the costs of organizing and managing economic activity across space.

By contrast, political forces, generally speaking, are acting as a break on globalization. Protectionism, which is largely a manifestation of economic nationalism, is still a powerful force and the success of GATT (now called the World Trade Organization) in removing non-tariff barriers to trade has at best been limited. In fact, protectionism is more entrenched as it is increasingly exercised by regional blocks rather than by individual countries. For example, the dispute between France and the USA relating to the former's restrictions on service imports was enmeshed in the dispute between the EU and the USA. The tensions within the EU itself also reveal the relevance of political forces. There is increasing resistance to further integration and some European countries show great reluctance to trading off national for regional sovereignty.

The slogan that marketers "should think globally and act locally" is meant to emphasize the fact that international marketers face a hierarchy of environments. Irrespective of how the linkages between different national marketing environments are construed, the environment of a particular country remains highly relevant to success or failure in that market. Environmental analysis should, therefore, concern itself with the international level as well as the national or local levels. International analysis should be used to indicate which countries may be avoided (on account, for example, of their instability or hostility to foreign business) and which countries could potentially be targeted. But the "real" marketing tasks relate to designing a MARKETING MIX for countries that are selected for entry or expansion programs, and clearly require a thorough understanding of the specific conditions of these countries. Furthermore, decisions regarding the feasibility and desirability of standardizing the marketing approach for several countries should be informed by a careful analysis of the relevant markets.

Even ardent advocates of globalization as the basis of marketing strategies cannot overlook the significant diversities that still divide national markets. Thus, it is obvious that differences in climate, topography, and other physical conditions will always be with us and will remain a significant influence on buyer behavior (*see*

CONSUMER BUYER BEHAVIOR). For example, it is unlikely that a product (e.g., a washing machine) designed to perform well in the arid climates of Greece or Spain will give an equally satisfactory service in Denmark or Sweden. More generally, the apparent homogeneity in customer preferences across countries, evidenced by their purchase of standardized products and global brands, may in fact mask significant behavioral or attitudinal differences of relevance to international marketers. Notably, recent research has shown that consumers in different countries and cultures show different degrees of involvement with a number of standardized global products (Zaichowsky & Sood, 1989; Sood, 1993). Cultural influences are clearly deeply rooted and are very durable and marketers should be highly sceptical of "evidence" of growing convergence (*see also* INTERNATIONAL MARKETING CULTURE). The key challenge facing practitioners concerns understanding how the interplay of global, regional, and local environments affects their decisions about what to offer to their international customers and how to implement a well-planned business approach that is responsive to local conditions. The point to emphasize is that these decisions span an exceptionally broad range of issues of a strategic and tactical nature, ranging from major decisions about the scale of investment in particular markets to minor decisions, which nevertheless require detailed market knowledge, such as the wording and format of labels.

## Bibliography

Badaracco, J. (1991). *The knowledge link: How firms compete through strategic alliances.* Boston, MA: Harvard Business Press School.

Levitt, T. (1983). The globalization of markets. *Harvard Business Review*, **22**, May–June, 41–53.

Prahalad, C. & Hamel, G. (1988). Creating global strategic capability. In N. Hood & J. Vahne (Eds), *Strategies in global competition.* London: Routledge.

Sood, J. (1993). A multi-country approach for multinational communication. *Journal of International Consumer Marketing*, **5**, (4), 29–50.

Zaichowsky, J. & Sood, J. (1989). A global look at consumer involvement and use of products. *International Marketing Review*, **6**, (1), 20–34.

MO YAMIN

**international marketing organization**  In the planning of their INTERNATIONAL MARKETING strategies firms must play close attention to the matter of organization. The creation of suitable organizational structures is in fact a central element of strategy formulation: it cannot be separated from the operational aspects of strategy. The creation of suitable organizational structures is, however, exceptionally complicated and is influenced by a host of factors, which cannot have quite the same significance for any two firms no matter how similar they may appear to be in their size (i.e., turnover and number of employees), product profile, and market specialization.

On the other hand, it is possible to identify eight main clusters of variables which firms need to take into account to ensure that their chosen organizational form serves as an effective mechanism of control for coordinating the international marketing effort within the firms and across the markets in which they operate. These eight variable clusters are: the size of the business – overall volume and the contribution of foreign sales; the number of markets in which the firm operates; the nature and level of involvement in foreign markets; the firm's international business goals; its international experience; the nature of its products, including its technical complexity and back-up needs; the width and diversity of the product line; and the precise nature of the marketing task.

In deciding on a suitable organization structure, companies traditionally choose between forms, which are based on four broadly alternative principles of divisionalization. The first principle is the international division, which is a specialist structure responsible for handling all aspects of a company's activities with foreign markets. These activities can be very diverse. In addition to overseeing relationships with all its international markets and intermediary partners, the international division will be called upon to: be responsible for foreign currency operations; deal with foreign governments and its own; handle all documentation pertaining to the supply of products to foreign customers; and work with key business partners such as exhibition contractors and advertising agencies. The establishment of a separate international marketing division is not favored by all companies on the grounds that such a structure creates an artificial distinction with domestic marketing operations. The argument for this organizational form is that international marketing is so specialized that it warrants this separation.

The second principle of organization is the product division. The rationale here, which is favored by several major international companies, is that a division based on a product (or suite of related products) enables the company to plan its business around products and product managers who will be exceptionally knowledgeable about them and fully aware of customer needs in all markets. The product division is popular with firms offering technical products requiring strong after-sales support and service. Therefore, a key role of the product manager is not only to advise on product marketing strategy, but also to act as a troubleshooter.

Against that form of organization, companies also make use of the geographical principle. In this case, companies divide their worldwide markets into distinct territories such as North America (i.e., USA and Canada), the Middle East, South America, the European Union etc. In this structure, the division is peopled by area specialists, one of whose skills may be knowledge of a foreign language. The rationale here is that doing business in specific geographically connected groups of markets requires considerable area knowledge, a kind of knowledge that the peripatetic product manager can never acquire, literally because he is never anywhere long enough. One problem with area-based structures is that the world's geography and the geopolitical associations that go with it do not lend themselves to tidy, self-contained, classification. For example, until the end of the 1980s it was convenient to treat the Soviet Union and the socialist countries of Eastern Europe as a more or less homogeneous region from a marketing point of view. Today, this region has become a set of increasingly distinctive business regions, each requiring a high degree of specialized knowledge.

The fourth divisional form is known as functional. This structure is prominent in the case of companies – such as those operating in the oil and gas industries – where production and marketing methods are homogenous. In reality, it is rare that one encounters a company that adopts one of these organizational structures in the pure form as described here. The need for specialization is ever to be balanced with the need to integrate functions and competencies across organizational boundaries. This state of affairs gives rise to a fifth structure known as the matrix organization. This structure takes account of the fact that foreign subsidiaries or intermediary partners may report to one group at company headquarters. Thus, it is organizationally straightforward for local managers to deal directly with HQ staff responsible for marketing, production, research and development and so forth. This arrangement has a certain elegance, while representing a pragmatic attempt to add flexibility to relationships between HQ and local representation. Nevertheless, there are drawbacks. For example, a principle of the matrix system is that the majority of interactions involve lower-level management and that adequate resources – human, financial, and technical – support these interactions. However, when senior managers are drawn into exchanges, this can lead to factionalism and time-consuming haggling over resource allocations. Despite these limitations, the matrix structure tends to be the favored form of organization in large, internationally operating, companies.

In operational terms, the key facet of any organizational structure is that it facilitates those activities for which it has been designed. It should not be overlooked that, in addition to serving as a means of achieving customer closeness, an effective organizational structure must prove amenable for the fulfilling of key tasks of international MARKETING MANAGEMENT. Companies frequently have difficulty combining operational effectiveness with managerial efficiency; and, as a result, breakdowns in communication occur between market places and the strategic center of the company. Organizational designers, therefore, need to be very clear about the organizational structure they opt for. The reality of international marketing operations is that the established structure will perforce undergo modification, planned or unplanned. A major influence in this respect concerns the management of information. Thus, the international marketing organization should be designed with a very clear view of information needs.

According to Dahringer & Mühlbacher (1991), there are a number of activities in respect of which an information system is needed for undergirding the formal organizational arrangements. These activities are: monitoring the INTERNATIONAL MARKETING environment; elaboration of strategic decisions (e.g., pertaining to market expansion or divestment); performance monitoring of product markets and geographical regions; assessment of resource-allocation decisions and their impact on the company's overall success; exchanging and integration of experiences gained in different parts of the company; and communicating information about the firm and its products, activities, and achievements to relevant business partners. The information system must be able to gather, store, update, and disseminate information efficiently.

Whatever organizational structure a firm adopts for its international marketing operations, a suitable information system (*see* MARKETING INFORMATION SYSTEMS) must be in place. Without this, competence for other major management tasks of international marketing, namely planning and control, will be severely impaired. It is still not fully appreciated by firms that international marketing success is closely correlated with a superior capacity to handle environmental information. This has been demonstrated by Japanese firms in the last two decades.

### Bibliography

Dahringer, L. D. & Mühlbacher, H. (1991). *International marketing: A global perspective.* Reading, MA: Addison Wesley.

NIGEL HOLDEN

**international marketing research**  International marketing research is intended to aid marketing decisions involving more than one country. The research can involve global products, large multinational companies active in several countries, or smaller companies interested in new export markets. International marketing research may involve routine yearly forecasting of sales of different products in many established markets, or decisions concerning the introduction of a product successful in one country into another country, or why a product's success varies from country to country. Although the same methods are used as in domestic marketing research, the international marketing research process is complicated by extra problems.

The MARKETING ENVIRONMENT varies from country to country. This is particularly true of the governmental, legal, economic, and cultural environments and secondary research (*see* SECONDARY DATA) will have to be carried out on these environments. This immediately multiplies the amount of search for relevant secondary data, and sources outside the domestic country will be needed. The potential for problems with secondary data is greater with international research than for domestic research. The level of information will vary with the informational environment, definitions vary from country to country; indeed, different sources frequently give different values for the same variables, e.g., country A's figure for its imports from country B will differ from country B's figure for its exports to country A. The level of accuracy may be expected to be better in developed countries than in developing countries. Data on national income based on tax returns will be affected by differing tax regimes and attitudes toward tax evasion.

Qualitative research becomes important in international marketing research as it is more likely that ignorance of foreign markets means that more exploratory research is needed. It may be difficult to recruit trained personnel with knowledge of both qualitative research methods and the culture and language of the country under study.

Survey research offers two types of problems relating to SAMPLING and QUESTIONNAIRE DESIGN respectively. Sampling problems include difficulties in population definition and the lack of suitable sampling frames which make it difficult to relate any sample results to a population. Low levels of telephone penetration or poor postal systems and low literacy levels may make telephone surveys or postal surveys impractical in developing countries. High transport costs in some countries may mean personal interviews are confined to urban areas. On the other hand, personal interviewing may be more economic in lower wage countries. Response rates depend upon cultural factors such as differing attitudes toward privacy, greater reluctance in some communities to communicate with strangers, and different attitudes toward some products such as food, personal hygiene, and alcohol.

Questionnaire problems begin with language problems. Language varies from country to country and in some countries several languages are spoken in different areas. Some words may have different meanings in different countries using the same language. Direct translation of a questionnaire from one language to another by a bilingual translator is frequently used. A translation needs to be checked by such means as back translation whereby the translated questionnaire is translated back to the original language by another translator and comparison of the original questionnaire and the back-translated version is carried out, allowing errors to be identified which can then be rectified. Piloting each language questionnaire in the country it is to be used in is another check. Other questionnaire problems occur when questions and scales appropriate to the one country are inappropriate to other countries. Thus, questions about car parking and out-of-town shopping centers may be inappropriate in countries where there are few cars. Again items in a scale designed to measure a particular concept and devised in one country may not be appropriate to another country.

*See also* **International marketing; Marketing research**

**Bibliography**

Malhotra, N. K. (1993). *Marketing research: An applied orientation.* Englewood Cliffs, NJ: Prentice-Hall. Chapter 25.
Moutinho, L. & Evans, M. (1992). *Applied marketing research.* Wokingham: Addison Wesley. Chapter 14.

MICHAEL GREATOREX

**international organizational structure**
The treatment of the structural issues within INTERNATIONAL MARKETING is highly influenced by the dominant paradigm in organizational theory. This holds that the structure of a firm reflects its strategy. In this paradigm, the most forceful statement of which is to be found

in Chandler (1962), structure is essentially concerned with the question "Who does what?," the answer to which is contingent, largely, on what strategy the firm is pursuing. Strategy, in turn (see also STRATEGIC MARKETING), is concerned with the question "What is to be done?," the answer to which is to be sought in environmental imperatives. There is a linear process of causation from environment to strategy to structure: a successful firm develops strategies that "fit" its environment and sets up an organizational structure that ensures their effective implementation. Thus, organizational structure defines in broad terms the prerogative and roles of different people or units within the firm. It also sets up an incentive structure of positive and negative rewards to motivate different groups within the firm to identify with, and pursue the goals of, the organization. Finally, an organizational structure creates a coordination or integration mechanism.

For international marketers, the key structure question concerns the appropriate balance between centralization at headquarters and the degree of local autonomy exercised by the subsidiaries. Subsidiaries have minimal input into strategy formulation which revolves around marketing standardization versus adaptation (see INTERNATIONAL PRODUCT ADAPTATION; INTERNATIONAL PRODUCT STANDARDIZATION). Subsidiaries also have little input to decisions relating to organizational "architecture" or organizational "surgery" (Goold & Campbell, 1989). For example, decisions regarding acquisitions, mergers, and the formation of alliances are made at the center alone. Likewise, decisions relating to the selling off, liquidation, or "downsizing" of particular units or subsidiaries are also usually the prerogatives of headquarters. Headquarters also decide whether international marketing activities are organized on a "separation" or an "integration" basis. The former treats foreign markets separately from the "home" market and all aspects of foreign marketing become the direct responsibility of the international division. The integration approach makes no distinction between domestic and foreign marketing; here the firm adopts a global structure organized around products, functions, or areas. An alternative (but one which is now out of favor (Achrol, 1991) is the matrix organization: this is a dual authority structure in which subsidiary managers are simultaneously accountable to regional and product managers.

The roles of subsidiaries are "residual" in the sense that these roles are specified in terms of the decisions that headquarters do not wish to be heavily involved in. This, in turn, depends on the overall MARKETING STRATEGY being pursued. Firms with a standardization strategy will have a tighter degree of supervision over various MARKETING MIX activities by the subsidiary. In terms of the role typology utilized by Queltch & Hoff (1986), headquarters will have "approving" and "directing" roles. On the other hand, a firm with an adaptation strategy will leave a greater degree of autonomy for subsidiaries and the center will confine itself to "persuading" and "coordinating." In practice, the autonomy enjoyed by subsidiaries is often greater than would be suggested by the range of formal roles assigned to them by the center. This is because effective monitoring and supervision is very expensive and needs information generated or filtered by subsidiaries. Subsidiary managers, particularly of subsidiaries in large and important markets, may in fact be able to largely ignore corporate level strategies. Effective control of subsidiaries is probably more feasible through an informal or organic socialization process whereby subsidiary managers identify with and adopt the corporate "mission" as their own. This may be easier to achieve if expatriates are employed in key managerial positions within the subsidiary.

The theoretical underpinning for the traditional view of the strategy/structure relationship has been criticized by Hedlund & Rolander (1990). The burden of their argument is to suggest that structure is not simply an instrument for implementation but that it influences how the firm "sees" the environment and what range of opportunities are perceived to be within its grasp. In other words, strategy depends on structure. In this view, structure is not only concerned with "who does what" but acts rather like the "nervous" or "sensing" system of the firm. Hedlund & Rolander (1990) argue that the environment-strategy-structure paradigm ignores the dynamic aspects of strategy which relate to the firm's learning capability. Corporate learning requires a structure that is tolerant of exploration and experimentation by different units. The "brain" functions of the organization cannot, therefore, reside solely at the center.

In a similar vein, Bartlett & Ghoshal (1989) discuss the drawbacks to the structural set-up within which the subsidiaries have implementation roles only. A potential advantage of multinationality is precisely that by operating in a number of diverse market environments it is possible to gain access to a wider range of ideas, skills, and capabilities. However, this potential is unlikely to be achieved if the roles of subsidiaries are confined to carrying out centrally determined strategy. In fact, Bartlett & Ghoshal (1989) have advocated a "transnational" structure in which subsidiaries, particularly those located in more dynamic markets, have a similar standing to headquarters and participate in strategy formulation.

**Bibliography**

Achrol, R. (1991). Evolution of marketing organisation: New forms for turbulent environments. *Journal of Marketing*, 55, (4), October, 77–93.

Bartlett, C. & Ghoshal, S. (1989). *Managing across borders: The transnational solution.* Boston, MA: Harvard Business School Press.

Chandler, A. (1962). *Strategy and structure.* Boston, MA: MIT Press.

Goold, M. & Campbell, A. (1989). *Strategies and styles.* Ashridge Management Centre.

Hedlund, G. & Rolander, D. (1990). Action in hetearchies – new approaches to managing the MNC. In C. Bartlett, Y. Doz, G. Hedlund (Eds) *Managing the global firm*, London: Routledge.

Queltch, J. & Hoff, E. (1986). Customizing global marketing. *Harvard Business Review*, 26, May–June.

MO YAMIN

**international pricing policy** Pricing decisions have long been held to be among the most difficult that managers must make. Chisnall (1995) points out five key factors which influence pricing decisions: nature and extent of demand; competitors' activities (influenced by trading structure); costs of production and marketing; pricing objectives (business policy); and product life cycle.

When it comes to pricing for international markets, these factors and the levels of complexity associated with them take on extra dimensions. The fact that all these factors play themselves out differently from market to market makes standard price policy a virtual impossibility and suggests that an international pricing policy must be one that is not narrowly focused on the setting of the product price. Ideally, as Dahringer & Mühlbacher (1991) note, an international pricing policy must take account of "the intended strategic position of the company as well as the positioning of its product lines and individual products."

International pricing decisions cannot be as easily standardized as decisions concerning product policy or promotional strategy. This is because so many uncontrollable influences can have a bearing on price. Furthermore, many of these influences are subject to rapid fluctuation: an obvious example of this kind concerns currency exchange rates. Other factors, such as changes to tax regimes in foreign markets or the rate of inflation there, can bring about significant changes in purchasing power, the degree of demand, and the nature of competition.

A number of factors which impact on pricing decisions for international markets have been classified by Daniels & Radebaugh (1994): different degrees of governmental intervention; greater diversity of markets; price escalation for exports; changing relative values of currencies; differences in fixed versus variable pricing practices; and strategies to counter international competitors.

Each of these factors is now considered. With respect to government intervention, this can take three main forms: exchange rate policies, balance of payments policies, and regulations. The first two influence the financial environment, having a direct bearing on business confidence. The third can manifest itself in the form of price controls. In order to protect a home industry or to avoid dumping, a government can use its regulations in various ways, for example to: impose price ceilings, restrict price changes, or tax profits (for example, by limiting the amount that can be expatriated).

Concerning diversity of markets, Dahringer & Mühlbacher (1991) isolate four general classifications of factors which vary significantly from country to country and which influence markedly the price that a market will tolerate for a given product: customers, competition, business groups, and economic conditions. Customers not only, in principle, establish through demand the real value of products, but also determine the theoretical price ceiling of a given product. Competition has a tendency to keep prices low. Business groups possibly, with their country's government, establish the framework of competition and may cooperate, formally or informally, to set the price parameters for a given industry sector. With respect to economic conditions, four factors exert the greatest influence over prices: growth rates, exchange rates, inflation, and income distribution. All of these factors are interrelated, and influence an economy's dynamism and its openness to foreign products.

Price escalation refers to the additional charges imposed on the basic production cost of a product. There may be as many as 20 of these cost elements on a product which is destined for export. These cover various ex-works transportation costs, administrative fees, international carriage and associated insurance, special packaging, and so forth.

Exchange rates not only establish monetary differentials among nations; they are also subject to fluctuation, and any currency in which goods may be finally quoted is subject to pressures which affect the ultimate perceived value of goods and therefore their relative value and affordability. One such pressure is inflation which can either be exported or imported. As Daniels & Radebaugh (1991) point out, inflationary pressures affect pricing in two significant ways: the receipt of funds in a foreign currency, when converted, buys less of the company's own currency than had been expected; and the frequent readjustment of prices is necessary to compensate for continual cost increases.

Changes in exchange rates have, of course, the effect of making goods appear either cheaper or more expensive. This means that an element of international pricing strategy must be to make best guesses about any such changes in order to set a price that does detract from consumers' perceived value. This form of prediction is far from easy. Nor should it be forgotten that exchange rates not only influence a company's prices, they also determine the cost of its own purchases from foreign sources.

A crucial aspect of pricing policy for international operations is that prices are often subject to extensive negotiation between suppliers and foreign customers, who may in the first instance be a market intermediary and not an end-user. In the case of a "one-off" capital project, such as a chemical plant or renovation of an airport, the purchaser would aim to secure a lower price, e.g., by modifying his requirements. There is also flexibility over payment and credit terms as well as over service arrangements or programs for training the purchaser's personnel. In other words, companies can shift their pricing strategy from one based on fixed price to one based on variable price.

A major consideration behind a variable price strategy is frequently a recognition of the need to counter international competitors. If the main competition in a foreign market comes from within, then the external supplier is able to set his price according to levels influenced by the domestic competition. Where, however, it encounters the same international competition in various markets, the company must develop a pricing policy which recognizes this fact. In other words, its pricing for international markets cannot be mainly influenced by internal market factors; the global competitive environment must be taken into account.

So far the discussion has concerned pricing as an element of business development linking suppliers to foreign markets. However, there is another form of international pricing that takes account of the fact that major internationally operating businesses supply goods internationally from one company location to another, e.g., from the point of production in one country to a subsidiary in another country. The pricing arrangement in this case is termed TRANSFER PRICING. A major motivation for this pricing option is that it provides major companies with a mechanism for side-stepping higher tax penalties in some countries.

As Daniels & Radebaugh (1994) explain: "If the corporate tax rate is higher in the parent company's country than in the subsidiary's country, the parent will set a low transfer price on products it sells to the subsidiary in order to keep profits low in its country and high in the subsidiary's country. The parent will also set a high transfer price on products sold to it by the subsidiary." In practice, transfer pricing may become very complicated, partly due to interdivisional rivalries within the same (vast) organization. Furthermore, because the transfer price is said to be arbitrary, i.e., is not set in accordance with market conditions, it can often prove difficult to evaluate subsidiary performance. It is for these reasons that transfer pricing is not always preferred to pricing methods that are market-oriented.

### Bibliography

Chisnall, P. (1995). *Strategic business marketing.* Hemel Hempstead, UK: Prentice-Hall.

Dahringer, L. D. & Mühlbacher, H. (1991). *International marketing: A global perspective.* Reading, MA: Addison Wesley.

Daniels, J. D. & Radebaugh, L. H. (1994). *International business: Environments and operations.* Reading, MA: Addison Wesley.

NIGEL HOLDEN

**international product adaptation** Marketing adaptation is the opposite of standardization and conveys the idea that marketers may tailor their marketing program to the specific conditions of the different countries in which they operate. A distinction is usually made between "mandatory" and "discretionary" adaptation (Hill & Still, 1984; Walters & Toyne, 1989). Mandatory adaptations are those that are dictated by the physical, legal, political, or economic factors in a country. For example, voltage levels and power sockets of electrical equipment need to conform to local requirements; in some countries safety or anti-pulsion/emission regulation may be particularly restrictive and may make it impossible for the firm to offer a standardized product. In fact, however, research indicates that the majority of adaptations are not mandatory and according to one estimate, more than 70 percent of adaptations made are discretionary (Hill & Still, 1984).

Jain (1989) provides a rigorous examination of factors that affect the balance between program standardization and adaptation and offers a number of specific hypotheses relating to their impact on the degree of standardization. These factors fall into five categories: the nature of the target market; the market position of the

firm in different countries; the nature of the product itself; environmental factors; and organizational factors. The observed pattern of standardization seems to confirm Jain's analyses. For example: the nature of the product is a strong predictor of standardization; standardization is more common for industrial as compared to consumer products; and products for which buyer behavior is culturally determined tend to be more adapted than products for which consumer choice is dependent on functional performance (e.g., food products compared to electrical goods).

*See also* **International product standardization**

### Bibliography

Hill, J. & Still, R. (1984). Adapting products to LDC tastes. *Harvard Business Review*, March–April, 92–101.

Jain, S. (1989). Standardisation versus adaptation: Some research hypotheses. *Journal of Marketing*, **53**, January, 70–79.

Walters, P. & Toyne, B. (1989). Product modification and standardization in international markets: Strategic options and facilitating policies. *Columbia Journal of World Business*, **29**, (3), Winter, 37–44.

MO YAMIN

**international product standardization** There is an inevitable tension between standardization and adaptation within marketing, whether domestically or internationally. The fact that customers have different preferences, and given marketing's commitment to customer "satisfaction," implies a pressure toward adaptation or even the customization of the offering to individuals or small groups. However, customization has been (until very recently, at any rate) considered to be prohibitively expensive due to the existence of economies of scale and other technological and economic constraints suggesting that most people (with the exception of the very rich) must tolerate some degree of standardization or uniformity in what they purchase and consume. The evolution of marketing from "mass" to "target" marketing reflects this tension; "mass" marketing simply ignores diversity or the desire for variety ("you can have any color as long as it is black"). Target marketing, by contrast, starts by assuming pervasive diversity and searches for groups or SEGMENTS that may have similar preferences for a particular offering. However, the tension between standardization and adaption is particularly important for the international marketer, as the potential for economic benefits from standardizing across countries could be very substantial while the diversities may be very great due to significant differences in culture and other environmental conditions between countries (*see* INTERNATIONAL MARKETING ENVIRONMENT).

In INTERNATIONAL MARKETING, complete program standardization means offering the same product or product line at identical prices through identical distribution systems and promotional policies to customers in different countries. Program standardization is, thus, concerned with the degree to which different elements in the MARKETING MIX are treated in the same or a similar manner by a firm that operates internationally. Process standardization, on the other hand, refers to the uniformity in the approach chosen by a multinational firm in analyzing market potential and the formulation of MARKETING PLANNING for different countries. The vast majority of the literature is concerned, however, with program standardization.

The main attraction of standardization is clearly the scale economics that may result from it, not only in production but also in R&D and product development and possibly in advertising and promotional expenditure. Levitt (1983) puts particular emphasis on technology and scale factors in advocating standardization. An uninterrupted production run from one center will allow the firm to move rapidly up the learning curve, thus reducing per-unit cost very rapidly. Operating on a large scale will also provide sourcing efficiencies, e.g., purchasing large amounts of raw materials and other inputs gives a multinational the power to bargain with suppliers. Doglus & Wind (1987) are more skeptical and point out that economies of scope and flexible manufacturing increasingly make it feasible to make adaptation without incurring increasing costs or diseconomies of scale. Economies of scope arise if it is cheaper to produce a number of different products or product varieties together in one plant than it is

to produce each in a separate plant. The basis for economies of scope is a number of interconnected technical developments known as "flexible" manufacturing systems.

In spite of much debate between the advocates of standardization and adaptation, little is known regarding the impact of standardization on corporate performance and until recently the performance issue had not received any research attention. Samiee & Roth's (1992) work is probably the first systematic investigation of the link between standardization and performance. They found no significant difference in performance between firms that stressed standardization and those that did not.

*See also* **International product adaptation**

**Bibliography**

Doglus, S. & Wind, Y. (1987). The myth of globalization. *Colombia Journal of World Business*, **22**, (4), 19–30.

Levitt, T. (1983). The globalization of markets. *Harvard Business Review*, **22**, May/June, 92–102.

Samiee, S. & Roth, K. (1992). The influence of global market standardisation on performance. *Journal of Marketing*, **56**, April, 1–17.

MO YAMIN

**international strategic alliances**  An alliance is any contractual or cooperative relationship between two organizations for a specific purpose. Relationships between firms can be conceived of in terms of a spectrum at one end of which is "arm's length" exchange. This is purely price-mediated and involves no commitment or promise regarding the future behavior of either party. At the other end of the spectrum is a merger or union between two organizations. Alliances occupy the mid-range between arm's length exchange and merger. Thus, an alliance involves some degree of long-term commitment between the parties manifested either through a legally binding contract or through a more informal agreement to cooperate. The duration of the relationship in an alliance is indeterminate but, unlike a merger, it is not permanent. Particular forms of alliances can be very varied and include LICENSING, subcontracting, FRAN-CHISING as well as INTERNATIONAL JOINT VENTURES.

Inter-firm alliances have a long history in international business. Until the early 1980s, these alliances were focused on market entry (see INTERNATIONAL MARKET ENTRY AND DEVEL-OPMENT STRATEGIES) into particular markets and were commonly between firms from developed economy markets and firms or government agencies in less developed or centrally planned economies. In such econo-mies, the option of direct investment was often ruled out or was made unattractive by govern-ment restrictions regarding foreign ownership and control. To generalize, these "traditional" alliances were a means of exploiting the Western or Japanese firms' existing capabilities (most often technological know-how, but also market-ing and organizational skills) and in this sense were essentially tactical. Any new skills or knowledge generated in the process were typically local market specific and of relatively little value to the rest of the organization.

Recent years have witnessed the rapid growth of various types of inter-firm alliances that are motivated very differently. The recent wave of alliances are not devices to avoid or circumvent government restriction but a means of gaining new capabilities. They are commonly between firms from developed country economies and their focus is on global competitiveness rather than entry into relatively unimportant markets in less developed or the ex-command econo-mies. Of course, capability acquisition may relate to a need to enter, or to enter more rapidly, a major or strategic market such as the USA or the European Union. For example, many of the alliances in the telecommunications field have taken place in order to give participating firms the technical and marketing capabilities to enter and operate in the deregu-lated US telecom market (Pisano, Russo & Teece, 1988). Similarly, given technological change and uncertainties, an alliance may give the firm an opportunity to "test the technical and market waters" of new or emerging technical fields before full, stand-alone, entry (Mody, 1993). This has, apparently, been the strategy behind many alliances between US and non-US firms in the medical diagnostic and imaging industry (Mitchell & Singh, 1992).

Why should firms rely on alliances to gain global competitive capability? The answer to this question lies in the fundamental new forces that are shaping the global competitive environ-ment. Sheth (1992) has characterized these forces in terms of the emergence of "borderless" markets and economies. Chief among these forces is the tremendous growth of scientific and technological knowledge and the diffusion of the capabilities to commercialize this vast stock of knowledge not only within the Triad economies but also to emerging competitors in East Asian countries such as Korea and Taiwan. A particularly important development in the technology field is rapid growth and specializa-tion within generic technologies such as IT, biotechnology, and new materials which have a wide variety of applications. Technological innovation, increasingly, requires the fusion of a large number of specialisms within generic and other technologies and even technologically powerful firms are not likely to possess all of these themselves. In fact, to obtain the full range of technical knowledge and skills firms may need to build or enter a *network* of alliances.

Another driving force behind strategic alli-ances is growing integration in economically important regions not only in Europe (where integration has progressed furthest), but also in North America and East Asia. Within Europe, for example, the establishment of the "single" market has persuaded many firms of the potential merit of collaboration through, for example, a joint venture and, frequently, full merger and acquisition. Intra-EU collaborative ventures not only facilitate greater cross-pene-tration of markets across Europe, but also, and more importantly, can assist European firms to develop pan-European capabilities and meet US and Japanese competition more effectively. At the same time, firms from outside the EU, anxious to create "beachheads" into the Eur-opean market, form alliances with EU firms in order to achieve this.

Strategic alliances raise difficult management issues. They are double-edged in as much as they can either be an effective short cut to global competitiveness or become a strategic traA realistic approach would be to regard them as the continuation of competition "by other means." Firms enter alliances for selfish rea-sons. They see alliances as a means of gaining capabilities for themselves cheaply or quickly, but also fear the risk of their own core capabilities being internalized by partners without adequate recompense. Some degree of genuine cooperation is essential as inter-organizational learning dictates a process of intense communication and dialogue which is only possible if an atmosphere of trust prevails. Nevertheless, cooperation is a means and not an end in itself. As Hamel (1991) has observed, within alliances there is often a "race to learn" between the partners; those that learn more quickly may lose interest in the continuation of the alliance. In fact, most alliances are seen as transitional arrangements by both parties and are terminated after a few years.

**Bibliography**

Hamel, G. (1991). Competition for competence and inter-partner learning within international strategic alliances. *Strategic Management Journal*, 12, 83–103.

Mitchell, W. & Singh, K. (1992). Incumbents' use of pre-entry alliances before expansion into new technical subfields. *Journal of Economic Behaviour and Organisation*, 18, 347–372.

Mody, A. (1993). Learning through alliances. *Journal of Economic Behaviour and Organisation*, 20, 150–170.

Pisano, G., Russo, M. & Teece, D. (1988). Joint ventures and collaborative arrangement in the telecommunication industry. In D. Mowery (Ed.), *International collaborative ventures in US manufacturing* (Chapter 2, pp. 23–69). Cambridge, MA: Balinger.

Sheth, J. (1992). Emerging marketing strategies in a changing macroeconomic environment: A commentary. *International Marketing Review*, 9 (1), 57–63.

MO YAMIN

**interpersonal communications** Interpersonal communications are the basis of informal channels of marketing communications, sometimes referred to as word-of-mouth communications (*see* WORD-OF-MOUTH COMMUNICATIONS), when consumers/buyers talk to each other about product-related issues. To understand interpersonal communications requires consideration of personal influence, group influence including reference groups, and opinion leaders.

Personal influence is the change in attitudes and/or behavior as a result of interpersonal communications. Personal influence can be initiated by a potential consumer seeking advice and information, or after purchase – as a provider of information and opinions. It is a two-way influence unlike that of the MASS MEDIA, and it may be visual as well as verbal.

The occurrence of personal influence depends on product variables (e.g., visibility, complexity, degree of perceived risk, stage in the diffusion process), and consumer variables (e.g., life stage, product experience, personality). Companies try to affect the extent of personal influence in their advertising and promotion, personal selling, and sales promotion activities. For example, in their advertising they may simulate personal influence with user stereotypes, testimonials, and group activities; or stimulate it, e.g., by encouraging people to talk about a product.

In the realm of interpersonal communications, not all individuals wield equal influence. Some, opinion leaders, are more influential and others may turn to them for information and advice. Katz & Lazerfeld (1955) believe that people are most influenced by those they are in contact with in everyday life, i.e., by people most like themselves, e.g., doctors for health issues and close friends for the purchase of consumer durables. Research has not been able to clearly identify opinion leader traits, e.g., with respect to demographics, personality, lifestyles, or media habits (e.g., Myers & Robertson, 1972). Further, it has not been possible to identify opinion leaders across product categories; opinion leadership is primarily product specific (e.g., King & Summers, 1979).

Group influence is an important aspect of social influence. All groups have values, beliefs, and norms, and expect individual members to share these and conform to them and behave in appropriate ways. Consumers are, therefore, influenced by a number of groups which may be categorized as primary (e.g., family, friends, neighbors, work associates) or secondary where there has been some deliberate choice in belonging and there is a more formal structure and rules (e.g., political parties, church affiliation, leisure and sporting clubs).

There are pressures on consumers to conform to group beliefs, values, and norms, and there is evidence in the consumer behavior literature that this does occur. The family is the most important source of group influence on an individual, in particular in his or her formative years. However, one of the distinguishing characteristics of Western culture (*see* CULTURE) is the declining influence of the family.

A specific type of group influence of interest to marketers is reference group(s) influence. These are groups which consumers identify with and are used as reference points in determining judgements, beliefs, and behavior. They set standards which are the source of personal behavior norms. They may be membership or aspirant groups. Examples of aspirant groups are personalities whose lifestyles are characterized by luxury products/consumption; and soccer stars who are emulated by small boys (and others) – as typified in the purchase of "football strips and apparel."

Bearden & Etzel (1982) studied reference group influence and the conspicuousness of a product and its brands, and suggested that reference group influence can be strong or weak for product and/or brand. For example, the purchase of a car and the model chosen are both subject to such influence, whereas for satellite television reference group influence prevails with respect to product ownership but not for "brand" choice.

Interpersonal communications are complementary to MASS MEDIA communications, and consumers use both types depending on the product, stage in the decision-making process, and perceptions of risk. Interpersonal communications provide a two-way communication process, are usually seen as more trustworthy than the mass media, and are harder to selectively ignore or tune out. However, they may also be providing unrealistic or inaccurate information and are, indeed, usually communicating evaluations and opinions rather than factual information.

## Bibliography

Bearden, W. O. & Etzel, M. J. (1982). Reference group influence on product and brand purchase decisions. *Journal of Consumer Research*, 9, (2), Sept., 183–94. Also in H. H. Kassarjian & T. S. Robertson (Eds) (1991). *Perspectives in consumer behaviour.* (4th edn). pp. 435–51. Prentice Hall.

Engel, J. F., Blackwell, R. D. & Miniard, P. W. (1990). *Consumer behavior* (6th edn). Orlando, FL: The Dryden Press. Chapter 5.

Hawkins, D. I., Best, R. J. & Coney, K. A. (1992). *Consumer behavior: Implications for marketing strategy* (5th edn). Homewood, IL: Irwin. Chapter 5.

Katz, E. & Lazerfeld, P. F. (1955). *Personal influence.* Glencoe, IL: Free Press.

King, C. W. & Summers, J. O. (1979). Overlap of opinion leaders across consumer product categories. *Journal of Marketing Research*, 7, Feb., 43–50.

Myers, J. H. & Robertson, T. S. (1972). Dimensions of opinion leadership. *Journal of Marketing Research*, 9, Feb., 41–6.

Schiffman, L. G. & Kanuk, L. Z. (1991). *Consumer behavior* (4th edn). Prentice-Hall. Chapters 11, 17.

Solomon, M. R. (1992). *Consumer behavior.* Needham Heights, MA: Allyn & Bacon, Chapter 11.

BARBARA LEWIS

**interviews**   *see* DEPTH INTERVIEWS; FOCUS GROUPS; SURVEY RESEARCH

**joint ventures** *see* INTERNATIONAL JOINT VENTURES

# K

**key account** "Account" here refers to a customer/supplier relationship, and as some accounts are more important than others they may be termed "key accounts" because of their implications for either or all parties. Many different factors can make an account "key" such as: the volume or value of the exchanges involved; the knock-on implications of failure in an account (e.g., faulty oil filters can immobilize vast machines); the anticipated flow of repeat business (e.g., from pilot projects); or the reputation of a particular customer (e.g., The Queen) or supplier (e.g., "Intel inside"). Other customer/supplier accounts may be particularly important because of indirect factors – e.g., a customer may be involved with a supplier in collaborative product development, or in quality improvement measures, or in mutual bench-marking. The importance of "key accounts" should be reflected in the sensitivity with which such accounts are managed – e.g., in the seniority of the account managers and the flexibility allowed in negotiations.

DOMINIC WILSON

# L

**latent demand**   *see* DEMAND

**learn-feel-buy model**   The learn-feel-buy models (*see* AIDA MODEL, HIERARCHY OF EFFECTS MODEL, INNOVATION-ADOPTION MODEL) in MARKETING COMMUNICATIONS propose that buyers/customers/consumers first learn about a product or service by seeing, reading, and understanding an advertisement or being the recipient of other marketing communications. They not only learn what benefits the product or service may give, but may also develop positive feelings about it, i.e., they are moving through stages of unawareness to awareness, interest, and liking. In turn, this may stimulate the potential customers/consumers to buy the product or service, and to develop loyalty toward it in the longer term. This sequence is most appropriate when the buyer/customer has high involvement with a product category with high differentiation, e.g., in the purchase of a car.

*See also* **Buy-feel-learn model; Feel-buy-learn model**

### Bibliography

Dickson, P. R. (1994). *Marketing management* (international edn). Fort Worth: The Dryden Press. Chapter 12.

Kotler, P. (1994). *Marketing management: Analysis, planning, implementation and control* (8th edn). Englewood Cliffs, NJ: Prentice-Hall, p. 602.

DAVID YORKE

**learning**   *see* CONSUMER LEARNING

**legal system**   The legal system is a powerful force in the MARKETING ENVIRONMENT surrounding any organization, both national and international. Legal systems vary from country to country, some being controlled wholly by government, others containing both statute law and precedent, i.e., judges may modify previous directions to meet changing circumstances. The principal features of any legal system as an element in the marketing environment relate first to the rights of the supplier, i.e., the legal conditions in which marketing activities may be undertaken, and secondly to the rights of the customer (*see*, for example, CONSUMER PROTECTION). Problems may arise when an organization seeks to internationalize its operations, as elements in different legal systems may preclude the use of a standardized marketing plan.

### Bibliography

Kotler, P. (1994). *Marketing management: Analysis, planning, implementation and control* (8th edn). Englewood Cliffs, NJ: Prentice-Hall. Chapter 6.

Palmer, A. & Worthington, I. (1992). *The business and marketing environment*. Maidenhead: McGraw-Hill. Chapter 12.

DAVID YORKE

**licensing**   Licensing is one of three indirect methods of market entry (*see* INTERNATIONAL MARKET ENTRY AND DEVELOPMENT STRATEGIES) that involve the transfer of industrial property rights and other resources, including capital. The other methods are FRANCHISING and production contracts (sometimes called management contracts). In the context of INTERNATIONAL MARKETING, the term licensing refers to specific contractual arrangements under which the foreign licensor empowers the licensee to make use of the former's technological know-how in exchange for financial compensation and access to the licensee's market. A common type of licensing arrangement would permit the licensee to manufacture and market the licensor's product, normally as an exclusive right, for an agreed period of time in return for an agreed payment, often in the form of a royalty payment. The attraction of licensing to licensors is that it allows them to establish a production base in a foreign market without committing considerable investments in capital and labor.

Before committing himself, a licensor will, depending on the nature of its business, endeavor to craft an agreement that offers it legal protection in relation to patents, copyright, trademarks, and know-how (which might involve trade secrets). The licensor will also wish to satisfy itself that a would-be licensee can meet all the performance criteria pertaining to production and marketing. If the licensee is inexperienced in these matters, the licensor will normally undertake to support the licensee through training of personnel or other means of support, ranging from access to the licensor's design and technical resources to its expertise in literature production and MARKETING RESEARCH.

In many instances the know-how of the licensor is ahead of, or superior to, that which is available in the licensee's country. Hence, license arrangements have proved to be a popular form of technology – and marketing know-how – transfer either to developing countries or to countries with "technological gaps," such as the former socialist countries. A striking example of a country that rapidly enhanced its technological expertise through a policy of entering license agreements and exploiting them to the full is Japan: from the end of the War (1945) until 1980 Japan had obtained some 2,500 licenses. Japan, in turn, is now a major licensor, passing on various technological benefits to its licensees in sectors such as electronics and automobile production.

Licensing can take many forms; one particular form is the joint venture (see INTERNATIONAL JOINT VENTURES). Another form, often involving the transfer of intangibles such as service know-how or trade-marks, is called

FRANCHISING. In industries characterized by frequent technological change such as chemicals, information technology, and electronics, companies resort to cross-licensing, which is a device for avoiding out-and-out technological competition which could be ruinous to both parties. Not surprisingly, perhaps, the closer parties are in technological parity, the more complex is the negotiation of licensing agreements and they can take months to arrange, especially where there has to be an exchange of secret information.

A study of licensing behavior of firms reveals: evidence of a considerable diversity of motives; an intention to transfer know-how that is (or is about to become) obsolete; a display of a commitment to a particular market that for political or other reasons may be difficult to penetrate by other means; a motive to internationalize business rapidly and with comparatively low risk; or a consolidation of a position in a foreign market where the company is well established in other product lines. There are cases of firms licensing know-how which their research and development has developed but which is not related directly to their major product portfolio.

NIGEL HOLDEN

life cycles  see LIFESTYLES

lifestyles  Consideration of consumer lifestyles incorporates an awareness of demographic variables and life cycles. Consumer behavior researchers and marketers are interested in trends in consumer DEMOGRAPHICS with respect to: birth rates and age profiles; marriage and divorce rates; number and spacing of children; size and composition of households/ families, and extent of single-person households; incomes and occupation; levels of employment including participation of women in the labor force; and type and location of residence. These all impact on consumer needs, attitudes, and behavior, and are often discussed in relation to life cycles and lifestyles.

The term life cycle refers to the progression of stages through which individuals and families proceed during their lives, with the consequent financial situation and needs for goods and services. The traditional life cycle stages were from: bachelor stage to newly married; full nest 1,2,3; empty nest 1,2; solitary survivor in labor force; and solitary survivor retired (*see* Wells & Gubar, 1966). However, several modernized family life cycles have been put forward (e.g., Murphy & Staples, 1979; Gilly & Enis, 1982) in response to demographic trends such as smaller family sizes, postponement of marriage, and rising divorce rates.

Consumer lifestyle refers to a consumer's pattern of living which influences and is reflected by consumption behavior. It is the result of interactive processes between social and personal variables surrounding individuals in childhood and throughout life, e.g., family, reference groups, CULTURE. It embodies patterns that develop and emerge from the dynamics of living in a society. Further, economic influences provide constraints and opportunities in the development of lifestyle.

Lifestyle encompasses a person's pattern of living in the world as expressed in terms of activities, interests, and opinions (e.g., *see* Wells & Tigert, 1971). Activities refer to how people spend their time: at work, home, community, special activities, hobbies, clubs, vacation, sport, and entertainment. Interests refer to what they place importance on in their immediate surroundings: family, home, job, community, recreation, fashion, and media. Opinions are in terms of their view of themselves and the world around them: e.g., social issues, politics, business, economics, education, and culture. These variables are considered together with demographics, and the basic premise of lifestyle research is that the more marketers know and understand about customers, the more effectively they can communicate and market to them. It provides a three-dimensional view of customers. The term PSYCHOGRAPHICS is used interchangeably with lifestyle, but may also include PERSONALITY variables.

One example of lifestyle is the VALS framework (*see* Solomon, 1992), which is based on some 30 to 40 demographic and attitudinal characteristics. From this, three broad groups of consumer are identified (in the US population): need-driven, outer-directed, and inner-directed. These are further divided into nine value

lifestyle groups: survivors, sustainers, belongers, emulators, "I am me," experientals, societally conscious, and integrated – with associated impact on consumer needs, attitudes, and behavior.

Another example of lifestyle is ACORN-typing (*see* CACI, 1993), used as an indicator of SOCIAL CLASS. This incorporates geodemographic data (*see* GEODEMOGRAPHICS), from the most recent census, to include: age, sex, marital status, occupation, economic position, education, home ownership, and car ownership: to provide a full and comprehensive picture of socioeconomic status. From this data, and postcode information, ACORN types are developed to profile consumers in terms of their attitudes and behavior – with respect to products and services bought, leisure activities, media habits, and financial position.

## Bibliography

CACI (1993). London: CAtx1CI Information Services.

Engel, J. F., Blackwell, R. D. & Miniard, P. W. (1990). *Consumer behavior* (6th edn). Orlando, FL: The Dryden Press. Chapter 21.

Gilly, M. C. & Enis, B. M. (1982). Recycling the family life cycle: A proposal for redefinition. In A. Mitchell (Ed.), *Advances in consumer research* (vol. 9, pp. 271–276). Ann Arbor, MI: Association for Consumer Research.

Hawkins, D. I., Best, R. J. & Coney, K. A. (1992). *Consumer behavior: Implications for marketing strategy* (5th edn). Homewood, IL: Irwin. Chapters 3, 7, 11.

Loudon, D. L. & Della Bitta, A. J. (1993). *Consumer behavior* (4th edn). McGraw-Hill Int. Chapter 7.

Murphy, P. E. & Staples, W. A. (1979). A modernised family life cycle. *Journal of Consumer Research*, June, 12–22.

Plummer, J. (1974). The concept and application of life style segmentation. *Journal of Marketing*, 38, Jan., 33–37.

Schiele, G. W. (1974). How to reach the young customer. *Harvard Business Review*, 52, Mar.–Apr., 77–86.

Schiffman, L. G. & Kanuk, L. Z. (1991). *Consumer behavior* (4th edn). Prentice-Hall. Chapter 5.

Solomon, M. R. (1992). *Consumer behavior*. Needham Heights, MA: Allyn & Bacon.

Wells, W. D. (Ed.) (1974). *Lifestyle and psychographics*. Chicago: American Marketing Association.

Wells, W. D. (1975). Psychographics: A critical review. *Journal of Marketing Research*, **12**, May, 196–213.

Wells, W. D. & Gubar, G. (1966). Life cycle in marketing research. *Journal of Marketing Research*, Nov., 355–363.

Wells, W. D. & Tigert, D. J. (1971). Activities, interests and opinions. *Journal of Advertising Research*, **11**, 27–35.

BARBARA LEWIS

**list price** In organizational markets price is often the result of negotiations based on a notional list price which is then either discounted (e.g., for volume purchases), or augmented (e.g., for customized orders). List prices are often quoted in product catalogues together with stipulated DISCOUNT levels for specified volumes – a practice referred to by some writers as administered pricing.

DOMINIC WILSON

**logistics** This is a management function concerning the process of physical distribution and stockholding. It deals with the planning, allocating, and controlling of a firm's resources and their movement around the organization or between organizations in a smooth, uninterrupted, and timely flow. Within a retail system this would include the flow of goods from the site of manufacture to the final consumer. The allocation of financial and human resources would also be the responsibility of logistics management.

Efficiency of allocation is of great importance to ensure that there is no over- or under-supply and that resources are distributed at lowest possible cost. This requires consideration of stockholding costs, packaging and transport costs, etc.

**Bibliography**

Christopher, M. (1977). *Distribution, planning and control, a corporate approach.* Farnborough, Hants: Gower.

STEVE WORRALL

# M

**macro environment**   The environment of an organization (*see* MARKETING ENVIRONMENT) is generally regarded as consisting of a MICRO ENVIRONMENT and a macro environment which is composed of several major elements over which the organization has little, if any, influence. The major forces in the macro environment tend to be viewed as: social, economic, legal, political, economic, and technological. It is generally assumed that organizations will identify the major trends and possible future developments in these various components of the macro environment and the possible threats to their existing business and the opportunities for future developments (*see* SWOT ANALYSIS). In this sense, organizations are often depicted as being reactive, although it is clear that they can be active in certain areas, through major technological innovation and attempts at influencing the policy-making and legislative processes. An organization's environmental analysts can be very selective with respect to those aspects of the macro environment on which they focus and in their interpretation of them.

*See also* **Environmental analysis**

Bibliography

Brownlie, D. B. (1994). In M. J. Baker (Ed.), *The marketing book* (3rd edn). Oxford: Butterworth-Heinemann. Chapter 7.
Sanderson, S. M. & Luffman, G. A. (1988). Strategic planning and environmental analysis. *European Journal of Marketing*, **22**, (2), 14–27.

DALE LITTLER

**macro marketing**   Macro marketing embraces marketing's role in society and can be defined as "the delivery of a standard of living to society." The aggregation of all organizations' marketing activities includes transportation and distribution, and so the efficiency of the system for moving goods from producers to consumers may substantially affect a society's well-being. Thus, macro marketing is the aggregate of marketing activities within an economy, or the marketing system within a society, rather than the marketing activities of a single firm.

Bibliography

Zikmund, W. G. & d'Amico, M. (1995). *Effective marketing: creating and keeping customers.* St Paul, MN: West Publishing Co. Chapter 1, p. 21.

BARBARA LEWIS

**magazines**   Magazines are publications which are purchased and read by people as part of their lifestyle (*see* LIFESTYLES). Magazine content may relate to: aspects of home life, e.g., cooking, gardening, do-it-yourself; leisure, sporting, and social activities; education (e.g., *The Times Higher Education Supplement*); and employment. Some magazines are industry specific and may be referred to as TRADE JOURNALS (e.g., *The Grocer, Drapers Weekly*), and so are bought by organizations as well as individuals; others are associated with professional business groups (e.g., *Investors' Chronicle, Accounting Age*).

The readership of magazines may, therefore, be specific (e.g., *Angling Weekly*) and perhaps also small (*Popular Bridge*), or much broader (*Woman's Weekly*), and possibly with a mass circulation (e.g., *Radio Times* and *TV Times*). Consequently, magazine readers may be profiled with respect to their demographic characteristics (*see* DEMOGRAPHICS) which has implications for MEDIA PLANNING (*see also* ADVERTISING).

Magazines typically provide full-color advertising at a reasonable cost, have a relatively long life and multiple readership, and can provide broad national coverage with, sometimes, flexibility through regional editions. Further, there is proven success of magazines' editorial offers and sales promotions. One drawback of magazine advertising is the relatively long lead time for copy dates.

DAVID YORKE

**mail order** Mail order is most readily associated with catalog shopping. Goods are selected from the catalog assortment and orders mailed or telephoned through to the retailer or a local agent. Mail order has traditionally been directed at lower social classes, with the attraction of easily obtainable credit terms, and at consumers living in more remote areas, where access to shops is restricted. More recently certain retailers, such as Next with the launch of the *Next Directory* in 1988, have successfully developed catalogs which appeal to more up-market consumers. These have helped to revitalize the mail order sector and improve the frequently dowdy and down-market image associated with this retail distribution channel. Greenland & McGoldrick (1991) identify over 40 different motives associated with catalog or mail order shopping, the key dimensions being:

- Hassle-free convenience
- Risk reduction
- Added value with credit, promotions, and free gifts
- Recreational experience
- Transaction efficiency
- Decision reassurance.

The mail order sector is a growth area, e.g., in 1993 US mail order sales were up 7 percent over 1992 (*Direct Marketing*, 1994). Key issues impacting on the future of this retail distribution channel include the image of direct marketing, merger and acquisition activity, alternative media, and an interactive market place (Petsky, 1994).

*See also* **Retail distribution channels**

### Bibliography

*Direct Marketing* (1994). 1994 mail order overview. *Direct Marketing*, 57, (4), 25–8.

Greenland, S. J. & McGoldrick, P. J. (1991). From mail order to home shopping – revitalising the non-store channel. *Journal of Marketing Channels*, 1, (1), 59–85.

Petsky, M. (1994). Critical issues and trends for the future of mail order. *Direct Marketing*, 57, (4), 29–32.

STEVE GREENLAND

**make/buy decision** An important alternative to PURCHASING goods or services is to supply them from internal sources. Equally, before undertaking internal production of goods or services it is important to consider whether external purchasing might provide a more efficient or preferable alternative. Make or buy decisions can also apply to internal services such as marketing, research, planning, accounting, and design, which may be better undertaken by external specialists with economies of scale and specialized investments (Anderson & Weitz, 1986). This issue has many strategic and operational implications beyond the relatively simple aspect of cost control. In-house supplier arrangements appear to offer potential advantages of management control, of cost manipulation (e.g., in TRANSFER PRICING), of acquitting minimum national content requirements where the alternative is international sourcing, of flexible production management, and of using what might otherwise be under-utilized assets. But there can also be significant problems of cost control, quality, delivery, and service where the commercial pressures of market forces are (or are perceived to have been) "suspended." Decisions in this area are frequently concerned with political, cultural, personal, historic, and strategic issues rather than with the more routine purchasing concerns.

**Bibliography**

Anderson, E. & Weitz, B. (1986). Make-or-buy decisions. *Sloan Management Review*, **27**, Spring, 3–19.

Ford, D., Cotton, B., Farmer, D. & Gross, A. (1993). Make-or-buy decisions and their implications. *Industrial Marketing Management*, **22**, Aug., 207–214.

Venkatesan, R. (1992). Strategic sourcing: To make or not to make. *Harvard Business Review*, **70**, (6), Nov.–Dec., 98–107.

DOMINIC WILSON

**margin**    Margin refers to the profit earned by a product or service at different stages of the VALUE CHAIN and is usually expressed as a percentage. Margins can be added at each stage of the production and distribution process (where these stages are treated as profit centers) in accordance with the competitive pressures prevailing at each stage. The sum of costs and margins for each stage of the value chain is reflected in the eventual price to the end user (DISCOUNT notwithstanding). "Margin" is a broad term and is more usually discussed under the slightly more specific variants of GROSS MARGIN and NET MARGIN.

DOMINIC WILSON

**marginal pricing**    Marginal pricing is a term used to refer to those occasions when price is calculated to cover only the variable costs of production and/or distribution and little or no CONTRIBUTION is required towards fixed costs and profit margins. Clearly, this is an unusual and uneconomic level for prices and one which could not be sustained for long. Marginal pricing might be used during a temporary fall in demand (e.g., during an economic recession or a price war) to keep assets "ticking over" pending the return of more normal trading conditions. The alternative is to reduce radically (or even suspend) operations which can lead to even less attractive consequences such as deterioration of skills, reduced customer loyalty, loss of reputation, and erosion of brands. Marginal

pricing might also be used to secure what is expected to be a favored position with respect to future sales (as with introductory offers).

DOMINIC WILSON

**market**    The term "market" is clearly an important concept in the field of marketing, yet while much debate has taken place on what constitutes an appropriate definition of "MARKETING," less attention has been directed in marketing literature toward the nature of markets. This is increasingly being recognized as an omission, given that many analytical techniques rely on concepts such as MARKET SHARE and MARKET SEGMENTATION (Curran & Goodfellow, 1990).

The original use of the term "market" referred to a physical location where buyers and sellers come together in order to exchange products and services. Since then, the term has been developed in the field of economics to refer variously to any network of dealings between buyers and sellers of a particular product, or to refer to products which are regarded as close substitutes. The latter is often referred to as the substitutability criteria, two products being contained in the same market where the cross-elasticity of demand between the two is greater than a pre-assigned number (x). However, there is little agreement in the field as to the criteria by which x might be specified.

Elsewhere, the term "market" has been used extensively to describe aggregate demand for a specific product (the "automobile" market) or in a specific physical area (the "European market"). Markets have also been viewed in broader "need" terms (the "transportation" market) and demographic terms (the "female" market) or any combination of these variables.

In contemporary marketing, however, the "market" is most commonly used to refer to the existing or target group of customers for a particular product or service. For example: "All the potential customers sharing a particular need or want who might be willing or able to engage in exchange to satisfy that need or want" (Kotler, 1991, p. 8). "Individuals who, in the past, have purchased a given class of product" (Sissors, 1966). "An aggregate of people who, as individuals or organisations, have needs for products in a product class and who have the ability, willingness and authority to purchase such products . . . people seeking products in a specific category" (Dibb et al., 1991). This view is endorsed in the literature on MARKET SEG-MENTATION, the process by which overall market definition is subdivided into identifiable sets of buyers similar in terms of demographic, psychographic, or other profiles.

The prevalent view is, then, one of markets as units of analysis with clearly defined boundaries. Yet perspectives offered elsewhere suggest a somewhat more complex understanding of markets. Strategic management literature offers a number of further perspectives, Abell (1980), for example, proposing a three-dimensional concept of markets, with the dimensions as customer group (who is being served with respect to factors such as demographics, user industry, or buyer behavior); customer function (what "need" is being satisfied); and technology (how the customer function is being satisfied). A "market" is consequently defined by the performance of given functions in given customer groups and includes all the substitutable technologies to perform these functions. Such definitions recognize that competing suppliers may define a market in different ways, as may individuals at different levels within the same organization, a recognition shared by Day (1981), who identifies two different perspectives for defining markets, top down and bottom uTop down, or strategic, definitions reflect the needs of strategists to understand the capacity and competitive potential of the business and specify markets in terms of organizational competitive capabilities and resource transferability. Bottom up, or operational, definitions reflect the narrower tactical concern of marketing managers and define markets in terms of patterns of customer requirements, usage situations, and "needs," which can be served in many ways.

Another dimension of market definition is apparent in the literature on BUSINESS-TO-BUSINESS MARKETING, where it is recognized that the importance of individual customers is often considerable and the relevance of aggregate markets therefore lessened. Here, the concept of a "market" might refer to only a single customer (*see* Grönroos, 1989, for further discussion of this).

A number of authors have also identified a disparity between the way markets are defined in marketing literature and in practice. Jenkins et al. (1994) elicited definitions of the term "market" from a sample of marketing managers and found that the majority tended to define markets in terms of products or channels (e.g., "the food retail market"), with only a minority of the sample offering definitions in terms of groups of consumers.

It is accepted by some authors at least, then, that the understanding of markets is likely to vary to a greater or lesser extent from marketer to marketer even within a particular organization, significantly from organization to organization with similar offerings, and radically from sector to sector. Others further assert that "the market," whether defined in terms of existing or potential customers, products, or organizational capabilities, is a volatile concept, where boundaries are arbitrary and seldom clear-cut, where definitions are multi-dimensional, and where perspectives shift with changing individual, corporate, and user views of product offerings and changes in the nature and availability of these offerings (*see* Curran & Goodfellow, 1990; Jenkins et al., 1994).

## Bibliography

Abell, D. F. (1980). *Defining the business: The starting point of strategic planning.* Englewood Cliffs, NJ: Prentice-Hall.

Curran, J. G. M. & Goodfellow, J. H. (1990). Theoretical and practical issues in the definition of market boundaries. *European Journal of Marketing*, **24**, (1), 16–28.

Day, G. S. (1981). Strategic market analysis and definition: An internal approach. *Strategic Management Journal*, **2**, 281–299.

Dibb, S., Simkin, L., Pride, W. M. & Ferrell, O. C. (1991). *Marketing: Concepts and strategies* (European edn). London: Houghton Mifflin Co.

Grönroos, C. (1989). Defining marketing: A market-oriented approach. *European Journal of Marketing*, **23**, (1), 52–60.

Jenkins, M., le Cerf, E. & Cole, T. (1994). How managers define consumer markets. In M. Jenkins & S. Knox (Eds), *Advances in consumer marketing.* The Cranfield Management Research Series. London: Kogan Page.

Kotler, P. (1991). *Marketing management: Analysis, planning, implementation and control* (7th edn). Englewood Cliffs, NJ: Prentice-Hall.

Sissors, J. (1966). What is a market? *Journal of Marketing*, **30**, (3), July, 17–21.

FIONA LEVERICK

**market demand**   The term market demand most usually refers to the total demand for a product or service over a specific period of time. It is used in relation to either individual products or services or product or service categories.

FIONA LEVERICK

**market exchange**   *see* EXCHANGE

**market manager**   Market managers are responsible for the marketing activities for particular markets or clusters of customers. They may have profit responsibility. A market manager structure is likely to be a feature of organizational markets where companies are marketing to several, perhaps diverse, customer groups with somewhat differing requirements. Thus, a manufacturer of paint will sell not only to consumer markets, but also to professional decorators as well as industrial users which will comprise possibly several markets (maritime, process plant, etc.).

Such managers can be expected to foster and maintain customer relationships (*see* RELATION-SHIP MARKETING) with key customers, develop an understanding of their requirements, and, increasingly in organizational markets, develop a problem-solving capability and provide a "solu-tions" package. They will, therefore, have to act as a focus for coordinating all the different activities, both internally and from external parties, involved in providing the appropriate offering. In some instances, managers may be appointed for key, major, customers. Such an approach contrasts with the product manager (*see* PRODUCT MANAGER) structure.

DALE LITTLER

**market penetration**   This is one of the strategies identified in Ansoff's (1965) direc-tional policy matrix (*see* DIRECTIONAL MATRIX). It is generally regarded as aiming at increasing the firm's MARKET SHARE within its existing markets. This can be achieved in at least one of three ways: increasing purchases by existing customers, winning over the consumers of competitors' offerings, and converting non-users to purchasers of the firm's offerings.

**Bibliography**

Ansoff, H. I. (1965). *Corporate strategy*. New York: McGraw-Hill. Chapter 6.

DALE LITTLER

**market segment**   *see* MARKET SEGMEN-TATION

**market segmentation**   Smith (1956) first defined market segmentation as "a rational and more precise adjustment of product and market-ing effort to consumer or user requirements, it consists of viewing a heterogenous market (one characterised by divergent demand) as a number of smaller homogenous markets." If it is assumed, or known, that all consumers in a market have similar needs and wants, then an undifferentiated or total market approach can be adopted by a company using a single MARKET-ING MIX to satisfy consumers. The Coca Cola company's early marketing of only one drink, of only one size, is an example of this approach. If the market has heterogeneous needs, then a TARGET MARKET approach can be adopted. Here, an organization attempts to subdivide the market into clusters of customers with similar requirements and tailor its marketing mix to each cluster. This approach involves additional costs for product modifications and associated administrative, promotional, and inventory costs. In completely heterogeneous markets, where each customer's requirements are differ-ent, the only way to satisfy everyone is by offering tailor-made or bespoke products. Nowadays, this is more prevalent in organiza-tional markets (*see* ORGANIZATIONAL MARKET-ING). However, in some consumer markets, producers still design their products for individual consumers, e.g., tailor-made clothes and shoes. This type of customized marketing is becoming increasingly possible, even in traditional mass markets, with the use of modern and flexible manufacturing technology, which allows shorter runs of products to be profitable. It should be noted that the idea of market segmentation can be used by profit-making and not-for-profit organizations alike (*see also* SEGMENTATION VARIABLES.

### The Process of Market Segmentation

The first step is usually some form of needs assessment, e.g., benefit segmentation, in order to decide whether or not groups of buyers seek different product benefits and hence will value different product features (*see* SEGMENTATION VARIABLES). (The starting point is not restricted to benefit segmentation, but must be something which is closely related to the customer needs.) Since markets are defined in terms of demand or customer needs/requirements, marketers must know how these needs vary by segment in order to design products to meet them. For example, the shoe market is best characterized by identifying customer needs of protection, durability, style, size, price, etc., rather than by the age, sex, or social class of the market. Green (1977) distinguished two methods commonly used when deciding on how a market should be segmented. First, is a priori segmentation in which management decides the basis for segmentation, such as product purchase, customer type, or respondent's favorite brand. Respondents are classified into favorite brand segments, for example, and then further examined in terms of their differences on other characteristics. The second, post hoc segmentation, is a cluster-based segmentation design in which segments are determined on the bases of a clustering of respondents on a set of relevant attributes, e.g., benefits, needs, attitudes.

The second step is to describe how the benefit segments differ in their buying loyalties, shopping behaviors, media usage, and sensitivity to various marketing tactics. In this descriptive phase are included all the "normal" SEGMENTATION VARIABLES which are discussed by numerous authors. If the benefit segments do not vary significantly on any of these descriptor variables, they will be very difficult to reach and target with tailored marketing mixes. The choice of descriptor variable is not easy, partly because of the enormous number of possible variables which could be used and partly because of the often questionable link between the selected base(s) for the segmentation and the descriptor.

A number of authors do not take needs as the starting point for segmentation and argue that, in practice, segmentation may not follow the logical two-step approach. Often descriptor or profile variables, which can be easily measured, are identified first, then the segments so described are examined to see if they show different behavioral responses. This approach of looking for measurable and identifiable variables, then examining their influence on behavior, can be criticized for moving the marketer's attention away from customer requirements and toward implementation issues. Sometimes a product is designed for a particular segment of consumers whose collective need also happens to be accurately characterized by a description of their group association; various clubs and organizations, e.g., the Brownies, or football supporters clubs, etc. might be examples. In these relatively few cases, the two approaches do overlap.

A recent survey found that the similarity of needs within segments and the feasibility of marketing action were the two most important criteria used to form segments. Stability of the segment over time was third most important, while the difference of needs between segments, and the potential for increased profit and return on investment were fourth and fifth. The simplicity of assigning customers to segments was least important (Abratt, 1993).

Good market segmentation can result in numerous advantages including: (1) a closer matching of a company's products with customers' needs, which leads to increased customer satisfaction and implementation of the MARKETING CONCEPT; (2) checking the basic assumptions and understanding about customers in the market, which can lead to improved communication with customers; (3) identifying new marketing opportunities from segments that have not been hitherto exploited; (4) increased COMPETITIVE ADVANTAGE by viewing a market in different ways from one's competitors; it also keeps organizations alert to changes in market conditions, competitors' actions, and environmental opportunities and threats; (5) better COMPETITIVE STRATEGY, because companies that do not understand how the market is divided up risk competing head on against larger organizations with superior resources; it can allow a company to dominate a segment – which is not often possible in the total market; and (6) enabling two different pieces of research containing separate data to be combined by means of a common classification (*see* GEODEMOGRAPHICS).

However, not all authors agree that market segmentation is necessarily a profitable strategy, especially when the market is so small that marketing to a portion of it is not profitable; when heavy users make up such a large proportion of the sales volume that they are the only relevant target; or when one brand dominates the market and draws its appeal from all segments of the market (Young, Ott & Feigin, 1978). In markets where consumers are willing to accept lower prices in exchange for less-tailored products and where there is a high potential for product and marketing economies by eliminating or fusing market segments, counter-segmentation should be considered (Resnik, Turney & Mason, 1979).

The question of profitability can be one of the principal limitations of market segmentation. Bonoma & Shapiro (1984) highlight two major cost factors associated with segmentation. One is the number of segments approached: the more a market is segmented the more costly it is. Second, is that some elements of the MARKET-ING MIX are more expensive to change than others. The least expensive tactic is tailoring communications. Specialized prices are harder to administer and can have a substantial impact on profits. By far the most expensive change to implement is product change. Bonoma & Shapiro advocate the practical strategy of using the least expensive tools first so long as the segments are responsive to these changes. In practice, however, Abratt (1993) found that product changes and sales promotion campaigns were the marketing actions most often used by companies to target different segments, while different advertising appeals and prices were used less often. Changing the sales force and distribution systems were used least often. A

further limitation is the inability to predict the nature and number of market segments that confront a new product in advance of the product being introduced (Frank et al., 1972). If the product has to be altered after introduction to meet the needs of different segments, this can be more expensive for the company and may reduce how well the company capitalizes on its first mover advantages. Conventional practice is to conduct an attitude and usage study in the test market area once the product has been introduced. However, from this it is impossible to tell if the segments which develop existed prior to being exposed to the product and advertisements, etc. One way to overcome this problem is to give written descriptions of concepts to consumers and ask them to indicate the concept's applicability to their situation and the benefits that could be derived therefrom (Moriarty & Venkatesan, 1978). A final limitation is that segments may not be stable in the longer term, because of changing consumer values, DEMOGRAPHICS, and LIFESTYLES.

*Target Segment Selection*

Many authors have written about the criteria used to assess the usefulness of segmentations, but one of the most commonly used sets includes the criteria of measurability, substantiality, accessibility, and actionability (Kotler, 1991). Measurability is the degree to which size and purchasing power of segments can be measured. Substantiality is the degree to which segments are large and/or profitable enough for the organization to pursue. Accessibility is the extent to which segments can be effectively reached and served, and actionability is the degree to which an effective marketing program can be formulated for attracting and serving the segments. Mitchman (1991) adds meaningful to the list, which relates to the similarity of needs within the segments, i.e., when there is low intrasegment variability. Wind (1978) considers other factors, namely: the reliability of the data from which the segments were derived and the temporal stability of resultant segments.

Piercy & Morgan (1993) suggest that little explicit concern has been shown about the difference between strategic and operational aspects of segmentation, and they study the "fit" between segment requirements and company strengths. If the proposed segments do not fit in with the company's long-run objectives or the company does not possess the relevant skills and resources to meet the needs of the segments, then the segmentation is less likely to be successful. Strategic marketing segmentation models may be better judged by such criteria as the ability to create and sustain competitive differentiation and advantage; INNOVATION in how the market is attacked; compatibility with the MISSION STATEMENT; providing a coherent focus for thinking in the organization; and consistency with corporate values and culture. It is important, however, that organizational compatibility does not become the governing criterion for segment selection, since organizations should be able and prepared to adapt to segments identified, rather than to target only those which are compatible with existing organizational strengths and weaknesses (*see* SWOT ANALYSIS).

Finally, some authors have advocated the use of Porter's five forces framework as criteria for determining a segment's structural attractiveness (*see* COMPETITIVE STRATEGY). A survey of marketing practice found that the ability to reach buyers in the market and the competitive position of their firm in the market were the two most highly rated criteria used by practitioners to select target segments. These were followed by the size of the market, compatibility of market with companies, objectives/resources, profitability, and expected market growth.

*See also* **Organizational segmentation; Segmentation variables**

### Bibliography

Abratt, R. (1993). Market segmentation practices of industrial Marketers. *Industrial Marketing Management*, 22, 79–84.

Bonoma, T. V. & Shapiro, B. P. (1984). Evaluating market segmentation approaches. *Industrial Marketing Management*, 13, 257–268.

Frank, R., Massy, W. & Wind, Y. (1972). *Market segmentation*. Englewood Cliffs, NJ: Prentice-Hall.

Green, P. E. (1977). A new approach to market segmentation. *Business Horizons*, 20, 61–73.

Kotler, P. (1991). *Marketing management: Analysis, planning, implementation and control* (7th edn). Englewood Cliffs, NJ: Prentice-Hall.

Mitchman, R. (1991). *Lifestyle market segmentation*. New York: Praeger.

Moriarty, M. & Venkatesan, M. (1978). Concept evaluation and market segmentation. *Journal of Marketing*, **42**, July, 82–86.

Piercy, N. F. & Morgan, N. A. (1993). Strategic and operational market segmentation: A managerial analysis. *Industrial Marketing Management*, **22**, 79–84.

Resnik, A. J., Turney, P. B. B. & Mason, J. B. (1979). Marketers turn to "Countersegmentation". *Harvard Business Review*, **57**, Sept–Oct., 100–106.

Smith, W. (1956). Product differentiation and market segmentation as marketing strategies. *Journal of Marketing*, **21**, July, 3–8.

Wind, Y. (1978). Issues and advances in segmentation research. *Journal of Marketing Research*, **15**, Aug., 317–337.

Young, S., Ott, L. & Feigin, B. (1978). Some practical considerations in market segmentation. *Journal of Marketing Research*, **15**, Aug., 405–412.

VINCE MITCHELL

**market share**    This is the ratio of a company's sales of a product or service (either by number of units or by value) during a specific time period in a specific market to the total sales of that type of product or service over the same period. It has been pointed out that calculations of market share are likely to vary considerably according to how the total market is defined (*see* MARKET).

The importance of market share has frequently been noted with, for example, a connection between market share and profitability identified in a project undertaken by the Marketing Science Institute on the PROFIT IMPACT OF MARKETING STRATEGIES (Buzzell et al., 1975). Other researchers (*see*, for example, Jacobson & Aaker, 1985) have suggested that the direct impact of market share on profitability, while not unimportant, is substantially less than is commonly assumed. Jacobson & Aaker express concern that efforts to maintain or increase market share by companies can be myopic, expensive, and detrimental to long-term profitability, and note that one of the premises of niche marketing (*see* MARKET SEGMENTATION) is that the smaller share competitors can also achieve high returns.

### Bibliography

Buzzell, R. D., Gale, B. T. & Sultan, R. G. M. (1975). Market share: A key to profitability. *Harvard Business Review*, **53**, (1), Jan.–Feb., 97–106.

Jacobson, R. & Aaker, D. A. (1985). Is market share all that it's cracked up to be? *Journal of Marketing*, **49**, Fall, 11–22.

FIONA LEVERICK

**marketing** Marketing was apparently first taught as a business subject in 1902, at the University of Wisconsin, although the first textbooks on the subject were not written until several years later (Bartels, 1962, 1970; Converse, 1951). The concept has no single universally agreed definition and perspectives on the nature of marketing have shifted considerably over time. Halbert (1965) has suggested that this is due to marketing having no recognized central theoretical basis such as exists for many other disciplines and the natural sciences in particular.

The development of "marketing" is often seen in terms of at least three "eras" (*see*, for instance, Gilbert & Bailey, 1990; Webster, 1988). The first of these is most commonly termed the "production" era (Keith, 1960) and is considered to have taken place between 1870 and 1930, when the primary focus of marketing was limited to overcoming constraints on supply, rather than paying attention to sales methods or customer requirements. The production era was apparently followed by the "sales" era, between 1930 and 1950, where marketing's responsibility was to sell what the organization produced, with a consequent focus on sales techniques. The shift from the production era to the sales era has been attributed to increased competition in many industrial sectors (Keith, 1960). Finally, the "marketing" era signified a widespread adoption of the "customer orientation" generally held to be part of the modern MARKETING CONCEPT. A number of authors, however, dispute the existence of either the production or sales eras (*see*, for instance, Fullerton, 1988), pointing to a number of varied and vigorous marketing efforts by manufacturers during these periods, especially the growth of chain stores (pre-1900), department stores (1850), advertising agencies (by 1900), and supermarkets focusing on self-service and low prices (by 1930 in the USA and by 1945 in Europe).

More recent examples of the various definitions of "marketing" include those of the UK's Chartered Institute of Marketing ("the management process which identifies, anticipates and satisfies customer requirements efficiently and profitably") and the American Marketing Association, which reviewed 25 definitions in 1985 and arrived at its own contribution ("marketing is the process of planning and executing the conception, pricing, promotion and distribution of ideas, goods and services to create exchanges that satisfy individual and organizational objectives"). EXCHANGE is seen by many authors as the central concept underlying marketing.

A number of attempts have been made to categorize definitions of "marketing." Crosier (1988), for example, reviewed over 50 definitions, placing them into three broad groups. The first group consisted of definitions which conceived of marketing as a process (*see* MARKETING PROCESS) connecting a producer with its market via a marketing channel, such as "the primary management function which organises and directs the aggregate of business activities involved in converting customer purchase power for a specific product or service into effective demand for a specific product or service and in moving the product or service to the final consumer or user so as to achieve company set profit or other objectives" (Rodger, 1971). The definitions of McCarthy & Perreault (1993) and Runyon (1982), among others, might be seen as falling into this category. The second group consisted of definitions which viewed marketing as a concept or philosophy of business (*see* MARKETING CONCEPT), e.g., "selling is preoccupied with the seller's need to convert his product into cash; marketing with the idea of satisfying the needs of the consumer by means of the product and the whole cluster of things associated with creating, delivering and finally consuming it" (Levitt, 1960). Crosier's third category of definitions emphasized marketing as an orientation present to some degree in both consumer and producer: the phenomenon which makes the process and the concept possible. However, only one example of such a definition was provided by Crosier, and this was felt by many researchers to be an unconvincing argument in favor of a third category of definitions (see MARKETING ORIENTATION).

A number of challenges to the definitions of the scope of marketing outlined by Crosier have emerged. The first of these might be seen as emanating from the field of NOT-FOR-PROFIT MARKETING, where Kotler & Levy's (1969) article extended the scope of marketing to cover activities undertaken for primary aims other than that of profit, including those of organizations such as educational establishments, churches, politicians, national interest groups, or charities, or, indeed, the activities related to INTERNAL MARKETING. Kotler & Levy referred to such not-for-profit marketing as SOCIETAL MARKETING, a term which has more recently come to develop a somewhat different meaning (see below and SOCIETAL MARKETING).

A second challenge developed from the area of SOCIETAL MARKETING, which has been described by some authors as the "fourth era" of the development of marketing (Bell & Emory, 1971; Abratt & Sachs, 1989). Societal marketing criticizes traditional marketing definitions for their emphasis on material consumption and short-term consumer gratification, without considering the long-term societal or environmental impact of marketing activities. It is often seen as a response to both the CONSUMERISM movement and wider criticisms of the ills of marketing. Societal marketing does not generally deny that the basic goal of a business enterprise is to ensure its long-term profitability and survival; however, it does counsel businesses to be fair to consumers, enabling them to make fully informed and intelligent purchase decisions, and to avoid marketing practices that have negative consequences for society. (See also Bartels, 1974; Dawson, 1969; Dickinson et al., 1986; Elliot, 1990; McGee & Spiro, 1990; SOCIAL RESPONSIBILITY; SOCIETAL MARKETING.)

A third challenge has stemmed from those who consider that definitions involving a focus on customer "needs" discourage major product innovations in favor of low-risk product changes, given that when consumers are asked to verbalize their needs, they tend to build on the familiar (Kaldor, 1971; Hayes & Abernathy, 1980).

A fourth challenge comes from authors like Grönroos (1989), who suggest that existing definitions do not capture the essence of BUSINESS-TO-BUSINESS MARKETING or SERVICES MARKETING, both of which revolve primarily around customer relationships (see RELATIONSHIP MARKETING). Grönroos offers an alternative definition of marketing as "to establish, develop and commercialise long term customer relationships, so that the objectives of both parties are met" (57).

Finally, marketing could be defined as an academic discipline, with a recognizable body of theory in relation to the study of the issues and processes described above, although, as Halbert (1965) suggests, there might be some disagreement among marketing academics as to the content of such a body of theory. Marketing is taught on the majority of university business and management degree courses throughout the world.

## Bibliography

Abratt, R. & Sacks, D. (1989). Perceptions of the societal marketing concept. *European Journal of Marketing*, **23**, (6), 25–33.

Bartels, R. (1962). *The development of marketing thought*. Homewood, IL: Irwin.

Bartels, R. (1970). Influences on development of marketing thought 1900–1923. In R. Bartels (Ed.), *Marketing theory and metatheory*, (pp. 108–125). Homewood, IL: Irwin.

Bartels, R. (1974). The identity crisis in marketing. *Journal of Marketing*, **38**, 73–76.

Bell, M. L. & Emory, C. W. (1971). The faltering marketing concept. *Journal of Marketing*, **35**, (4), Oct., 37–42.

Converse, P. D. (1951). Development of marketing theory: Fifty years of progress. In H. Wales (Ed.), *Changing perspectives in marketing* (pp. 1–31). Urbana, IL: University of Illinois Press.

Crosier, K. (1988). What exactly is marketing? In M. J. Thomas & N. E. Waite (Eds), *The marketing digest* (pp. 16–27). London: Heinemann.

Dawson, M. (1969). The human concept: The new philosophy for business. *Business Horizons*, **12**, 29–38.

Dickinson, R., Herbst, A. & O'Shaughnessy, J. (1986). Marketing concept and customer orientation. *European Journal of Marketing*, **20**, (10), 18–23.

Elliot, G. R. (1990). The marketing concept: Necessary but sufficient? An environmental view. *European Journal of Marketing*, **24**, (8), 20–30.

Fullerton, R. A. (1988). How modern is modern marketing? Marketing's evolution and the myth of the "Production" Era. *Journal of Marketing*, **52**, (1), Jan., 108–125.

Gilbert, D. & Bailey, N. (1990). The development of marketing: A compendium of historical applications. *Quarterly Review of Marketing*, 15, (2), Winter, 6–13.

Grönroos, C. (1989). Defining marketing: A market-oriented approach. *European Journal of Marketing*, 23, (1), 52–60.

Halbert, M. (1965). *The meaning and sources of marketing theory*. Marketing Science Institute Series. New York: McGraw-Hill.

Hayes, R. H. & Abernathy, W. J. (1980). Managing our way to economic decline. *Harvard Business Review*, 57, July–Aug., 67–77.

Kaldor, A. G. (1971). Imbricative marketing. *Journal of Marketing*, 35, (2), Apr., 19–25.

Keith, Robert J. (1960). The marketing revolution. *Journal of Marketing*, 24, 35–38.

Kotler, P. & Levy, S. (1969). Broadening the concept of marketing. *Journal of Marketing*, 33, (1), Jan., 10–15.

Levitt, T. (1960). Marketing myopia. *Harvard Business Review*, 37, July–Aug., 45–56.

McCarthy, E. J. & Perreault, R. (1993). *Basic marketing* (11th edn). Homewood, IL: Irwin.

McGee, L. W. & Spiro, R. K. (1990). The marketing concept in perspective. *Business Horizons*, 31, (3), 40–5.

Rodger, L. W. (1971). *Marketing in a competitive economy*. London: Associated Business Programmes.

Runyon, K. E. (1982). *The practice of marketing*. Columbus, OH: C. E. Merrill.

Webster, F. E. Jr (1988). The rediscovery of the marketing concept. *Business Horizons*, 31, (3), 29–39.

FIONA LEVERICK

**marketing audit**    A marketing audit is an analysis, conducted from the perspective of the marketing function, of the environment surrounding an organization and its offerings (*see also* ENVIRONMENTAL ANALYSIS). The aim of the audit is to examine systematically an organization's operations, offerings, markets, and environment so as to find ways to improve marketing performance. This could result, for example, in recommendations that products be adapted to meet new customer requirements, or that old markets be exited, or that fresh investments be considered.

The marketing audit is generally conducted in two interrelated parts: the INTERNAL AUDIT (examining the internal operations and assets of the organization) and the EXTERNAL AUDIT (examining the environment surrounding the organization). This process is similar to the SWOT ANALYSIS recommended for strategic marketing planning where strengths and weaknesses (the "SW" of SWOT) equate to the internal audit, while opportunities and threats (the "OT" of SWOT) correspond to the external audit.

**Bibliography**

Kotler, P., Gregor, W. & Rodgers, W. (1977). The marketing audit comes of age. *Sloan Management Review*, 18, Winter, 25–43.

Wilson, A. (1982). *Marketing audit checklists*. Maidenhead: McGraw-Hill.

DOMINIC WILSON

**marketing channels**    *see* CHANNELS OF DISTRIBUTION; RETAIL DISTRIBUTION CHANNELS; WHOLESALERS

**marketing communications**    Organizations are involved in a range of marketing communications exchanges; e.g., a manufacturer may communicate with its middlemen, customers (existing and potential), and various publics. Its middlemen communicate with their customers and various publics. Customers engage in WORD-OF-MOUTH COMMUNICATIONS with other customers and consumers, and each group can provide communication feedback to every other group, especially through the MARKETING RESEARCH activities of organizations.

Marketing communications comprise a mix of techniques or tools known as the COMMUNICATIONS MIX (and sometimes referred to as the promotional mix), by which a MESSAGE is delivered from one party in the communications exchange to another.

Schramm (1971) was one of the first to discuss the marketing communications process. This is summarized in Kotler (1994). This model answers the questions (1) who (2) says what (3) in what channel (4) to whom (5) with what effect? All communications involve "senders" and "receivers;" the "senders" being concerned with messages and channels, i.e., the ways in which messages are carried/ delivered to an audience. Marketing communicators require that the message sent is the one that is received, but they are aware of consumers' selective processes (of exposure, attention, distortion, and recall), and intervening variables, referred to as NOISE (i.e., factors over which the communicator has no control, not least of which are messages being sent to target groups simultaneously), which may interfere with the process.

Kotler (1994) refers to the five major tools of the marketing communications mix available to an organization, namely: ADVERTISING, DIRECT MARKETING, SALES PROMOTION, PUBLIC RELATIONS and PUBLICITY, and PERSONAL SELLING. An alternative consideration of the mix is a classification into two broad dimensions: first, whether or not the communications are paid for, and second, whether they are personal, i.e., where there is some direct contact between the sender and the receiver, or impersonal where there is not. Examples include:

Paid and personal: PERSONAL SELLING, TELEMARKETING
Paid and impersonal: ADVERTISING, SALES PROMOTION, PUBLIC RELATIONS, DIRECT MAIL, PACKAGING
Non-paid and personal: social channels, i.e., WORD-OF-MOUTH COMMUNICATIONS, INTERPERSONAL COMMUNICATIONS
Non-paid and impersonal: PUBLICITY

Personal communications tend to be more important when products are expensive, risky, have social significance, or are purchased infrequently; and buyers seek information, product experiences, and the knowledge of others. Impersonal communications are less insistent than personal channels, and so can easily be avoided or tuned out. Further, they are subject to the consumer psychological processes of selective attention, perception, and retention (see CONSUMER PERCEPTIONS; SELECTIVE EXPOSURE).

This classification allows for the communication to be initiated by consumers as well as supplier organizations (see TWO STEP FLOW MODEL).

Effective communication/promotion involves a number of activities. These include: identify-

ing the target audience and its characteristics, e.g., individuals, groups, families, and businesses, and their socioeconomic profiles, personality, perceptions of risk, and stages in the buying process, etc.; determining the COMMUNICATIONS OBJECTIVES, e.g., to create awareness, knowledge, liking, preference, conviction, or purchase; designing the message; selecting the communication channels, both personal and impersonal, which will vary between consumer and organizational markets; allocating the communications budget and deciding on the promotional mix, which will be influenced by funds available, the nature of the market, and the stage in the product life cycle, etc.; measuring the communications results; and managing the marketing communications program.

### Bibliography

Dibb, S., Simkin, L., Pride, W. M. & Ferrell, O. C. (1994). *Marketing concepts and strategies* (European edn). Boston, MA: Houghton Mifflin Co. Chapter 14.
Kotler, P. (1994). *Marketing management: Analysis, planning, implementation and control* (8th edn). Englewood Cliffs, NJ: Prentice-Hall. Chapter 22.
Schramm, W. (1971). How communications works. In W. Schramm & D. F. Roberts (Eds), *The process and effects of mass communications*. Urbana, IL: University of Illinois Press.

BARBARA LEWIS

**marketing concept**   The marketing concept has been seen variously as a statement of the philosophy of marketing, an approach to doing business, or a broad umbrella governing business activity. It is seen by many as synonymous with "marketing" itself, definitions of marketing as a concept or philosophy of business comprising one of the three types of definitions of "marketing" identified by Crosier (1988) (see MARKETING).

The marketing concept is generally held to have three major components (see McGee & Spiro, 1990). The first of these is a so-called "customer orientation," whereby an understanding of customer "needs," wants, and behavior is the focal point of all marketing action. The second is a focus on what is usually termed either coordinated activities or integrated effort, with the entire organization sharing the customer orientation by emphasizing the integration of the marketing function with areas such as research, product management, sales, and advertising. The third is a profit orientation, with attention directed primarily toward profit, as opposed to sales volumes, although clearly a profit focus is not appropriate for all organizations (e.g., NOT-FOR-PROFIT MARKETING). Reflecting these three areas, Kotler (1994) defined the marketing concept as "a customer orientation backed by integrated marketing as the key to attaining long term profitable volume." Other authors have gone on to emphasize a fourth component: a long term-orientation, in order to deflect criticisms of the marketing concept as focused only on the current, articulable "needs" of consumers (see MARKETING).

There has been some concern that the marketing concept as defined above is not broad enough to cover the more recent developments in the scope of marketing. In particular, developments in the area of SOCIETAL MARKETING have led to a number of restatements of the marketing concept to include a focus on consumers' and society's long-term interests (see SOCIETAL MARKETING; SOCIAL RESPONSIBILITY). This had led some authors to produce a more "modern" statement of the marketing concept based on the three elements of consumer satisfaction, company profits, and community welfare (Abratt & Sacks, 1989).

### Bibliography

Abratt, R. & Sacks, D. (1989). Perceptions of the societal marketing concept. *European Journal of Marketing*, **23**, (6), 25–33.

Crosier, K. (1988). What exactly is marketing? In M. J. Thomas & N. E. Waite (Eds), *The marketing digest* (pp. 16–27). London: Heinemann.

Kotler, P. (1994). *Marketing management: Analysis, planning, implementation and control* (8th edn). Englewood Cliffs, NJ: Prentice-Hall.

McGee, L. W. & Spiro, R. K. (1990). The marketing concept in perspective. *Business Horizons*, **31**, (3), 40–45.

FIONA LEVERICK

**marketing control** It is clear that effective strategic marketing management (*see* STRATEGIC MARKETING; MARKETING MANAGEMENT)

suggests establishing predetermined targets against which actual performance can be assessed. This is the essence of marketing control.

There are at least two major areas where marketing control will be applied: to the marketing strategy; and to the marketing budget. In the case of marketing strategy, control is viewed as the final phase of the four-stage strategy process (*see* STRATEGIC PLANNING), and is primarily concerned with ensuring that the strategy is developing according to plan so that the established objectives will be realized. If deviations are identified, the implications can be analyzed and appropriate action taken. It may be necessary to adjust expectations or even the strategy where the outcomes differ significantly from expectations and cannot be reconciled with the original strategy. In some instances, the strategy may have to be abandoned where the deviations are such as to make it commercially unviable.

Budgetary control involves monitoring the extent to which the various cost and revenue streams match with those defined in the budget. Assessments are likely to be undertaken regularly (in some cases daily, made possible by the use of computerized data capture and processing systems). Among the variables managers may monitor are: sales/profits and sales/profit variances; market share; and expenses to sales ratios. In addition, it is important to watch more qualitative indicators such as customer attitudes (say, through tracking studies) and complaints.

Firms also need to evaluate periodically the profitability of products, channels of distribution, customers and order sizes, as well as the efficiency of key marketing activities, such as advertising and sales. Firms may employ benchmarking, i.e., compare their costs and efficiencies against the "best practice" elsewhere.

### Bibliography

Bureau, J. R. (1995). Controlling marketing.In M. J. Baker (Ed.) *The marketing book* (pp. 565–585). Oxford: Butterworth-Heinemann.

DALE LITTLER

**marketing decision support systems** A marketing decision support system is an information system that allows marketing decision-makers to interact directly with both databases and models. As such, it is an improvement on MARKETING INFORMATION SYSTEMS. A decision support system consists of the computer hardware and communication interface, databases, relevant marketing models and software, and the marketing decision-maker. The aim is to help the decision-maker, not only by allowing access to past and current data, but also by providing answers to "what if . . . " questions through the incorporation of marketing models deemed appropriate by the decision-maker.

To be effective a marketing decision support system should have the following characteristics: it should be understood by the managers using it; it should be perceived as useful by these users; it should be complete on important issues (e.g., on important factors where hard objective data are not available, the system should allow the use of the subjective assessments of the user rather than ignore those factors); it should be easy for the manager to use and interact with without the need for an intermediate computer expert; it should be flexible and give sensible answers; and it should be evolutionary in the sense that it is capable of being extended at a later date.

One of the problems is getting marketing decision-makers to use decision support systems. This will be helped if: the potential users are involved in the design of the system; the decision-makers specify the decisions where they would like support (probably frequently occurring decisions); the marketing models/theories and databases being used have the decision-makers' approval; and successful use of the system can be demonstrated, probably, in the first instance, by helping with simple problems.

Examples of marketing decisions that have been aided by decision support systems include media scheduling, sales force management, store location, warehouse location, and competitive bidding.

**Bibliography**

Churchill, G. A. (1991). *Marketing research: Methodological foundations* (5th edn). Chicago: The Dryden Press. Chapter 2.

MICHAEL GREATOREX

**marketing environment** The marketing environment is made up of the actors and forces that directly or indirectly influence the company's marketing operations and performance and which are generally thought to be outside the company's power of control. The distinction is often made between the MICRO ENVIRONMENT, which is made up of actors in the company's immediate environment, such as suppliers, market intermediaries, customers, or competitors, and the MACRO ENVIRONMENT, which is made up of wider societal forces that affect all of the actors in the micro environment, such as legal, cultural, economic, technological, demographic, or political trends.

*See also* **Marketing management**

FIONA LEVERICK

**marketing ethics** Marketing ethics can be seen as the moral principles that define "right" or "wrong" behavior in marketing. "Unethical" marketing activity might include, for example, deceptive advertising, misleading selling tactics, price fixing, and the deliberate marketing of harmful products. While marketing ethics are frequently referred to in conjunction with the concept of SOCIAL RESPONSIBILITY, the two areas have been differentiated by the criteria that social responsibility is an organizational concern while ethics are the concern of the individual manager or business decision-maker (Carroll, 1981). Other authors have identified the process of ensuring that marketing decisions are taken according to ethical principles as just one aspect of a wider concept of corporate social responsibility (*see* SOCIAL RESPONSIBILITY).

The study of marketing ethics has become an important area for research, paralleling a growing body of literature in the field of business ethics more generally (*see* Smith & Quelch, 1993 for a more thorough discussion of ethical issues in marketing). While there exists no totally accepted statement about what is ethical in marketing, two major philosophies, deontology and utilitarianism, have dominated the study of ethics and these have been used as the basis for a general theory of marketing ethics (*see* Hunt & Vitell, 1986).

Deontology refers to the existence of prima facie ideals that can direct our thinking, behavior being judged on the basis of whether or not it infringes these universal rules. Kant (1964 translation) suggests that ethical actions should be based on reasons the decision-maker would be willing to have others use. That is, one should not act unless one is willing to have the maxim on which one acts become a universal law. This approach would, for example, require a marketer to ask if he or she would be willing to live in a world where all producers were making a product known to be harmful to some people in its normal use. Rawls (1971) provides a more modern statement of deontology, suggesting that an action is ethical if it involves true freedom of choice and action, is available to all, injures no one, and is of benefit to some.

Utilitarianism, on the other hand, is concerned with maximizing the greatest good for the greatest number of people. Alternative marketing actions would thus be judged on the basis of the consequences for all the people affected by the actions, according to a cost-benefit analysis. If the net result of all benefits minus all costs is positive, the action would then be ethically acceptable. Compared to deontology, which views the individual as the major concern and unit of analysis, utilitarianism is societal in nature, being more concerned with the welfare of society as a unit.

Utilitarianism, in particular, has been criticized on a number of points. First, difficulties are likely to be encountered in attempting to quantify "benefits" and "costs." It also involves the problem of concealing major negative occurrences to a small segment of people by allowing them to be offset by a relatively minor increase in "benefits" to large segments.

### Bibliography

Carroll, A. B. (1981). *Business and society*. Boston, MA: Little, Brown & Co.

Hunt, S. D. & Vitell, S. (1986). A general theory of marketing ethics. *Journal of Macromarketing*, **6**, Spring, 5–16.

Kant, I. (1964). *Groundwork of the metaphysics of morals*. Translation by H. J. Paton. New York: Harper & Row.

Rawls, J. (1971). *A theory of justice*. Cambridge, MA: Harvard University Press.

Smith, N. C. & Quelch, J. A. (1993). *Ethics in marketing*. Boston, MA: Irwin.

FIONA LEVERICK

**marketing exchange**   *see* EXCHANGE

**marketing information systems**   A marketing information system is designed to generate, analyze, store, and distribute information to appropriate marketing decision-makers on a regular basis. The definition of marketing information systems is similar to that of MARKETING RESEARCH except for the emphasis on the regular supply of information to marketing managers in marketing information systems as opposed to the emphasis on the gathering of information in marketing research. The growth in the use of marketing information systems has been facilitated by improvements in computer hardware and software, and contemporary marketing information systems are very much computer driven.

Marketing information systems are designed around individual decision-makers, the decisions they are required to make, and the information needed to make those decisions. The information includes both that required on a regular and that required on an ad hoc basis. The underlying data may be collected internally or externally. The information is presented in a form requested by the decision-maker. The key task is to specify what information each individual decision-maker requires, when it is required, and in what format. The end result is a series of customized reports that go to the appropriate decision-makers.

As the volume of information in a marketing information system increases over time, a large memory and easy access becomes important; technical improvements in the form of laser compact discs are meeting this need.

Marketing information systems are being superseded by MARKETING DECISION SUPPORT SYSTEMS which are more versatile in the way the decision-maker is able to interact with the database and which, because of the ability to include marketing modeling in marketing decision support systems, permit the decision-maker to ask "what if . . . " questions rather than merely retrieve data.

## Bibliography

Churchill, G. A. (1991). *Marketing research: Methodological foundations* (5th edn). Chicago: The Dryden Press. Chapter 2.

MICHAEL GREATOREX

**marketing management** The term "marketing management" is generally used to refer to the management activities undertaken in the practice of marketing in organizations. The conventional view of marketing management found in most standard marketing textbooks is of a process whereby the marketing manager uses marketing resources to perform a highly defined and "logical" series of activities and responsibilities (*see* Baker, 1991; Dibb et al., 1991; Kotler, 1994; McCarthy & Perreault, 1993). Dibb et al. (1991), for instance, see marketing management as the process of "planning, organising, implementing and controlling marketing activities to facilitate and expedite exchanges effectively and efficiently." The execution of this process defines the marketing manager's areas of responsibility and the nature of his or her work.

The specific activities involved in marketing management will depend to a great extent on the type of markets the business is operating in. The activities involved, for instance, in marketing to consumers and marketing to other businesses may differ significantly (*see* BUSINESS-TO-BUSINESS MARKETING; CONSUMER MARKETING). At a general level, however, standard marketing textbooks frequently divide marketing management activities into the four areas of analysis, planning, implementation, and control.

Analysis refers to the gathering and preparation of information about the markets the organization is currently operating in or which it plans to enter, in terms of identifying and evaluating present and emergent customer "needs" and potential opportunities for business expansion. Such analysis is often seen as being undertaken by studying both the organization's current MARKETING ENVIRONMENT and identifying future trends.

Planning is most commonly seen as a systematic process of assessing opportunities and resources, setting marketing objectives, developing a MARKETING STRATEGY, and formulating measures for implementation and control (*see* MARKETING PLANNING). In this way, marketing managers are required to make decisions on target markets, market positioning, product and service development, pricing, distribution channels, physical distribution, communication, and promotion. The result of these activities is often contained in a marketing plan.

Implementation refers to the activities necessary to translate the marketing plan into action. It might include organizing marketing resources and developing the internal structure of the marketing unit, coordinating marketing activities, motivating marketing personnel, and effectively communicating within the unit. Bonoma (1985), however, reviewed 17 marketing textbooks and found implementation to be a generally neglected area of marketing management, with most emphasis directed toward analysis, planning, and control.

Finally, the marketing control process involves the measurement of results and evaluating progress according to standards of performance such as MARKET SHARE, cost sales ratios, advertising/sales ratios, or, more commonly in the case of BUSINESS-TO-BUSINESS MARKETING, techniques such as customer PORTFOLIO ANALYSIS or customer profitability analysis. Expected performance standards against which results are judged would commonly be specified as part of the marketing plan. Indeed, analysis, planning, implementation, and control might be seen as a continuous marketing management process in which during planning, guidelines for implementation are set and expected results specified for the control process, and feedback from the control process is used in the development of new plans.

This "textbook" view of marketing management embedded in the work of, for example, Kotler (1994) and McCarthy & Perreault (1993) has, however, been criticized on a number of counts (*see* Brownlie, 1991 for a summary of criticisms). In particular, the view of the marketing management process driven by "rational" marketing planning has been questioned by authors such as Brownlie (1991) and

King (1985), who suggest that such a normative model of marketing management bears little relation to what practicing marketing managers actually do, being based instead on what textbook writers think marketing managers *ought to* do. According to Brownlie, much marketing management literature overlooks the part played by individual managerial judgement, vision, and experience, qualities seen as especially relevant in the area of marketing as opposed to, say, finance or production, given that the data on which marketing decisions are made are often unreliable and consumers often behave "irrationally" or unexpectedly, making a focus purely on analytical techniques inappropriate. Whereas marketing management may be reduced to a sole focus on analysis and planning in junior brand management jobs in fast-moving consumer goods sectors, it is questioned whether this is representative across other sectors and levels of responsibility.

References are frequently made on this point to the work of authors such as Kotter (1982) and Mintzberg (1973), who have both looked at the nature of managerial work. Kotter, for instance, followed 15 general managers for a month and found that activities such as building networks, developing agendas, executing marketing activities, establishing values and norms, maintaining relationships, working through meetings and dialogues, establishing multiple objectives, spending time with others, and using rewards to secure support and desired behavior were more common in successful organizations than were planning and analysis activities. Mintzberg (1973) found that managers spend a great proportion of their time in oral communication and face-to-face contact rather than in formulating written plans.

A more accurate portrayal of marketing management might also reflect the increasingly wider focus of marketing itself (*see* MARKETING), to include the activities undertaken in SERVICES MARKETING, BUSINESS-TO-BUSINESS MARKETING, and NOT-FOR-PROFIT MARKETING, and also marketing activities directed toward parties in the organization's MARKETING ENVIRONMENT other than those individuals and organizations who purchase goods and services, such as stakeholders, publics, or employees (*see* INTERNAL MARKETING).

**Bibliography**

Baker, M. J. (1991). *Marketing: An introductory text* (5th edn). Basingstoke: Macmillan.

Bonoma, T. V. (1985). *The marketing edge: Making strategies work*. New York: Free Press.

Brownlie, D. T. (1991). Putting the management into marketing management. In M. J. Baker (Ed.), *Perspectives on marketing management*, Vol 1. Chichester: John Wiley.

Dibb, S., Simkin, L., Pride, W. M. & Ferrell, O. C. (1991). *Marketing: Concepts and strategies* (European edn). London: Houghton Mifflin Co.

King, S. (1985). Has marketing failed or was it never really tried? *Journal of Marketing Management*, 1, (1), 1–20.

Kotler, P. (1994). *Marketing management: Analysis, planning, implementation and control* (8th edn). Englewood Cliffs, NJ: Prentice-Hall.

Kotter, J. (1982). *The general managers*. New York: Free Press.

McCarthy, E. J. & Perreault, R. (1993). *Basic marketing* (11th edn). Homewood, IL: Irwin.

Mintzberg, H. (1973). *The nature of managerial work*. New York: Harper & Row.

FIONA LEVERICK

**marketing mix**   The term "marketing mix" was first used by Professor Neil Borden of Harvard Business School to describe a list of the important elements or ingredients that make up marketing programs, the idea having been suggested to him by Culliton's (1948) description of a business executive as a "mixer of ingredients" (Borden, 1964). More recently, McCarthy & Perreault (1987) have defined the marketing mix as the controllable variables that an organization can coordinate to satisfy its target market. The essence of the concept is the idea of a set of controllable marketing variables or a "tool kit" (Shapiro, 1985).

Some diversity of opinion exists as to the components of the marketing mix. Borden's own list is probably the longest, containing merchandising/product planning, pricing, branding, channels of distribution, personal selling, advertising, promotion, packaging, display, servicing, physical handling, fact finding and analysis, and market research. The best-known marketing mix is McCarthy's 4Ps, product, price, promotion, and place. However, this has been widely criticized as simplistic and misleading, especially in the areas of BUSINESS-

TO-BUSINESS MARKETING, SERVICES MARKET-ING, and NOT-FOR-PROFIT MARKETING, and more recently Kotler (1986) has added politics and public relations and Booms & Bitner (1981), participants, physical evidence, and process to McCarthy's 4Ps.

*See also* **Marketing management.**

**Bibliography**

Booms, B. H. & Bitner, M. J. (1981). Marketing strategies and organization structures for service firms.In J. Donnelly & J. R. George (Eds), *Marketing of services* (pp. 47–51). Chicago: American Marketing Association.

Borden, Neil H. (1964). The concept of the marketing mix. *Journal of Advertising Research*, 2–7.

Culliton, J. W. (1948). *The management of marketing costs*. Division of Research, Graduate School of Business Administration, Harvard University.

Kotler, P. (1986). Megamarketing. *Harvard Business Review*, **64**, (2), Mar.–Apr., 117–124.

McCarthy, E. J. & Perreault, W. D. Jr (1987). *Basic marketing* (9th edn). Homewood, IL: Irwin.

Shapiro, B. P. (1985). Rejuvenating the marketing mix. *Harvard Business Review*, **63**, Sept.–Oct., 28–34.

FIONA LEVERICK

**marketing organization** The modern marketing department has had an evolution consisting of at least five phases, ranging from the simple sales department to the modern marketing company. In the early stages, many of the activities now associated with marketing would have been undertaken by a number of different functions, often in an uncoordinated manner. Thus, the sales department may have been responsible not only for managing the sales activity, but also for advertising and rudimentary market research; pricing may have been shared by accounting, sales, and production; while design and product development may have been the responsibility of research and development. As the importance of marketing became increasingly recognized, it emerged as a distinct corporate activity responsible for at least managing in a more coordinated fashion different activities that were seen to have some bearing on the development of the product and more generally on the relationship with the customer.

Contemporarily, marketing is widely acknowledged as a core organizational activity, often with representation at board level.

The marketing activity can be structured according to functions; geographical areas; products; and customer types.

In the functional form, marketing is organized in terms of distinct specialisms, such as marketing research, sales, and product development, that report to a marketing manager or director. However, in organizations with complex PRODUCT PORTFOLIOS that may also operate in several markets, there is clearly a need for marketing responsibility to be shared among several managers, each of whom may have responsibility for particular products and/or market areas. Marketing may also be organized in terms of geographical regions. A naive division may be between overseas and domestic operations. However, companies operating in several countries may have managers for different groups of countries, e.g., Asia Pacific; South America; Europe; or even specific countries. Within countries, there may also be managers for particular areas, such as the South West or the North East.

The product manager system developed as individual products became increasingly important. Under the general marketing management structure, "assistant" marketing managers were appointed to manage various aspects of the increasingly complex product portfolio. Individual managers, often referred to as brand or product managers, are given responsibility for coordinating all the marketing activities, such as advertising, marketing research, product development as well as, in some cases, responsibility for profit, of specific major products or brands.

Alternatively, marketing may be organized according to the customers or markets it serves, this being particularly appropriate where the firm markets to diverse customer groups with significantly differing requirements. Individual managers may be responsible for all the marketing effort for customer groups or markets and even for individual customers where the level of demand merits this. Hanan (1974) has termed this approach "market centring" and argues that it provides the company with a distinct competitive advantage because of the detailed knowledge of the customer or market that in theory the market manager should acquire.

Such a structure would appear to support RELATIONSHIP MARKETING.

These approaches to marketing organization are not mutually exclusive, and the marketing activity may be a combination of two or more of these forms. For example, marketing may have functional managers supporting product and market managers. There may, in addition, be managers responsible for geographical regions.

Marketing may have representation at board level and may be expected to be an active participant in the development of overall organizational strategy. It may be a service activity providing marketing advice both to the board and to individual business or operating units. Individual business units or divisions may have individual marketing activities or departments; while marketing may be part of the matrix structure of an organization ensuring that marketing contributes to every major activity. Increasingly, it is argued that marketing should be embedded in the culture of an organization and that it should be recognized that all those whose activities in any way have some impact on the customers should be seen as, in effect, part-time marketers.

All decision makers can have access to customer information which can be disseminated throughout the organization using computerized information systems (*see* MARKETING INFORMATION SYSTEMS). It could be argued that this might herald the end of the era of marketing as an important functional activity. Marketing may at best in the future be a minimal service activity, advising managers, responsible for particular relationships, on various facets of marketing, much of which may be outsourced to specialist agencies.

### Bibliography

Hanan, M. (1974). Recognize your company around its markets. *Harvard Business Review*, November–December.

Spillard, P. (1994). Organisation for marketing. In M. J. Baker (Ed.), *The marketing book* (3rd edn). (pp. 54–88). Oxford: Butterworth-Heinemann.

DALE LITTLER

**marketing orientation**   A marketing orientation is usually seen as the company orientation necessary in order that the MARKETING CONCEPT is put into practice. It is often contrasted with the "production orientation" and "sales orientation" associated with the "production era" and "sales era" of the development of marketing thought respectively (*see* MARKETING; MARKETING CONCEPT).

A number of writers have gone into more detail on the precise nature of a "marketing orientation" in relation to the various activities associated with MARKETING MANAGEMENT. For example, according to McCarthy & Perreault (1993), marketing activities and the product offering are seen as guided primarily by customer "needs;" the role of market research is seen as to determine customer "needs" and how well the company is satisfying them; innovation activity is focused primarily on locating new opportunities, in, for example, products or technologies; profit (as opposed to sales volume) is the critical objective of marketing activity; packaging is designed for customer convenience and as a selling tool (over and above simply the protection of the product); inventory levels are set with customer requirements and costs in mind (rather than at the convenience of the supplier); the focus of advertising is to promote the needs-satisfying benefits of the product or service; the role of sales force, coordinated with the efforts of the rest of the firm, is to help customers to buy only if the product fits their needs; and so on. Somewhat more succinctly, Shapiro (1988) notes three key features of a marketing orientation: information on all important buying influences permeates every corporate function; strategic and tactical decisions are made interfunctionally and interdivisionally; and divisions and functions make well coordinated decisions and execute them with a sense of commitment.

Many authors (Doyle, 1985; Hooley & Lynch, 1985; Saunders & Wong, 1985; Witcher, 1990) have argued that UK companies in particular have found it difficult to develop a marketing orientation and that this has been a significant contributor to the decline in the UK's worldwide competitive position (*see also* Kheir-El-Din, 1991, for a review of this literature). Doyle et al. (1987), for example, found that almost 50 percent of a sample of UK companies acknowledged that they were unclear about the main types of customer in their markets and what the requirements or preferences of these customers were. The corresponding figure for a sample of Japanese companies was 13 percent. More recently, similar deficiencies were found in a sample of UK manufacturers involved in business-to-business marketing (Chartered Institute of Marketing/University of Bradford Management Centre, 1995).

**Bibliography**

Chartered Institute of Marketing/University of Bradford Management Centre (1995). *Manufacturing: The marketing solution.* Oxford: Chartered Institute of Marketing Report.

Doyle, P. (1985). Marketing and the competitive performance of British industry. *Journal of Marketing Management*, 1, (1), 87–98.

Doyle, P., Saunders, J. & Wright, L. (1987). *A comparative study of US and Japanese marketing strategies in the British market.* Warwick University Report.

Hooley, G. J. & Lynch, J. E. (1985). Marketing lessons from the UK's high flying companies. *Journal of Marketing Management*, 1, (1), 67–74.

Kheir-El-Din, A. (1991). The contribution of marketing to competitive success. In M. J. Baker (Ed.), *Perspectives on marketing management*, Vol. 1. Chichester: John Wiley.

McCarthy, E. J. & Perreault, R. (1993). *Basic marketing* (11th edn). Homewood, IL: Irwin.

Saunders, J. & Wong, V. (1985). In search of excellence in the UK. *Journal of Marketing Management*, 1, (2), 119–137.

Shapiro, B. P. (1988). What the hell is market-oriented? *Harvard Business Review*, 66, Nov.–Dec., 119–125.

Witcher, B. J. (1990). Total marketing: Total quality and the marketing concept. *Quarterly Review of Marketing*, 15, (2), Winter, 1–6.

FIONA LEVERICK

**marketing performance**   MARKETING PLANNING may involve the definition of targets or performance indicators. Measures commonly employed include product sales, costs, and market share. The company may also monitor the ability to meet customer specifications, delivery times, stock levels, tender success rates, the efficiencies of various operations, and such like.

DALE LITTLER

**marketing plan**   *see* MARKETING PLANNING

**marketing planning**   Marketing, like other functions and the organization as a whole, may have a plan which sets out the objectives and the means of achieving these. The plan can be viewed as a blueprint for future action. It will also set out targets against which performance can be monitored (*see* MARKETING CONTROL; MARKETING PERFORMANCE). The process of marketing planning, frequently prefaced with "strategic," is often depicted as consisting of a number of stages (Leppard & McDonald, 1991) involving: the gathering of information on the company's internal operations and its external environment; the identification of the strengths, weaknesses, opportunities, and threats (*see* SWOT ANALYSIS); the definition of the assumptions regarding the company and its environment; the setting of the marketing objectives in the light of the first three stages; the formulation of strategies aimed at achieving these objectives; the devising of programs setting out the timing of activities, costs, and revenues; the definition of responsibilities and the means of monitoring performance. The plan should ensure that the organization has in place the rudiments for implementing, monitoring, and controlling the strategy (Bonoma & Crittenden, 1988). The plan might contain specific objectives in terms of: sales, profits, and market share; the pricing strategy and policies; the communications strategy; and various other elements of the traditional MARKETING MIX necessary for the organization to meet its strategic objectives.

Such marketing plans may be undertaken, inter alia, at the level of the product or at the level of the strategic business unit (*see* STRATEGIC BUSINESS UNITS).

In the marketing literature the distinction between corporate, strategic, and marketing planning has become blurred: all are often depicted as involving a similar methodology, for example. However, it is reasonable to assume that corporate planning embraces all of the different activities of the organization, whereas marketing planning should be regarded as focusing on the means by which marketing can play its part in facilitating the attainment of corporate objectives. In this sense then, (strategic) marketing planning is operational, a stance which appears compatible with that adopted by Greenley (1986).

It could be argued that marketing planning would apply particularly to large firms, which have the resources to direct the extensive analysis that such planning demands, and which operate in stable, and therefore relatively predictable, environments (see Mintzberg, 1973).

### Bibliography

Bonoma, T. V. & Crittenden, V. L. (1988). Managing marketing implementation. *Sloan Management Review*, **29**, Winter, 7–14.

Leppard, J. W. & McDonald, M. H. B. (1991). Marketing planning and corporate culture: A conceptual framework which examines management attitudes in the context of marketing planning. *Journal of Marketing Management*, **7**, (3), July, 213–36.

Greenley, G. E. (1986). *The strategic and operational planning of marketing*. Maidenhead: McGraw-Hill, 89–139.

Mintzberg, H. (1973). Strategy making in three modes. *California Management Review*, **16**, (2), Winter, 44–53.

DALE LITTLER

**marketing process**   Two levels of understanding of the marketing process are common in the marketing literature. The first refers to the organizational process concerned with directing goods and services from producer to consumer. Indeed, the marketing process is often seen as synonymous with "marketing" itself, with process-related definitions of marketing forming one of the three categories of definition identified by Crosier (1988). The extent to which the activities involved in the marketing process are specified varies from author to author. Kotler (1994) proposes a highly specific marketing process consisting of "analyzing marketing opportunities, researching and selecting target markets, designing marketing strategies, planning marketing programmes, and organizing, implementing and controlling the marketing effort." In this way, the marketing process is seen as inseparable from structured, normative approaches to MARKETING MANAGEMENT, the activities involved being essentially the same (see MARKETING MANAGEMENT). The marketing process of an organization involved in SERVICES MARKETING or BUSINESS-TO-BUSINESS MARKETING, in particular, is likely to differ substantially from this model (see BUSINESS-TO-BUSINESS MARKETING; SERVICES MARKETING; RELATIONSHIP MARKETING).

A second level of understanding of the marketing process is concerned with the whole marketing system and describes a wider social process that directs an economy's flow of goods and services from producers to consumers in a way that effectively matches supply and demand and accomplishes the objectives of society (see McCarthy & Perreault, 1993).

### Bibliography

Crosier, K. (1988). What exactly is marketing? In M. J. Thomas & N. E. Waite (Eds), *The marketing digest* (pp. 16–27). London: Heinemann.

Kotler, P. (1994). *Marketing management: Analysis, planning, implementation and control* (8th edn). Englewood Cliffs, NJ: Prentice-Hall.

McCarthy, E. J. & Perreault, R. (1993). *Basic marketing* (11th edn). Homewood, IL: Irwin.

FIONA LEVERICK

**marketing research**

Marketing research is the function which links the consumer, customer and public to the marketer through information – information used to identify and define marketing opportunities and problems; generate, refine and evaluate marketing actions; monitor marketing performance; and improve understanding of marketing as a process. Marketing research specifies the information required to address these issues; designs the method for collecting information; manages and implements the data collection process; analyses the results; and communicates the findings and their implications. (American Marketing Association, 1987, quoted in Malhotra, 1993, 10)

Malhotra, who emphasizes the need for information for decision-making, defines marketing research as "the systematic and objective identification, collection, analysis, and dissemination of information for the purpose of assisting management in decision making related to the identification and solution of problems and opportunities in marketing" (Malhotra, 1993, 10).

Marketing research, therefore, is closely linked with decision-making by marketing managers. O'Dell, Ruppel, Trent & Kehoe (1988) suggest a five-stage marketing decision-making process: identify the decision problem; formulate alternative solutions; establish criteria; evaluate the alternative solutions; and resolve the decision. They see change, especially in the environment, as the source of decision problems. If a manager feels that things, e.g., sales, profits, etc., are not as expected, based on historical or budgeted levels, the question arises "Why?." The answer to this question often lies in environmental (in its widest marketing meaning) change. Information concerning the environment may enable changes to be detected or predicted and linked to current or likely marketing problems. Appropriate solutions can be suggested and evaluated when the cause of the problem is known.

Problem solving is the name O'Dell et al. give to their first two stages, the identification of the decision problem and the formulation of alternative solutions, and they suggest the need at these stages is for "environmental data and information." The final three stages, the establishment of criteria, the evaluation of the alternative solutions, and the resolution of the decision-making process, are called decision-making and the authors suggest the need here is for "actionable data and information." Environmental data indicate what is, while actionable data are pertinent to what should be done. Environmental data become available and are used prior to and during the formulation of alternative solutions. Actionable data are data sought after the alternative solutions have been formulated and for the specific purpose of evaluating the alternatives. Sometimes environmental and actionable data are collected jointly in a single information-gathering effort but usually they are gathered separately. Experience has shown that environmental data need not be as precise, relatively, as actionable data. Different methods may be appropriate, depending on the stage in the decision-making process and the type of data required. Thus, secondary data, either from external or internal sources, may be satisfactory as environmental data, while a well-designed experiment may be called for to provide actionable data.

Malhotra (1993, 11–13) suggests two types of marketing research: problem-identification research and problem-solving research. Problem identification is undertaken to help identify problems which are, perhaps, not apparent on the surface and yet exist or are likely to arise in the future. Examples of problem-identification research include research into market potential, market share, brand or company image, market characteristics, sales analysis, short-range forecasting, long-range forecasting, and business trends. When a problem has been identified, problem-solving research is undertaken to arrive at a solution. Problem-solving research includes segmentation and marketing mix research – what will be the effects of a price change, new packaging, change in sales promotion or advertising, change in service levels to retailers, etc.?

Marketing research involves both SECONDARY and PRIMARY DATA. Secondary data are data collected for a purpose other than the problem under consideration. Internal secondary data are available from within the organization from records such as sales records kept for accounting purposes, general management information systems, etc. External secondary data come from governments, trade associations, and marketing research organizations and are accessible from printed publications and, increasingly, from computer databases by way of CD-ROM or computer network.

Primary data are data collected specifically for the problem under consideration. Two types of data are identified, qualitative and quantitative data. Qualitative data mainly provide insights into the problem by looking at the underlying motives, needs, opinions, etc. of respondents using techniques such as DEPTH INTERVIEWS, FOCUS GROUPS, and PROJECTIVE TECHNIQUES. Quantitative techniques look to provide quantitative data which sometimes are used in exploratory research but which are usually associated with the decision-making stage. Quantitative techniques also seek to enable results from a sample to be generalized to a population. Techniques include observations, surveys (see SURVEY RESEARCH) using structured questionnaires, and experiments. While much primary research is ad hoc or one off, an increasing amount is continuous involving the repeated use of the same design or questionnaire, sometimes with different samples, sometimes with the same sample or panel.

The increasing use of electronic capture of data, e.g., at retail store checkouts or in consumer scanner panels or, potentially, in two way in-home communications associated with cable systems, is capable of providing a continuous flow of data that enables the tracking of key measures that are useful to marketing decision-makers.

The information that marketing research provides becomes part of an organization's MARKETING INFORMATION SYSTEM. A marketing information system is a system designed to generate, analyze, store, and distribute information to appropriate marketing decision-makers on a regular basis. However, marketing information systems are limited to supplying past and current data in a prescribed, even if customized, form for each manager. Further developments have lead to MARKETING DECISION SUPPORT SYSTEMS which incorporate databases, marketing modeling, and facilities for the user to communicate easily with the data and models. The easy communication allows improved interaction with databases and the inclusion of models and databases allows the user to ask "what if. . . . " questions and so raise analysis to a different level.

### Bibliography

Malhotra, N. K. (1993). *Marketing research: An applied orientation.* Englewood Cliffs, NJ: Prentice-Hall. Chapter 7.

O'Dell, W., Ruppel, A. C., Trent, R. H. & Kehoe, W. J. (1988). *Marketing decision making: Analytical framework and cases* (4th edn). Cincinnati, OH: South-Western Publishing Co.

MICHAEL GREATOREX

**marketing strategy** In essence, marketing strategy embraces the customer targets or segments and the means, in terms of the MARKETING MIX elements, to be employed for these. Foxall (1981), for example, regards marketing strategy as being an indication of how each element of the marketing mix will be used to achieve the marketing objectives. Some such as Kotler (1994) argue that corporate or business strategy should be heavily influenced by marketing, on the grounds that strategy is concerned with the match between the organization and its environment, and that marketing, because of its unique position at the interface between the organization and the environment, must therefore be a prime mover in strategy formulation. It seems reasonable that marketing should be regarded as having a perspective critical to strategic management because it is primarily concerned with operationalizing the MARKETING CONCEPT. However, the other functional activities, such as those concerned with technological development, must also take into account wider environmental considerations; while many activities (finance, manufacturing, logistics, research and development) all contribute to the development and achievement of wider corporate goals.

Others, such as Greenley (1986) take a more limited view of marketing strategy, arguing that it is operational, i.e., it is oriented towards implementing the overarching strategy of the organization. It is likely that marketing strategy is shaped by and also shapes overall CORPORATE STRATEGY.

Greenley (1993) suggests that marketing strategy has five elements: market positioning and segmentation, involving the selection of segments for each product market; product positioning, involving decisions on the number and type of products for each segment; the selection of the marketing mix; market entry – how to enter, re-enter, position, or reposition products in each segment; and the timing of strategy and implementation given that, as Abell (1978) argues, there are only limited periods during which the fit between key requirements of a market and the particular competencies of a firm competing in that market is at an optimum. The marketing strategy is likely to be modified according to different stages of the PRODUCT LIFE CYCLE.

### Bibliography

Abell, D. F. (1978). Strategic windows. *Journal of Marketing*, **42**, (3), 22–25.

Foxall, G. R. (1981). *Strategic marketing management.* London: Croom Helm.

Greenley, G. E. (1986). *The strategic and operational planning of marketing.* Maidenhead: McGraw-Hill.

Greenley, G. (1993). An understanding of marketing strategy. *European Journal of Marketing*, **23**, (8), 45–58.

Kotler, P. (1994). *Marketing management: Analysis, planning, implementation and control* (8th edn). Englewood Cliffs, NJ: Prentice-Hall. Chapter 3.

DALE LITTLER

**markets**  A market comprises all the individuals and organizations who are actual or potential customers for a product or service, and those in a market are involved in market exchange with companies and others providing goods and services.

Markets have several requirements. First, those in the market for a product or service must need the product; they must also have the ability to purchase the product, i.e., buying power, which can include credit purchase. In addition, they must be willing to use their buying power; and also have the authority to make purchase decisions, e.g., those under 18 years do not have authority in the UK to purchase alcohol.

Markets may be categorized as consumer markets, to include individuals and households who buy or acquire goods and services for personal consumption/use, i.e., for final consumption without further transactions; or organizational markets. Organizational markets comprise: producer or industrial markets, i.e., individuals or organizations buying goods and services for the purpose of manufacturing products; reseller markets (wholesalers and retailers) who buy finished goods and services and resell them; and government markets at local and national level where goods and services are bought to provide citizen services or, more broadly, to carry out government functions, e.g., defence, health, education, and welfare. Institutional markets, such as hospitals and schools, may be in the private as well as the government sector.

Finally, one can consider international markets which may embrace all the other types of markets.

BARBARA LEWIS

**Maslow's hierarchy of needs**  *see* CONSUMER NEEDS AND MOTIVES

**mass media**  Mass media are impersonal channels by which the communicator can communicate directly with the target audience. The major mass media are cinema, TELEVISION, RADIO, POSTERS, NEWSPAPERS and MAGAZINES. Although the communicator has a high degree of control over the content of the MESSAGE, mass media channels are relatively inflexible in that in general the message cannot be adapted to suit the particular requirements of the audience. They can often be seen to involve the imposition of a message on an audience, and they cannot be adapted to suit specific moods or relevant wants. The use of domestic video recorders enables consumers to be more discerning in their consumption of television advertising messages, while SELECTIVE EXPOSURE, selective perception, and SELECTIVE RETENTION can be powerful filtering processes affecting the effectiveness of mass media communications. Technological developments, such as advertising via the Internet, are already facilitating greater interactivity between the consumer and the communicator.

It may not be possible to aim communications at narrowly defined targets through mass media channels, because by definition these channels tend to have a wide appeal, although the readership of, for example, many magazines and the viewers of certain television programs and cinema films can be specialized. In the future, it is likely that the proliferation of cable, satellite, and terrestrial digital television will enable the targeting of specific clusters of consumers.

*See also* **Communications mix; Marketing communications**

DALE LITTLER

**media**  *see* MASS MEDIA

**media planning**  Media planning is concerned with the selection of the most appropriate media to deliver marketing communications messages to target audiences. Before making media plans, organizations should have decided on their target MARKETS and COMMUNICATIONS OBJECTIVES. Media selection may be affected by such factors as the desired REACH,

FREQUENCY, IMPACT, and continuity of advertisements. Overall, they wish to be cost-effective in their choice of media and so choices will be closely related to the relative costs of the available media.

*See also* **Advertising**

**Bibliography**

Rust, R. T. (1986). *Advertising media models: A practical guide.* Lexington, MA: Lexington Books.

DAVID YORKE

**media schedule** A media schedule is an operational activity which results from MEDIA PLANNING, designed to achieve particular objectives with respect to REACH, FREQUENCY, and IMPACT. The schedule relates to the timing of ADVERTISING expenditures which depends on the product/service, the stage in its life cycle, seasonality of purchase, and COMMUNICATIONS OBJECTIVES.

Macro scheduling relates to choices between schedules over a year or a season (e.g., with respect to tourism services), with allowances for lagged effects and advertising carry-over. Micro scheduling is concerned with allocation over a shorter period of time, and possible advertising timing patterns, namely, concentrated, continuous, or intermittent, which in turn relates to the rate at which new buyers appear in the market, purchase frequency, and forgetting rates.

In making media scheduling decisions, organizations are inevitably also concerned with the individual media costs of reaching target audiences (*see* COST PER THOUSAND) and, hence, to achieve a cost-effective mixture of reach and frequency of message exposure.

**Bibliography**

Crosier, K. (1994). In M. J. Baker (Ed.), *The marketing book* (3rd edn). Oxford: Butterworth-Heinemann. Chapter 21.

DAVID YORKE

**message** Message is central to the communication between the sender (the organization) and the receiver (the various publics) and captures the values that an organization wishes to convey to its various publics. Messages emanating from organizations – products, brands, and corporate identity – are expressions of their "corporate voice," of their heritage and personality and serve to differentiate and support their POSITIONING in the market place. The choice of the company name "Rockwater," for example, was chosen because "it implied strength and stability. It was substantial, appropriate internationally in the English-speaking offshore industry and did not have negative connotations in other languages. It sounded mature and authoritative and gave the impression that it had always been there" (Lee, 1991).

The message can be conveyed in various forms (or media), such as TV advertisements, printed leaflets, billboards, corporate identities, electronically via multimedia systems, Internet, and so on (*see* COMMUNICATIONS MIX). Regardless of the form used to convey the message and reach different publics, certain organizational values will be presented and perceptions and opinions of the organization formed by the publics it reaches. Levi advertisements, for example, reinforce the company's heritage and its American birthright, the product's quality and durability, as well as a progressive, youthful, and sexual image.

If the messages coming from an organization fail to match with expectations, then the publics may be confused and communication can be made more difficult. A recent example is Lever's "Persil Power" washing liquid which was launched as a safe and effective product. However, after numerous washes it was claimed that the innovative ingredient had a deleterious effect on certain fabrics. After a few months in the marketplace, the product was withdrawn but at significant cost, including a fall in MARKET SHARE of Persil products. Lever had then to build up the public's belief and trust that their existing products were effective and safe. Perrier had faced a similar situation when a potentially harmful ingredient was discovered and the product was withdrawn from the market. Again, the company had to regain the public's trust in the product.

**Bibliography**

Aaker, D. A. & Myers, J. G. (1987). *Advertising management* (3rd edn). Englewood Cliffs, NJ: Prentice-Hall. Chapter 11.

Dibb, S., Simkin, L., Pride, W. M. & Ferrell, O. C. (1994). *Marketing: Concepts and strategies* (European edn). Boston, MA: Houghton Mifflin Co. Chapter 15.

Lee, S. (1991). The Rockwater story. *Design Management Journal*, Winter, 22–28.

MARGARET BRUCE

**micro environment** The environment of an organization is generally viewed as comprising two components: the MACRO ENVIRONMENT and the micro environment which, unlike the former, consists of elements or activities with which the organization interacts directly and over which it can therefore exert influence, if not control. The major aspects of the micro environment are: competitors; SUPPLIERS; CHANNELS OF DISTRIBUTION; CUSTOMERS; and the media (*see* MASS MEDIA).

DALE LITTLER

**minitab** Minitab is a computer software package used to analyze data, including data obtained in MARKETING RESEARCH surveys. The components of the package concern data input, data modification, data analysis, presentation of results, and communication with other packages. The range of statistical procedures that can be specified is very large and includes all types of DESCRIPTIVE STATISTICS, HYPOTHESIS TESTING, UNIVARIATE ANALYSIS, BIVARIATE ANALYSIS, and MULTIVARIATE METHODS (ANALYSIS).

Bibliography

Miller, R. B. (1988). *Minitab handbook for business and economics*. Boston: PWS-Kent Publishing.

MICHAEL GREATOREX

**mission statement** The mission statement is generally presented as the first stage in the strategic planning (*see* MARKETING PLANNING; STRATEGIC PLANNING) process, depicted as consisting of a number of stages, although it may in fact be formulated at any time. Greenley (1986) suggests that the mission statement has several aims, including: to provide the purpose for the organization; to express the philosophy that will guide the business; to articulate the vision of where the firm will be in the future; to define the business domain, i.e., the customer groups and needs, and the technology to be employed; and to motivate employees by providing them with a clear sense of purpose and direction. Campbell & Tawadey (1992) have devised the Ashridge Mission Model which has four elements: purpose ("why the company exists"); strategy ("the commercial rationale" which embraces the business domain in which the firm is aiming to compete and the competitive advantages that it aims to exploit); standards and behaviors ("the policies and behavior patterns that guide how the company operates"); and values ("the beliefs that underpin the organization's management style, its relations to employees and other stakeholders, and its ethics"). Overall, the mission statement might be expected to provide answers to the questions posed by Drucker (1973): What is our business? Who is the customer? What is value to the customer? What will be our business? What should our business be? It is believed that the mission statement should be aspirational and provide a shared sense of purpose, thereby giving a focus for the efforts of all in the organization. It has various audiences, often with different requirements, including customers, shareholders, employees, and suppliers.

However, mission statements may often be general and bland, perhaps for fear of providing competitors with information about future strategies and because they need to appeal to different constituencies. They may also reflect what the company has been or is doing, rather than what it intends to do.

Bibliography

Abell, D. (1980). *Defining the business: The starting point of strategic planning*. Englewood Cliffs, NJ: Prentice-Hall. Chapter 3.

Campbell, A. & Tawadey, K. (Eds), (1992). *Mission and business philosophy*. Oxford: Butterworth-Heinemann. Chapter 1.

Drucker, P. (1973). *Management: Tasks, responsibilities, practices*. New York: Harper & Row. Chapter 7.

Greenley, G. E. (1986). *The strategic and operational planning of marketing*. Maidenhead: McGraw-Hill.

DALE LITTLER

**modified re-buy** Robinson, Faris & Wind (1967) suggest a division of organizational buying into three categories: NEW TASK, modified re-buy, and STRAIGHT RE-BUY. The category of modified re-buy refers to those occasions when there are significant differences in the terms of the purchasing contract under review (e.g., changes in price, technical specifications, delivery arrangements, packaging, design, quality). The significance of these differences might reflect changes in the customer's requirements (e.g., changed specifications or delivery arrangements), or in the customer's competitive position (e.g., entering new markets, developing improved products), or in a supplier's offerings (e.g., increased price, new product features), and will generally require a significant renegotiation of the contract though not usually a change of supplier.

**Bibliography**

Robinson, P. T., Faris, C. W. & Wind, Y. (1967). *Industrial buying and creative marketing.* Boston, MA: Allyn & Bacon.

DOMINIC WILSON

**multidimensional scaling** Multidimensional scaling is a generic name given to a number of procedures related to attitude and image research. Its main uses in marketing are in attribute mapping, product positioning, and finding ideal brand points. Two types of variables form the starting blocks for much multidimensional scaling: perceptions (of attributes, of similarities between brands, etc.); and preferences (e.g., between brands).

Brands are perceived by customers in terms of attributes, e.g., for cars the attributes could be performance, safety, size, style, country-of-origin, price, etc. Different brands may be perceived in different ways; brands can be represented on maps and some brands will be close together (hence, likely to be competing), while other brands will be apart. It may be possible to discover for individual buyers their ideal positions on these maps and hence, taken with the product map, predict which brand is likely to be purchased. The ideal point has another interpretation as an indicator of the importance of the dimensions identified. Gaps

in the offerings to the customers may be spotted, hence helping with the design of new products. Dimensions used in the maps indicate the attributes used by respondents to characterize the brands.

Different types of measurement scales include ratio, interval, ordinal, and categorical scales. The latter two scales are known as non-metric scales for obvious reasons. Another scale, known as an ordered metric scale, is used in the commonest type of multidimensional scaling. In an ordered metric scale, all possible intervals between positions on the scale are ranked.

Thus, one technique of multidimensional scaling requires all pairs of brands to be ranked in order of similarity. The brands on offer in a market are listed in pairs and the respondent has to say which pair is the most similar, the next most similar, and so on right down to the least similar. This information is fed into a computer, attribute maps are prepared showing the relative positions of the brands, and a metric measure of the similarities (or differences) between brands is obtained, even though originally the data were merely an ordered metric scale. It may take only two dimensions to map the brands, when it is easy to represent the maps graphically. When three or more dimensions are to be used, several two-dimensional graphs are prepared. The dimensions are not named; they have to be named by the researcher from the grouping of the brands and further knowledge of the brands' attributes. The dimensions identify the attributes used by the respondent to evaluate and compare the brands.

The ideal point can be discovered, based upon the respondent being able to rank the brands in order of preference either overall or on each of several attribute scales according to the program used. The maps, based on similarities data, are produced for each individual. The dimensions that are thrown up may differ from map to maIt is difficult to aggregate maps over individuals; this is unfortunate as it makes it hard to use the knowledge gained about ideal points to discover clusters of respondents with close ideal points. Usually, clustering takes place first; this is followed by obtaining a map to represent each cluster either for an average individual in each cluster, or based on averaging similarities data from each cluster. Ideal points for individuals in the cluster can be mapped in relationship to the positions of the brands on the map.

**Bibliography**

Green, P. E., Carmone, F. J. & Smith, S. M. (1989). *Multidimensional scaling: Concepts and applications.* Boston, MA: Allyn & Bacon.

MICHAEL GREATOREX

**multivariate methods (analysis)** Multivariate methods of data analysis involve the consideration of relationships between more than two variables and as such extend UNIVARIATE ANALYSIS and BIVARIATE ANALYSIS of data. Multivariate methods require the use of computer-based statistical analysis packages such as the STATISTICAL PACKAGE FOR THE SOCIAL SCIENCES, or SPSS, and MINITAB.

The best-known methods are Multiple Regression (*see* REGRESSION AND CORRELATION) which seeks to find the relationship between a dependent variable and several independent variables, PRINCIPAL COMPONENT ANALYSIS and FACTOR ANALYSIS which are looking for interrelationships within a set of variables, DISCRIMINANT ANALYSIS which seeks the best combinations of variables to discriminate between groups of respondents, CLUSTER ANALYSIS which is a range of grouping techniques, MULTIDIMENSIONAL SCALING which is used to obtain perceptual maps of how customers perceive brands, and CONJOINT ANALYSIS which can be used to obtain indirect evaluations of the utilities of product attributes. STRUCTURAL EQUATION MODELS (or latent variable path models) bring together the many parts the MARKETING RESEARCH effort and the software, such as LISREL, PROC CALIS, or EQS, used to estimate the parameters of these models can be seen as superseding in a holistic way some of the multivariate methods mentioned above.

**Bibliography**

Hair, J. F., Anderson, R. E. & Tatham, R. L. (1987). *Multivariate data analysis* (2nd edn). New York: Macmillan. Chapter 1.

MICHAEL GREATOREX

# N

**natural environment**   The natural environment is one of the elements of the MARKETING ENVIRONMENT. This aspect is concerned with ecological issues such as trends in the availability of raw materials and energy, and increasing measures to protect the natural environment.

*See also* **Environmental analysis**

DOMINIC WILSON

**needs**   *see* CONSUMER NEEDS AND MOTIVES

**negotiation**   It has been argued that customer/supplier negotiations have traditionally tended to be part of a "zero-sum game" and that an advantage for one side (e.g., a discount) was "won" through a disadvantage for the other (Dion & Banting, 1988). This is, of course, an oversimplified view of the complex field of customer/supplier negotiations and there would have been many exceptions to this exaggeratedly aggressive picture of negotiation. Nevertheless, this image seems to have had a powerful influence on the sales negotiation literature, much of which has focused on techniques for manipulating customers into sales agreements which, by definition, they would otherwise have negotiated further or even declined. A more sophisticated view of marketing negotiation now prevails whereby "win-win" situations are sought in which both supplier and customer gain from negotiation. An example of this mutually beneficial approach is the idea of long-term customer/supplier partnerships (*see* SUPPLIERS) where commitment and trust on both sides replace the traditional image of suspicion and hostility. In reality, different circumstances and personnel will require different negotiating styles and this has always been the case. The fundamental principle remains that effective negotiation depends not just on skill and techniques but on understanding the position of all parties involved – a principle which lies at the heart of marketing more generally.

**Bibliography**

Carlisle, J. & Parker, R. (1990). *Beyond negotiation.* Chichester: John Wiley.
Dion, P. A. & Banting, P. M. (1988). Industrial supplier–buyer negotiations. *Industrial Marketing Management*, 17, (1), Feb., 43–48.
Fisher, R. & Brown, S. (1988). *Getting together: building a relationship that gets to Yes.* Boston, MA: Houghton Mifflin Co.
Lancaster, G. & Jobber, D. (1985). *Sales technique and management.* London: Pitman.
Lidstone, J. B. J. (1991). *Manual of sales negotiation.* Aldershot: Gower.
McCall, I. & Cousins, J. (1990). *Communication problem solving.* Chichester: John Wiley. Chapter 6, 89–115.

DOMINIC WILSON

**net margin**   Net margin (generally expressed as a percentage) refers to the excess of sales revenues over cumulative costs, after subtracting fixed costs but before taking account of any extraordinary, exceptional, or non-product-related issues.

*See also* **Margin**

DOMINIC WILSON

**network**    The research of the IMP (Industrial Marketing and Purchasing) Group of researchers into European buyer–seller PURCHASING relationships has developed the concept of interaction (*see* INTERACTION APPROACH) whereby supplier–customer relationships are understood in terms of a set of evolving and mutually-dependent exchanges bound not only by commercial logic but also by factors of social and operational "comfortableness." The IMP research evolved from studies of procurement practices between suppliers and customers in European industrial markets where the importance of an informal network of personal contacts was quickly recognized as crucial to the day-to-day work of procurement personnel. At a more aggregated level, organizations in a market will share many such relationships in what can be analyzed as a network of bilateral and multilateral relationships (Håkansson & Snehota, 1989). It may even be useful to define organizational markets in terms of the common factors shared by a network of organizational relationships rather than the more usual simplistic reference to products or services. More recently, the network concept could be seen as an important stimulus to research interest in issues of interorganizational collaboration and strategic alliances (*see* INTERNATIONAL STRATEGIC ALLIANCES), e.g., in terms of NEW PRODUCT DEVELOPMENT (Håkansson, 1987) and technology management (Håkansson, 1990).

*See also* **Relationship marketing**

**Bibliography**

Håkansson, H. (1987). Product development in networks. In H. Håkansson (Ed.), *Industrial technological development – A network approach* (pp. 84–128). London: Croom Helm. (Also (abridged) in D. Ford (Ed.), *Understanding business markets: Interaction, relationships and networks.* (pp. 487–507). London: Academic Press.)

Håkansson, H. (1990). Technological collaboration in industrial networks. *European Management Journal,* 8, (3), 371–9.

Håkansson, H. & Snehota, I. (1989). No business is an island: The network concept of business strategy. *Scandinavian Journal of Management,* 4, (3), 187–200.

DOMINIC WILSON

**new product development**    New product development, or NPD, "is the process that transforms technical ideas or market needs and opportunities into a new product that is launched onto the market" (Walsh et al., 1992, 16). New products can make a profound contribution to competitiveness and this is particularly acute in an era of accelerating technological change, general shortening of the PRODUCT LIFE CYCLE, and increasingly intense competition. The most common representation of the NPD process is as a series of decision stages or activities (Kotler, 1984, 5th edn). Cooper & Kleinschmidt (1986) identify 13 stages of the NPD:

(1)  screening of new product ideas;
(2)  preliminary market assessment;
(3)  preliminary technical assessment;
(4)  detailed market study/market research;
(5)  business/financial analysis;
(6)  physical product development;
(7)  in-house product testing;
(8)  customer tests of product;
(9)  test market/trial sell;
(10) trial production;
(11) pre-commercialization business activities;
(12) production start-up; and
(13) market launch.

However, the traditional sequential model of NPD has been criticized for ignoring the interactions that occur between the stages and the interactions between different departments, as well as with external agencies, such as customers and suppliers (Hart, 1995). The uncertainties of NPD are recognized and relate to both market uncertainties and technological uncertainties (*see* UNCERTAINTY). The more radical the NPD, then the greater the difficulty in making ex ante assessments of the technical and market opportunities. A considerable amount of research has been devoted as to how to improve the likelihood of new product success. However, there is little agreement as to what constitutes "success," and various indicators have been used, such as different financial measures and different units of analysis, which means that direct comparison of the results of separate studies is not feasible. Nonetheless, some themes have emerged from the different studies that appear to have some bearing on the positive outcome of NPD. These include: people factors, such as commitment of senior managers (Maidique & Zirger, 1984); organizational factors, e.g., effective interfunctional cooperation (Pinto & Pinto, 1990); and operational factors, such as the use of market research (Johne & Snelson, 1988). Marketing has been identified as having a significant role. Rothwell (1977) points to the role of marketing and publicity and of understanding "user needs," and Cooper (1994) notes the value of having a "strong market orientation and customer focus." The constant interaction of R&D, design, production, and marketing from the very early stages of NPD to market launch have been associated with success (e.g., Cooper & Kleinschmidt, 1986). The presence of a "PRODUCT CHAMPION" has also been acknowledged as a "success" factor. Product development is not always about new products – product modifications, extensions, and style change are also aspects of product development.

To devise, produce, and implement new products and modifications to existing products entails input from different functions, notably marketing, R&D, and production. Their input has to be integrated to ensure that products are made that correspond with customer needs and are made economically and without time delays. Different approaches to the management of product development activities have been identified. "Over the wall" refers to a functionally divided organization wherein product ideas are continually passed back and forth between functions, so that marketing undertakes some development work, then passes this onto R&D which carries out more development and then passes the ideas back to marketing, and so on. This process can mean that the idea stays in development for a long time. A different approach is that of the "rugby scrum" whereby product development teams are formed with representatives from each function, all of which make an ongoing contribution to the product's development. This organizational approach can facilitate a quicker time to market than the "over the wall" approach (Walsh et al., 1992).

Different functions may not communicate easily with one another and the interface between R&D and marketing, in particular, has received attention (Gupta, Raj, & Wileman, 1995). A recent study found that effective interface between marketing and design was likely to occur in organizations with a culture of openness, close location of marketing and design functions and a multidisciplinary team approach to product development (Davies-Cooper & Jones, 1995).

## Bibliography

Cooper, R. G. (1994). New products: The factors that drive success. *International Marketing Review*, 11, (1), 60–77.

Cooper, R. G. & Kleinschmidt, E. J. (1986). An investigation into the new product process: Steps, deficiencies and impact. *Journal of Product Innovation Management*, 3, (1), 71–85.

Davies-Cooper, R. & Jones, T. (1995). The interfaces between design and other key functions in product development. In M. Bruce & W. Biemans (Eds), *Product development: Meeting the challenge of the design–marketing interface.* Chichester: John Wiley.

Gupta, A. K., Raj, S. P. & Wileman, D. (1985). R&D and marketing dialogue in high-tech firms. *Industrial Marketing Management*, 14, 289.

Hart, S. (1995). Where we've been and where we're going in new product development research. In M. Bruce & W. Biemans (Eds), *Product development: Meeting the challenge of the design–marketing interface.* (Chapter 1) Chichester: John Wiley.

Johne, F. A. & Snelson, P. (1988). Marketing's role in successful product development. *Journal of Marketing Management*, 3, (3), 256–268.

Kotler, P. (1984). *Marketing management: Analysis, planning and control.* (5th edn). Englewood Cliffs, NJ: Prentice-Hall. Chapter 10, p. 309.

Maidique, M. A. & Zirger, B. J. (1984). A study of success and failure in product innovation: The case of the US electronics industry. *IEEE Transactions on Engineering Management*, EM-31, (4), Nov., 192–203.

Pinto, M. B. & Pinto, J. K. (1990). Project team communication and cross functional co-operation in new program development. *Journal of Product Innovation Management*, 7, 200–212.

Rothwell, R. (1977). The characteristics of successful innovations and technically progressive firms (with some comments on innovation research). *R&D Management*, 7, (3), 191–206.

Walsh, V., Roy, R., Bruce, M. & Potter, S. (1992). *Winning by design: Technology, product design and international competitiveness.* Oxford: Basil Blackwell. Chapters 1 & 5.

MARGARET BRUCE

new task   Robinson, Faris & Wind (1967) suggest a division of organizational buying into three categories: new task, MODIFIED RE-BUY, and STRAIGHT RE-BUY. Of these categories, new task is the most complex and refers to those occasions when it is necessary to identify new sources for goods or services. This may be because a previous source is no longer satisfactory, or because the requirement itself is new. In principle, all stages of the PURCHASING PROCESS will be involved in new task buying but in practice this will depend on the scale and significance of the purchase in question. Thus, new task purchasing in the defence sector (e.g., for an aircraft carrier) might take years, whereas new task purchasing for ballpoint pens (e.g., in a bank) might be done very quickly.

### Bibliography

Robinson, P. T., Faris, C. W. & Wind, Y. (1967). *Industrial buying and creative marketing.* Boston, MA: Allyn & Bacon.

DOMINIC WILSON

newspapers   Newspapers are a communications medium (*see* COMMUNICATIONS MIX), usually using print but they are also being developed via the Internet. Newspapers can be local, regional, national, or international in terms of readers and distribution; and are usually published daily or weekly. They are a major ADVERTISING medium, the main advantages for which are: mass, regular, coverage of major target groups; geographical flexibility through regional editions; positioning opportunities; and very short lead times. However, some newspapers have limited regional flexibility and they have limited opportunities for color, which is expensive, and presentation (i.e., creative scope); poor reproduction quality; a short life; and are less intrusive than other media, e.g. TELEVISION. Further, measurement of newspaper "readership" as opposed to "the number of copies sold" is difficult.

DAVID YORKE

noise   Noise usually refers to physical disturbance to a communication MESSAGE during the process of its transmission. For example, a member of the SALES FORCE may be interrupted during a presentation, readers of MAGAZINES or NEWSPAPERS may be distracted, and, more broadly in the market place, any one MARKETING COMMUNICATIONS technique has to compete for space in a buyer/customer/consumer's mind with all others.

### Bibliography

Schramm, W. (1971). How communication works. In W. Schramm & D. F. Roberts (Eds), *The process and effects of mass communication.* Urbana, IL: University of Illinois Press.

DAVID YORKE

non-price factors   Products are bought for a variety of reasons relating to cost, convenience, BRAND LOYALTY, and quality of the alternatives. Products compete on the basis of price and non-price factors. The non-price factors are those related to the quality and DESIGN of a product, such as reliability, performance, appearance, safety, and maintenance ("intrinsic" non-price factors); and those related to the quality of the service offered by the manufacturer or supplier, such as delivery time, after-sales service, and availability of spare parts ("associative" non-price factors) (Saviotti et al., 1980). Non-price factors, such as the environmental impact of the product, can influence consumers. Price factors include financial arrangements for purchase or hire, depreciation, running costs, servicing and parts costs as well as the sales price after discount. If two products of similar quality are on sale for different prices, the theory is that a rational purchaser will choose the cheaper product. However, this choice will be influenced by brand loyalty, company image, and advertising, which affect the consumer's perception of quality and price. Several studies have investigated purchasers' decisions to assess the relative importance of price and non-price factors and it is clear that non-price factors affect purchase decisions but these vary from market to market. Rothwell's (1981) study of agricultural machinery, for example, showed that even where British products were cheaper, farmers were in favor of more expensive, often imported, products on grounds of superior reliability and technical features. Moody (1984) indicated in his study of medical equipment that technical, aesthetic, and ergonomic features were all reasons for doctors' preferences when choosing such products.

*See also* **Competitive advantage; Product differentiation**

### Bibliography

Moody, S. (1984). The role of industrial design in the development of new science-based production. In R. Langdon (Ed.), *Design policy, vol. 2: Design and industry*. London: Design Council.

Rothwell, R. (1981). Non-price factors in the export competitiveness of agricultural engineering goods. *Research Policy*, **10**, 260.

Saviotti, P., Coombs, R., Gibbons, M. & Stubbs, P. (1980). Technology and competitiveness in the tractor industry. A Report of the Department of Industry. Department of Science and Technology Policy, University of Manchester, UK.

Walsh, V., Roy, R., Bruce, M. & Potter, S. (1992). *Winning by design: Technology, product design and international competitiveness*. (Chapter 2, pp. 64–68). Oxford: Basil Blackwell.

MARGARET BRUCE

**not-for-profit marketing**   Not-for-profit marketing is part of "non-business" marketing (together with SOCIAL MARKETING) which relates to marketing activities conducted by individuals and organizations to achieve some goal other than ordinary business goals of profit, market share, or return on investment. Marketing concepts and techniques can be applied to not-for-profit organizations in both the public and private sectors and includes, for example: government agencies, health care organizations, educational institutions, religious groups, charities, political parties, performing arts.

For example, universities facing increasing costs may use marketing to compete for both students and funds, e.g., defining markets better, improving their communication and promotion, and responding to needs of students and other publics. One of the main characteristics of many not-for-profit organizations is that their support does not come directly from those who receive the benefits which the organization produces, e.g., funding for students' education comes from student fees, government sources, endowments, industry sponsorship, research grant awarding bodies.

### Bibliography

Blois, K. J. (1994). Marketing for non-profit organisations. In M. J. Baker (Ed.), *The marketing book*. London: Heinemann.

Christy, R. (1995). The broader application of marketing. In G. Oliver (Ed.), *Marketing Today*. (Chapter 24, pp. 500–527). Hemel Hempstead, UK: Prentice-Hall.

BARBARA LEWIS

# O

**observation** Observation is a method of collecting data on a topic of interest by watching and recording behavior, actions, and facts. Informal, unstructured, observation is an everyday means of collecting marketing information. However, planned observation is likely to produce better information than casual observation. Observation can in fact be structured or unstructured, with disguised or undisguised observers, in a natural or a contrived setting, using human and/or electronic/mechanical observers.

Observation is used instead of, or in conjunction with, surveys involving interviews utilizing questionnaires or depth interviews. Observation is less suitable than interview techniques for measuring attitudes, needs, motivations, opinions, etc., except where the subjects being studied are unable to communicate verbally, e.g., children and animals. Observation is unsuitable for studying events that occur over a long period of time or that are infrequent or unpredictable when an excessive amount of time and money may be required to carry out the research. Observation is suitable for traffic counts, for packaging experiments, for retail audits, etc., where data are more economically gathered through observation than through interviews. Sometimes data are collected by observation and through questionnaires and the results compared.

Structured observation is used when a problem has been defined precisely enough for there to be a specification of the behavior and actions to be studied and the ways in which the actions will be coded and recorded. Unstructured observation is used in exploratory research where the problem has not been identified and where the observer has less guidance about what to note and record.

Structured observation implies prior knowledge of the subject under study, of hypotheses to be tested, or inferences to be made. For this latter reason, trained human observers may be preferred to mechanical observers as a human observer can make such inferences in a way that a machine cannot. Perversely, this is a potential weakness of the method, relying as it does on the subjective and possibly biased judgement of the observer.

In disguised observations the subjects do not know that they are being observed. Disguised observations are used in order to overcome the tendency for subjects to change their behavior if they know that they are being watched. Mystery shopping, where observers take on the role of store or bank customers in order to assess the level of service offered by sales staff, is one example of disguised observation. Other examples of disguised observation include the use of two-way mirrors or hidden cameras. Undisguised observations include the measurement of TV audiences based on a sample of households in which on-set meters record when a TV set is in use and to which channel it is tuned.

Sometimes it is possible to study behavior in natural settings. Counting how many people turn right and how many turn left at the top of an escalator in a department store can be done in a natural setting. Likewise, the effect of new point of sale display material for a product may be studied by observing the sales of the product in a supermarket by counting the numbers in stock at the beginning and at the end of a period and adjusting for additions to stock; this is observation research done in a natural setting. However, the researcher often wants to control for intervening variables by researching in a laboratory, which is obviously an unnatural setting. As well as controlling intervening variables, laboratory research allows stimuli to be invoked and response measured in situations where occurrences of the stimulating event in real life might be uncommon. This is one way in which laboratory research can be a quick way of obtaining data. Laboratory research also permits easier use of electronic and mechanical devices to record behavior.

Among the electronic and mechanical devices that are used to record behavior are those that record physiological changes in subjects when they are subject to stimuli. For example, the galvanometer is used to measure the emotional arousal of subjects exposed to advertising copy by measuring the changes in electrical resistance caused by the sweating that is brought on by emotional arousal. The eye camera records eye movements of subjects looking at newspaper advertisements. Other electronic/mechanical devices include the on-set meters used to measure TV audiences and the scanners that are used by panels of shoppers to read the bar-codes on their purchases.

### Bibliography

Malhotra, N. K. (1993). *Marketing research: An applied orientation*. Englewood Cliffs, NJ: Prentice-Hall. Chapter 7.

MICHAEL GREATOREX

**off the page**   Off the page is a technique for communication or selling using catalogs (either print or electronic) to which a buyer/customer responds directly in person, in writing, or by telecommunication (*see* DIRECT MARKETING; INBOUND COMMUNICATIONS). The number of responses may be used as a prima facie measure of the cost-effectiveness of the activity, and the names of respondents may be entered onto a DATABASE in order to build a profile of likely future buyers/customers for specific products or services who then may be targeted more precisely.

**offering**   Marketing has traditionally differentiated between products and services (*see* SERVICE CHARACTERISTICS). The PRODUCT has been viewed as consisting of a bundle of tangible and intangible attributes. Thus, Littler (1984) suggests that a product has three dimensions: the core, consisting of the essential benefit or service; the tangible product, including the color, taste, design, brand name, and packaging; and the augmented product, such as the back-up service, warranty, and delivery. The "product," then, is a set of benefits, many of which can be seen as involving service, offered to the customer. Firms can be viewed as making an offering of a package of values to customers, rather than selling a pure service or physical product. In some cases, especially in organizational markets, firms will act as "problem solvers" and provide complete systems (the design, development, installation, and implementation of, for example, management information systems) (*see* SYSTEMS MARKETING).

### Bibliography

Littler, D. A. (1984). *Marketing and product development*. Oxford: Philip Allan. Chapter 6.

DALE LITTLER

**one step flow model**   The one step flow model of communications presents mass communications (*see* MASS MEDIA), mainly ADVERTISING, as acting directly on each member of the target audience. This often-called "hypodermic needle" model of communications (the communication passing directly to individual members of the audience) contrasts markedly with the TWO STEP FLOW MODEL, which depicts communications as being filtered through intermediaries called opinion leaders (*see* INTERPERSONAL COMMUNICATIONS). Many individuals are likely to receive information from mass communications, although SELECTIVE EXPOSURE, SELECTIVE PERCEPTION, and SELECTIVE RETENTION will act as filters. Mass communications may create awareness and even interest, but then further information may be sought or received through interpersonal channels, such as from opinion leaders (*see* INTERPERSONAL COMMUNICATIONS).

DALE LITTLER

**opinion leaders**   *see* INTERPERSONAL COMMUNICATIONS

opportunities  *see* SWOT ANALYSIS

**organizational buying behavior** The exchange relationship between BUYERS and sellers (*see* SUPPLIERS) has long been studied in the context of consumer markets and is now also recognized as being central to an understanding of organizational markets, though with significant differences. Research into organizational buying behavior has developed from an analysis of individual purchases in organizational markets, to an examination of the broader strategic implications of buyer/seller relationships and of the environmental, corporate, and personal influences permeating the purchasing context.

Much of the early research was concerned with attempts to develop models of organizational buying behavior and three models of organizational buying behavior are discussed here. For a concise review of this research see Parkinson & Baker, 1986 (especially Chapters 4, 5 & 7), while Turnbull provides a convenient discussion of the Sheth, Webster & Wind model, and interaction models (Turnbull, 1994). It should be noted that none of these "models" claims to be predictive; all three are attempts to describe a complex process as a necessary preliminary to further analysis. Consequently, it is difficult to "test" the theoretical status of these models.

Webster & Wind modeled the process as a set of four contextual influences (macro environment, organization, group, individual) with particular emphasis on the role of organizational culture and individuals as the ultimate decision-makers in the buying process (Webster & Wind, 1972). Although Webster & Wind present their model as a sequence with each area of influence leading progressively to the next, it is important to understand that the relationship between these influences is generally iterative rather than sequential. Sheth's (1973) model included the concept of multiple sources (*see* SINGLE/MULTIPLE SOURCING) and participants in a buying process which was acknowledged as having significant psychological aspects as well as rational aspects. Both the Sheth and the Webster & Wind models take the buying decision as the unit of analysis, yet much of the work undertaken by the IMP (Industrial Marketing and Purchasing) Group of researchers suggests that greater insights into the buying process may be available from taking the relationship between organizations as the unit of analysis (*see* INTERACTION APPROACH). The IMP research has developed a model of buying behavior in organizational markets as an interaction between individuals within organizations, conducted in an atmosphere formed by the context and experience of previous exchange episodes and surrounded by the macro-environmental features common to previous models (Håkansson, 1982; Campbell, 1985). In this presentation, decisions could be thought of as the "punctuation" in a continuing stream of interaction, and best understood in the long-term context of the relationship.

Arguably, there are also many contemporary macro-environmental and competitive dynamics which could be regarded as stimuli to inter-organizational relationships, such as acceleration of the widely recognized phenomena of globalization, increasing competition, environmental complexity (*see* MARKETING ENVIRONMENT), and escalating R&D costs. Under these pressures a routine purchasing relationship can evolve into a strategic alliance (*see* INTERNATIONAL STRATEGIC ALLIANCES), especially as the foundation for such relationships may have as much to do with mutual familiarity and trust as it does with strategic logic. This encourages a much wider understanding of the scope and significance of "buying behavior" in organizational markets than has generally been recognized and emphasizes the importance of understanding such relationships in their long-term dynamic and strategic context rather than, perhaps, as a series of recurring exercises in cost control. Research into the process of how such relationships develop over time, and the implications arising for MARKETING MANAGEMENT, are therefore increasingly relevant to organizations seeking to develop their competitiveness through strategic alliances.

Buyer–seller relationships in organizational markets are now accepted as a highly complex area and one of considerable strategic importance. Research continues into both these aspects: e.g., the work of Johnston & Bonoma (1981) examining the intricate dynamics and systems at work in the BUYING CENTER itself;

and Ford's (1984) further work arguing that skill in the management of such relationships can itself become a strategic asset and an important factor in the selection of interorganizational partners. Nevertheless, it is difficult to avoid the conclusion that research into organizational buying behavior seems to have been less productive than that into CONSUMER BUYING BEHAVIOR, perhaps because organizational buying is highly complex, difficult to categorize (other than simplistically), and explanations depend on many personal and contingent variables.

*See also* **Relationship marketing**

**Bibliography**

Campbell, N. C. G. (1985). An interaction approach to organizational buying behaviour. *Journal of Business Research*, **13**, (1), 35–48.

Ford, D. (1984). Buyer–seller relationships in international industrial markets. *Industrial Marketing Management*, **13**, (2), May, 101–112.

Håkansson, H. (Ed.) (1982). *International marketing and purchasing of industrial goods – An interaction approach*. New York: John Wiley.

Johnson, W. J. & Bonoma, T. V. (1981). The buying centre: Structure and interaction patterns. *Journal of Marketing*, **45**, Summer, 143–156.

Parkinson, S. T. & Baker, M. J. (1986). *Organisational buying behaviour: Purchasing and marketing management implications*. Basingstoke: Macmillan.

Sheth, J. N. (1973). A model of industrial buyer behaviour. *Journal of Marketing*, **37**, (4), Oct., 50–56.

Turnbull, P. W. (1994). Organizational buying behaviour. In M. J. Baker (Ed.) (1994). *The marketing book* (3rd edn). London: Heinemann, pp. 216–237.

Webster, F. E. Jr & Wind, Y. (1972). *Organizational buying behavior*. Englewood Cliffs, NJ: Prentice-Hall.

DOMINIC WILSON

**organizational marketing**    Organizational marketing can be thought of as the activity of marketing between organizations, as opposed to marketing between organizations and individual customers, usually referred to as CONSUMER MARKETING. However, such a simple clarification masks many problems of interpretation and definition. For example, the term "organization"

includes many groups which are not primarily concerned with generating profit, such as charities, political parties, military groups, local societies, hospitals, and so on.

It is worth highlighting two central issues in organizational marketing which have profound implications for marketing and for understanding organizations more generally. The first issue concerns organizational objectives (*see* STRATEGIC OBJECTIVES), the guiding light of marketing activities. With the increasing realization of how widely marketing can be applied to organizational activities, organizational devices can no longer be thought of in quite such straightforward terms as "profit maximization" or "shareholder asset growth." For example, it is clear that, at least in principle, charities are concerned with altruism, that orchestras have cultural objectives that armies aim at enforcement, and that government agencies are directed at efficient administration rather than generating profits. No doubt, many of these objectives are also applicable to conventional business organizations and their constituent sub-units. It is important to appreciate this multi-faceted and overlapping nature of organizational objectives because this kaleidoscope of objectives provides the direction and momentum for marketing activities.

The second issue is the importance of understanding relationships (*see* RELATIONSHIP MARKETING) between organizations as continuing interactions, rather than as an episodic series of encounters where "manipulative suppliers" engage with "suspicious customers" (Han et al., 1993). Understanding interorganizational relationships as continuing interactions (*see* INTERACTION APPROACH) is important not only to understanding organizations but also to understanding the competitive and strategic dynamics of markets (Håkansson & Snehota, 1989). While the idea of a collaborative interactive relationship is implicit in the idea of marketing as a mutually advantageous exchange, as Chisnall (1995) points out, marketing (more accurately "selling") in business markets has long been presented as an antagonistic zero-sum game where the customer's gain is the supplier's loss. This raises many conceptual and practical questions, not least of which is the difficulty of reconciling traditional views of organizational relationships as necessarily competitive with the increasing representation of these relationships as fundamentally mutually dependent and collaborative.

Both these issues are inextricably linked also with the role of the manager in STRATEGIC MANAGEMENT as an individual with personal objectives and discretionary power rather than, as seems to have been assumed in much of the marketing literature, as a strictly rational organizational servant routinely enacting corporate executive policies (Pettigrew, 1975).

It could be argued, therefore, that organizational marketing is not only an important aspect of marketing but also that it has raised issues with profound implications for a better understanding of marketing and of organizations more generally. In line with these developments in the understanding of the role of marketing, organizational marketing can be seen not simply as the marketing of products and services between organizations but more broadly as the management and development of EXCHANGE relationships between organizations.

As a rule, organizational markets are more complex and larger than consumer markets, if only because for every consumer market there are usually several upstream organizational markets manufacturing and supplying the products marketed to consumers. There are also many large and complex organizational markets providing services where conventional payment may not be involved (e.g., churches, charities, schools, hospitals) or where there may be no direct connection with consumers at all (e.g., military forces).

Another important distinguishing feature of organizational markets is the nature of DEMAND. Demand in organizational markets is derived from a combination of many factors, depending on the market in question. For example, in industrial markets demand is derived from the requirements of downstream suppliers of various consumer goods and services. In government markets demand may also be a function of political and legislative commitments, economic circumstances, political priorities, and lobbying. Forecasting this derived demand is, therefore, highly complex and depends on understanding the needs and circumstances not only of immediate organizational customers, but also of subsequent supplier/customer exchanges right down the

VALUE CHAIN to the eventual consumer. Inevitably, many organizations are unable to do much more than respond to the anticipated requirements of their immediate customers. One potentially useful approach to this problem of forecasting demand in organizational markets is to build particularly close relationships with selected customers in various key segments. There can, of course, be many other reasons for building such relationships but the advantage with respect to forecasting problems is that such relationships can provide intimate insights not otherwise available into the competitive position of strategic customers and so of their markets and customers more broadly. (*See also* RELATIONSHIP MARKETING.)

Much of the theory discussed above seems most obviously appropriate to the more important occasions of organizational marketing – to NEW TASK purchasing and major accounts, to complex customer requirements and intensely competitive markets. However, it should not be forgotten that much of organizational marketing is concerned with routine purchasing in relatively familiar circumstances and with few immediate implications for competitive positions or strategic dynamics. On such occasions the application of the processes and principles discussed above remains relevant but the practice of organizational marketing is more likely to reflect compromises based on experience, work priorities, and common sense.

### Bibliography

Chisnall, P. M. (1995). *Strategic business marketing* (3rd edn). Englewood Cliffs, NJ: Prentice-Hall.

Håkansson, H. & Snehota, I. (1989). No business is an island: The network concept of business strategy. *Scandinavian Journal of Management*, **4**, (3), 187–200.

Han, S-L., Wilson, D. T. & Dant, S. P. (1993). Buyer–supplier relationships today. *Industrial Marketing Management*, **22**, (4), Nov., 331–338.

Pettigrew, A. M. (1975). The industrial purchasing decision as a political process. *European Journal of Marketing*, **5**, Feb., 4–19.

DOMINIC WILSON

**organizational purchasing**   *see* ORGANIZATIONAL BUYING BEHAVIOR

**organizational segmentation**   The goal of organizational segmentation is to divide a large organizational MARKET into smaller components that are more homogeneous with respect to product needs. Griffith & Pol (1994) argue that segmenting organizational markets is generally a more complex process than segmenting consumer markets since: organizational products often have multiple applications, organizational customers can vary greatly from one another, and it is sometimes difficult to decide which product differences are important.

Bonoma & Shapiro (1984) identify a general approach to segmentation, characterized by ease of implementation, which reflects a major trend in and criticism of organizational segmentation studies. Recently, Dibb & Simkin (1994) have reiterated the complaint that selection of segmentation variables is related to the ease of implementation rather than to how valid the segments are in terms of grouping customers with similar requirements. While academics stress VALIDITY, the priority of the practitioner is often to identify segments which can be effectively targeted with a marketing program. In a recent survey of the variables which industrial marketers use in segmentation, the results suggest that variables are chosen more for convenience and actionability than for grouping purchasers with similar needs. The survey found that geographic segmentation bases were the most often used – by 88 percent of the sample. PSYCHOGRAPHICS, e.g., purchaser risk perceptions, were used by only 50 percent of companies, while the most theoretically sound and meaningful base, that of benefit segmentation, was used by only 38 percent of companies (Abratt, 1993). Bonoma & Shapiro (1984, 259) argue that: "Clearly a benefits-orientated approach is the more attractive in the theoretical sense, but more difficult for managers to implement . . . often management and researchers face an interesting 'segmentation tension' between the theoretically desirable and the managerially possible."

While it is acknowledged that any starting point for segmentation should be user requirements in the form of needs and benefits (*see* MARKET SEGMENTATION and SEGMENTATION VARIABLES), the discussion here focuses on the additional descriptor variables which are only used in organizational markets. These have been grouped into macro variables, based on organizational characteristics, and micro variables based on decision-making characteristics.

*Macro Variables*

These include standard industrial classification (SIC), organizational size, and geographic location. SIC describes an organization's main type of business, e.g., forestry, and is one of the most common variables used to describe business segments. Although this type of information is quite superficial, it is widely available in a standardized and comprehensive form and allows a firm to assess the potential size of a market segment. When using SIC codes, two cautions must be noted. First, all establishments with the same SIC code do not necessarily engage in the same activities. For example, in the grocery store category, large grocery stores sell more than just grocery items. Second, establishments in a given category do not necessarily account for all, or even a large proportion, of the activity in that category.

Organizational size data in terms of total sales volume or number of employees can easily be obtained and related to an organization's need for some products, e.g., insurance and health care plans which can be modified depending on the number of employees in an organization. However, size can be measured in many ways: total size, size by division, size and number of individual branches, sales value, asset value, other types of activity measure, and number of employees, which can sometimes be related tangentially to purchaser requirements. Dickson (1994) describes two "natural" organizational segmentation variables as being the size of the account and growth potential of the account. If an organization has much of its business with a relatively small number of clients, it cannot help but adopt a RELATIONSHIP MARKETING approach. Such individual relationship segmentation makes consideration of other broader segmentation variables somewhat redundant, but not all companies are in a position to adopt this relationship approach.

Geographic location can indicate purchaser needs when the industry itself is dependent upon the geography of the area, for example, coal mining and other natural resource industries. Purchasing practices and expectations of companies may also vary by location, e.g., in

Central and Eastern Europe. Convenient though it may be to use simple spatial geography to separate complicated purchasing practices or expectations, the variable used to segment the market in this case should be purchasing practice) not geographic location. Using simple geography as anything other than a descriptor variable can be problematic if further criteria are not specified. For example, which geographical location of the business should be used: the site of the buying office, where the products are received, or where they are used? As Griffith & Pol (1994) point out, the first is of concern to sales management, the second to logistics managers, and the third to field service people, installation crews, etc.

*Micro Variables*

These include choice criteria such as productivity and price. This is akin to benefit segmentation (*see* SEGMENTATION VARIABLES). DECISION-MAKING UNIT (DMU) characteristics identify the nature of the individuals within the DMU and the benefits they perceive. Different members within an organization may value different attributes and benefits. The type of purchasing structure in organizations can also be important, e.g., centralized purchasing is usually associated with purchasing specialists who become experts in buying a range of products.

*See also* **Market segmentation; Positioning**

**Bibliography**

Abratt, R. (1993). Market segmentation practices of industrial marketers. *Industrial Marketing Management*, **22**, 79–84.
Bonoma, T. V. & Shapiro, B. P. (1984). *Segmenting the industrial market.* Lexington, MA: D. C. Heath & Co.
Dibb, S. & Simkin, L. (1994). Implementation problems in industrial market segmentation. *Industrial Marketing Management*, **23**, 55–63.
Dickson, P. R. (1994). *Marketing management* (international edn). Orlando, FL: The Dryden Press.
Dickson, P. R. & Ginter, J. L. (1987). Market segmentation, product differentiation and marketing strategy. *Journal of Marketing*, **51**, 1–10.
Griffith, R. L. & Pol, L. G. (1994). Segmenting industrial markets. *Industrial Marketing Management*, **23**, 39–46.

VINCE MITCHELL

**original equipment manufacturer** An original equipment manufacturer (often abbreviated to OEM) is the original manufacturer of goods and components which are subsequently sold to be included within the products of a customer. Thus, OEM goods tend to be "invisible" to the eventual customer. An example would be the use of OEM diesel engine components in automobiles, or OEM microprocessors in washing machines.

DOMINIC WILSON

**outbound communications** Communications in DIRECT MARKETING may be either inbound (*see* INBOUND COMMUNICATIONS) or outbound. The former are initiated by the buyer/customer as a response to a stimulus received from INDIRECT COMMUNICATIONS in the media. Outbound communications are initiated by the supplier organization. The two principal techniques are DIRECT MAIL and TELEMARKETING. Each is designed to target members of a specific market segment and to communicate directly with them with the intention of obtaining a positive response. Evaluation of the cost-effectiveness of each of the techniques may be in terms of the number of positive responses, i.e., the volume, or value of sales ultimately generated.

**Bibliography**

Roberts, M. L. & Berger, P. D. (1989). *Direct marketing management.* Englewood Cliffs, NJ: Prentice-Hall.

DAVID YORKE

**outsourcing** This refers to the activity of purchasing goods or services from external sources, as opposed to internal sourcing (either by internal production or by purchasing from a subsidiary of the organization). In practice, the term tends to be used in connection with a purchasing decision to change from an internal source to an external source. For example, an organization may decide that in future it will "outsource" part of its distribution operation by purchasing distribution services from an organization specializing in this field. The advantages of "outsourcing" can include cost reduction (external sources may enjoy scale economies), access to specialist expertise, and greater concentration on an organization's "core competence" (by avoiding "peripheral" operations). The potential disadvantages of outsourcing can include reduced control over the operations involved and so less flexibility in responding to unexpected developments. It is, therefore, important to take into account both the strategic and the operational implications of outsourcing.

There has been a notable increase in the use of outsourcing during the 1980s and 1990s, for example in UK local government and health markets. It could be argued that this has arisen as a direct consequence of increasing competitive pressures which have forced organizations (often against their cultural predispositions) to outsource "uncompetitive" activities to external specialists and to focus on areas of more sustainable and profitable differentiated competence.

*See also* **Make/buy decision**

DOMINIC WILSON

**own branding**    This is the process whereby a product or service name is developed for or by a retailer for their exclusive use. In some cases the producer of a branded good will produce a similar product for a retailer giving it a different name as chosen by that retailer. In other cases the retailer may contract to have the product manufactured independently. Examples would include Marks and Spencer's "St Michael" range and Sainsbury's "Classic Cola."

Own brand goods are usually positioned in the market place to compete directly with the manufacturers' brands (often appearing next to them in the store) and may even have a very similar appearance and usage characteristics. In other cases stores may stock only their exclusive brands (e.g., Body Shop).

In pursuing such a marketing strategy the retailer may be attempting to create consumer loyalty for his brand and take market share from the competitors. This strategy may also raise the retailer's profile in the consumer's mind. In addition, own branding may allow a retailer to gain an advantage over competitors without own brand products as the perceived quality of own brands increases while still being offered to the customer at a price lower than manufacturers' brands. Dore (1976) recommends a 15 percent discount on similar branded goods.

Problems with an own brand strategy can include increased pressure on limited store display space, and the possible confusion of customers due to an abundance of very similar products.

**Bibliography**

Dore, B. (1976). Own labels – are they still worth the trouble to grocers? *Advertising and Marketing*, 13, (2), 58–63.

James, G. & Morgan, N. J. (Eds) (1994). *Adding value: Brands and marketing in food and drink.* London: Routledge.

STEVE WORRALL

# P

**packaging**  In the past, commodities were typically sold as loose items, the most widely used form of packaging was a paper bag, and packaging had a purely functional role, i.e., to protect the product. Today, however, the plethora of competing products from which the prospective buyer has to choose points to packaging's role in product promotion by communicating the product's features, benefits, and image. Yavas & Kaynak (1981) argue that an effective package design is a promotional tool and should: attract the prospective buyer, communicate rapidly and clearly, create a desire for the product, and trigger a sale. Southgate (1994) suggests that creative packaging adds value and helps to achieve brand preference. A badly designed package may communicate to the consumer that the product it contains is of low value. Conversely, a well-designed package is evidence of the care and attention that has gone into the product. A package has to sell the product at the point of sale and act as the sales tool in self-service environments.

## Bibliography

Southgate, P. (1994). *Total branding by design.* London: Kogan Page, p. 21.

Yavas, V. & Kaynak, E. (1981). Packaging: The past, present and the future of a vital marketing function. *Scandinavian Journal of Materials Administration,* 7, (3), 35–53.

MARGARET BRUCE

**Pareto's rule**  The 20/80 rule, attributed to the Italian economist and political philosopher, Vilfredo Pareto, suggests that 20 percent of the products/customers account for approximately 80 percent of the revenues/profits. The major customers or products might then act as a focus of the organization's activities, which begs the question of what to do with the often long tail of products or customers. Important and obvious criteria are whether or not the benefit to cost ratio of servicing customers or supplying products in the "tail" is or could be increased, and there are strategic reasons for retaining these customers or products in the PRODUCT MIX.

DALE LITTLER

**partnership sourcing**  There is considerable evidence to suggest that managing sourcing relationships as partnerships, whether upstream or downstream, can generate a significant COMPETITIVE ADVANTAGE for both partners (Johnston & Lawrence, 1988; CBI, 1991; Han et al., 1993; Lamming, 1993). Partnership sourcing refers to the practice of sourcing on an exclusive basis from a single supplier over an extended period of time and with extensive customer access to the operations and management systems of the supplier. This provides obvious benefits to the supplier in the guaranteed demand for their offerings to the customer. Customer benefits include the guarantees of fair prices, appropriate quality, and continuity of supply which are underwritten by the customer's access to the supplier's operational systems and accounts. Both organizations benefit from the increasing experience, mutual understanding, and personal relationships which develop as the partnership becomes established. Naturally, as with all collaborative relationships, these benefits may become "vulnerabilities" if one of the parties attempts to take advantage of the other. For many organizations the requirement to trust their suppliers or customers – often against a background of relatively antagonistic bargaining – can be a major psychological and cultural barrier to accessing the benefits of partnership sourcing. Partnership sourcing is more relevant to those markets where long-term guarantees of supply continuity are important and it is difficult to switch swiftly between sources, perhaps because of product complexity or scarcity or high competitive differentiation.

*See also* **Relationship marketing**

**Bibliography**

CBI (1991). *Partnership sourcing*. London: Confederation for British Industry.

Han, S-L. Wilson, D. T. & Dant, S. P. (1993). Buyer–supplier relationships today. *Industrial Marketing Management*, **22**, (4), Nov., 331–338.

Johnston, R. & Lawrence, P. R. (1988). Beyond vertical integration – The rise of the value-added partnership. *Harvard Business Review*, **66**, July–Aug., 94–101.

Lamming, R. (1993). *Beyond partnership*. Prentice-Hall.

DOMINIC WILSON

**payback**   Payback (or payback period) refers to the time taken to reach the break-even point (*see* BREAK-EVEN ANALYSIS) for the profitability of a particular product or service. Payback is reached when cumulative fixed and variable costs are matched by cumulated sales revenues and so is crucially influenced by PRICING decisions. Many organizations use payback as a key internal measure to prioritize alternative product/service offerings but there is a danger that this may encourage managers to plan unrealistic or short-term pricing policies.

DOMINIC WILSON

**penetration pricing**   Penetration pricing is the term used to describe a PRICING strategy whereby an organization uses a low price in marketing a new product so as to develop a large MARKET SHARE very quickly. For example, penetration pricing might be used by a new entrant aiming to develop a substantial competitive position in a market dominated by an established rival. Alternatively, the strategy might be used to launch a new product where the initial barriers to competitive entry were thought to be low and there was a risk of rivals developing imitative products quickly.

Following successful entry to a market using a penetration pricing strategy, price levels can subsequently be raised (e.g., where the price had been promoted as a temporary introductory DISCOUNT), although raising prices is often problematic and can generate undesirable market signals. More usually, prices set through a penetration policy are held largely unchanged and become profitable as unit costs decrease in line with the economies of scale made available through growing market share. Scale economies and capital investment requirements in production and distribution can then provide significant barriers to deter new entrants. Thus, the effect of successful penetration pricing is often to accelerate not only the rate of adoption (*see* ADOPTION PROCESS), but also the early stages of the PRODUCT LIFE CYCLE and the emergence of competitive market structures. Alongside these potential advantages, penetration pricing also carries the risks associated with commitment to relatively long-term policies (including reduced competitive flexibility). In short, penetration pricing is likely to be appropriate where there is widespread potential demand for the offering, where this demand can be accessed quickly by the supplier, where significant scale economies are available, and where rivals could otherwise develop imitative offerings promptly.

DOMINIC WILSON

**perceived risk**   The concept of perceived risk can be looked on as an extension of the general conceptual framework of the CONSUMER DECISION-MAKING PROCESS, which may be described as problem-solving activity in which a consumer attempts to identify product performance and psychological goals (*see* CONSUMER NEEDS AND MOTIVES) and to match them with products/brands. However, consumer decision-making involves risk in the sense that any action will produce consequences which cannot be anticipated with anything approaching certainty, and some of which are likely to be unpleasant. Consumers cannot conceive of all possible consequences and those which they are aware of they cannot anticipate with a high degree of certainty.

Consumers may be uncertain with respect to buying goals; their nature, acceptance levels, relative importance, and current levels of goal attainment. They may be uncertain as to which products/brands will best satisfy acceptance levels of buying goals, i.e., the problem of matching goals with purchases. Further, consumers may see adverse consequences if a purchase is made, or not made, and the result is a failure to satisfy buying goals. These consequences relate to: performance goals, i.e., functional ones; psychosocial goals; and the time, money, and effort invested to attain the goals. So one can refer to types of risk as: financial, which is a function of price, length of commitment to a product; social, related to visibility of a product; and physiological, e.g., to do with consumption and harmful physiological effects as with smoking. Roselius (1971) refers to time, hazard, ego, and money losses or risks.

Consumers develop strategies to reduce perceived risk so that they can act with relative ease and confidence in buying situations where information is inadequate and where the consequences of their actions are in some way unknown or incalculable. They either increase certainty (decrease uncertainty) by information handling, or decrease the amount at stake – i.e., the consequences which would occur. Typically, risk handling is largely concerned with dealing with uncertainty and so can be equated with information handling. In respect of buying goals and needs, consumers generate information needs and to satisfy them they acquire, process, and transmit information.

Information acquisition may be accidental or sought from marketer dominated channels, INTERPERSONAL COMMUNICATIONS, or from neutral sources – e.g., consumer reports. Information processing involves evaluation and decisions with respect to use, storage, and forgetting, followed by possible transmission of information to others. Alternatively, to reduce the consequences, consumers can reduce or modify their goals and expectations, avoid or postpone purchases, or purchase and absorb any unresolved risk.

Numerous strategies for reducing risk have been researched (see, e.g., Bauer, 1967; Cox, 1967; and Cunningham, 1967) and include: BRAND LOYALTY, to economize on effort, substitute habit for deliberate action/decision; reliance on advertising, to give confidence; consumer reports, to provide objective information – e.g., evidence of government or private testing; personal influence, e.g., word-of-mouth communication with those with experience of the product/brand; group influence, usually stronger when the wisdom of one's choice is difficult to assess; impulse buying, to suppress possible consequences from consciousness and rush through the buying process; store used, its image, reputation, and product range; most or least expensive brand; demonstration, e.g., test driving of cars; special offers; service, to include money-back guarantees and exchanges; reliance on well-known brands; and endorsements, e.g., testimonials from experts and personalities.

People use different styles in their choice between increasing certainty and decreasing the consequences of purchases, which depend on their buying goals, products under consideration, personality, and degree of buying maturity or experience. These may relate to: clarifying the purchase situation – typically reacting to ambiguity by seeking new information and increasing understanding; or simplifying – typically avoiding new information and relying on experience of other people.

## Bibliography

Bauer, R. A. (1967). Consumer behavior as risk taking. In D. F. Cox (Ed.), *Risk taking and information handling in consumer behavior*. Division of Research, Harvard Business School.

Cox, D. F. (Ed.) (1967). *Risk taking and information handling in consumer behavior*. Division of Research, Harvard Business School.

Cunningham, S. M. (1967). The major dimensions of perceived risk. In D. F. Cox (Ed.), *Risk taking and information handling in consumer behavior*. Division of Research, Harvard Business School.

Roselius, T. (1971). Consumer rankings of risk reduction methods. *Journal of Marketing*, **35**, Jan., 56–61.

Taylor, J. W. (1974). The role of risk in consumer behavior. *Journal of Marketing*, Apr., 54–60.

BARBARA LEWIS

**personal influence**  *see* INTERPERSONAL COMMUNICATIONS

**personal selling**  Personal selling is the process of informing customers and potential customers and persuading them to purchase products and services through oral personal communication in an exchange situation, either face to face or on the telephone (*see* TELE-MARKETING). It is a two-way channel of communication (*see* MARKETING COMMUNICA-TIONS) which has a number of advantages: customers can inquire, discuss, or even bargain; there is immediate, interactive response; a company can get feedback; and the company can relate to specific consumer needs. Personal selling aids in the cultivation of buyer–seller relationships (*see* RELATIONSHIP MARKETING), especially in organizational buying (*see* ORGANI-ZATIONAL BUYING BEHAVIOR).

The characteristics and personality of sales people is important, in particular because persuasion techniques, including the use of inducements, may be relevant. Customers may see personal selling activities as biased and react negatively to their obligation to listen and to persuasion techniques, etc. It is an expensive form of communication, and potential customers may not always be accessible.

Personal selling takes place in the home, in stores and other organizations (i.e., in business-to-business interactions) and involves the SALES FORCE and sales persons who as well as providing information may be active in tasks such as order taking, delivery, and market research.

*See also* **Communications mix; Marketing communications; Sales management**

**Bibliography**

Dalrymple, D. J. & Cron, W. L. (1995). *Sales management: Concepts and cases.* New York: John Wiley.

Lidstone, J. (1994). In M. J. Baker (Ed.), *The marketing book* (3rd edn). Oxford: Butterworth-Heinemann. Chapter 19.

DAVID YORKE

**personality**  Personality refers to those characteristics that account for differences among people and are predictive of their behavior. Such differences evolve from heredity, personal experience, and environmental influence. Personality includes intelligence but is usually defined as accounting for non-cognitive behavior, referring chiefly to emotional and social qualities together with drives, sentiments, and interests – characteristics significant in daily living and social interactions. Personality is usually described in terms of traits such as self-confidence, dominance, autonomy, deference, sociability, defensiveness, and adaptability. In understanding personality and its resulting impact on consumer product and brand choice, media preferences, etc., various frameworks have been considered; these include Horney's classification of compliant, aggressive, and detached people (Horney, 1958), and Reisman's typology of tradition, inner and other-directed people (Reisman et al., 1960). Further, numerous research investigations have focused on consumer personality and product/brand choice (e.g., Cohen, 1967; Kassarjian, 1971; Alpert, 1972; Villani & Wind, 1975; and Kassarjian & Sheffet, 1991).

**Bibliography**

Alpert, M. I. (1972). Personality and the determinants of product choice. *Journal of Marketing Research*, **9**, Feb., 89–92.

Cohen, J. B. (1967). An interpersonal orientation to the study of consumer behavior. *Journal of Marketing Research*, **4**, Aug., 270–278.

Engel, J. F., Blackwell, R. D. & Miniard, P. W. (1990). *Consumer behavior* (6th edn). Orlando, FL: The Dryden Press. Chapter 12.

Foxall, G. R. & Goldsmith, R. E. (1994). *Consumer psychology for marketing.* London: Routledge. Chapter 6.

Horney, K. (1958). *Neurosis and human growth.* New York: Norton.

Kassarjian, H. H. (1971). Personality and consumer behavior: A review. *Journal of Marketing Research*, Nov., 409–418.

Kassarjian, H. H. & Sheffet, M. J. (1991). Personality and consumer behavior: An update. In H. H. Kassarjian & T. S. Robertson (Eds), *Perspectives in consumer behavior* (pp. 281–303). Englewood Cliffs, NJ: Prentice-Hall.

Loudon, D. L. & Della Bitta, A. J. (1993). *Consumer behavior* (4th edn). McGraw-Hill Int. Chapter 9.

Reisman, D, Glazer, N. & Denney, R. (1960). *The lonely crowd*. New Haven, CT: Yale University.

Schiffman, L. G. & Kanuk, L. Z. (1991). *Consumer behavior* (4th edn). Prentice-Hall. Chapter 4.

Villani, K. E. A. & Wind, Y. (1975). On the usage of "modified" personality trait measures in consumer research. *Journal of Consumer Research*, 2, Dec., 223–226.

BARBARA LEWIS

**physical distribution**   *see* CHANNELS OF DISTRIBUTION

**PIMS**   *see* PROFIT IMPACT OF MARKETING STRATEGIES

**planning style**   Planning is traditionally associated with a process (*see* STRATEGIC PLANNING; SWOT ANALYSIS) which involves formal analysis of the organization and its environment and the development of appropriate means of meeting the objectives which the organization has established. There are some major advantages of planning per se. Quinn (1978) suggests that planning imposes a discipline on managers to look ahead periodically; results in communication of "goals, strategic issues, and resource allocation;" and helps the implementation of strategic changes. It provides a baseline against which to assess performance, while as Loasby (1967) notes, the major value of formal planning "is in the raising and broadening of important issues that are liable otherwise to be inadequately considered."

One possible pitfall of much planning is to extrapolate into the future without taking account of possible discontinuities. Some would suggest that UNCERTAINTY undermines much formal planning, although this would point to the necessity of engaging in CONTINGENCY PLANNING and of ensuring that the plans have scope for flexibility to take account of the unexpected. Mintzberg (1973) suggests that planning is one of three possible strategic modes (*see* ADAPTIVE STRATEGY; ENTREPRENEURIAL STRATEGY) and is most appropriate for stable environments.

**Bibliography**

Loasby, B. J. (1967). Long range formal planning in perspective. *The Journal of Management Studies*, 4, Oct., 300–8.

Mintzberg, H. (1973). Strategy making in three modes. *California Management Review*, 16, (2), Winter, 44–53.

Quinn, J. B. (1978). Strategic change: "Logical Incrementalism". *Sloan Management Review*, 1, (20), Fall, 7–21.

DALE LITTLER

**point of purchase**   Point of purchase is the place at which the purchase (by an individual or a group) of a product or service is made. This may be, for example, in the home, in a retail store, or at a place of work. In terms of MARKETING COMMUNICATIONS, it is argued that the most effective techniques to be used at the point of purchase are PERSONAL SELLING, SALES PROMOTION, and PACKAGING, as each can have a direct and immediate impact on the decision to purchase. Some ADVERTISING (usually in retail stores) may also be used, although its effectiveness is difficult to measure.

**Bibliography**

Kotler, P. (1994). *Marketing management: Analysis, planning, implementation and control* (8th edn). Englewood Cliffs, NJ: Prentice-Hall. Chapter 24.

Quelch, J. A. & Cannon-Bonventre, K. (1983). Better marketing at the point of purchase. *Harvard Business Review*, 61, Nov.–Dec. 162–169.

DAVID YORKE

**political environment**   The political environment is one of the elements of the MARKETING ENVIRONMENT. This aspect is concerned with political developments such as new and proposed legislation at local, national, regional, and global levels, as well as attempts to influence such regulatory developments through lobbying and disseminating information.

*See also* **Environmental analysis**

DOMINIC WILSON

**portfolio analysis** In marketing, portfolio analysis is used at both a business and a product level, but the discussion here will be in terms of businesses. The aim is to assess the current mix of businesses in terms of balance of, for example, growing as against maturing businesses. Portfolio analysis techniques generally prescribe the actions to be taken with regard to these businesses, such as, invest, abandon, etc.

The most popular framework for portfolio analysis is that proposed by the Boston Consulting Group (*see* BCG MATRIX) which classifies businesses in terms of two major parameters (relative MARKET SHARE and market growth). Other analytical frameworks which employ a composite of variables have subsequently been developed, although essentially they all have the same end in view: of providing an easily employable means of evaluating a mix of businesses and prescribing the courses of action to be adopted.

Two of these, the Shell directional policy matrix and the A. D. Little competitive position-industry maturity matrix, are reviewed in Abell & Hammond (1979) and Hofer & Schendel (1978). The limitations of these approaches are discussed in Day, 1977 and Wensley, 1981. Some criticisms made are that: strategy aimed at securing a high market share regardless of context is questionable; there are difficulties in defining the market, and the cut-off points to decide between "high and low" of market share and growth; and the approaches focus on generalized strategic recommendations which might stifle creative solutions.

### Bibliography

Abell, D. F. & Hammond, S. (1979). *Strategic market planning*. Prentice-Hall, 213–219.

Day, G. (1977). Diagnosing the product portfolio. *Journal of Marketing*, 41, Apr., 29–38.

Hofer, C. W. & Schendel, D. (1978). *Strategy formulation: Analytical concepts*. St Paul, MN: West Publishing.

Wensley, R. (1981). Strategic marketing: Betas, boxes or Basics. *Journal of Marketing*, 45, 173–182.

DALE LITTLER

**positioning** In an attempt to emphasize the non-product aspects of positioning, Ries & Trout (1982) define it as: "not what you do to the product. Positioning is what you do to the mind of the prospect." Ries & Trout's focus on the end product of positioning strategies, namely, the "position" the product holds in the minds of consumers, brings to the fore Kelly's work (1955) on the idiosyncratic way in which people see the world. Recently, Marsden & Littler (1995) have argued that only in terms of the consumers' own construing of products will marketers find meaningful "units" of segmentation, and it remains important that marketers define, categorize, and describe products from the consumers' point of view. However, psychological positioning must be supported by the reality of the product otherwise the positioning created by other elements of the MARKETING MIX will be undermined by the use experience and will not be sustainable in the long term.

When developing a positioning strategy, marketers need a good understanding of how their product differs from others. Kotler (1991) suggests that differences should be: (1) important to a sufficient number of buyers; (2) distinctive, i.e., the difference is not offered in the same way, or at all, by competitors; (3) superior to others in achieving the same/more benefit; (4) communicable and visible to buyers; (5) difficult to copy; (6) affordable to the target market; (7) profitable and possible for the company to engineer.

Few products are superior to their competitors on all their attributes. What is required is that they differ on key dimensions that are important to the target customers. Some marketers advocate promoting only one benefit – a unique selling proposition or USP, since buyers tend to remember "number one" messages better than others – particularly in today's over-communicated society (Reeves, 1960; Ries & Trout, 1982). Others believe that it is possible to employ a double-benefit positioning strategy, e.g., Volvo is positioned on two benefits, safety and durability. One of the main advantages of using benefit or need-based segmentation is that it is the most useful in determining the positioning strategy. If other variables, e.g., age, are used initially, at some stage the marketer needs to return to benefits in order to effect a positioning strategy. When deciding which position to adopt, a company should promote its major strengths, provided that the target market values these strengths.

To overcome the problem that many companies face of how to unlock the psychological grip which large brands have on the market, a company can: strengthen its own position with the message of "because we're number two we try harder;" unlock new unoccupied positions which are valued by consumers; and deposition or reposition the competition, e.g., identify a competitor's weakness through comparative advertising (Ries & Trout, 1982). A further strategy is the "exclusive club strategy." Since people tend to remember number one, it is important to become number one on something. What counts is to be number one on some valued attribute, not necessarily size. However, if the number one position along a meaningful attribute cannot be achieved, a company can promote the idea that it is one of, for example, the Big Three in the industry. The idea was first used by the third largest US car manufacturer Chrysler, although the concept can be extended to any reasonable number (below ten) in any industry where there is some justification for it in the industry's structure (Kotler, 1991).

Occasionally, products will require repositioning because of changing customer tastes and/or poor sales performance. Jobber (1995) identifies four repositioning strategies: (1) *image repositioning*, where the product is kept the same in the same market, but its image is altered via changes to the COMMUNICATIONS MIX. This is akin to what Ries & Trout (1982) view as positioning and is the purest form of repositioning proposed by Jobber as it focuses solely on changing perceptions, not the reality of a product, in consumers' minds; (2) *product repositioning* in which the product is adapted to meet the needs of the target market more closely; (3) *intangible repositioning* which involves a different market segment being targeted with the same product, e.g., Lucozade's attempts to target sporty young adults; (4) *tangible repositioning* when both target market and product are changed.

*See also* **Market segmentation; Segmentation variables**

**Bibliography**

Jobber, D. (1995). *Principles and practice of marketing.* Maidenhead: McGraw-Hill. Chapter 7, 200–233.

Kelly, G. A. (1955). *The psychology of personal constructs*, vols 1 and 2, New York: Norton.

Kotler, P. (1991). *Marketing management: Analysis, planning, implementation and control* (7th edn). Englewood Cliffs, NJ: Prentice-Hall. Chapter 10, 262–277.

Marsden, D. & Littler, D. (1995). *Product construct systems: A personal construct psychology of market segmentation.* Association for Consumer Research Conference, Copenhagen, June.

Reeves, R. (1960). *Reality in advertising.* New York: Knopf.

Ries, A. & Trout, J. (1982). *Positioning: The battle for your mind.* New York: Warner Books.

VINCE MITCHELL

**posters**    Posters, or street advertising hoardings, are the principal medium of outdoor ADVERTISING, and they are targeted at those people who are thought to pass by them. They are one element in the marketing COMMUNICATIONS MIX and are used, for example, to provide visual support for other media (e.g. TELEVISION) or to achieve long-term exposure.

Posters have public visibility, cover a high percentage of the population, are able to reach the light television viewer, are geographically (i.e., regionally) highly flexible, provide repeated exposure, are relatively low cost (i.e., COST PER THOUSAND reached), and can be changed quickly.

However, they are not suitable for complex advertising (e.g., there are limitations to the length of the MESSAGE which may be communicated), coverage is wasted in terms of the audience reached (i.e., specific targets are not possible), audience selectivity is limited, there may be site control by town planning authorities, and measurement of (sales) effectiveness is virtually impossible.

DAVID YORKE

**potential demand**    *see* DEMAND

**predatory pricing**    Predatory pricing is where heavy discounting (*see* DISCOUNT) is used as a deliberate attempt to drive out competition with a view to achieving a subsequent monopoly situation where prices can be raised to exploitative levels. Predatory pricing is illegal in many countries, although it can sometimes be difficult to distinguish unambiguously between vigorous discounting (e.g., in "price wars") and more unethical or illegal practices such as dumping and predatory pricing.

DOMINIC WILSON

**pressure groups**   *see* CONSUMERISM

**price discrimination**   Price discrimination is where different prices are charged to different customers. There are many reasons why it may be necessary to vary the price of a particular product or service, though this practice can sometimes seem inequitable and so may be resisted by customers and avoided by suppliers. Important variables which can affect costs and so provide a basis for reasonable price discrimination include: the costs of distribution to differing markets, the shelf life of the product in different climatic conditions, discounting for volume, the need for incentives to ease supply management, the imposition of local taxes, and the adoption of SKIMMING PRICING or PENETRATION PRICING strategies in new markets. There can also be considerable variation in price sensitivity and demand within the market for a particular offering which may lead to variation in pricing (Shapiro et al., 1991) although the ruthless exploitation of vulnerable demand through inflated prices (profiteering) is both unethical and illegal in many countries.

*See also* **Discount; Price elasticity**

**Bibliography**

Shapiro, B. P., Rangan, V. K., Moriarty, R. T. & Ross, E. B. (1991). Managing customers for profits (not just sales). In R. J. Dolan (Ed.), *Strategic marketing management* (pp. 307–319). Boston, MA: Harvard Business School.

DOMINIC WILSON

**price elasticity**   Price elasticity refers to the effect on demand of changes in price and is similar to the concept of price-sensitivity. In elastic (or price-sensitive) markets a small change in price can result in a large change in demand (e.g., interest rates in money markets), whereas in inelastic (or price-insensitive) markets even substantial changes in price tend to have relatively little effect on demand (e.g., luxury goods). Traditionally, inelastic demand has been seen as typical of "basic" needs such as food, health, housing, and education but it is notable that in all these cases the element of inelasticity refers only to aggregated demand and there can be very considerable price elasticity within subsections of these markets (e.g., respectively, for delicacies, health insurance, mansions, private education). The elasticity (or price-sensitivity) of demand may also be affected by variables such as the availability of product alternatives, variants, and substitutes, or the availability of product prerequisites (e.g., driving lessons, petrol supplies, and spare parts for would-be motorists) (Reibstein & Gatiguan, 1984). The concept of price elasticity continues to be important in many markets and even small price changes can have significant consequences for consumer loyalty (e.g., supermarket groceries, newspapers). The following formula can be used to estimate price elasticity:

Price elasticity of demand = % change in demand / % change in price

**Bibliography**

Hanssens, D. M., Parsons, L. J. & Schultz, R. L. (1990). *Market response models: Econometric and time series analysis.* Boston, MA: Kluwer Academic Publishers.
Hoch, S. J., Kim, B.-D., Montgomery, A. L. & Rossi, P. E. (1995). Determinants of store-level price elasticity. *Journal of Marketing Research*, **32**, (1), Feb., 17–29.
Reibstein, D. J. & Gatiguan, H. (1984). Optimal product line pricing: The influence of elasticities and cross elasticities. *Journal of Marketing Research*, **21**, (3), 259–267.

DOMINIC WILSON

**price leadership**   Where an organization is able to exert considerable influence (whether active or tacit) over rivals' PRICING decisions then it is said to be the price leader. This influence is often a reflection of a dominant

MARKET SHARE (as with IBM in mainframe computer markets during the 1960s and 1970s) but it can result from other factors such as reputation for quality (Marks & Spencer clothing) or reputation for value (MFI furniture). Where a group of suppliers together dominate a market in an effective oligopoly (as with petrol retailing, sports shoes, broadcasting) then they may exercise price leadership collectively (though one or two of them may well be more influential than the others) and this might have to be regulated by government or independent administrators to avoid price collusion and unfair practices.

DOMINIC WILSON

**price promotions** Some pricing decisions involve a short-term adjustment to the price of an existing product/service, possibly prompted by disappointing sales caused by an economic downturn, competitors' activities, seasonality, etc. Such adjustments should be made using an estimate of price elasticity, i.e., how much will sales volumes change with a change in price and what will be the likely contribution margin, i.e., the difference between price and average variable cost? Price promotions need not result in a net profit increase in the short term – they may be used to attack competitive offerings. However, price promotions must be used with care. While they might have a beneficial short-term effect, their continuing use may demean the product/service in the mind of the customer/buyer.

*See also* **Pricing; Pricing methods; Pricing objectives**

**Bibliography**

Day, G. S. & Ryans, A. B. (1988). Using price discounts for a competitive advantage. *Industrial Marketing Management*, 17, (1), Feb., 1–14.
Wilcox, J. B., Howell, R. D., Kuzdrall, P. & Britney, R. (1987). Price quality discounts. Some implications for buyers and sellers. *Journal of Marketing*, 51, (3), July, 60–70.

DAVID YORKE

**price sensitivity**   *see* PRICE ELASTICITY

**pricing** At its simplest, price is the value placed on that which is exchanged between a supplier and a customer. However, price is a highly complex and multi-faceted issue, reflecting the complexity of EXCHANGE processes. For example, price can be expressed in many different forms – rent, royalties, interest rates, taxes and gratuities are all forms of "price" – and need not be expressed in monetary terms at all (as in barter, or countertrade). It could be argued that pricing is the most important of the MARKETING MIX elements since the price an organization sets for its offerings will play a large part in determining an organization's revenues, profitability, and competitiveness. Whereas this is a useful reminder of the significance of pricing, it should also be understood that no single element of the marketing mix can be isolated from the mix as a whole in terms of its effects and significance. Thus the factors, objectives, and strategies relevant to pricing will also be relevant to other aspects of the mix and, indeed, to other functional aspects of the organization's operations.

Management decisions concerning price should reflect PRICING OBJECTIVES which in turn should be consistent with the overall objectives of marketing strategies (*see* MARKETING STRATEGY) and of business and corporate strategies (*see* CORPORATE STRATEGY). Pricing decisions are arrived at, in principle, through PRICING METHODS and can result in prices which are high, low, or neutral with respect to rival offerings, costs, or customer perceptions. To illustrate the complexity of objectives and strategies in pricing, consider the example of a product which may be priced well above the cost of its production and distribution though well below that charged by less efficient rivals and yet still be perceived by potential customers as being poor value (perhaps because of weak promotional strategies). Many organizations will find it necessary to adopt a range of pricing strategies, reflecting differences among the products in their portfolio of offerings, while also attempting to ensure a degree of consistency, perceived fairness, and competitiveness in pricing necessary to generate profit and satisfy customers. It is this mix of complex, and sometimes conflicting, dynamics which makes pricing so difficult and so important.

Much of the specialist literature on pricing refers to consumer products and relatively little attention has been paid to pricing issues in the contexts of organizational markets (Laric, 1980), services markets (Schlissel & Chasin, 1991), or international marketing (Lancioni, 1989). Nevertheless, there are several well-established and excellent general guides to the theory and practice of pricing (e.g., Nagle, 1987; Gabor, 1988; Winkler, 1989), while a convenient brief review of the literature is provided by Diamantopoulos (1991).

### Bibliography

Cohen, S. S. & Zysman, J. (1986). Countertrade, offsets, barter, and buybacks. *California Management Review*, **28**, Winter, 41–56.

Diamantopoulos, A. (1991). Pricing: Theory & practice – A literature review. In M. J. Baker (Ed.), *Perspectives on marketing management*, Vol. 1. Chichester: John Wiley.

Gabor, A. (1988). *Pricing: Concepts and methods for effective marketing* (2nd edn). Aldershot: Gower.

Korth, C. M. (Ed.) (1987). *International countertrade.* New York: Quorum Books.

Lancioni, R. A. (1989). The importance of price in international business development. *European Journal of Marketing*, **23**, (11), 45–50.

Laric, M. V. (1980). Pricing strategies in industrial markets. *European Journal of Marketing*, **14**, (5/6), 303–321.

Monroe, K. B. (1973). Buyers' subjective perceptions of price. *Journal of Marketing Research*, **10**, Feb., 70–80.

Nagle, T. T. (1987). *The strategy & tactics of pricing: A guide to profitable decision-making.* Englewood Cliffs, NJ: Prentice-Hall.

Schlissel, M. R. & Chasin, J. (1991). Pricing of services: An interdisciplinary review. *Service Industries Journal*, **11**, (3), July, 271–286.

Winkler, J. (1989). *Pricing for results.* London: Heinemann Business Paperbacks.

DOMINIC WILSON

**pricing methods**   "Pricing methods" refer to the methods by which prices are decided for any particular product or service. There is an important distinction to be made between price decisions for existing offerings and those for new offerings. Setting the price for an existing (or "established") product is relatively straightforward as substantial market data are often available (reflecting customer response to previous price levels). However, it should be recognized that not all organizations collect such data rigorously, nor is it always easy to isolate the effect of price variation from shifts in other elements of the MARKETING MIX. It is also the case that even established offerings can experience sudden changes in the market environment (*see* MARKETING ENVIRONMENT) which can undermine the relevance of previous data and so question long-standing pricing policies – e.g., in times of economic recession; or at the launch of rival offerings; or when there are dramatic changes in legislation, technology, or consumer expectations.

Nevertheless, the pricing of new products is generally more complex than that of established products as crucial issues such as cost, demand, and competitive response are likely to be relatively unfamiliar. The problems of setting prices for innovative offerings can be so complex that sometimes these decisions are, in effect, intuitive and heuristic (Oxenfeldt, 1973). However, three more rigorous methods have also been identified for determining prices for relatively new products and services: cost-plus pricing, demand-based pricing, and going-rate pricing, each of which is discussed below.

The cost-plus pricing method is an approach which, with deceptive simplicity, sums the costs incurred in producing and distributing a good, adds an appropriate profit margin (or mark-up) according to company policy, and so generates an appropriate price (also known as mark-up pricing). A significant variant of this approach is rate-of-return or target return pricing which adds in to these calculations the cost of the capital investment involved in production and distribution, aiming to fix a price which will yield a target rate of return on this investment. This variant is more typical of those occasions when substantial investment is required for the development, production, and launch of a new product or service, resulting in particular priority to achieving a prompt return on such investment. The problem with such an approach to pricing is that it makes assumptions about DEMAND and competitive response which can be frail, especially for a new product or service (one might consider the UK Channel Tunnel as an example here). An interesting reversal of this target return approach, which responds to these problems, is that of target costing, favored by some Japanese multinational suppliers of consumer goods. This approach reverses the stream of calculations mentioned above, starting not with the costs but with what is thought to be an appropriate price. The desired profit margin is then deducted leaving a figure to cover all costs. The issue then is whether or not the offering can be produced and marketed within these costs.

The calculation of these prices is based on the following crude formulae:

> Cost-plus or Mark-up price = unit cost / (1 − % markup)
>
> [where Unit cost = variable cost + (fixed cost/forecast unit sales)]
>
> Target return price = unit cost + ((% target return x capital invested) / forecast unit sales)

While ensuring an important priority to cost issues, cost-plus pricing methods have a number of difficulties. First, it can be surprisingly difficult to allocate all relevant costs to individual product variants, even where a standard cost accounting system is already in use. Some costs can only be allocated very approximately (e.g., production, inventory, customer service, central administration, R&D, strategic planning, multiple product, or non-specific promotions). Second, this approach takes no account of the discounting (see DISCOUNT) and competitive flexibility which provide the area of discretion necessary for negotiating contracts in organizational markets. Third, the approach takes no direct account either of competitive offerings or of the price sensitivity of demand (see PRICE ELASTICITY). And fourthly, costs can vary considerably over time yet it is impractical (and undesirable) constantly to vary price. Nevertheless, the approach is useful for its apparent reasonableness (assuming appropriate margins), its focus on cost control, and its compatibility with existing management accounting systems.

The second fundamental approach is that of the demand-based pricing method which uses a mix of market research, managerial experience, and intuition to arrive at a price which, it is assumed, reflects demand. Here too, there are

problems. First, the assessment (at best) reflects demand prior to the introduction of the new product which is, presumably, differentiated from previous offerings in some significant way. This problem can be anticipated to some extent through MARKET RESEARCH techniques (such as focus groups, price recall tests, and buyer response surveys) and by TEST MARKETING. Second, difficult assumptions have to be made about the future response not only of demand but also of competitors. Third, demand is often influenced by qualitative factors such as self-image or risk tolerance, factors which may not easily be registered in the quantitative terms necessary for pricing decisions. Fourth, demand-based prices in consumer markets can only reflect an aggregate assessment of demand since it would be impractical in most cases to vary prices for each purchase in response to the specific motivations and circumstances of individual customers (an important exception here is pricing by auction). In organizational markets, the individual nature of many supplier–customer relationships makes it possible (even common) to adjust prices in response to specific demand. So consumer prices cannot usually reflect demand directly, even if this could be measured accurately. And fifth, the widespread market and competitive research required by this approach can be costly and time-consuming (and may risk leaking news of the product to rivals). Despite these difficulties, the demand-based pricing method is likely to ensure that priority is given to the customer's perspective.

A third method of determining prices for new products is one which seeks to minimize competitive disruption by setting prices which are thought to reflect what might be the going rate for a parallel product or service. This is sometimes also referred to as imitative pricing. Relatively few "new" products or services are completely different to anything already on the market and most will compete, in effect, with existing alternatives or substitutes. By setting prices in line with such established offerings it may be possible to sidestep some of the problems of assessing price-sensitivity to new products (see PRICE ELASTICITY) while also perhaps avoiding immediate competitive response. Prices can subsequently be adjusted to reflect observed demand for whatever differentiating features may be offered by the new product. It may well be sensible to avoid provoking strong competitive responses during the initial, vulnerable, stages of a new product's life cycle, especially perhaps where the extent of differentiation is not immediately apparent or involves significant changes in customer learning.

The three main methods of pricing discussed above reflect the three principal problems of determining prices for new products – uncertainty about costs, demand, and competitive response. Cost-based pricing focuses on costs and assumes that demand and competitive response are predictable; demand-based pricing focuses on customer response while paying relatively little attention to cost or rivals; going-rate pricing prioritizes maintaining the competitive status quo over issues of cost or demand. All approaches have difficulties and advantages and all should ideally be considered when making pricing decisions (Gabor, 1988).

A fourth method of setting prices is also worth mentioning: hedonic pricing or perceived value pricing (Kortge & Okonkwo, 1993). This is an interesting approach originating from the field of economics which regards products and services as "clusters of desirable attributes" and attempts to allocate a "price" component to each attribute such that the eventual price calculation is the sum of the hedonic price components. For example, a washing machine may merit different price components according to such variables as its spin speed, the time taken by its wash cycles, the availability of economy settings, the strength of its brand, the ease of servicing, its appearance, its power consumption, and so on. Statistical REGRESSION AND CORRELATION analysis of existing washing machines can identify the apparent price which the consumer seems prepared to pay for these attributes in existing washing machines and so new models can be designed and priced accordingly (Hartman, 1989). This approach presents problems in researching consumer response to genuinely innovative attributes and in its apparent disregard for cost issues, but the concept seems useful, especially perhaps in high-price mature consumer markets such as white goods, cars, furniture, holidays, and housing.

Sensible pricing decisions will, of course, draw on all four pricing methods (Tellis, 1986) though perhaps with a mixture of formal and more intuitive methodologies which will reflect not only the logic of the products/services and their anticipated markets, but also the culture of the organizations involved and the personal preferences of individual decision-makers. As with all organizational decision-making processes, it would be foolish to ignore the sociopolitical dynamics and personal interests which are likely to be powerful factors affecting the individual decision-makers involved.

## Bibliography

Cooper, R. & Kaplan, R. S. (1988). Measure cost right: Make the right decisions. *Harvard Business Review*, 66, Sept.–Oct., 96–103.

Gabor, A. (1988). *Pricing: Concepts & methods for effective marketing* (2nd edn). Aldershot: Gower.

Hartman, R. S. (1989). Hedonic methods for evaluating product design and pricing strategies. *Journal of Economics & Business*, 41, (3), Aug., 197–212.

Kortge, G. D. & Okonkwo, P. A. (1993). Perceived value approach to pricing. *Industrial Marketing Management*, 22, (2), May, 133–140.

Nagle, T. T. (1987). *The strategy and tactics of pricing*. Englewood Cliffs, NJ: Prentice-Hall.

Nagle, T. T. (1993). Managing price competition. *Marketing Management*, 2, Spring, 36–45.

Oxenfeld, A. R. (1973). A decision-making structure for price decisions. *Journal of Marketing*, 37, Jan., 48–53.

Smith, G. E. & Nagle, T. T. (1994). Financial analysis for profit-driven pricing. *Sloan Management Review*, 35, (3), Spring, 71–84.

Tellis, G. J. (1986). Beyond the many faces of price: An integration of pricing strategies. *Journal of Marketing*, 50, Oct., 146–160.

DOMINIC WILSON

**pricing objectives** An organization might have many objectives in determining its pricing policies. Some of the more typical pricing objectives include: ensuring continuity of cash flow (encouraging attention to PAYBACK period); increasing market share (favoring low price strategies such as PENETRATION PRICING; maintaining the competitive status quo (favoring neutral pricing strategies and a focus on non-price competition); and, of course, achieving sufficient profit to offset the costs and risks involved in making the offering available. Finally, in times of economic or competitive difficulty the prime objective of organizations may simply be to survive, resulting in pricing policies such as MARGINAL PRICING which would not normally be considered. It is particularly important that pricing objectives be consistent with the objectives of other elements of the MARKETING MIX, e.g., a product priced to imply quality and prestige (such as a perfume or a liqueur) would seem absurd if promoted and packaged as a commodity product. Equally, the pricing objectives should be consistent with the STRATEGIC OBJECTIVES of the business and the organization as a whole, for example, a supermarket aiming to appeal to a wide range of customers would offer some products such as coffee or beer in several forms (economy, premium, luxury) with different levels of quality and price.

### Bibliography

Marn, M. V. & Rosiello, R. L. (1992). Managing price: Gaining profit. *Harvard Business Review*, 70, Sept.–Oct., 84–94.
Oxenfeldt, A. R. (1973). A decision-making structure for price decisions. *Journal of Marketing*, 37, Jan., 48–53.

DOMINIC WILSON

**pricing process**   In theory, the pricing process can be represented as having several interconnected but distinguishable "stages," though in practice it will rarely be appropriate to go through all of these stages completely except on the most elaborate and important occasions of new task purchasing (*see* Corey, 1991 for a concise overview). According to this theoretical and idealized model, the pricing process starts with the identification of PRICING OBJECTIVES (derived from strategic marketing objectives), then analyzes the level of DEMAND and PRICE SENSITIVITY in the target market, while also analyzing the relevant cost structure and profit expectations, and evaluating rival offerings, before selecting an appropriate pricing policy (such as PENETRATION PRICING or SKIMMING PRICING), and an actual set of prices for the product range. In effect there are four broad and overlapping phases in this "process": first, the setting of objectives; second, the analysis of costs, demand, rival offerings,

potential profits, and the development of varying scenarios to test the assumptions involved; third, the determination of specific prices and the degree of discretion to be associated with each nominal price; fourth, the monitoring and (if necessary) adjustment of the pricing decisions compared to assumptions concerning demand and competitive response. It would, of course, be sensible to assume that this pricing process was a seamless part of the product development and marketing process rather than a discrete sequence.

### Bibliography

Corey, E. R. (1991). Pricing: The strategy and process. In R. J. Dolan (Ed.), *Strategic marketing management*. Harvard Business School, 253–269.

DOMINIC WILSON

**primary data**   Primary data are collected specifically to address a particular research issue. Primary data are required when SECONDARY DATA are unavailable or insufficient. They are more likely to be used in the later decision-making stages of a research project. Primary data are collected about such things as the demographic, socioeconomic, psychographic, and lifestyle characteristics of the subjects of research as well as their attitudes, opinions, awareness, knowledge, intentions, motives, and behavior. Methods of collecting primary data are set out in the section on PRIMARY RESEARCH.

### Bibliography

Churchill, G. A. (1991). *Marketing research: Methodological foundations* (5th edn). Chicago: The Dryden Press, 305–314.

MICHAEL GREATOREX

**primary research**   Primary research collects data (*see* PRIMARY DATA) specifically to address a particular research issue. The broad categories of methods of collecting primary data are qualitative (*see* QUALITATIVE RESEARCH) and quantitative, which can be broken down into OBSERVATION, surveys (*see* SURVEY RESEARCH) involving the questioning of respondents, and experiments (*see* EXPERIMENTATION).

Qualitative methods include DEPTH INTERVIEWS, FOCUS GROUPS, and PROJECTIVE TECHNIQUES and are often used in exploratory research. Surveys use structured questionnaires to obtain the desired information, usually from a sample of the population of interest. The questionnaires may be administered personally by an interviewer, in the street or in the home or using the telephone; alternatively a computer or the postal system may be used. Responses are numerically analyzed using computer statistical packages.

Both qualitative methods and surveys aim to obtain information on respondents' attitudes, opinions, motives, etc., with unstructured (qualitative methods) or structured (surveys) interviews. Qualitative methods are aimed at discovering the hidden or underlying factors that more direct methods may not reveal.

OBSERVATION is a method of collecting data on a topic of interest by watching and recording behavior, actions, and facts.

EXPERIMENTATION is a type of primary marketing research in which the experimenter systematically manipulates the values of one or more variables (the independent variables), while controlling the values of other variables, to measure the effect of the changes in the independent variables on one or more other variables (the dependent variables).

Primary research may be done on an ad hoc basis, where the data are collected from the respondents once only, or continuously, where data are collected from the same respondents on a regular basis. Examples of continuous research include CONSUMER PANELS, members of which keep diaries about their purchases, TV audience measurement by the Broadcasters' Audience Research Board (BARB), and retail audits. One advantage of continuous research is the opportunity to observe trends.

**Bibliography**

Churchill, G. A. (1991). *Marketing research: Methodological foundations* (5th edn). Chicago: The Dryden Press. Chapter 7.

MICHAEL GREATOREX

**principal component analysis** Principal component analysis and FACTOR ANALYSIS are two closely associated multivariate statistical techniques. Principal component analysis attempts to represent the interrelationships within a set of variables; it tries to reduce the number of variables required to represent a set of observations.

The method first finds the linear function of the variables with the largest variance, so that this newly created artificial (or latent) variable represents as much as possible of the variability in the original data. It then chooses a second linear function, independent of the first principal component, which explains as much as possible of the remaining variability in the original data. This continues until one chooses to stop the process. The idea is to account for the variability in, say, the p variables by m (where m < p) components and, thus, obtain some economy in the representation of the data.

The components may or may not have meaningful interpretations as constructs related to theoretical concepts. Interpreting components offers a challenge to the imagination of the researcher. Thus, a set of 18 variables on consumer attitudes and intentions could be reduced to three components interpreted as measuring views on general economic conditions, personal financial circumstances, and household durable buying intentions.

Component analysis is best carried out using a computer package such as the STATISTICAL PACKAGE FOR THE SOCIAL SCIENCES or SPSS where it is an optional variation in the factor analysis procedure.

*See also* **Multivariate methods (analysis)**

**Bibliography**

Hair, J. F., Anderson, R. E. & Tatham, R. L. (1987). *Multivariate data analysis* (2nd edn). New York: Macmillan. Chapter 6.

MICHAEL GREATOREX

**procurement**   *see* PURCHASING

**product**   A product can be an idea, a service, a good, or a combination of these. For Kotler (1984) a product "is anything that can be offered to market for attention, acquisition, use or consumption that might satisfy a want or need." Obviously, the products of manufacturing firms are tangible, while those of service industries are intangible. A household insurance package is an example of a product that is a service. Such examples indicate the difficulty of clearly distinguishing between a product and a service (*see* SERVICE PRODUCT). The product is regarded as encompassing a set of benefits and is often referred to as the product (or service) offering.

**Bibliography**

Kotler, P. (1984). *Marketing management: Analysis, planning and control* (5th edn). Englewood Cliffs, NJ: Prentice-Hall. Chapter 15, pp. 462–463.

MARGARET BRUCE

**product champion**  Product champion is a term used to refer to those individuals with a commitment to, or belief in, a new product, which is strong enough to overcome organizational resistance to the new product idea (Maidique, 1980). Schon (1963) studied 15 major inventions of the 20th century and observed that certain highly committed individuals, or champions, were likely to play a role in successfully commercializing these inventions: "no ordinary involvement with a new idea provides the energy to cope with the indifference and resistance that major technical change provokes;" champions of new innovations "display persistence and courage of heroic quality." Various studies have associated the existence of a product champion as a differentiating factor between innovations regarded as successful and those regarded as less successful (SPRU, 1972; Roberts & Fusfield, 1981). Roberts & Fusfield (1981) suggest that product champions are critical in NEW PRODUCT DEVELOPMENT, "recognizing, proposing and pushing a new (product) idea." However, the product champion may serve to play a detrimental role precisely because of his/her unshaking commitment to, or belief in, the new product in question in order to overcome resistance to the new idea. This may occur when commitment leads to continued expenditure on a relatively unpromis-

ing venture, rather than withdrawing resources before considerable losses are incurred (Leverick & Littler, 1994).

**Bibliography**

Leverick, F. & Littler, D. A. (1994). Marketing in the process of managing ambiguity: The development of telepoint in the UK.Manchester School of Management Working Paper, UMIST: UK.
Maidique, M. A. (1980). Entrepreneurs, champions and technological innovation. *Sloan Management Review*, 3, 299–307.
Najak, P. R. & Ketteringham, J. M. (1985). *Breakthroughs.* London: Mercury Books.
Roberts, E. B. & Fusfield, A. R. (1981). Staffing the innovation technology based organization. *Sloan Management Review*, **22**, (3), 19–34.
Schon, D. A. (1963). Champions of radical new inventions. *Harvard Business Review*, **41**, (2), 77–86.
SPRU (1972). *Project SAPPHO: A study of success and failure in innovation.* SPRU, University of Sussex, UK.

MARGARET BRUCE

**product concept**  The product concept is a basic outline of the features and values of the product. This should be based on the core benefit(s) proposition which is a summary of the advantages the product will offer to the customer. In addition, the proposition should highlight the main features which differentiate it from the competition. The first definition of the product concept will tend to be general, but over time, as a result of market research and management deliberation, it will gradually become more refined. Examples of product concepts are: a kettle that can be easily filled through the spout and enables the user to boil only small quantities of water at a time; and an ergonomically designed secretarial chair that adapts with ease to different tasks of the secretary and prevents backache. In these cases, more work is required to define some of the basic features outlined, for example, what is a "small volume of water?"

**Bibliography**

Kotler, P. (1984). *Marketing management: Analysis, planning and control* (5th edn). Englewood Cliffs, NJ: Prentice-Hall. Chapter 10.

Littler, D. A. (1984). *Marketing and product development*. Oxford: Philip Allan. Chapter 7.

MARGARET BRUCE

**product deletion**   This is the process of eliminating a product that does not perform at a level considered adequate according to certain criteria. Most companies base their decisions to delete weak products on poor sales and profit potential, low compatibility with the firm's business strategies, and unfavorable market outlook (Lambert & Sterling, 1988). The decision to eliminate a product is based on its impact on the overall PRODUCT MIX of the firm and if a weak product is no longer making a contribution and the resources employed can be more effectively deployed, then it may be deleted. Once the decision to delete has been made, the need to minimize costs and to retain customer goodwill (e.g., providing assurances that spare parts will be available for a certain period) may affect whether the "weak" product is immediately dropped, or phased out gradually. The phase out approach can either attempt to exploit any strengths left in the product, e.g., by a price reduction to boost sales, or let the product decline with no change in marketing strategy.

### Bibliography

Dibb, S., Simkin, L., Pride, W. & Ferrell, O. C. (1994). *Marketing: Concepts and strategies* (2nd European edn). Boston, MA: Houghton Mifflin Co. Chapter 9, pp. 242–244.
Lambert, D. M. & Sterling, J. U. (1988). Identifying and eliminating weak products. *Business*, July–Sept., 3–10.

MARGARET BRUCE

**product development**   *see* NEW PRODUCT DEVELOPMENT

**product differentiation**   Although in some markets, such as commodities, price remains a primary determinant of demand, in general customers will seek an optimum combination of price and non-price variables, such as technical features, delivery, service support, and brand image (Rothwell, 1981). A possible exception is some luxury goods markets, where price may be relatively disregarded. Suppliers may aim to secure a COMPETITIVE ADVANTAGE by developing offerings providing sets of values tailored to the requirements of different clusters of customers. In this way, suppliers effectively steepen their demand curves and aim to prevent their products reaching commodity status. Over time, though, because of imitation by competitors, it may be increasingly difficult to implement and sustain effective differentiation. Chamberlain (1956) was among the first to highlight the principle of product differentiation in his exposition of monopolistic (or "imperfect") competition.

### Bibliography

Chamberlain, E. H. (1956). *The theory of monopolistic competition* (7th edn). Cambridge, MA: Harvard University Press. Chapters 2 & 5.
Rothwell, R. (1981). Non-price factors in the export competitiveness of agricultural engineering goods. *Research Policy*, 10, 260–288.

DALE LITTLER

**product innovation**   This is the "first introduction of a new product into commercial or social use" (adapted from Freeman, 1992). The process of product innovation is concerned with all of the various activities – R&D, marketing, production, etc. – involved in converting a new idea or discovery into a novel product in commercial or social use. The term can cover a spectrum of different possibilities, ranging from minor adaptations or extensions, such as a new formulation and a new flavor or color of an existing product, to the more technologically advanced, such as a compact disc player. Innovations can be categorized in terms of their effects on demand and their perceived degrees of "innovativeness." Robertson (1971) defines three categories of innovation:

*Continuous:* this is the least disruptive and is likely to involve a modification to an existing product, rather than the creation of something new;

*Dynamically continuous:* this can involve the development of something new or alterations to existing products, but not the creation of new consumption patterns;

*Discontinuous:* the creation of new consumption patterns and the development of previously unknown products.

The new product may entail changes in form, components, materials, packaging, or technology, so that products may have different dimensions of "newness." They may: be functionally new or perform an existing function in a new way; be technically new, involving new materials, new ingredients, and sometimes new forms; or have new styles. What really matters is that consumers perceive a product as new, e.g., stylistic innovations, such as changes to packaging, often are intended to generate a perception of newness.

### Bibliography

Freeman, C. (1982). *The economics of industrial innovation.* London: Frances Pinter.

Robertson, T. J. & Thomas, S. (1971). *Innovative behaviour and communication.* New York & London: Holt, Rinehart & Winston.

MARGARET BRUCE

**product life cycle**   This is a representation of a product in the market place from market launch to maturity and decline. The product life cycle or PLC is based on the belief that most products go through a similar set of stages over their lives, much like living organisms. Typically, the PLC is represented with a graph of sales over time and is divided into four main stages: introduction, growth, maturity, and decline.

In the *introduction* stage, sales will be low because people will not know of the product and may be reluctant to try it out because of its novelty. They may be unsure of its features, e.g., its reliability, its "true" costs, and so perceive a risk in its purchase. One of the main purposes of advertising and promotion (*see* MARKETING COMMUNICATIONS) is to create AWARENESS of the product and stimulate TRIAL, and, as a consequence, the expenditure for this purpose will be high. Other costs may

also be high, such as R&D. Overall, the net losses will intensify in this period.

The *growth* stage implies a growth in sales as people learn (*see* CONSUMER LEARNING) of the product and try it out. PERCEIVED RISK will lessen as consumers learn of the actual effects of product usage. Advertising and promotion costs, while still high, will reduce as a proportion of total product price. Unit costs will fall as output increases and the product should make profits. Competition will enter the market but, if demand increases, then there should be room for competitors. Advertising emphasis will shift from "buy my product" to "buy my brand."

In the *mature* phase, a fall in sales growth will occur as the market becomes saturated and there is little growth in DEMAND. Demand will consist largely of repeat sales. Competition will intensify, prices will tend to fall, and selling effort will be more aggressive. Profits will then be squeezed.

In the *decline* period, actual sales will fall with product competition and changing consumer tastes and preferences. Prices and profits will decline. Some firms will delete mature products and reallocate resources to other activities.

As a product moves through its life cycle, marketing strategies may be adapted; e.g., in the growth stage, it is important to develop brand loyalty and market position. In the maturity stage, a product may be modified, or new market segments may be developed, to stimulate sales. In a period of decline, decisions have to be made about whether to eliminate the weak product, or to reposition it to extend its life.

It is argued (Kotler, 1984) that the PLC can be employed as a planning tool as a basis for timing the development and launch of new products. However, its usefulness as a planning tool is questionable. Some products display a "fad" cycle that has no, or a short, maturity phase, e.g., video games; others display one or more recycles between the growth and maturity stage. This can be caused by new technology that extends the uses of the product, e.g., more powerful personal computers. Dhalla & Yaspeth (1976) note that another PLC is that of the growth-decline plateau where the growth phase is followed by a partial decline to a stable volume that is considerably lower than peak sales, e.g., packaged goods. The four stages of the PLC are not clearly definable, e.g., it is not always clear at what point the introductory phase ends and that of growth begins. It is important to note that a distinction exists between the life cycles of a product class (e.g., cars, beer), product type (e.g., sports car, lager), and brands (e.g., Rover Metro, Fosters). The PLC of a class can last several or even more decades and within the class life cycle there can be several product-type cycles, while, typically, brands have shorter life cycles.

### Bibliography

Dhalla, N. K. & Yaspeth, S. (1976). Forget the product life cycle. *Harvard Business Review*, **54**, (1), 102–112.

Dibb, S., Simkin, L., Pride, W. & Ferrell, O. C. (1994). *Marketing: Concepts and strategies* (2nd European edn). Boston, MA: Houghton Mifflin Co.

Kotler, P. (1984). *Marketing management: Analysis, planning and control* (5th edn). Englewood Cliffs, NJ: Prentice-Hall.

Littler, D. A. (1984). *Marketing and product development*. Oxford: Philip Allan.

Moore, W. L. & Pressemier, E. A. (1993). *Product planning and management: Designing and delivering value*. New York: McGraw-Hill.

MARGARET BRUCE

**product line analysis** A product line includes a group of items that are related because of marketing, technical, or end use considerations. An optimum product line consists of items that reflect different consumer needs and target methods. A balanced PRODUCT MIX is needed to ensure that new products are being developed and marketed to replace or augment those products that are in decline.

### Bibliography

Dibb, S., Simkin, L., Pride, W. & Ferrell, O. C. (1994). *Marketing: Concepts and strategies* (2nd European edn). Boston, MA: Houghton Mifflin Co. Chapter 7, 201-202.

MARGARET BRUCE

**product manager** The product manager is responsible for a product, a product line, or several distinct products in a group. A product manager plans the marketing activities for the product by coordinating a mix of functions including distribution, promotion, and price. The areas the product manager has to deal with include packaging, branding, R&D, engineering, and production and s/he has to continually appraise the product's performance in terms of growth targets, market share, working capital targets, and return on assets managed. Littler (1984) highlights two main criticisms of the product manager approach for product development. First, a lack of authority commensurate with the responsibilities of the position and, second, the relatively low status of the product manager function so that young and often inexperienced recruits are placed at this position.

### Bibliography

Littler, D. A. (1984). *Marketing and product development*. Oxford: Philip Allan.

MARGARET BRUCE

**product market** Two broad categories of products and services exist: consumer and organizational. Consumers buy products to satisfy their personal wants, whereas organizational buyers seek to satisfy the goals of their organizations. Consumer goods can be divided into different categories: convenience, shopping, specialty, and unsought products. Convenience goods are relatively inexpensive, frequently purchased, and rapidly consumed items on which buyers exert only minimal purchasing effort, e.g., bread, soft drinks, and newspapers. Shopping products are items that are chosen more carefully than convenience products, e.g., shoes, furniture, and cameras. Specialty products possess one or more unique features and buyers will expend considerable effort to obtain them, e.g., a Gucci watch. Unsought products are bought irregularly to solve a given problem, e.g., emergency car repairs. Organizational products include raw materials; major equipment; accessory equipment, e.g., tools, calculators; component parts; process materials which are used indirectly in the production of other products, e.g., fiber for products such as computer print ribbon; consumable supplies; and industrial services. The same item can be a consumer and an industrial product, e.g., when consumers buy envelopes for their homes, they are treated as consumer goods; when a company buys envelopes, then they are classified as organizational goods. The ultimate use of the product – for consumers to satisfy their personal wants and for companies to use in the firm's operations – governs the classification.

### Bibliography

Kotler, P. (1994). *Marketing management: Analysis, planning and control* (5th edn). Englewood Cliffs, NJ: Prentice-Hall.

MARGARET BRUCE

**product mix**    This refers to the total array of products that a company markets, and it consists of new, growing, mature, and declining products. A product mix may, in turn, consist of one or more product lines. A product line is composed of variations of a basic product, e.g., Cadbury's chocolate bars. The depth of the product mix is measured by the number of different products offered in each product line and the width of the product mix measures the number of product lines offered by a company. Some companies have a narrow product mix, e.g., Perrier's Mineral Water, whereas a company selling ice-cream with many flavors, such as Haagan-Daz, has a narrow product mix but great product depth. A "balanced" product mix or portfolio is required to ensure that new products are being developed to replace or augment those in decline or in maturity and that there are products with a positive cash flow to finance the development of new products.

### Bibliography

Dibb, S., Simkin, L., Pride, W. & Ferrell, O. C. (1994). *Marketing: Concepts and strategies* (2nd European edn). Boston, MA: Houghton Mifflin Co.

MARGARET BRUCE

**product modification**    This means changing one or more of the product's characteristics and may involve reformulation and repackaging to enhance its customer appeal. Modifications can give a competitive advantage, e.g., a company may be able to charge a higher price and enhance customer loyalty. Dibb et al. (1994) classify modifications into three distinct types: quality, function, and style. Quality modifications relate to the product's dependability and durability; functional modifications relate to the effectiveness, convenience, and safety of products (e.g., washing machines that use less heat and water), and style modifications alter the sensory appeal of the product (such as its taste, texture, sound, and appearance). Such modifications can act to differentiate products in the market place, e.g., BMW cars have an immediately recognizable style.

A number of issues have to be considered before deciding whether or not to keep the product, change it, or eliminate it. What is the customer appeal? The product may have lost its distinctiveness because of the introduction of new products or improvements of its main rivals. By reformulating the product, it may be possible to regain its competitive edge. What is the vulnerability of the product to technological innovation and competition? The company needs to assess the opportunities and threats posed by technological change. What are the interdependencies of the product and others in the mix and how would modification impact upon the overall cost structure?

### Bibliography

Dibb, S., Simkin, L., Pride, W. & Ferrell, O. C. (1994). Identifying and eliminating weak products. *Business*, July–Sept., 3–10.
Littler, D. A. (1984). *Marketing and product development*. Oxford: Philip Allan.

MARGARET BRUCE

**product planning**    The product life cycle suggests that there is a need to monitor the performance of existing products, to devise appropriate policies for those products, and to develop new products where necessary. All this is the essence of product planning. Littler (1984) points out that product planning entails the creation of procedures to evaluate product performance, and to plan the modification, where necessary, of existing products aimed at extending their lives; the deletion of weak products that have reached the terminal stage of their lives; and the development and marketing of new products. The thrust of product planning is to ensure that companies have a "balanced" product mix in the sense that there are new products being developed or marketed to replace or augment those in decline, or maturity, and that there are products with a positive cash flow that can be used to finance the development of new products. In addition, it is important to ensure that there is a balanced portfolio of new products so that those which are highly risky (but offer the prospect of a high return) are balanced by those which have a low element of risk but also a correspondingly low return. Companies should periodically review their products and identify those products that are satisfying customer needs and yielding returns and those that are not. Managers have to consider the potential of the market and company objectives and set performance criteria to review product performance. Action should be taken to modify or delete those products which do not meet the company's performance criteria. Such criteria may include: sales and profit history of the product, relative profitability, future potential, customer appeal, and vulnerability to technological developments and competitors' actions. As well as considering weak products, new product opportunities need to be identified and investment put into new product development. Innovative products have to be developed as the differential advantages of existing products are undermined by technological change and competitors' actions. In some sectors, the pace of technological change is so rapid that product life cycles are less than one year old (Cane, 1991). New products generate additional sales and profits. They can add value by offering more perceived customer values and so help to sustain a COMPETITIVE ADVANTAGE. Thus, the development of new products should be a facet of the overall product planning process to ensure that new products are available to replace the loss in sales and profits resulting from the maturity and demise of existing products.

## Bibliography

Cane, A. (1991). A race that does not lose face. *Financial Times*, May 19, 1991.

Littler, D. A. (1984). *Marketing and product development*. Oxford: Philip Allan.

MARGARET BRUCE

**product portfolio**    The product portfolio covers all the products that a company markets. The portfolio may consist of several product lines; or alternatively different individual products; or a blend of both. In theory, an organization will strive to ensure that it has products at different stages of the PRODUCT LIFE CYCLE so that, for example, there are new products being introduced to replace those products entering their decline stage. The firm may also strive for a balanced product portfolio in terms of risk and/or cash flow. Frameworks such as the BCG MATRIX, developed for business portfolio analysis, can also be employed in the analysis of product portfolios.

DALE LITTLER

**product positioning**    This concerns the decisions and activities intended to create and maintain a firm's PRODUCT CONCEPT in the customer's mind. Attempts are made by companies to position new products so that they are seen to possess the features most desired by the target market. Product positioning is linked to segmentation so that effective product positioning helps to serve a specific market segment by creating an appropriate concept in the minds of customers in that market segment. A product can be positioned to compete directly with another product, e.g., Pepsi with Coca Cola, or it can be positioned to avoid competition, e.g., 7UP in relation to other soft-drink products.

Every product offered to a market needs a positioning strategy so that its place in the total market can be communicated to the target market. Alternative bases for constructing a product-positioning strategy have been identified. Wind (1982) includes positioning on specific product features, positioning for a specific user category, and positioning against another product. Perceptual maps visually summarize the dimensions or primary needs that customers use to perceive and judge products and they present the relative position of brands in terms of these dimensions. For pain relievers, for example, "effectiveness" and "gentleness" may be used as the dimensions to construct the perceptual maps and different offerings can be plotted according to these two dimensions. More than two dimensions of primary needs can be used to create perceptual maps; e.g., alternative modes of transport can be compared on the basis of "quickness and convenience," "ease of travel," and "psychological comfort." Plotting the perception of the new and existing brands on perceptual maps can help evaluate the brands and assess their competitive position and can point to new opportunities. Measures of preference are needed which suggest what potential buyers might want in a new product to determine whether or not the product is desirable (Thomas, 1993).

### Bibliography

Thomas, R. J. (1993). *New product development: Managing and forecasting for strategic success.* New York: John Wiley.

Urban, G. L. & Hauser, J. R. (1993). *Design and marketing of new products* (2nd edn). Englewood Cliffs, NJ: Prentice-Hall.

Wind, Y. J. (1982). *Product policy: Concepts, methods and strategy.* Reading, MA: Addison Wesley.

MARGARET BRUCE

**product/service profit center**    The traditional form of financial accountability in an organization is where profit centers are based on products or services, as opposed to customer profit centers. All revenues and direct costs (of manufacturing and distribution) are allocated to specific products/services. Indirect costs (of manufacturing, sales, and promotion) are apportioned in some way, usually by determining how much of each can be attributed to each product/ service. This is called activity-based costing. The product or brand manager may be held accountable for such profitability and the profit center may also then be used as the basis for future MARKETING PLANNING.

### Bibliography

Cooper, R. & Kaplan, R. S. (1988). Measure costs right: Make the right decisions. *Harvard Business Review*, **66**, (5), Sept.–Oct., 96–103.

DAVID YORKE

**profit**    Profit is a concept which refers to the financial benefit of engaging in commercial activities. It is usually calculated as the excess of sales revenues over total costs (fixed and variable) but there are many forms of profit and measures are subject to accounting conventions. Profit is an important issue in PRICING as products and services are generally not marketed unless profit is anticipated. However, the profit involved may not necessarily be anticipated exclusively in financial terms (as with charities), or in the short term (as with nuclear power), nor even with respect to the specific product or market in question (through cross-subsidization).

DOMINIC WILSON

**Profit Impact of Marketing Strategies**
Profit Impact of Marketing Strategies (PIMS) is a data bank originating in the early 1970s that provides a source of cross-sectional and time series data. The database contains information on a number of environment, strategy, performance, competition and firm related variables for approximately 3,000 businesses (or STRATEGIC BUSINESS UNITS) collected from over 200 participating companies. The database contains annual data as well as averages for various four-year periods.

The most publicized use of the PIMS data is in a regression (*see* REGRESSION AND CORRELATION) model which contains 37 independent variables grouped into seven categories: attractiveness of the business environment; the strength of competitive position; the differentiation of competitive position; the effectiveness of use of investment; discretionary budget allocations; the characteristics of the owning corporation; and the current change in position variables. This explains 80 percent of the variance in the dependent variable, pre-tax return on investment. A similar model has been developed to assess the impact on cash flow.

Schoeffler (1977) summarized the findings and noted that: investment intensity has a negative impact on percentage measures of profitability and cash flow; businesses producing high value added per employee are more profitable than those with low value added; the absolute and relative market share have a positive impact on profit and cash flow; the served market growth rate has a positive impact on dollar measures of profit, no effect on percentage measures of profit, and a negative effect on all measures of cash flow; product and/or service quality in relation to competitors' offerings (as viewed by the customer) has a favorable impact on all measures of financial performance; a business's extensive actions with regard to new product introduction, R&D, marketing effort, etc. have a positive impact on its performance, but only if the business is in a strong position to begin with; VERTICAL INTEGRATION, for businesses competing in mature and stable markets, has a favorable impact, but the opposite is the case for rapidly changing markets; the effect of cost push factors, such as wage and salary increases, increases in raw material prices, etc. depends on the ability of the firm to pass on the increase to its customers and/or its ability to absorb these higher costs; with regard to current strategic effort, the direction of change may be opposite to that of the factor itself, so that attempts to increase market share of high market share firms have a negative effect on cash flow.

## Bibliography

Abell, D. F. & Hammond, J. S. (1979). *Strategic marketing planning.* Englewood Cliffs, NJ: Prentice-Hall, pp. 328–332.
Johnson, G. & Scholes, K. (1993). *Exploring corporate strategy* (3rd edn). Prentice-Hall, pp. 263–269.
Schoeffler, S. (1977). *Nine basic findings on business strategy.* Cambridge, MA: The Strategic Planning Institute.

DALE LITTLER

**projective techniques**   Projective techniques are a group of QUALITATIVE RESEARCH methods which are useful when it is felt that a typical direct questionnaire may not be appropriate in providing the information sought. Projective techniques include word association tests where the respondent is required to give the first word that comes to mind after the interviewer presents a word, e.g., a brand name, in a sequence that includes the words of interest along with several neutral words. Two further techniques are sentence completion and story completion where it is felt that respondents will give revealing answers as they relax their conscious defense. Construction techniques require the respondent to construct dialogue, e.g., to fill in a balloon on a cartoon, or to compose a story behind a picture. Third person techniques allow the respondents to project their own attitudes and opinions on to someone else, such as an average person, rather than acknowledge that they are their own attitudes, opinions, etc.

Projective techniques, based on methodologies devised by clinical psychologists, require specialists to conduct and to interpret the responses.

## Bibliography

Malhotra, N. K. (1993). *Marketing research: An applied orientation.* Englewood Cliffs, NJ: Prentice-Hall. Chapter 6.

MICHAEL GREATOREX

**promotion**   *see* MARKETING COMMUNICATIONS; PRICE PROMOTION; SALES PROMOTIONS

**psychographics**   Psychographics is the general term used to describe the measurement of psychological characteristics of consumers. While personality traits and values are of major concern, many authors also include, in this category, lifestyle data such as activities, interests, hobbies, and opinions (*see also* LIFESTYLES; PERSONALITY). Mitchman (1991) argues that the great diversity of consumer lifestyles in the 1980s and '90s has made market segmentation more difficult in many markets. The general increasing wealth of Western countries, the rise in demand for more psychological value in products, increasing competition, and the better-tailored MARKETING MIX, are factors pushing marketers to develop more precise and effective SEGMENTATION VARIABLES.

Numerous comparisons show that the predictive VALIDITY of psychographic variables is likely to be substantially higher than for demographic variables, e.g., Burger & Schott (1972), King & Sproles (1973), Nelson (1969), Wilson (1966) (*see* SEGMENTATION VARIABLES).

In the light of this, psychographics have become more popular over the past two decades. However, there is still no single widely-accepted definition. When Wells (1975) published his critical review of the subject, he found no less than 32 definitions in 24 articles. Some researchers have used standard personality tests, while others have developed their own scales unique to their purpose. The dominant method of developing psychographic measures has been to use long scales of items/questions which are rated/answered by respondents. The highly-structured nature of these questionnaires allows easy administration to relatively large samples of consumers. Once the data are collected, a common set of statistical procedures is used to derive the psychographic segments which usually involves the use of FACTOR ANALYSIS, CLUSTER ANALYSIS, and DISCRIMINANT ANALYSIS.

An example of a generic psychographic segmentation tool is VALS–2 (Values and Lifestyles). SRI International (of Menlo Park, California) attempted to develop a standard psychographic framework to be used in analyzing US consumers. They identified eight major groups: Strugglers, Makers, Strivers, Believers, Experiencers, Achievers, Fulfilled, Actualizers. It is obvious from the SRI analyses that the categories broadly reflect Maslow's hierarchy of needs ranging from Strugglers at the bottom, who are powerless, narrow focused, risk averse, and conservative, to the Actualizers at the top, who are optimistic, self-confident, involved, outgoing, and growth orientated (see CONSUMER NEEDS AND MOTIVES).

An acclaimed alternative to VALS is LOV (List of Values) which includes segments based on self-respect, security, warm relationships with others, being well-respected, self-fulfilment, self-accomplishment, sense of belonging, fun and enjoyment of life (Kahle & Kennedy, 1988). The researchers have claimed that LOV: (1) has greater predictive VALIDITY than VALS in consumer behavior trends; (2) is easier to administer; and (3) is better able to diminish communication errors, because it is easier to preserve the exact phrase from a value study and incorporate it into an advertisement.

A European value-based segmentation includes: Material Hedonists, Rational Materialists, Empathetic Risk-takers, Self-actualizers, and Safety-orientated (Puohiniemi, 1991). Other research on European lifestyles by the RISC organization has identified six "Eurotypes" from 24 Eurotrends, namely: Traditionalists, Homebodies, Rationalists, Pleasurists, Strivers, and Trendsetters. Whereas most lifestyle research provides only a "snapshot" analysis, the RISC approach offers a continuous measurement of sociocultural trends.

Lifestyle and value-based segmentation have been criticized for being too general to be of great use and their international application is limited because lifestyles vary from country to country (Sampson, 1992). Sampson argues that it is possible to understand human social behavior to a limited degree only, by studying values in isolation. This is because values are too general and cannot deal with issues that relate to specific product consumption and brand-choice behavior in different markets. Therefore, while it may be important to understand value change in longer-term strategic marketing planning, in the short term, value analysis is of limited worth. Sampson advocates a model which has four psychological axes: outward expressiveness to inward repression, and stereotype masculinity (e.g., strength) to stereotype femininity (e.g., softness). The model has been tested in the USA, South Africa, South East Asia, Japan, and 17 European countries, and claims to be superior to lifestyle and value-based segmentation because peoples' loves, hates, fears, hopes, aspirations, and hang-ups are more similar than their lifestyles.

A number of psychographic segmentations have been developed for specific markets. For example, Moschis (1992) has developed a segmentation tool for the 55 years+ market. The "gerontographic" clusters include: Healthy Hermits, Ailing Out-goers, Frail Recluses, and Healthy Indulgers. Pernica (1974) reported that purchasers of stomach remedies can be divided into Severe Sufferers, Active Medicators, Hypochondriacs, and Practicalists.

Despite the usefulness of some psychographic segmentation studies in understanding consumers, the technique is not without its problems. Cost is one major problem, since the time and money involved in developing questionnaires and obtaining, analyzing, and interpreting psychographic and lifestyle data can be significant. It is also difficult to draw firm conclusions based upon the results of any single study and reported replications of studies, which would allow discernible patterns to be seen, are few (*see* e.g. Novak & MacEvoy, 1990). The consumer research literature also contains several critical articles questioning the RELIABILITY (and VALIDITY) of psychographic concepts and measures (*see* Lastovicka, 1982; Wells, 1975).

*See also* **Market segmentation; Segmentation variables**

**Bibliography**

Burger, P. C. & Schott, B. (1972). Can private brand buyers be identified? *Journal of Marketing Research*, **9**, May, 219–222.

Kahle, L. & Kennedy, P. (1988). Using the list of values (LOV) to understand consumers. *The Journal of Services Marketing*, **2**, Fall, 49–56.

King, C. W. & Sproles, C. B. (1973). The explanatory efficacy of selected types of consumer profile variables in fashion change agent identification.Institute Paper No. 425, Krannert Graduate School of Industrial Administration, Purdue University.

Lastovicka, L. (1982). On the validity of life style traits: A review and illustration. *Journal of Marketing Research*, **19**, Feb., 126–138.

Mitchman, R. (1991). *Lifestyle market segmentation.* New York: Praeger.

Moschis, G. (1992). Gerontographics: A scientific approach to analysing and targeting the mature market. *Journal of Services Marketing*, **6**, (3), Summer, 17–27.

Nelson, A. R. (1969). A national study of psychographics.Paper delivered at the International Marketing Congress, American Marketing Association, June.

Novak, T. P. & MacEvoy, B. (1990). On comparing alternative segmentation schemes: The list of values (LOV) and lifestyles (VALS). *Journal of Consumer Research*, **17**, June, 105–109.

Pernica, J. (1974). The second generation of market segmentation studies: An audit of buying motivation. In W. D. Wells (ed.), *Life style and psychographics* (pp. 277–313). Chicago: American Marketing Association.

Puohiniemi, M. (1991). Value-based segmentation, social change and consuming orientations. In ESOMAR Seminar on The Growing Individualisation of Consumer Life-styles and Demand: How is Marketing Coping With It? *Helsinki Proceedings.*

Sampson, P. (1992). People are people the world over: The case for psychological market segmentation. *Marketing and Research Today*, Nov., 236–245.

Wells, W. (1975). Psychographics – A critical review. *Journal of Marketing Research*, **12**, May, 196–213.

Wilson, C. L. (1966). Homemaker living patterns and marketplace behavior – A psychometric approach. In J. S. Wright & J. L. Goldstucker (Eds), *New ideas for successful marketing* (pp. 305–347). Chicago: American Marketing Association.

VINCE MITCHELL

**public relations**   Public relations is an element in the marketing COMMUNICATIONS MIX and may be defined as "the deliberate, planned and sustained effort to establish and maintain mutual understanding between an organisation and its publics" (Jenkins, 1988). Thus, it is a conscious and positive attempt to maintain an organization's image. Groups, or publics, at whom public relations activities are aimed, include customers and potential customers, shareholders, employees, competitors, suppliers, and government. A variety of techniques may be used in implementing a positive public relations program, including press releases/conferences, newsletters, the production of brochures, posters, and videos, and the support of community activities.

*See also* **Publicity; Sponsorship**

**Bibliography**

Jenkins, F. (1988). *Public relations techniques.* London: Heinemann.

Kotler, P. (1994). *Marketing management: Analysis, planning, implementation and control* (8th edn). Englewood Cliffs, NJ: Prentice-Hall. Chapter 23.

DAVID YORKE

**publicity**   Publicity is "non-personal communications in news story form, regarding an organisation and/or its products and services, that is transmitted through a mass medium at no charge (to the organisation)" (Dibb et al., 1994).

Media editors wish to publish information and news stories about organizations and their products, services, etc. to encourage favorable consumer response to the media sources (e.g., sell more newspapers). At the same time, organizations want the information presented in the media to be favorable, so as to stimulate consumer demand for their product/service or create favorable attitudes toward the company (e.g., as a result of community involvement). Many organizations will, therefore, prepare publicity material, i.e., company- and product-oriented information and news, which is made available to the media editors (and sometimes directly to consumers and other interested parties), in the hope that this may reach the company's target audience. However, publicity is generally controlled by the MASS MEDIA and, therefore, may be favorable or unfavorable with respect to a company and its products (e.g., in consumer reports).

The main advantage of publicity for the receiver/consumer is its credibility, typically attributed to an independent source.

### Bibliography

Dibb, S., Simkin, L., Pride, W. & Ferrell, O. C. (1994). *Marketing: Concepts and strategies* (European edn). Boston, MA: Houghton Mifflin Co. Chapter 15.

DAVID YORKE

**purchase decisions**   *see* CONSUMER DECISION-MAKING PROCESS

**purchase intentions**   *see* CONSUMER DECISION-MAKING PROCESS

**purchasing**   Purchasing (sometimes also referred to as procurement) is the professional activity of buying goods and services on behalf of organizations. In practice, purchasing tends to be more professionally organized in larger organizations and can be quite informally organized in smaller organizations. The importance of a professional approach to purchasing is now widely recognized as organizations pay increasing attention to issues of cost and quality control where purchasing can make a major contribution. Heinritz illustrates the importance of professionalism in organizational purchasing at the macroeconomic level by pointing out that

the combined purchasing of the largest 100 US corporations amounts to about 10 percent of the entire US economy (Heinritz, 1991) – clearly it is important to manage such a vast responsibility in an efficient and professional manner. At an organizational level, the importance of purchasing can be illustrated by noting that in a typical manufacturing operation there is likely to be about three times as much investment in materials (depending on inventory and production policies) as there is in labor. Thus, equal percentage reductions would return much greater economies in purchasing costs than in labor costs. Nevertheless, much greater managerial attention has generally been paid, historically, to achieving economies in the labor process than in the material side of organizational management. Baily & Farmer (1990) suggest that the importance of purchasing in an organization will significantly increase when the PRODUCT LIFE CYCLE of the organization's output becomes shorter (e.g., computer suppliers), or when the organization's markets become particularly volatile (e.g., TV production companies), or when the cost of the organization's purchases form a particularly large proportion of its income (e.g., armed forces). Other factors likely to increase the significance of purchasing could be suggested, including economic recession, increasing competition, the introduction of new technology (reductions of labor costs through automation leave a higher priority on managing purchasing costs), and legislation requiring open tendering (as opposed to routine re-ordering).

### Bibliography

Baily, P. J. H. & Farmer, D. (1990). *Purchasing principles and management* (6th edn). London: Pitman.

Heinritz, S. (1991). *Purchasing: Principles and applications* (8th edn). Prentice-Hall.

DOMINIC WILSON

**purchasing process**   The purchasing process or buying process in ORGANIZATIONAL MARKETING has been analyzed and modeled as a cycle with various "phases" or "stages." Robinson, Faris & Wind (1967) not only distinguished three "buy classes" (which they refer to as "NEW

TASK," "MODIFIED RE-BUY," and "STRAIGHT RE-BUY") but also correlated these "buy classes" with eight "buy phases" in a BUYGRID MODEL derived from their empirical research. These eight "buy-phases" are:

(1) Anticipation and/or recognition of need
(2) Determination of features and quantity of required item
(3) Specification of purchase requirement
(4) Search for potential sources
(5) Acquisition and analysis of proposals from potential sources
(6) Selection of one (or more) supplier(s)
(7) Negotiation of purchase arrangements and terms
(8) Feedback and evaluation of the flow of purchase

(Robinson, Faris & Wind, 1967 – as cited in Webster & Wind, 1972, 24)

This representation of the purchasing process as a cycle of buy phases is useful for descriptive purposes but it should not be taken literally as a managerial model since it lacks any predictive power or causative explanation of buying decisions (Webster & Wind, 1972). Nor would it be appropriate to regard the buygrid model as necessarily sequential, or serial, or involving all the identified steps and no others. Nevertheless, the buygrid model is not without value. It supports various practical observations and intuitive conclusions, such as what Robinson et al. refer to as "creeping commitment" (the increasing reluctance of customers to consider new suppliers as the purchasing process unfolds); and the different significance of the buy phases in different buy class situations.

It may be more realistic to envisage an extended purchasing process as continuing beyond the stages of "receipt" and "inspection" through a subsequent stage of "payment" (a stage prone to its own complexities and problems) and then through periodic "review" phases towards eventual re-buy situations (if the supply has proved to be acceptable) or reverting to the new task process (if the supply is no longer acceptable). Purchasing practice can, of course, be very different from the theoretical and full-blown process described here for illustrative purposes. Twelve approximately discernible stages (which may overlap or be

omitted depending on circumstances) might be envisaged in such an extended purchasing process and these twelve stages are presented below as an illustration in general terms of how the process might be observed for more complex new task purchases:

(1) Perception of requirement
(2) Analysis and assessment (including establishment of provisional specifications, probable size and frequency of order, possible costs, MAKE/BUY DECISION, profiles of potential suppliers)
(3) Criteria setting (identification and ranking of the most important purchasing criteria)
(4) Negotiation (including request for quotations, prototype submission, pilot studies, trials, visits to suppliers' premises and reference sites, pursuit of references, capacity and liquidity assessment)
(5) Value engineering (systematic evaluation of the functions of the short-listed offerings to assess which of the offerings is best able to provide the customer's needs at the lowest net cost taking into consideration all relevant aspects)
(6) Decision (the outcome of the previous stages is considered in the context of broader aspects, where appropriate, and final negotiations may be conducted at senior levels to adjust any residual uncertainties until agreement is struck with one favored supplier)
(7) Delivery and receipt (delivery procedures will have been agreed but receiving procedures are often overlooked, can vary considerably and can often lead to administrative confusion, frustrating delays, deterioration of goods, and problems of disputed payment)
(8) Inspection (usually on arrival and before receipt but this may not be practicable because of weather, nature of packaging, type of good/service, or congestion in receiving area)
(9) Storage (preferably only briefly but this will vary according to contract terms, storage life, cost of storage, safety stocks, and so on)
(10) Payment
(11) Review (all procurement arrangements should be subject to review which should

take close account of the views of production management and workers as well as consulting finance (for scrap and obsolescence rates), goods receiving (for delivery performance), quality control, and product engineering (for compatibility with any proposed changes to product design or production systems)

(12) Reassessment of requirement in anticipation of major changes (e.g., in product design, in suppliers, in technology).

*See also* **Purchasing**

**Bibliography**

Robinson, P. T., Faris, C. W. & Wind, Y. (1967). *Industrial buying and creative marketing.* Boston, MA: Allyn & Bacon.

Webster, F. E. Jr & Wind, Y. (1972). *Organizational buying behavior.* Englewood Cliffs, NJ: Prentice-Hall.

DOMINIC WILSON

# Q

**qualitative research** Qualitative marketing research aims to find out what is in a consumer's mind. It is a major methodology used in exploratory research by helping the researcher become familiar with a problem from the respondent's point of view. Qualitative research studies feelings, opinions, needs, motives, attitudes, beliefs, past behavior, etc., which are difficult to observe directly or to obtain data on using structured approaches such as questionnaire surveys (*see* SURVEY RESEARCH).

Qualitative methods include (one-to-one) DEPTH INTERVIEWS and FOCUS GROUP interviews; these methods are less structured than the major alternative quantitative approaches such as those using questionnaires. They also include PROJECTIVE TECHNIQUES which concentrate on association, completion, and construction techniques.

There are several reasons for the use of the less structured qualitative approach. People may be unwilling to answer, truthfully and directly, embarrassing questions or questions that reflect on their status or which are subject to social pressure. The interviewer may, then, have to investigate such topics indirectly. The researcher may be unable, especially at an exploratory stage, to devise a questionnaire that will allow respondents to describe fully their emotions, behavior, etc. in a complicated situation. An unstructured approach allows the respondents to choose how to report on their feelings, needs, motives, attitudes, values, etc. In a depth interview, a well-trained interviewer is able to follow up a respondent's answer to a question and probe deeper into the respondent's thinking and this may lead in unanticipated ways to the uncovering of underlying or hidden information.

A major difficulty of qualitative research is the subjective nature of the analysis, interpretation, and reporting of the results. A problem is the requirement for highly trained interviewers, usually psychologists. Interviewer bias can also be a problem. Samples are often small and unrepresentative and, thus, it is difficult to generalize results from qualitative studies to the population of interest as a whole.

Qualitative research is most useful in the problem definition stage of the MARKETING RESEARCH process where the researcher, while aware that there is a marketing problem, is trying to define or articulate the problem prior to attempting to solve it. Quantitative research, on the other hand, is more useful at the later, decision-making, stage of the marketing research process.

**Bibliography**

Malhotra, N. K. (1993). *Marketing research: An applied orientation.* Englewood Cliffs, NJ: Prentice-Hall. Chapter 6.

MICHAEL GREATOREX

**questionnaire design** Questionnaires are associated mainly with SURVEY RESEARCH but are used sometimes as part of experimental research (*see* EXPERIMENTATION). A questionnaire is a formalized set of questions for obtaining information from respondents. A questionnaire can be administered in a face-to-face personal interview, by telephone, by computer, or by post.

Questionnaires are used to measure: (1) behavior; past, present, or intended; (2) knowledge; (3) attitudes and opinions; and (4) demographic and other characteristics useful for classifying respondents.

The critical concern in questionnaire design is the minimization of measurement error, i.e., minimizing the difference between the information sought by the researcher and that produced by the questionnaire. The factors that need to be considered in questionnaire design include (1) specification of required information; (2) question content; (3) question wording; (4) response format; (5) question order; (6) physical characteristics; and (7) pilot testing.

Software is available to aid the design of questionnaires and in telephone and computer interviewing to provide the questions and collect the responses as they are made.

The specification of the required information is an essential part of the research process and a necessary prerequisite of good questionnaire design. It is also necessary to consider who the respondents will be and what the interview technique will be – postal, computer, telephone, or personal.

The next consideration is to determine individual question content. Are the data to be produced by a particular question needed? Will a particular question produce the specified data? Are several questions needed rather than one? A common error is to ask two questions in one, resulting in a question that the respondent has difficulty in answering unambiguously. Will the respondent not answer the question because (1) it is outside the competence of the respondent, (2) the respondent has forgotten the answer, (3) the respondent cannot articulate the answer, or (4) the subject is embarrassing or private and the respondent is unwilling to provide an answer?

The wording of the question is important. Simple, frequently used, and well-understood words are preferred. Leading questions such as "Most people agree that corporal punishment is wrong, do you?" or "Do you think patriotic Britons should buy Japanese cars?" should be avoided. Questions should give alternatives equal prominence, for instance a resident of Glasgow might be asked "Do you prefer to travel by air, train, or road when going to London?"; just asking whether they prefer to travel by air would bias the answers (*see* Tull & Hawkins, 1987). When using a battery of RATING SCALES, say, Likert scales, the state-

ments should be a positive and negative mixture; indeed, different questionnaires, with the direction of the statements varying, could be prepared and distributed randomly to the respondents.

The response format is a choice between open-ended and closed questions. In open-ended questions the respondent is free to offer any reply using his/her own words. This precludes the influencing of the respondent by the list of response categories. Responses that are different to the researcher's expectations can be forthcoming, making open-ended questions suitable for exploratory research. On the other hand, respondents dislike writing answers on questionnaires and so this reduces the usefulness of self-completion questionnaires; for interviewer-administered questionnaires, the summarization and recording of answers is left to the interviewers, whose abilities and biases may vary. Eventually, responses to open-ended questions have to be coded, which may lead to misinterpretation of responses and certainly adds to cost.

In closed questions a list of possible response categories is provided for respondents to choose and record their choice. Closed, or multiple choice questions, are easier for the interviewer and the respondent. They increase response rates, reduce interviewer bias, and data analysis is easier. However, multiple choice questions are more difficult to compose as the list of possible answers needs to be complete, a problem whose solution requires preliminary research. The list can bias answers, not only because some response categories may be omitted but also due to the order in which the categories are listed. For this reason, several questionnaires with different response category orders may be produced and distributed at random in postal surveys; in computer surveys the order may be easily varied; and in personal interviews several prompt cards with different orders of alternatives may be produced and used at random.

The question sequence can affect replies: the rule is to start with general topics and gradually become more specific. Routes through the questionnaire may need to be devised depending on the responses to early questions: thus, owners of a product may be asked one set of questions, non-owners a different set. Initial questions should be simple and interesting, otherwise respondents may refuse to complete the interview. For the same reason, demographic and classification questions should be left until the end unless they are needed immediately, e.g., to establish whether or not the respondent is qualified to fill a quota in quota sampling.

The physical characteristics should make the questionnaire easy to use, especially when branching questions are used to decide on routes through the questionnaire. Physical appearance is especially important in postal surveys in order to secure the cooperation of the respondent.

Questionnaires should be piloted in order to see if the questions are understood by the respondents and mean the same thing to the respondent as the researcher intended, that the lists of response categories are complete, that the questionnaire is not too long, and that the routes through the questionnaire are appropriate and can be followed by the interviewers or respondents.

### Bibliography

Malhotra, N. K. (1993). *Marketing research: An applied orientation*. Englewood Cliffs, NJ: Prentice-Hall. Chapter 12.

Tull, D. S. & Hawkins, D. I. (1987). *Marketing research: Measurement and method* (4th edn). New York: Macmillan. Chapter 7.

MICHAEL GREATOREX

# R

**radio**  Radio is a broadcasting medium which depends for its efficacy on the spoken word. The development of commercial, as opposed to government-controlled, radio stations, provides ADVERTISING opportunities.

Radio advertising has the advantages of: local and regional flexibility; cheap production and media costs; very short lead times; strength of communication with target audiences; and the ability to reach people who are on the move (e.g., driving) and at work. However, there is limited national coverage, and creative opportunity, and many "listeners" are using the radio as a background while involved in other primary activities (both at work and at home). These elements relate to the IMPACT that radio advertising has in reaching its targets and, in turn, its cost-effectiveness.

## Bibliography

Crosier, K. (1994). Promotion. In M. J. Baker (Ed.), *The marketing book* (3rd edn). (Chapter 21, pp. 484–533. Oxford: Butterworth-Heinemann.

DAVID YORKE

**rating scales**  Rating scales allow measurements of objects to be recorded. They are used in MARKETING RESEARCH questionnaires to measure a respondent's attitudes towards products, beliefs concerning product attributes, importances of product attributes, intentions to buy, etc. The respondent is required to provide an estimate of the magnitude of an attitude, belief, importance, or likelihood by placing a mark on a numerical scale or by selecting one of a series of numbered ordered categories on the scale.

A continuous rating scale requires the respondent to indicate a rating by placing a mark at the appropriate position on a line that runs from one extreme to the other. For instance, the answers to questions concerning the likely outcome of some event may be recorded on a scale going from impossible to certain. Alternatively, the end points of the scale may be marked as 0 and 100 with intermediate points marked along the scale in intervals of 20. Typically, the researcher treats the recorded scores as interval data.

In an itemized rating scale, the respondent records a rating on a scale that has a small number of categories. Associated with each category is a number or a series of descriptions that are ordered. Itemized rating scales are popular in marketing research and often form part of more complicated multi-item rating scales. Commonly used rating scales are the Likert and semantic differential scales.

A Likert scale requires the respondent to record his/her degree of agreement with each of a series of statements about the object of the research. Each scale has a small number of categories, typically five categories, ranging from strongly disagree to strongly agree. For data analysis purposes each category is given a number going from, say, 1 for strongly disagree to 5 for strongly agree. Analysis can be carried out on an item-by-item basis using frequency distributions or arithmetic means (profile analysis). Use of arithmetic means assumes that the scales are interval. Alternatively, to get an overall assessment of the object being studied, summated scores over the battery of scales can be calculated for each respondent, remembering to reverse the scores for negative statements so that strongly agreeing to a positive statement and strongly disagreeing with a negative statement both score the same.

The semantic differential is a rating scale, usually with seven points, with end points given labels that have opposite meanings. Usually respondents rate the object under study on several bipolar rating scales with ends given adjectives such as clean–dirty, hot–cold, soft–hard, slow–fast, etc. Each scale can be scored 1 to 7 and analysis can be carried out item by item (profile analysis). A summated measure can be constructed, remembering to reverse some scales so that positive adjectives are consistently scored. Again this assumes, controversially, that the scales are interval.

Other types of rating scales are also used. Examples include 5- or 7-point importance scales going from very unimportant to very important to record the importance of each of several product attributes, or usefulness scales to record the usefulness of each of several risk relievers, such as obtaining the advice of friends or relatives or buying the most popular brand.

The major issues in the construction of itemized rating scales include (1) the number of scale categories; (2) balanced (equal number of positive and negative categories) or unbalanced; (3) odd or even number of categories (with an even number of categories, respondents cannot sit on the fence); (4) forced or unforced (the latter has a don't know category); and (5) the amount of verbal description (*see* Tull & Hawkins, 1987).

Multi-item rating scales build upon the individual rating scales discussed above. The simplest multi-item scales are simple sums of selected individual scales, remembering to reverse negative scales. More complicated scales include weighted sums of the individual scales with the weights being suggested by multivariate statistical methods, e.g., FACTOR ANALYSIS and the use of STRUCTURAL EQUATION MODELS. Tests for RELIABILITY, such as Cronbach's alpha, and VALIDITY are appropriate before such multi-item scales can be recommended.

An alternative to directly measured rating scales are scales obtained indirectly by methods such as MULTIDIMENSIONAL SCALING and CONJOINT ANALYSIS. In the latter, "products" are assessed overall and the "part-worths" or "utilities" of individual product attributes are derived mathematically.

**Bibliography**

Bearden, W. O., Neteymeyer, R. G. & Mobley, M. F. (1993). *Handbook of marketing scales*. London: Sage.

Tull, D. S. & Hawkins, D. I. (1987). *Marketing research: Measurement and method* (4th edn). New York: Macmillan. Chapter 8.

MICHAEL GREATOREX

**reach**   When organizations are planning their ADVERTISING and, in particular, deciding on which media to use (i.e., MEDIA SCHEDULE), they have to consider the desired reach of their advertising, i.e., the number of persons, households, or organizations exposed to a particular media schedule at least once during a specified period of time.

The effective reach is the percentage of the target MARKET exposed to the advertisement for the minimum number of times (FREQUENCY) that is judged necessary for the advertisement to be effective. Calculation of effective reach is discussed by Kotler (1994).

*See also* **Advertising**

**Bibliography**

Kotler, P. (1994). *Marketing management: Analysis, planning, implementation and control* (8th edn). Englewood Cliffs, NJ: Prentice-Hall. Chapter 23, pp. 638–639.

DAVID YORKE

**realizable demand**   *see* DEMAND

**reference groups**   *see* INTERPERSONAL COMMUNICATIONS

**regionalism**   The global economy and society contains a number of regions which share a degree of commonality in culture, language, political outlook, and, to a lesser degree, economic circumstance. For example, one can mention "the Arab World," "the Indian subcontinent," "Latin America," or north-west Europe. One may expect, all things being equal, that the individual countries within these regions would have reason to engage in extensive trade and economic transactions with each other. In practice of course all things are rarely equal and, for example, European colonization introduced a major distortion into the structure of trade relations. Many countries in Asia and Africa, for example, tended to trade mainly with the European colonial powers rather than with each other as the trading infrastructure (transport links, insurance etc.) tended to discourage this. The UK's pattern of trade was also to some degree distorted away from its neighboring countries in the European continent and towards the Commonwealth.

Since the War, the demise of European colonialism has been responsible, along with other factors, for restoring the "natural" regional pattern of world trade. The regionalization of international trade has developed most fully in Europe and, in recent years, has also progressed in East Asia and North America. However, it has not progressed so much in other regions such as the Middle East as many of these countries are still poor or have economies dominated by one commodity (oil), the demand for which still comes predominantly from the West. The emergence of the "Triad" economies in Western Europe, the Pacific, and North America is thus a manifestation of the uneven spread of regionalization in these three regions compared with the remainder of the global economy. These three regions have become the natural focus for international business activities; virtually all innovations stem from these regions; the bulk of international merchandise trade is within and between these regions, and in more recent years there has been a growing number of alliances (*see* INTERNATIONAL STRATEGIC ALLIANCES) between firms from these regions (Ohane, 1985).

Regionalization has important consequences for the study and practice of INTERNATIONAL MARKETING. One can interpret regionalization as a stepping-stone to GLOBALIZATION; gaining the capability to pursue a pan-European strategy may be a prelude or preparation fordeveloping full-blown global strategies. On the other hand, regionalization may in fact stultify the process of globalization. Progress towards global integration can be reversed if the world economy is divided into regional trading blocks, each centered on a major currency and closed to outsiders. Regional blocks may impose tariff and non-tariff barriers that depress the volume of world trade. The World Bank's view is that the overall impact of regionalization is liberalizing: "concerns about regional protectionist tendencies are easily overstated. Unlike their predecessors, the new blocks go beyond liberalisation of trade to include liberalisation of investment. This, in turn, necessitates the liberalisation of national production standards that would otherwise raise the cost of regionally integrated production" (The World Bank, 1993, p. 364)

From the marketing practitioner's point of view, regionalization is an important element in the emergence of "borderless" economies (Sheth, 1992). Regional integration is beginning to dilute some of the differences between "domestic" and international marketing. Thus, even for those firms whose marketing horizon is basically local, competition may in fact be international. For those firms whose marketing horizon is already international and global too, regional integration has important implications. The integrated European "single" market, for example, can be viewed as a testing ground for the viability of standardization of marketing program. Western Europe is probably the most integrated region in the world economy (unless, of course, one regards the USA as a region as well as a country). If a company's standardization of the MARKETING MIX does not work within Europe, it is unlikely that it will work beyond Europe.

### Bibliography

Ohame, K. (1985). *Triad power: The coming shape of global competition.* New York: Free Press.

Sheth, J. (1992). Emerging marketing strategies in a changing macroeconomic environment: A commentary. *International Marketing Review,* **9,** (1), 57–63.

The World Bank (1993). *The East Asian miracle: Economic growth and public policy.* Oxford: Oxford University Press.

MO YAMIN

**regression and correlation**   The possibility of a relationship between a pair of variables can be investigated in a scatter diagram where each pair of values is plotted as a point on a graph where the axes are used to represent the variables.

Simple correlation measures the strength of a relationship between two variables. If both variables are measured on metric scales, the best measure is the simple product-moment correlation coefficient which ranges from $-1$ to $+1$. A correlation coefficient numerically equal to 1 indicates a perfect linear relationship while a value of zero indicates no relationship at all and values in between indicate the amount of scatter among the points on the scatter diagram. High values of correlation coefficients indicate strong linear relationships while low values indicate weak relationships. A positive correlation coefficient indicates that high values for one variable are associated with high values for the other, similarly low values of the two variables occur together; a negative coefficient indicates that high values on one variable are associated with low values of the other variable and vice versa.

Correlation between pairs of variables measured on ordinal scales can be measured using measures such as Kendall's tau and Spearman's rank correlation coefficient.

Bivariate regression measures the (linear) relationship between a pair of variables; it fits the straight line to the scatter of points that best represents the form of the relationshiOne variable (Y) is designated as the dependent variable and the other (X) is the explanatory or independent variable. The relationship is specified as $Y = a + b*X + u$ where u is the error term that accounts for the scatter of points around the straight line $Y = a + b*X$. The "least squares" method is the basis of the procedure for obtaining numerical estimates of the parameters a and b (*see* Jain, 1994, pp. 166–167).

Multiple regression is an extension of simple regression where more than one independent variable is used to explain variations in the dependent variable.

Regression equations, while usually linear, may be non-linear. The dependent variable could be the sales of beer, the several explanatory variables could be the price of beer, the price of wines and spirits, beer advertising

expenditure, consumers' income, and temperature, with quarterly data for ten years being available for each variable. Relationships are estimated using computer programs, e.g., MINITAB, the STATISTICAL PACKAGE FOR THE SOCIAL SCIENCES or SPSS, etc. Coefficients are estimated, t-tests and F tests are used as tests of significance covering individual variables or groups of variables, although in complicated situations these tests may be approximate only. Regression equations can be built up using step-wise methods based on appropriate test procedures. Regression is probably the most frequently used statistical technique. Fitting a regression equation allows a researcher to see the influence of each independent variable on the dependent variable; in particular some variables may be seen to have little or no effect. Once a regression equation has been obtained, predictions of the dependent variable can easily be obtained given values of the independent variables.

Regression works best when all the variables involved are measured on metric scales, but can be adapted, sometimes with difficulty, for use with other types of measure. For instance, a variable measured on a nominal scale can be replaced by several dummy variables.

Mathematical statisticians have shown that the least squares estimation procedure has optimal properties under certain assumptions. Among the assumptions are that the errors are independent of each other (no auto-correlation), have zero mean and constant variance (no heteroscedasticity), there is no relationship between the dependent variables and the errors, and there is no exact or very strong relationship between the dependent variables (no multicollinearity). In addition, it is advantageous if the errors are normally distributed. The computer packages used in estimation have tests to see if these assumptions hold and part of the skill of the user is to know what variation of the basic least squares technique is appropriate in circumstances where particular assumptions have been shown to be inapplicable.

Econometricians have developed special estimation techniques for models involving interdependent variables where there are several simultaneous relationships to estimate. For instance, sales may depend upon prices, advertising expenditures, and the weather but at the same time prices may depend upon sales, competitors' prices, and the cost of production; advertising expenditure might depend upon last year's profits and competitors' advertising expenditure; and so on. To describe this situation, several equations involving some of the same variables are needed. Special econometric estimation techniques are available to fit these equations in computer packages such as Shazaam.

### Bibliography

Jain, D. (1994). Regression analysis for marketing decisions. In R. P. Bagozzi (ed.), *Principles of marketing research* (Chapter 5). Cambridge, MA: Blackwell.

MICHAEL GREATOREX

**regulated pricing**  Regulated pricing is a convenient term to refer to the practice of setting prices externally, usually through regulatory agencies (e.g., legal fines, wage councils) or political decisions (e.g., prescription charges, income tax). Some prices can be very closely influenced by such external agencies without necessarily being completely determined by them (e.g., interest rates, gas tariffs), while other prices can vary within a range which may be limited by such agencies (e.g., telephone and electricity tariffs). There are also some international regulatory agencies which can have a similar effect on national pricing levels (e.g., OPEC, GATT, EEC).

DOMINIC WILSON

**relationship marketing**  Relationship marketing can be seen as stemming from a growing body of literature expressing dissatisfaction with conventional marketing theory when applied to the areas of BUSINESS-TO-BUSINESS MARKETING and SERVICES MARKETING, with Berry (1983) being one of the first researchers to introduce the concept. The major concern is that the traditional marketing paradigm, based on the marketing mix and the concept of exchange, was developed using assumptions derived from studies of the US market for consumer goods and the resulting short-term transactional focus

is inappropriate for business-to-business and services marketing where establishing longer term relationships with customers is critical to organizational success.

In contemporary marketing, the term relationship marketing is most commonly used to describe a long-term approach to marketing strategy, in which developing and maintaining relationships with individual customers is seen as of fundamental importance, rather than taking a "one sale at a time" approach. It has many similarities with the International Marketing and Purchasing (IMP) Group's approach to business-to-business marketing (*see* BUSINESS-TO-BUSINESS MARKETING), where the notion of building long-term relationships with business customers is well documented. Relationship marketing has been used to refer to the development and enhancement of relationships with bodies other than external customers, such as the organization's own staff (*see* INTERNAL MARKETING), as well as its suppliers, referral sources, influence markets, and recruitment markets.

Writing on relationship marketing, Grönroos (1990) proposed a marketing strategy continuum, ranging from "transaction marketing," which was seen as more suitable for consumer packaged goods, through to relationship marketing, which was seen as more suitable for business-to-business marketing and, especially, services marketing. However, the relationship marketing concept has been extended to the area of CONSUMER MARKETING. Copulsky & Wolf (1990), for example, use the term in a highly specific sense to refer to the building of a database of current and potential consumers which records a wide range of demographic, purchase, and lifestyle information. The database is then used to select suitable customer targets for the promotion of products or services (direct mail is particularly commonly used), the message contained in the promotion being differentiated according to customer characteristics and preferences. The response of each customer to this and any further promotional activity is tracked to monitor the cost of acquiring the customer and the lifetime value of his or her purchases.

The rationale forwarded for the use of the relationship marketing concept in consumer markets is the high degree of correlation between customer retention and profitability. Established customers, it is suggested, tend to buy more, are predictable, and usually cost less to service than new customers. They also tend to be less price-sensitive and may provide free word-of-mouth advertising and referrals. Retaining customers makes it more difficult for competitors to enter a market or increase share in that market and also avoids the often considerable cost of recruiting new customers.

Relationship marketing has been linked in its later development to issues of organizational structure, with advice to base organizational design around company-wide processes, as opposed to business functions (*see*, for example, McKenna, 1991).

### Bibliography

Berry, L. L. (1983). Relationship marketing. In L. L. Berry et al. (Eds), *Emerging perspectives on services marketing* (pp. 25–28). Chicago: American Marketing Association.

Copulsky, J. R. & Wolf, M. J. (1990). Relationship marketing: Positioning for the future. *Journal of Business Strategy*, July–Aug., 16–20.

Grönroos, C. (1990). Relationship approach to marketing in service contexts: The marketing and organisational behaviour interface. *Journal of Business Research*, **20**, Jan., 3–11.

McKenna, R. (1991). *Relationship marketing*. London: Century Business.

FIONA LEVERICK

**reliability**   Reliability is the extent to which a scale (*see* RATING SCALES), for example in a marketing research questionnaire, produces consistent results if repeated measurements are made. Systematic error (or bias) has no effect on reliability; it is the error that occurs randomly each time something is measured that causes unreliability.

Tests for reliability include test-retest reliability, alternative forms reliability, and internal consistency reliability. In test-retest reliability, the same scale items are presented to the same respondents at different times under conditions that are as similar as possible. In alternative forms reliability, two equivalent forms of a scale are constructed and presented to a respondent in the same questionnaire. Strictly speaking, the respondent should give the same answer but

reliability is usually measured in these two approaches by the simple correlation coefficient; the bigger the correlation coefficient the greater the reliability.

Internal consistency reliability is used to assess the reliability of a summated scale by measuring the intercorrelation among the scores on the individual items. Cronbach's alpha is one well-known measure of internal consistency reliability and measures of less than 0.6 are taken to indicate unsatisfactory internal consistency. The formula for Cronbach's alpha is

$$\alpha = (\ n/n - 1)*(1 - \Sigma\ s_i^2/s_t^2)$$

where n is the number of scales, $s_i^2$ is the variance of scale i, and $s_t^2$, is the variance of the total scale formed by summing the scales. A measure called beta identifies any inconsistent scales used in the total scale. Other tests of internal consistency are available with packages involving STRUCTURAL EQUATION MODELS.

### Bibliography

Tull, D. S. & Hawkins, D. I. (1987). *Marketing research: Measurement and method* (4th edn). New York: Macmillan, pp. 222–225.

MICHAEL GREATOREX

**retail buying**   This is concerned with the acquisition by retailers of a suitable range of stock from suppliers for sale within their stores (or in the case of mail order – catalogs). The organization of the function varies widely among retail firms. The retail buying team takes on the role of implementing corporate strategy by offering to the consumer an assortment of goods that is consistent with that strategy. Decisions have to be taken by the buying team concerning the desired quality, price to the consumer, profit levels, and contract terms with suppliers.

The buyer's role is vital in securing a "good" deal that allows the retailer to compete successfully in the market place. This may entail purchasing the goods at the lowest possible price thus allowing greater profits. The buyer needs negotiating skills and an in-depth understanding of the supplier's business. In addition, the buyer should have an understanding, often based on a combination of intuition, experience, and market research, of what the final consumer might buy, often (depending on manufacture and distribution lead times) several months before the goods are available in the high street. In increasingly competitive markets the buyer must also have an eye for something new to offer the consumer.

Buying mistakes can be costly, especially if a chosen product does not sell well or the right price has not been achieved with the manufacturer. This may allow competitors to undercut the retailer's price.

The main responsibilities of the buyer are likely to include product and supplier selection, negotiation, pricing, evaluation of past purchase decisions, market monitoring, and forecasting – depending on the size of the organization and the structure of its buying department.

Buying decisions may be taken individually or in committee, again depending on the individual company. It may be that the decision to move into a new line of merchandise would be taken at board level, leaving the individual product decisions to the buying team.

The role of the buyer is becoming increasingly important within the commercial environment and more sophisticated as levels of competition increase and the consumer becomes more knowledgeable about the products available (McGoldrick, 1990).

**Bibliography**

Fulop, C. (1964). *Buying by voluntary chains.* London: George Allen & Unwin.
McGoldrick, P. J. (1990). *Retail marketing.* Maidenhead: McGraw-Hill, p. 207.

STEVE WORRALL

**retail distribution channels**    Retail distribution channels include both store and non-store selling media such as mail order and catalog shopping, home shopping, and teleshopping. These represent the end of the manufacturer–wholesaler–retailer distribution channel and serve consumers directly. In some channels each activity is performed by independent firms but there is a growing trend toward vertical integration, whereby companies are performing more than one level of activity in

the channel, e.g., most large grocery retailers, such as Safeway and Aldi, do their own wholesaling and also control physical distribution tasks. Others, such as Marks & Spencer and The Gap, are involved at all levels including product design, manufacture, and quality testing. "Indeed, Marks and Spencer has been described as a manufacturer without factories" (McGoldrick, 1990).

Vertical integration enables the retailer to make significant cost savings, enhancing the efficiency of the distribution channel through greater control over the planning and operation of the flow of merchandise to the stores. Many retailers are investing in quick response (QR) delivery systems, which are highly efficient inventory management systems. EPOS and EFTPOS collect information concerning the day's sales at store checkouts and relay the data to enormous, highly efficient, and automated warehouse or distribution centers. Here, stock orders are rapidly made up and dispatched to the stores the same or the following day. The enhanced efficiency minimizes the handling of goods, reducing stock damage and shrinkage, and has eliminated the need for large in-store stock rooms, allowing additional store floor area to be devoted to selling activities, e.g., Next, the high street clothing retailer, has a highly efficient EPOS system and a centralized automated distribution network, that have eliminated the need for in-store stock rooms altogether.

Manufacturers' exclusive hold over merchandise production and design matters has gradually been eroded since the 1950s and "[b]ecause of the growing number of regional, national and international retail chains, retailers have more power in the distribution channel than ever before" (Berman & Evans, 1995). The retail multiples' control of the distribution channel stems from their enormous buying power, through which they are able to dictate production terms and prices, driving down manufacturer margins and further strengthening their own position. Even retailers which are smaller in terms of asset base have been able to gain economies of scale, rapid growth, and channel buying power through establishing networks of retail franchises.

O'Reilly (1984) recognized four key economic factors which might reduce the retailers' channel power:

(1) Surplus floor space, arising from rapid expansion.
(2) Intensification of retail competition.
(3) Serious decline in high street property values.
(4) The massive scale of retailers' long-term investment in their distribution systems.

Since 1984, with world recession and continued retail property investment in shopping malls and out-of-town shopping centers, all of these factors have begun to take effect to varying degrees. It remains to be seen whether or not this will impact upon the retailers' control and power in the distribution channel.

The store distribution channel produces by far the main retail sales volume. However, new retail formats and technology associated with the distribution of goods, such as home shopping and interactive teleshopping, dictate that the precise level of distribution assigned to each channel will continue to be dynamic until equilibrium between the different retail distribution channels is reached.

*See also* **EFTPOS; EPOS; High street retailing, Home shopping; Mail order; Retail franchises; TV-based home shopping; Wholesalers**

Bibliography

Berman, B. & Evans, J. R. (1995). *Retail management.* Englewood Cliffs, NJ: Prentice-Hall.
McGoldrick, P. J. (1990). *Retail marketing.* Maidenhead: McGraw-Hill.
O'Reilly, A. (1984). Manufacturing versus retailers; the long term winners? *Retail and Distribution Management,* **12**, (3), 40–41.
Rosenbloom, B. (1990). *Marketing channels.* Orlando, FL: The Dryden Press.

STEVE GREENLAND

**retail environment**    *see* RETAILING

**retail franchises** These are franchising grants selling rights within a given geographical area for franchising goods and services. The franchising company provides a recognized brand name, goods, equipment, and services, such as training in merchandising and management, receiving in return a fee or a percentage of turnover, or both. Franchising has a long history but emerged as a major element in retailing during the 1980s when it accounted for around 10 percent of the retail market. This distribution method is continuing to grow in the retail sector due to the numerous advantages franchising has to offer both franchiser and franchisee (Baron & Schmidt, 1991). Facilitating rapid and reduced risk expansion opportunity, franchising has assisted national and international network development for retailers such as Kentucky Fried Chicken, Blockbuster Video, Benetton, and The Body Shop.

*See also* **Retail distribution channels**

Bibliography

Baron, S. & Schmidt, R. A. (1991). Operational aspects of retail franchises. *International Journal of Retail and Distribution Management,* **19**, (2), 13–19.
Morgenstein, M. & Strongin, H. (1992). *Modern retailing.* Englewood Cliffs, NJ: Prentice-Hall.

STEVE GREENLAND

**retail hierarchy** A retail hierarchy is the organization of stores within a chain according to size or sales per unit of area. The larger stores within the chain (in terms of selling floor space or total sales) would appear higher up the hierarchy than those with lower sales or selling floor space. Larger stores may offer an extended range of goods and services. So-called "flagship" stores tend to be seen by the retailer as being at the top of the hierarchy and are often situated in prestige locations in major cities.

STEVE WORRALL

**retail image** Retail image refers to the way in which the retailer is perceived by the public. One of the earliest definitions, specifically in relation to retail stores, was provided by Martineau (1958), who describes retailer image as: "the way in which the store is defined in the shopper's mind, partly by its functional qualities and partly by an aura of psychological attributes."

*See also* **Store design**

**Bibliography**

Martineau, P. (1958). The personality of the retail store. *Harvard Business Review*, **36** (1), 47–55.
McGoldrick, P. J. (1990). *Retail marketing*. Maidenhead: McGraw-Hill.

STEVE GREENLAND

**retail location**  Retail location is one of the most important considerations facing the retailer. "Although a good location is unlikely in itself to compensate for mediocre overall strategy, a poor location can be a deficit that is very difficult to overcome. Even very small physical differences between locations can exert a major influence upon the stores' accessibility and attractiveness to customers" (McGoldrick, 1990).

The location decision is multidimensional in scope, moving from regional analysis, to trade area analysis, to smaller scale site-specific and premises considerations. Despite their importance to retail success, location decisions "appear, until comparatively recently, to have been taken in a decidedly cavalier fashion and on the basis of obscure rules of thumb, rudimentary calculations, past experience, intuition, and/or entrepreneurial flair" (Brown, 1992).

Today, most retailers adopt a far more systematic approach to location. The main techniques used to evaluate retail sites include:

*Checklists* – which provide details of numerous factors, such as geodemographic, competitor, market, and site-specific information, to be considered when evaluating a site's potential.
*Analogs* – (also known as the same store approach) where other outlets with similar characteristics to the location in question have their key store features and catchment areas described quantitatively. These data are then extrapolated and used to estimate the likely turnover and profitability of the site in question.

*Trade area mapping* – where customer catchment areas for stores or shopping centers are mapped out geographically to identify consumer shopping patterns. Gaps in the market place and potentially profitable locations can then be identified.
*Mathematical modeling* – more systematic approaches to assist the retail planner have been developed using multiple regression techniques and spatial interaction models:

(1) *Multiple regression* involves developing equations, using existing store data, that represent linear relationships between branch performance indicators and location attributes. The regression analysis identifies the key factors in a store's catchment area and site-specific data, concerning factors such as premises size, that determine performance. The regression equation, by incorporating various data from proposed retail sites, can then be used to forecast performance.

(2) *Spatial interaction* or gravity models predict that a retailer's store patronage will exhibit a distance decay relationship with its hinterland, or surrounding area. They work on the principle that a store's sphere of influence will be a function of its size, its distance, and customers' journey times in relation to other outlets in the surrounding area. For example, the Reilly model, an early and basic type of spatial interaction model, predicts that the breaking point or boundary between the trading areas of store A and store B will be equal to:

$$\frac{\text{the distance between store A and store B}}{1 + \sqrt{\dfrac{\text{size of store A}}{\text{size of store B}}}}$$

Since Reilly's model, more complicated gravity models have been developed which involve a greater number of variables, such as patterns of store distribution, road networks, physical features, center attractiveness values, and population values, and which assess the interaction between more than just two places. They are used to predict a store's catchment areas, which is then used to anticipate retail performance at particular retail locations. The gravity models can also be used to calculate the probable impact of adding or removing stores from retail distribution networks. In this way store locations can be planned to achieve an optimum pattern of distribution for the retailer.

Retail location techniques are not only used to identify sites to open new stores on, but also to assist in the:

(1) Closure of non-profitable stores with markets that offer little promise of improvement.
(2) Downgrading of retail provision at certain outlets and upgrading at others to lower costs and improve the efficiency of the retail distribution network.
(3) Relocation of stores that are underperforming due their poor retail location.

These are three key areas of network rationalization that have become common practices of the major retailers as a result of the current economic and competitive situation (e.g., *see* Greenland, 1994). Focusing upon retail location and network planning has therefore become an even more important issue.

*See also* **Retail distribution channels**

**Bibliography**

Brown, S. (1992). *Retail location: a micro-scale perspective*. Aldershot: Avebury.
Davies, M. & Clarke, I. (1994). A framework for network planning. *International Journal of Retail and Distribution Management*, **22**, (6), 6–10.
Greenland, S. J. (1994). Branch location, network strategy and the high street. In P. J. McGoldrick & S. J. Greenland (Eds), *The retailing of financial services* (pp. 125–153). Maidenhead: McGraw-Hill.
McGoldrick, P. J. (1990). *Retail marketing*. Maidenhead: McGraw-Hill.

STEVE GREENLAND

**retail merchandising**    Retail merchandising encompasses primarily the merchandise mix, store space allocation, and the placement of products within it (Rogers, 1985). This is the general definition accepted by many UK retailers. In the USA, however, merchandising has a far broader meaning, e.g., "[t]he process of developing, securing, pricing, supporting and communicating the retailer's merchandise offer-

ing" (Lewison, 1994). As a consequence, the function of merchandising within different companies varies enormously. McGoldrick (1990) suggests sparing use of the term "[b]ecause of its many different definitions and connotations?" (For aspects of visual merchandising *see* STORE DESIGN.)

**Bibliography**

Lewison, D. (1994). *Retailing*. New York: Macmillan.
McGoldrick, P. J. (1990). *Retail marketing*. Maidenhead: McGraw-Hill.
Rogers, D. (1985). Research tools for better merchandising. *Retail and Distribution Management*, **13**, (6), 42–44.

STEVE GREENLAND

**retail positioning**    Retail positioning aims to provide competitive advantage by differentiating the retailer from its competitors through a retail offering that appeals to and is readily identifiable by its specific target markets. Frequently, differentiation is achieved on the basis of image, price, product, and service. As Martineau (1958) noted: "It is high time we retailers recognize that we cannot be all things to all people. When we do that we end up with no particular appeal to anybody."

**Bibliography**

Harris, D. & Walters, D. (1992). *Retail operations management*. Prentice Hall.
Martineau, P. (1958). The personality of the retail store. *Harvard Business Review*, **36**, (1), 47–55.

STEVE GREENLAND

**retail pricing**    This is the process for deciding the price to be charged to the customer for a product or service. This may be a complex activity involving a number of considerations such as the desired profit level; the price charged by competitors; an understanding of what the market will bear; and promotions being run on a particular product. Within a competitive retail market customers tend to be relatively price aware, holding a perception of the price competitiveness of the major retailers.

A number of pricing options are open to the retailer, depending on whether, for example, market penetration, profit maximization, under-cutting the competition, or creating a quality image are the desired goals. For most retailers maximizing sales and/or profitability are the key intentions. In order to achieve this, an under-standing of how price will affect demand is required.

The pricing decision cannot be taken in isolation from other MARKETING MIX decisions. A consistent strategy of merchandise choice, promotion/advertising, store location, and pri-cing should be adopted in order to attract and retain customers.

Once decided, the price charged for a good or service tends to be varied from time to time such as at the "end of season sale," upon the arrival of updated and improved goods, or as a competitive response to the activities of other retailers.

Across many sectors of retailing, the phe-nomenon of price discounting has come to the fore. This tends to dilute the power of the seasonal "sale" as customers come to expect low prices and adequate levels of service and product quality all year round.

A number of marketing promotions can be offered to the customer based upon the price charged for an item. The "two for the price of one" device is widely used as is the "price promise" where a retailer will promise to beat any price available for the same product else-where.

*See also* **Pricing**

**Bibliography**

Gabor, A. (1988). *Pricing concepts and methods for effective marketing* (2nd edn). Aldershot: Gower.

STEVE WORRALL

**retail product range**    The retail product range is the assortment of goods and services offered for sale by a retailer. The particular range offered may be tailored closely to the needs of the target customers. The retailer may seldom stock the full range of a manufacturer's goods unless there is the demand for them.

A retail product range is made up of a number of "lines," i.e., closely related products. A product line will have a certain "depth,"

depending on the number of variants offered. The more variants available in store the deeper the product range.

In addition, the product range has a certain width depending upon the number of product lines stocked. A large supermarket will have a wider range than a specialty store. The product range of a supermarket may be in excess of 20,000 product items.

The retailer needs to decide how deep and wide the range should be. By offering the largest possible range the retailer may be able to extend the appeal to a wide range of customers. Conversely, a more focused product range may appeal to selected market segments. In this way the retailer is able to position itself in the market place.

Within certain specialist markets, for instance where a great degree of product knowledge is needed, the retailer may benefit from selling only a limited product range. On the other hand, certain so-called "category killer" stores may offer a very wide range of products within a specialist market at a discount to their compe-titors.

STEVE WORRALL

**retail promotion**    This involves communi-cating (by the retailer as opposed to the manufacturer) with the organization's target customers. This is typically different to other types of promotion in that the retailer brand (i.e., the store fascia or trading name) is promoted instead of or alongside the products in the store. This may take one or more of several forms including:

PERSONAL SELLING – the one-to-one selling of a product to a customer;
PUBLICITY – non-personal, mass communica-tion with the audience;
PUBLIC RELATIONS – developing and mana-ging publicity;
ADVERTISING – paid-for communication; and
SALES PROMOTION – monetary and other incentives to purchase a particular good or service.

Together these form the so-called "promotional mix" and can be used collectively or individually to create a promotion strategy. The level of emphasis placed on the use of each technique should be decided by the retailer based upon the nature, behavior, and interests of the customer group at which the promotion is aimed as well as the objectives of the promotion, the nature of the product to be promoted, and any wider market considerations.

The purpose of such communication may be to encourage sales by informing the customer about new products, new price structures, special offers, or other arrangements, such as philanthropic causes helped by the donation of a proportion of each sale.

In order to be effective, the communicated message should be encoded in a manner understood by the target customers. Hence, retail promotions are carefully devised to convey the desired meaning to the customer. This may include straightforward information about a product and/or some element of persuasion to buy. If this meaning is misunderstood, the communication will be lost and the promotion expense wasted. In many societies, the consumer is typically bombarded with numerous commercial communications on a daily basis. Therefore, in order to be noticed, a retail promotion needs to attempt to convey something different. The promotion also needs to be remembered by the consumer who may require repeat exposure to it.

The promotion itself needs to be targeted at key customer groups, be they existing, new, or potential. It is unlikely that a blanket promotion would appeal to all customer segments.

The main measure of promotional effectiveness is the number of extra sales gained that can be attributed to it.

Regulations for conducting such activity are laid down by statute.

### Bibliography

Burnett, J. J. (1993). *Promotion management.* Boston, MA: Houghton Mifflin.

STEVE WORRALL

**retail security**   Retail security concerns several main areas including in-store shoplifting, staff pilferage, premises security regarding shopbreaking, hold-ups and the personal security of staff members, as well as customers. The relative significance and incidence of each varies between different retail activities. Prevention measures include, inter alia, store detectives, electronic merchandise tag systems, closed-circuit television, security mirrors, chain and loop alarms on merchandise, fitting room tags, secure merchandising cabinets, well-lit high-visibility store layouts, strong rooms, security systems, frontage grilles and shutters, external bollards preventing ram raiding, appropriate security procedures and practices, and general staff training on security matters (Cox, 1978; Green, 1986). Activities involving large-volume cash handling and transactions, such as financial services retailing, are particularly vulnerable and security is an even greater and growing concern. The number of armed raids on financial services outlets in the UK more than doubled between 1989 and 1992, and appears to be doubling every 12 months in London (Hughes, 1994). Risk of violence to both customers and staff members are real worries and extra security measures and procedures are required. Since financial service activities have become more retail orientated, considerable research has been undertaken to develop more flexible security systems required for the modern open-plan branch formats, that have replaced the more traditional branch "bunker" security concepts. More effective staff security training is essential, particularly with the increasing threats of violence and the frequency of hostage-taking. The use of high-profile security systems, bullet-proof shop furniture and bandit screens, vacuum tubes transporting cash directly to and from counters to strongrooms, safes, rising security screens and shutters that seal off the sales area are all common practices. Counseling provision for victims is also desirable to combat any post-raid trauma.

*See also* **Financial services retailing**

### Bibliography

Cox, R. (1978). *Retailing.* Plymouth: Macdonald & Evans.

Green, W. R. (1986). *The retail store.* New York: Van Nostrand Reinhold.

Hughes, M. (1994). Retail branch security. In P. J. McGoldrick & S. J. Greenland (Eds), *Retailing of financial services* (pp. 154–162). Maidenhead: McGraw-Hill.

STEVE GREENLAND

**retail service**   Retailing is a service industry. Many companies have recognized that good customer service can differentiate them from the competition. Providing a good service is desirable in that it may encourage customers to return. This may entail enhancing the shopping experience to make it more enjoyable, relaxing, and rewarding.

Service to the customer can be incorporated into every element of retail activity from the selection of goods for sale to the convenience to the customer of store location and opening times.

In order to provide a level of service deemed appropriate, the retailer may engage in extensive staff training, provide a modern and comfortable store environment, and develop policies designed to reduce customer dissatisfaction, such as money-back guarantees and easy exchange of goods.

Although retailing can be seen as a service sector industry, both goods and services can be purchased from stores. Recently, financial service providers such as banks and building societies have begun to see themselves as retailers.

The current use of self-service within stores can be seen as a reduction of customer service although it is not necessarily viewed negatively by consumers (Bateson, 1985). Conversely, retailers are becoming adept at providing different forms of customer service, the more innovative of which are often copied by competitors. They key is to find elements of service that are valued by consumers.

Bibliography

Bateson, J. E. G. (1985). Self service consumer: An exploratory study. *Journal of Retailing*, **61**, (3), 49–76.

STEVE WORRALL

**retail strategy**   *see* RETAILING

**retailer patronage**   This is the adoption of an outlet or supplier by a customer, especially on a frequent basis. Understanding the basis for store patronage may allow retailers to develop their MARKETING MIX such that they increase their attractiveness to target customer groups, possibly raising market share and profitability.

The reasons for patronizing a given store are many and varied and include the convenience of store location; previous experience with the store; reputation; pricing; availability and suitability of merchandise; and word of mouth.

In addition to patronizing a certain store, the consumer may develop loyalty toward a certain BRAND or product. These two examples of shopping behavior should not be confused.

Bibliography

Berman, B. & Evans, J. R. (1995). *Retail management: A strategic approach* (6th edn). Prentice-Hall.
Walters, D. (1994). *Retailing management: Analysis, planning and control.* Basingstoke: Macmillan. Chapter 10.

STEVE WORRALL

**retailers**   *see* RETAILING

**retailing**   This embraces those activities concerned with selling goods or services to the final consumer or another person acting on his/her behalf.

Retailing need not take place exclusively in a shop setting. Home shopping via a printed catalog and mail order is a firmly established phenomenon. Less widely available is television-based shopping through a fiber optic cable, although this continues to grow. The future is likely to see wider use of computer-based shopping "online" with the use of a modem and standard telephone line.

Retailing takes place in many forms. The typical examples include everyday shopping for clothing and food, etc. However, retailing is also the method by which we acquire mortgages or investment policies from banks and building societies. It is also the medium through which dental treatment is received and paid for; airline or concert tickets are booked over the telephone or through an agent; soft drinks are bought from vending machines.

Although highly visible to the consumer on the high street or through catalogs and home shopping systems, the retail industry is heavily involved in a wide range of activities. These include storage, distribution, and selling a product or service at a price that is competitive, of a quality that is appropriate, at a time that is convenient, and at the greatest possible convenience to the customer.

In order to fulfil this role, the most successful retailers have become highly effective in a number of management disciplines, including personnel management, financial control and accounting, LOGISTICS, STRATEGY development, DISTRIBUTION, and MARKETING. In some cases retailers have also become involved in manufacturing.

For a store-based retailer, siting the outlet at the best possible location is a primary concern. In order to achieve high visibility, and thus achieve passing trade, the best store site is likely to be in the high street of a town or in a shopping mall. The better locations tend to command higher rents, leaving the retailer faced with a trade-off between higher operating costs but potentially higher sales. For some stores, notably larger supermarkets and DIY outlets, an "out-of-town" site may be more appropriate given the importance of car-borne trade and the need for large car parking lots. Other retailers may choose to locate in a "retail park;" these tend to include electrical goods superstores, furniture stores, and car accessory retailers.

Retail companies should also develop a strong understanding of their customer profile. By targeting different segments of the population, retailers are able to tailor their offerings closely to the needs of customers. Some retailers may aim themselves at the affluent, fashion-conscious section of society, whereas others appeal to the less well off or the price conscious.

By understanding their customers' socio-economic background, lifestyles, and beliefs, retailers are able to develop marketing strategies in order to serve their target customers more profitably. Such strategies entail manipulating the various elements of the "MARKETING MIX" to provide an image and service appropriate to the customer. Therefore, merchandise would be selected, pricing levels decided, store interiors designed, and marketing communications developed (advertising, promotions, etc.) to appeal to the target customer.

Retailers' performance in the market place is heavily influenced by the forces within the business environment (*see* MARKETING ENVIRONMENT). These consist of economic, political, sociocultural, demographic, technological, and physical influences (Kotler, 1988). In recent years, increasing competition and recessionary forces affecting many retail sectors have, in part, led to cost cutting, price reductions, and lowered profits. Other forces include the growing internationalization of retailing, with a number of operators expanding overseas as international trade becomes less restricted. Other issues such as Sunday trading, EPOS and scanning services, legislation affecting part-time workers, and possible planning restrictions on out-of-town sites are likely to continue to impinge on retail activity.

Retail companies are typically organized into chains of stores and may own several hundred outlets across the country all trading under the same "fascia." Other forms of organization include franchise agreements where a trader pays a proportion of his profits to the parent retailer in exchange for trading under his name (e.g., Benetton); concessions involving a retailer trading from a small store sited within a larger store; market traders who pay a local authority for the use of a market stall site; and independent retailers who may own one or two stores (e.g., the traditional corner shop, butcher, or baker).

Non-store retailing through the medium of a printed catalog is also a highly competitive business. In recent years, the quality of such publications has increased dramatically and the manner of trading has vastly improved with better customer service through telephone ordering, credit and debit card payment facilities, easier exchange policies, and quick postal or vehicle delivery. This has been largely due to the innovative practices of companies such as Next, Cotton Traders, and Racing Green, along with a number of overseas operators which have succeeded in selling or giving away catalogs as supplements to Sunday newspapers. Sales agents are still used by some catalog retailers although recruiting, motivating, and retaining such staff has proved difficult.

**Bibliography**

Ghosh, A. (1990). *Retail management*. Chicago: The Dryden Press.

Kotler, P. (1988). *Marketing management: Analysis, planning, implementation and control* (6th edn). New York: Prentice-Hall, 135.

Morgenstein, M. & Strongin, H. (1992). *Modern retailing, management principles and practices* (3rd edn). Prentice-Hall.

STEVE WORRALL

**risk reduction**   *see* PERCEIVED RISK

# S

**sales call cycle** SALES FORCE management (*see* SALES MANAGEMENT) usually involves defining the number of calls that a salesperson would be expected to make to particular customers. Customers may be classified according to their importance in terms of sales volume, profitability, reputation, and growth potential, and the number of calls during a period specified according to the importance of the account. The number of hours that sales representatives are expected to spend with customers may be an additional or alternative target. A distinction may be made between servicing existing customers as against prospecting for new accounts. Companies may expect sales representatives to spend a proportion of their time seeking new accounts, and establish a target for the number of unsuccessful calls to be made to a prospect.

Some flexibility is required in establishing a sales call cycle in order to allow the sales representative the discretion to deal with, for example, unexpected demands of customers.

Bibliography

Dalrymple, D. J. & Cron, W. L. (1995). *Sales management – Concepts and cases.* New York: John Wiley. Chapters 5, 11.

DALE LITTLER

**sales force** In many, although not all, organizations, the sales force is the principal means of obtaining orders. This will be achieved by PERSONAL SELLING, either by visiting customers or by TELEMARKETING (telephone selling) on a planned basis. Each member of the sales force may have a territory or group of customers which is organized geographically, by product/service type, by customer type, or by some combination of these. Sales targets (by volume or value) may be set but, in addition, members of the sales force may have other defined activities such as customer service (e.g., problem solving and training), attendance at EXHIBITIONS, and collecting overdue accounts.

A feature of SALES MANAGEMENT, in its planning and control of the sales force, is to balance sales potential with workload. For instance, in the case of SALES TERRITORY, two territories may contain an equal potential, in terms of actual and likely potential customers and their demand for certain products/services, but the geographical spread of the customers may be totally different with one territory needing much more travel. If sales persons' remuneration is to be equitable, the workload, however measured, must be perceived to be similar. Much will depend on the job definition of the sales force as laid down by sales management in the quest to satisfy both customer needs and its own corporate objectives.

Bibliography

Cravens, D. W. & LaForge, R. W. (1983). Salesforce deployment analysis. *Industrial Marketing Management*, **12**, July, 179–192.

Dalrymple, D. J. & Cron, W. L. (1995). *Sales management – Concepts and cases.* New York: John Wiley. Chapter 24.

Kotler, P. (1994). *Marketing management: Analysis, planning, implementation and control* (8th edn). Englewood Cliffs, NJ: Prentice-Hall. Chapter 25.

Wilson, M. T. (1983). Managing a sales force. (2nd edn). Aldershot: Gower.

DAVID YORKE

**sales management** Sales management is responsible for the organization and performance of the SALES FORCE. More specifically, this will include: defining the task of the sales force, organization into sales territories, planning sales call cycles, recruiting and training of personnel, setting objectives, establishing budgets, motivation of personnel, and performance evaluation against objectives. From the evaluation, sales management can determine strengths and weaknesses and initiate any changes in line with corporate objectives and support.

## Bibliography

Adams, T. (1988). *Successful sales management.* London: Heinemann.
Churchill, G. A. Jr, Ford, N. M. & Walker, O. C. Jr (1985). *Sales force management: Planning, implementation and control.* Homewood, IL: Irwin.
Kotler, P. (1994). *Marketing management: Analysis, planning, implementation and control* (8th edn). Englewood Cliffs, NJ: Prentice-Hall. Chapter 25.

DAVID YORKE

**sales promotion**    Sales promotion(s) is a part of the marketing COMMUNICATIONS MIX and is an activity and/or material that acts as a direct inducement, offering added value and incentive for a product to resellers, sales persons, or end customers.

Sales promotions are designed to stimulate dealer or trade purchases and, in turn, in consumer markets to: get customers to try a new brand; encourage favorable opinions; match competitors' actions; increase sales frequency and amounts, etc. Most sales promotions are short term, and they tend to be used more intensively in the marketing of fast-moving-consumer goods where BRAND switching and perceived homogeneity of the offerings prevails. They are relatively more easy to isolate and evaluate than other elements in the communication mix.

Trade promotions include buying allowances, free goods, cooperative advertising, dealer sales contests, and display materials. Consumer promotions include samples, COUPONS, PRICE PROMOTIONS, redeemable vouchers for gifts, contests, combination offers, trading stamps, and clubs (e.g. Tesco Club Card). Promotions may also be targeted at the SALES FORCE, e.g. contests and prizes.

## Bibliography

Blattberg, R. C. & Nelsin, S. A. (1990). *Sales promotion: Concepts, methods and strategies.* Englewood Cliffs, NJ: Prentice-Hall.
Kotler, P. (1994). *Marketing management: Analysis, planning, implementation and control* (8th edn). Englewood Cliffs, NJ: Prentice-Hall. Chapter 23.
Peattie, S. & Peattie, K. (1994). Sales promotion. In M. J. Baker (Ed.), *The marketing book* (3rd edn). (Chapter 22, pp. 534–554). Oxford: Butterworth-Heinemann.
Wilmhurst, J. (1993). *Below-the-line promotion.* Oxford: Butterworth-Heinemann.

DAVID YORKE

**sales territory**    A SALES FORCE needs, typically, to be structured in order to achieve its objectives effectively. It can be structured entirely geographically, by product type, by customer type, or by some combination of these. Whichever form is used, each sales person will be allocated a territory, ranging from a few square kilometers/miles to the whole country or, indeed, a number of countries. The simplest form of sales territory is one where all customers are visited or telephoned by one person responsible for all products/services. Where the product range is wide and/or where customer types with differing needs can be readily identified, territories will tend to occupy more than one sales person and, in the former case, customers may be visited/telephoned by more than one person.

There is a need to balance the costs of implementing different structures with the benefits/problems as perceived by individual customers. A particular feature will be the frequency with which each customer needs to be contacted, thus necessitating the planning of sales call cycles within each territory. Such SALES CALL CYCLES will also attempt to balance workload with potential, for each territory.

## Bibliography

Dalrymple, D. J. & Cron, W. L. (1995). *Sales management – Concepts and cases.* New York: John Wiley. Chapter 5.

Kotler, P. (1994). *Marketing management: Analysis, planning, implementation and control* (8th edn). Englewood Cliffs, NJ: Prentice-Hall. Chapter 25.

DAVID YORKE

## sampling

### Census or Sample?

Research is usually undertaken to obtain information about the characteristics or parameters of a population. A population comprises all the individuals or cases or elements that make up the universe of interest in the MARKETING RESEARCH problem being studied. Information about the population may be obtained by taking a census or a sample. A census involves taking measurements from each and every member of the population and population parameters can be computed directly from the measurements obtained. A sample is a subgroup of the population chosen to be representative of the population as a whole. Measurements are taken from each member of the sample, sample characteristics, or statistics, are computed for the sample, and these statistics are used to make inferences or test hypotheses about population parameters and characteristics.

Should a census of the whole population be carried out or should a sample representative of the population be taken? Common sense suggests that when possible a census of the whole population is better but there are compelling reasons for taking samples. These include cost, time, population size, population variability, cost of errors and accuracy required and the destructive nature of some measurements.

### The Sampling Process

A requirement of the sampling process is that the sample should be representative of the population and so permit, if other factors are also satisfactory, accurate estimates of the population parameters and characteristics. The steps in the sampling process are: definition of the population; specification of the sampling frame; selection of the type of sample; determination of the sample size; and implementation of the sampling plan.

Defining the population is often not simple, especially in industrial marketing research. The population may be all organizations in a specified industry, but defining an industry precisely may be difficult. Many organizations operate in several establishments at different sites, so is the population to comprise organizations or establishments? Who is to provide the information? Industrial marketing researchers are aware that buying decisions in organizations are often made by formal decision-making units made up of changing personnel. Will one individual be able to answer for the whole group? If so, which individual should be approached? Or should several individuals be questioned so that interactions within the group and with suppliers' personnel can be studied?

The sampling frame is a list of the population. Examples of frames include the electoral roll, telephone directories, membership lists of professional organizations, and trade directories listing organizations by activity, geographical location, etc.

Any discrepancy between the population and the sampling frame will lead to sampling frame error. For example, electoral rolls are often incomplete even at the time of compilation due to the ineligibility of some members of the population to vote (e.g., those under 18 years of age) and the failure to register by some people. Internal migration, deaths, etc. cause the rolls to become out of date quickly. The electoral roll may not be an appropriate list of the specified population, e.g., the purchase of home owners in a particular area.

A frame is not needed for non-probability samples; rather the sample is chosen on the basis of convenience or by referral in sampling methods such as quota sampling, purposive sampling, snowballing, etc.

There are several considerations to bear in mind when selecting the type of sample. The most important consideration is whether or not to use a probability or a non-probability sample. Probability samples are of various types but involve the use of a frame listing the entire population of interest and the selection of individuals for the sample in such a way that the chance of each individual in the population being chosen for the sample is known. In non-probability samples, methods other than chance selection procedures are used. Probability samples are difficult to select and expensive and time-consuming to use but are preferred by statisticians as rules and formulae derived by mathematicians can be used to allow results from the sample to be related to the population. Non-probability samples are quicker and cheaper to implement and are often preferred by practicing market researchers.

The sample size depends on a number of factors such as the importance of the decision and the level of accuracy desired, the number of variables, the variability of the data, the extent of the decomposition of the sample in order to study segments, and finally, a factor often overlooked by statisticians, the resources available to the researcher.

The sampling plan involves the implementation of the preceding decisions and leads to the actual selection of the sample. The elements selected for the sample are contacted and measurements taken. This involves a substantial amount of office and field work. Data, concerning all the cases in the sample, are collected together and analyzed. The results are interpreted and suggestions for action or further research are made in a report submitted to the client.

### Probability Samples

In probability samples, the probabilities of the individual elements in the population being selected for the sample are known.

*Simple random samples.* In simple random sampling, all of the individual elements in the population have an equal chance of being selected for the sample. A frame or list of the entire population of interest is essential. All of the elements in the frame are given numbers and the numbers of the elements who are to make up the sample are selected at random, by drawing from a hat, by using tables of random numbers, or by a computer using a random number generator. In telephone sampling, the numbers are selected and dialled automatically using a technique called random digit dialing.

It is important to note that an interviewer standing on the street and subjectively selecting people as they walk past will not obtain a random sample. Such samples should not be called random or probability samples and could better be described by a non-technical term such as haphazard samples.

*Systematic samples.* This is very close to simple random sampling. A list of individuals or items in the population is available. The sampling fraction (ratio of the desired sample size to the size of the population) is determined, say, 1 in 20, then a number is chosen at random in the range 1 to 20, say, 8: then the 8th item in the list and every subsequent 20th item, i.e., the 8th, 28th, 48th, 68th, etc. individual is selected for the sample. This is a random sample for at the outset of the process every individual in the population has an equal chance of selection. A possible danger occurs if there is a cyclical pattern to the list that leads to the sample being unrepresentative of the population, but this danger is usually slight. One advantage of systematic sampling over simple random sampling is that the mechanism of selecting the individuals for the sample is simpler – the random selection is done only once – and the effort required is less. Another possible advantage is that a fully detailed frame is not required. For instance, if every 20th customer passing a store is intercepted and interviewed a systematic random sample of people passing by the store can be obtained without knowing the full sampling frame. Thus, for some populations, systematic sampling can be used in shopping mall surveys.

*Stratified samples.* The population is divided into strata (the equivalent marketing term is segments,) such that every element of the population is in precisely one of the strata. Stratified sampling is most suitable when there is much similarity between the elements within each stratum but differences between elements in different stratum. A probabilistic sample, usually a simple random sample, is selected from each stratum, thus ensuring that each stratum is adequately represented. Stratified sampling differs from quota sampling in that the sample elements are selected probabilistically rather than by judgement or convenience as is the case with quota sampling.

Stratified samples can be of two kinds, either with uniform or variable sampling fractions. In the former, the sizes of the samples drawn from the strata are proportionate to the sizes of the populations in each stratum, thus using uniform sampling fractions for each stratum. The latter method, when the sampling fractions of the different strata vary, can be used to increase the efficiency of the sampling by reducing the sampling error of the estimate of the sample mean. Maximum efficiency is obtained when the sampling fractions of the different strata are proportionate to the variance within each stratum. Thus, small sampling fractions occur when there is little within-strata variation; larger sampling fractions are taken in strata where there is more variability. This makes common-sense as when the elements within a stratum are very similar only a small sample needs be taken to get an accurate measure, while larger samples are required to get similar accuracy for strata containing much variability.

Stratified random sampling with variable sampling fractions requires some estimates for the different strata, e.g., the variances, within each stratum, of the variable of interest. It may be possible to base such estimates on information from previous surveys or on the results of pilot surveys.

*Cluster samples.* (Also referred to as multi-stage sampling and area sampling). The population is divided into groups; again every member of the population belongs to precisely one group. Cluster sampling works best when each group is similar and typical of the population as a whole. A random sample of the groups is selected and within each selected group a random sample of individuals is selected. The idea can be extended to more than two stages, but at each stage it is essential that each selection is by use of a probability sampling method.

Often the division into groups is done geographically to reduce interviewing costs by having samples of individuals living close together. Thus, if the basic frame is the electoral roll, a number of parliamentary constituencies are chosen at random, then within the chosen constituencies a number of wards are chosen at random, then within the chosen wards a number of individuals are chosen at random. However, while this reduces interviewing costs, it is likely that the clusters differ from one another and thus it is possible that the clusters selected at the first stage are not typical of the population as a whole.

### Non-probability Samples

*Convenience samples.* Individuals are chosen because they are handy for the researcher. For example, students make up many convenience samples in research carried out by university marketing lecturers, retailers interview their customers, magazines invite their readers to use tear-out questionnaires, etc. It becomes difficult to generalize the results to any sensible population and there is the danger that the sample is untypical of a population, should the researcher have actually specified a population in the first place.

*Purposive samples.* Individuals are selected with some purpose in mind, e.g., in research concerning a new computer, university lecturers may be selected because they are (supposed to be) intelligent, articulate, opinion leaders, etc., whose opinions might be more useful than the views of a purely random sample of the population.

*Judgement samples.* Individuals are chosen to get a sample that, in the judgement of the researcher, is typical of the population. Thus, examples of judgemental samples are: (1) the stores selected for testing new product packaging, (2) constituencies selected for opinion polling, and (3) individuals to take part in focus group sessions. Experience has shown that biases inevitably enter into judgement and that the samples may be non-typical of the population.

*Snowball samples.* Initial respondents are selected and after being interviewed, these respondents are asked to suggest other individuals who belong to the target population. These respondents in turn are asked for suggestions and the sample snowballs. This method has use in industrial buyer–seller research where buyer–seller relationships are being studied; buyers are asked to nominate sellers who nominate other buyers who nominate other sellers, etc. It is useful when the researcher has initial difficulty in identifying members of the target population and without such a method may have many unproductive interviews.

*Quota samples.* The researcher first of all selects variables to be used as control variables so that the selected sample matches the population for these variables. Typical control variables in consumer research are demographic variables such as age, sex, income, geographic location, etc. From knowledge of the composition of the population in terms of the control variables, the researcher gives interviewers quotas of respondents with the specified characteristics. The choice of the individuals is left to the interviewer as long as his sample matches his quota on the specified variables.

Unfortunately, there is no guarantee of fulfilling the hope that because the sample is typical of the population for the control variables it will be typical for all variables. For one thing, it may not be possible to use a key control variable, e.g., education level, due to practical difficulties. For another, the choice of respondents by interviewers may be biased, e.g., interviewers may avoid poorly dressed people, or foreigners who may have difficulties with the language, or people whose location makes interviewing difficult.

Quota sampling is a popular sampling method with market researchers because it attempts to provide representative samples at a low cost. It is like stratified sampling in that samples are chosen from all groups in the population. It can be like area (cluster) sampling in that sample members can be located close together to minimize interviewers' travelling costs. However, at the final step, individuals are not selected probabilistically but according to the judgement of the interviewers. Attempts can be made subsequent to the polling to validate the sample by comparing sample characteristics with known population characteristics other than those used in quota specification. If the sample differs from the population on these characteristics, it indicates bias in the subjective selection procedure.

*Quota Versus Probability Samples*

*Arguments for probability samples.*
(1) Formulae are available so that estimates of population parameters can be made based on data from the sample. Thus, the sample mean and sampling errors can be calculated and used in formulae for CONFIDENCE INTERVALS. The distributions of some statistics are known, enabling hypotheses to be tested. None of this

is possible with quota samples. (Note, the formulae, e.g., for the sampling error, differ according to the type of probability sample used. The formulae for simple random sampling are well known; equivalent formulae for stratified, cluster, etc. samples are more complicated but can be seen in textbooks on sampling.)
(2) It is difficult to ensure quota samples are representative due to interviewer selection bias within quotas and/or with respect to variables not used to define quotas.
(3) It is difficult to check fieldwork in quota samples.

*Arguments for quota samples.*
(1) Quota samples are economical and quick because they are independent of frames, involve no callbacks, and suffer from less non-response.
(2) With proper controls, quota samples can be representative.
(3) Because of non-response, so-called random samples are not random anyway, hence the use of formulae that assume samples are random is questionable.

**Bibliography**

Malhotra, N. K. (1993). *Marketing research: An applied orientation.* Englewood Cliffs, NJ: Prentice-Hall. Chapter 7.

MICHAEL GREATOREX

**scenario building**    Differing assumptions on the future performance of environmental factors (*see* MARKETING ENVIRONMENT) may lead to different predictions or forecasts. These may then be used to construct a range of possible future situations or scenarios, which are often difficult to quantify but may involve complex relationships. Scenarios may be formally constructed at different levels – global, national, regional, or local and may be based on the probability of certain "events" occurring. They may also be totally unstructured when individuals, who are constantly scanning the environment in an informal way by conversations and the monitoring of the media and other sources of information, meet to exchange views. Depending on the product or service, the future time span will vary. Scenario building and the probability of each scenario occurring may be important in deciding on future strategies.

**Bibliography**

Beck, P. W. (1982). Corporate planning for an uncertain future. *Long Range Planning*, 15, (4), 12–21.

Johnson, G. & Scholes, K. (1993). *Exploring corporate strategy*. Prentice-Hall. Chapter 3.

DAVID YORKE

**secondary data**  Secondary data are data that are collected for some purpose other than the problem at hand. The development of commercially available databases and the use of computers has seen a large increase in the use of secondary data. While secondary data are used in all stages of the MARKETING RESEARCH process, they are mainly used in the initial exploratory stages.

Secondary data come from sources internal to the company such as accounting and sales records, and from external sources such as government, industry, and marketing research sources. In addition, libraries have access to books, reports, and articles on a wide range of topics.

The advantage of secondary data is that they can be obtained quickly and, usually, inexpensively. However, secondary data on the required topic may not be available. Secondary data that are available in the general area under study may not fit precisely the requirements of a particular problem. For instance, the geographic area for which the data are available may not coincide with the area for which the data are required. The definitions of the variables may differ; e.g., secondary data on unemployment may be of the numbers of people claiming unemployment benefit which may be different from the numbers available for work. Government data based on the governmental administration process may contain unquantifiable biases, e.g., national income data based on tax returns will be affected by tax evasion. Definitions used in the collection of secondary data may change over time. Secondary data may be published annually when quarterly or monthly data are required. Secondary data may be out of date by the time they are published, e.g., input-output tables.

Internal sources of secondary data include accounting records and sales reports. Sales invoices form the bases of internal accounting records of much of the internal secondary data of interest to marketers. These data when reanalyzed can give a picture of sales over time by product, by customer, by sales territory. Marketing expenditures on such variables as the sales force, advertising, promotion, distribution, new product development, and marketing research can also be determined from internal accounting records. Reports by salespersons on customers and market potential are another internal source of marketing data. The trend toward developing MARKETING INFORMATION SYSTEMS means that a coordinated effort is taking place to collect internal information and make it available on a regular basis to marketing decision-makers.

External sources of information include the growing services from computerized commercial database providers who gather together data from a wide variety of secondary sources. The majority of these provide numerical data but bibliographical databases provide references to articles, reports, and books based upon abstracts and key words. The best-known bibliographical database for marketers is ABI/Inform.

The government and its agencies and associates collect and make available data on a wide range of business and economic topics of interest to marketers. Topics include national income data, production, imports and exports, price data, agriculture, travel and tourism, consumer confidence, etc. UK government publications include the *Annual Abstract of Statistics*, the *Monthly Digest*, *Economic Trends*, the *National Income Blue Book*, the *Business Monitor Series* which give production systems for many different products, the *Family Expenditure Survey*: some of this data is available from the ESRC archives.

Many trade associations collect data about their industries, including size of markets, and distribute this information to members.

Marketing research organizations collect information for sale to customers or on behalf of syndicates of clients. Examples of surveys of the flow of products at the retail level in the UK are Nielsen's Retail Audits which measure sales of a large number of brands through retailers which in turn allows trends in brand shares in total or through different types of outlets or in different regions to be observed and reported to clients. Electronic point of sale scanner equipment which is improving the amount of such data and the speed with which they can be gathered is revolutionizing the provision and use of this kind of data. An example of a survey of consumers in the UK is the Target Group Index (TGI), a large annual survey based on diaries kept by a panel which provides information on who buys what product and prefers which brand. One example of a survey of interest to advertisers in the UK is the National Readership Survey which measures the readership of 200 leading newspapers and magazines, together with a lot of classification information, and is used by media owners to sell, and advertisers and advertising agencies to buy, press advertising. A survey for the UK Broadcasters Audience Research Board (BARB) provides data on TV audiences for the BBC and ITV companies and for advertisers and their agents.

A number of marketing research companies collect data on specific products, industries, or markets in order to sell to many clients. In the UK, Market Intelligence (Mintel), Retail Business, and Keynotes publish monthly reports on different markets.

The amount of secondary data available is great. The examples mentioned above are just a few of the sources of secondary data. The problem is to track down what is available on the topic of interest.

**Bibliography**

Moutinho, L. & Evans, M. (1992). *Applied marketing research*. Wokingham: Addison Wesley, pp. 12–14.

MIKE GREATOREX

**segment**   *see* MARKET SEGMENTATION

**segmentation**   *see* GEODEMOGRAPHICS; MARKET SEGMENTATION; ORGANIZATIONAL SEGMENTATION; POSITIONING; PSYCHOGRAPHICS; SEGMENTATION VARIABLES

**segmentation variables**   The segmentation model requires a selection of a basis for segmentation (the dependent variables) as well as descriptors (the independent variables) of the various segments. Descriptor variables are used to understand more about identified market segments and include: reference group (*see* REFERENCE GROUPS) influences, where people live, where and when they shop, their media habits, what social backgrounds they come from, etc. One of the main reasons for using descriptor variables to profile segments is that readership and viewership data on newspapers, magazines, and television programs tend to be expressed in this way.

Segmentation variables fall into two broad groups: customer characteristics, which include geographic and demographic variables; and consumer responses to a particular product, such as benefits sought, usage occasions, brand loyalties (Kotler, 1991).

*Customer Characteristics*

These include demographic and geographic variables. Demographic variables are most prevalent because consumers can be placed into categories which are easily understood, easily interpreted, relatively easily gathered, widely available from government sources, and easily transferable from one study to another. Demographics are often the best descriptors of identified segments. They include: age; sex; family size; type of residence, whether it be a flat or semi-detached house; income; occupation; education, e.g., secondary, graduate, postgraduate; religion; ethnic origin, e.g., African, Asian, Caribbean, European; nationality; and socioeconomic grouping (SEG). In the UK, one SEG which is commonly used is the A,B,C1, C2,D,E categorization, where A refers to those at the top of their professions such as judges, directors, etc. and E to those on a subsistence level, e.g., state pensioners.

Some markets can easily be segmented by age, e.g., the holiday market has 18–30 holidays and holidays for the over-fifties. However, it is important for marketers to realize that their target can be psychologically, rather than chronologically, young. Age stereotype needs to be guarded against. One can have a 70-year-old who is house bound and another who still actively engages in voluntary work.

Wells & Gubar (1966) identified nine life cycle stages, from a bachelor stage to a retired solitary survivor. The problems with their classification are that it takes no account of the number of single-parent families within many countries, or the increasing number of childless and single sex couples. In addition, the cycles are distorted because more women are postponing having children until later in their lives and family size has declined. Murphy & Staples (1979) devised a more modern family life structure, as follows: (1) Young single. (2) Young married without children. (3a) Young divorced without children. (3b) Young married with children, infant, 4–12 years old, adolescent. (3c) Young divorced with children, infant, 4–12 years old, adolescent. (4a) Middle-aged married without children. (4b) Middle-aged divorced without children. (4c) Middle-aged married with children, young, adolescent. (4d) Middle-aged divorced with children, young, adolescent. (4e) Middle-aged married without dependent children. (4f) Middle-aged divorced without dependent children. (5a) Older married. (5b) Older unmarried, divorced, widowed. (6) Others.

*Geographic segmentation* is used when consumer patterns and preferences vary by geographical location. This can involve looking at the: postcode; city; town; village; coastal or inland; county; region, e.g., television region; country; continent; climate; or population density. For example, a franchise restaurant organization may only locate in cities with a population greater than 100,000 people, while other companies may choose to locate in cities with less than 100,000 people to avoid well-entrenched competitors. Unlike population density, market density refers to the number of potential customers within a unit of land (such as a square kilometer). Unfortunately, many of the measurable geographic variables are not closely related to needs. Only those which are related to local climate or terrain and natural resources can truly be said to have a direct influence on consumers' needs. For example, the market for snow tires is greater in certain mountainous parts of the USA than in Florida; and differences in hobbies such as mountain climbing, surfing, and other recreational activities can clearly be seen to be related to geography.

One major advancement in segmentation in the last two decades has been geodemographics (*see* GEODEMOGRAPHICS). These identify groups of consumers by combining a large number of demographic and geographic variables together. Their advantage is that they are able not only to characterize consumers, but also to identify (to postcode level) where consumers are located. This helps enormously in market measurement and market accessibility.

*Customer Response Characteristics*

These are the second major category of segmentation variables. Basic demographic variables such as age and sex can determine needs well in certain markets, e.g., denim jeans, perfume, and jewelry, but they can result in market segments within which there is considerable variation in consumers' needs and outlook. The use of any variable as a base for market segmentation is ultimately related to the extent to which it can be correlated with product purchase or use. Therein lies the fundamental limitation of using customer demographic characteristics, since they are usually only indirectly related to behavior. Although highly reliable in measurement terms, there is evidence that demographic data have generally failed to explain consumption behavior (*see* Mitchman, 1991; Sheth, 1977). Much more important are customer response variables such as benefits sought, usage patterns, and price sensitivity.

*Benefit segmentation* is the division of a market according to the benefits consumers want from a product. For example, the benefits sought in the soft/drinks market may be: energy; vitamins; low in calories; or low cost. One of the earliest attempts at benefit segmentation was made by Yankelovich (1964) who identified three main benefit segments for watches. These were: a price-sensitive segment, a durability and general product-quality segment, and a segment buying watches as symbols or gifts for some important occasion. Problems are sometimes encountered with benefit segmentation in terms of determining the size of the resultant benefit group and differences in the semantic variations of the stated benefits. Nonetheless, it remains one of the most conceptually-valid approaches to take.

*Volume of consumption* can be one way of segmenting markets, e.g., into non-users, light users, and heavy users of a product. Each user category can have different informational needs. For example, an advertisement to a non-user might give more information about the product class in general, while a regular user might be told the merits of one product versus another. Research has found fewer than half of the consumers can account for between 70 percent and 80 percent of total consumption (Twedt, 1974; Cook & Mindak, 1984). Heavy users of products often have common demographics, PSYCHOGRAPHICS, and media habits as well as needs which make them suitable for targeting with tailored marketing activities.

Another response characteristic is loyalty status (*see also* BRAND LOYALTY). Brand-loyal consumers are of greater value to marketers since it is estimated to cost five times more to attract a new customer than to retain an existing one. Kotler (1991) identifies four categories of loyalty status: hardcore loyals, who buy one brand all the time; softcore loyals who buy two or three brands regularly; shifting loyals, who shift from favoring one brand to another; and switchers who show no loyalty to any brand. By studying softcore loyals a company can pinpoint which brands are most competitive with its own, and by analyzing motives of customers who are shifting away from its brands a company can learn about its marketing weaknesses. Sometimes what appears to be a brand-loyal purchase pattern may reflect habit, indifference, low price, or the non-availability of alternatives. Following this line of argument, Dickson (1994) describes several types of brand loyalty which relate to the reasons for being loyal. These include: emotional loyalty, e.g., to a hospital that saves a child's life; identity loyalty, which is an expression of the self that bolsters the self-esteem, e.g., Porsche cars; differentiated loyalty, which is based on the perceived superiority of features and attributes of a particular appliance; contract loyalty, when the consumer believes that continued loyalty will earn him or her special treatment and that a social contract exists, e.g., loyalty schemes in petrol and grocery retailing; switching-cost loyalty, when the effort involved in considering alternatives and adapting to new alternatives is not worth the expected return, e.g., loyalty to a particular computer system; familiarity loyalty, the result of top-of-the-mind brand awareness, e.g., Coca Cola; and convenience loyalty, which is based on buying convenience, e.g., the most convenient snack at a counter.

*Image segmentation* involves the consumer's self-image or self-concept and its relationship to the image of the product, e.g., perfumes which try to differentiate themselves from each other by having their own distinctive image. While image-oriented features can be difficult to create in new brands, once established in the consumer's mind they can generate many years of consumer loyalty. Landon (1974) discusses two forms of self-concept: one is the regular concept, i.e., how we see ourselves; the other is the ideal concept, i.e., how we would like ourselves to be seen. One criticism of the use of self-image research is the difficulty in identifying cause and effect. If one considers self-image in relation to a product already purchased by the consumer, the consumer's self-image may have already been altered by the purchase of the product. In addition, there is the problem of the non-availability of products which exactly match a person's self-image (*see also* PSYCHOGRAPHICS).

*Purchase occasion* can influence the needs for a particular product. For example, products may be bought as gifts or as self-purchases. In purchase-occasion segmentation, consumers are grouped based on the reasons or times they purchase products. Consumers can also be divided by their *attitudes toward risk* (*see* PERCEIVED RISK) or their *willingness to purchase new products*. Dickson (1994) examines how *time pressure* can affect the purchase of new products and, therefore, be used as a possible segmentation variable. He argues that while the "wealthy" may have more money to buy innovative products, many do not have the time to invest in learning how to use them. The real innovators, then, are likely to be consumers who have more leisure time to devote to their interests. One can observe an interesting role reversal where teenagers teach their parents how to use selected products, particularly electrical equipment. In addition, at any given time, people are at different stages of *readiness to purchase* a product: some are unaware of the product, some are aware, some are informed, some are interested, some have a desire to buy, and some have an intention. Consumers can also be categorized by their *degree of enthusiasm* for a product, e.g., enthusiastic, positive, indifferent, negative, or hostile, as well as by their *price sensitivity*, e.g., during economic recession segments tend to be more price sensitive.

Finally, buyers may differ in their *search behavior* and the way they can be "contacted" by marketers. They use different retail outlets, different shopping styles, are exposed to different media, and are sensitive to different creative advertisements. It is suggested that in mature markets it may be effective to segment by this *contact sensitivity* (Dickinson, 1994). Contact segmentation may also be less obvious to competitors and, therefore, more difficult to imitate.

*See also* **Market segmentation**

**Bibliography**

Cook, V. J. & Mindak, W. A. (1984). A search for constants: The "heavy user" revisited. *Journal of Marketing*, **48**, (4), 79–81.
Dickson, P. R. (1994). *Marketing management*. Orlando, Fla: The Dryden Press (international edn).
Kotler, P. (1991). *Marketing management: Analysis, planning, implementation and control* (7th edn). Englewood Cliffs, NJ: Prentice-Hall.
Landon, E. L. (1974). Self concept, ideal self concept, and consumer purchase intentions. *Journal of Consumer Research*, 1, Sept., 44–51.
Mitchman, R. (1991). *Lifestyle market segmentation*. New York: Praeger.
Murphy, P. E. & Staples, W. A. (1979). A modernized family life cycle. *Journal of Consumer Research*, 6, June, 12–22.
Sheth, J. (1977). *What is multivariate analysis? Multivariate methods for market and survey research*. Chicago: American Marketing Association.
Twedt, D. W. (1974). How important to marketing strategy is the "Heavy User?". *Journal of Marketing*, **38**, Jan., 70–76.
Wells, W. C. & Gubar, G. (1966). Life cycle concept in marketing research. *Journal of Marketing Research*, 3, Nov., 355–363.
Yankelovich, D. (1964). New criteria for market segmentation. *Harvard Business Review*, **42**, Mar.–Apr., 83–90.

VINCE MITCHELL

**selective exposure**   In response to MARKETING COMMUNICATIONS and, in particular, ADVERTISING, consumers are selective in their exposure, perceptions, selection, and retention (*see* CONSUMER PERCEPTIONS). Consumers are potentially exposed, on a daily basis, to many thousands of communications messages. However, they are aware of only a small proportion of these, and selective exposure and perception depends on variables such as congruence with beliefs and attitudes, needs and values, personal characteristics, personality, characteristics of the company and its products/services, and the messages and channels being used.

**Bibliography**

Ries, A. & Trout, J. (1986). *Positioning: The battle for your mind*. New York: McGraw-Hill.
Schramm, W. (1971). How communication works.In W. Schramm, D. F. Roberts (Eds), *The process and effects of mass communication*. Urbana: University of Illinois Press.

DAVID YORKE

**selective perception**   *see* CONSUMER PERCEPTIONS

**selective retention**   Retention of a positive MESSAGE in the mind of a buyer/customer/consumer is a prime objective of MARKETING COMMUNICATIONS. However, before a message is received it is, first of all, subject to SELECTIVE EXPOSURE. Should it overcome this problem, the message still may not have enough IMPACT to compete with others to be stored in the receiver's limited memory. Organizations rely heavily on the expertise of an AGENCY to develop creative and memorable messages for their products and services.

**Bibliography**

Ries, A. & Trout, J. (1986). *Positioning: The battle for your mind*. New York: McGraw-Hill.
Schramm, W. (1971). How communication works.In W. Schramm, D. F. Roberts (Eds), *The process and effects of mass communication*. Urbana: University of Illinois Press.

DAVID YORKE

**self-regulation**   *see* CODES OF PRACTICE

**service characteristics**  A number of generic characteristics of services distinguish them from products, namely, intangibility, inseparability, heterogeneity, and perishability (*see* Lovelock, 1983 & 1991 (Chapter 2); Gronroos, 1990).

*Intangibility*

Services are generally characterized as intangible although tangible elements may prevail (*see* SERVICE PRODUCT). Services may be seen as "performances" rather than products (e.g., entertainment, professional services, education), and are consumed rather than possessed (e.g., legal, hairdressing). They cannot be seen, touched, or used prior to use and often the results of use cannot be seen (e.g., medical treatment, insurance policies, education). This leads to problems for both service providers, e.g., patenting is not possible, promotion is difficult, and quality standards (*see* SERVICE QUALITY) are difficult to set and adhere to; and for the consumer, e.g., testing prior to purchase is not available (*see* Flipo, 1988).

*Inseparability of Production and Consumption*

For most services, creating or performing the service (production) may occur at the same time as partial or full consumption of it (e.g., entertainment, hairdressing). Further, services may be sold before they are produced and consumed (travel services, private and university education). In addition, many services cannot be separated from the person of the service provider (e.g., lawyer, real estate agent), and the service provider is often present when consumption takes place (e.g., hairdresser, advice services). In general the role of service providers' personnel (both customer-contact and "back-room" employees) has implications for human resource management issues. And customers may be involved in the production of a service (e.g., dentist, hairdresser, meal in a restaurant) and affect the service process (*see* SERVICE PROCESS) and the consumers' perceptions of service quality (*see* SERVICE QUALITY). In many instances, inseparability of production and consumption implies that direct sale is the only channel of distribution (*see* SERVICE DISTRIBUTION).

*Heterogeneity*

Heterogeneity of services refers to the variability or lack of standardization or uniformity in the "assembly," "production," and delivery of services. Service standards may not be precise due to a lack of mass production (in most services), i.e., the characteristics of the service product (*see* SERVICE PRODUCT) – e.g., haircuts, football team performance, professional services. There will also be variability with respect to the service environment (*see* SERVICE ENVIRONMENT), i.e., the mix of physical facilities involved, and the involvement of people (both service personnel and customers) in the production and delivery process.

Lovelock (1983 & 1991) also refers to variation with respect to customization and judgement in service delivery, i.e., the extent to which the service is customized to meet consumer needs (high for professional services, health care, education, restaurants), and the extent to which customer-contact personnel exercise judgement in meeting individual customers' demands.

*Perishability*

Services are perishable and so cannot be stored. Perishability is manifested in various ways: e.g., if theater seats and hotel rooms are not sold and occupied then their capacity is wasted; "no-shows" and vacant appointments with dentists and other service professionals represent an element of lost capacity although the provider may be able to use the time for some other, more peripheral, purpose; under-enrollment in a class is also wasted capacity and revenue – although it might improve the quality of service provided to those in the class. Potential perishability is exacerbated by fluctuating demand which service providers may be able to manage (e.g., with respect to utilities) or which may present problems (e.g., with respect to transport, accommodation, theater seats). Excess demand may lead to delays, unmet demand, and dissatisfied customers.

Service providers manage their supply and demand in a number of ways (*see* Sasser, 1976; Maister, 1985; Lovelock, 1991 (Chapter 6); Mudie & Cottam, 1993; Palmer, 1994). Demand may be managed by:

- differential pricing and price incentives at non-peak times (*see* SERVICE PRICE)

- developing and promoting non-peak demand

- developing complementary services for consumers while they are waiting

- creating reservation systems to reduce waiting

- using technology/computers in service delivery.

Alternatively, service companies aim to manage supply through a combination of:

- part-time employees

- increased customer participation (to reduce labor input)

- shared capacity and services

- multiple jobs for employees

- a substitution of machines for labor

- attempts to maximize efficiency.

**Bibliography**

Flipo, J. P. (1988). On the intangibility of services. *The Service Industries Journal*, 8, (3), 286–298.

Gronroos, C. (1990). *Service management and marketing*. Chapter 2 Lexington, MA: Lexington Books.

Lovelock, C. H. (1983). Classifying services to gain strategic marketing insights. *Journal of Marketing*, 47, Summer 9–20.

Lovelock, C. H. (1991). *Services marketing* (2nd edn). Prentice-Hall. Chapters 2 & 6.

Maister, D. H. (1985). The psychology of waiting lines. In J. A. Czepiel, M. R. Solomon, C. F. Surprenant (Eds), *The service encounter*, Lexington, MA: Lexington Books.

Mudie, P. & Cottam, A. (1993). *The management and marketing of services*. Oxford: Butterworth-Heinemann. Chapter 8.

Palmer, A. (1994). *Principles of marketing*. Maidenhead: McGraw-Hill. Chapter 7.

Sasser, W. E. (1976). Match supply and demand in service industries. *Harvard Business Review*, 48, Nov.–Dec., 133–140.

BARBARA LEWIS

**service delivery**  The consumer may be actively involved in the production and delivery process, e.g., in applying for a loan, providing information for tax returns, using salad bars in restaurants, and explaining symptoms to a health care professional. The organization may have to "manage" the customer input; e.g., to tell him/her how to use equipment in a gym, to clear the table in McDonalds, and "how to behave" in DisneyWorld. This will facilitate and enhance the service encounter (*see* SERVICE ENCOUNTERS). Customers' participation in service delivery may provide them with some control in the service delivery process, allow more customization, and a faster service, and may lead to lower prices.

Technology is typically central to service delivery, and also integral to the SERVICE PRODUCT, SERVICE PROCESS, and SERVICE ENVIRONMENT, and technological advances have made major contributions to facilitating customer–company exchanges and to increasing levels of service. For example, mechanization and computerization can increase speed, efficiency, and accuracy of service (e.g., in stock-taking, ordering and distribution, operations, reservations systems, management and marketing information systems, and security systems), but can also depersonalize service. Depersonalized service can free employees for other activities which may detract from customer contact and lead to less customer loyalty; or it may allow employees time to concentrate on developing interactions and relationships to maintain customer loyalty. Ultimately, technology will not replace people in the provision of service(s), and "high-tech" and "high-touch" go hand in hand – better personal service with enhanced technological efficiency.

*See also* **Service distribution; Service guarantees; Service process**

**Bibliography**

Kelley, S. W., Donnelly, J. H. & Skinner, S. J. (1990). Customer participation in service production and delivery. *Journal of Retailing*, 66, (3), Fall 315–335.

BARBARA LEWIS

**service design**  Design management is relevant in the context of the SERVICE PRODUCT and also relates to other elements of the marketing mix, in particular the extended marketing mix for the services sector (*see* Booms & Bitner, 1981). Service design is discussed in a special issue of the *Design Management Journal* (1992) and by Mudie & Cottam (1993). A particular aspect of service design is service blueprinting which is basically a flowchart of the service process (*see* SERVICE PROCESS) in which all the elements or activities, their sequencing, and interactions can be visualized (*see* Shostack, 1984 & 1987; Kingmann-Brundage, 1989).

### Bibliography

Booms, B. H. & Bitner, M. J. (1981). Marketing strategies and organizational structures for service firms. In J. H. Donnelly & W. R. George (Eds), *Marketing of services* (pp. 47–51). Chicago: American Marketing Association.

*Design Management Journal* (1992). Special issue: Design in service industries. *Design Management Journal*, **3**, (1), Winter

Kingmann-Brundage, J. (1989). *Blueprinting for the bottom line*. Proceedings of the Annual Services Marketing Conference. Chicago: American Marketing Association.

Mudie, P. & Cottam, A. (1993). *The management and marketing of services*. Oxford: Butterworth-Heinemann. Chapter 3.

Shostack, G. L. (1984). Designing services that deliver. *Harvard Business Review*, **62**, Jan.–Feb., 133–139.

Shostack, G. L. (1987). Service positioning through structural change. *Journal of Marketing*, **51**, Jan., 34–43.

BARBARA LEWIS

**service distribution** Service distribution channels comprise service firms, their intermediaries, and their customers. Typically, there are high levels of direct sale due to the inseparability of services and the provider organizations, e.g., business and professional services, utilities, personal services; together with the existence of intermediaries, e.g., agents for tourism, insurance, employment, and retailers. Quasi-retail outlets are also used to sell services: e.g., banks, building societies, launderettes, hotels, real estate agents.

In addition, one needs to consider the ways in which the customer is involved in service distribution (*see also* SERVICE DELIVERY). Sometimes the customer travels to the service-providing organization, e.g., theater, airplane, hotel; and at other times the provider comes to the customer, e.g., business and household

cleaning services. Various services may have both types of distribution, e.g., taxi services, hairdressing, beauty services, professional business services. A third scenario may involve no direct personal interaction, e.g., TV and radio services, and other remote service operations.

A recent trend in service distribution is the growth of franchising; this happens when standardization is possible and includes industries such as fast food, hotel chains, car rental, dry cleaning, and employment services. Technology also has increasing impact on services distribution, e.g., in: financial services with delivery from remote locations; the use of software packages to facilitate "best deals" for buying insurance and mortgages; and reservation systems for tourism and hospitality organizations, professional services, health care, etc.

### Bibliography

Cowell, D. W. (1984). *The marketing of services*. London: Heinemann. Chapter 10.

Palmer, A. (1994). *Principles of marketing*. Maidenhead: McGraw-Hill. Chapter 10.

BARBARA LEWIS

**service encounters** The extent of direct interaction between a service provider and its customers in the service delivery process is referred to as service encounters or "moments of truth" or "critical incidents" (*see* Carlzon, 1987; Czepiel et al., 1985).

A service encounter may take varying forms. For example, a bank customer wishing to make account enquiries may choose between an interaction with an ATM, or with a bank employee by telephone, letter, or face to face in a branch. Every time the customer comes into contact with an aspect of the bank and its employees there is an opportunity to form an impression and evaluation of the bank and its service(s). Service encounters, in particular those involving employees, have a high impact on consumers and the quality of the encounter is an essential element in the overall quality of service experienced by the customer (*see* SERVICE QUALITY).

Service encounters also have an impact on employees in relation to their motivation, performance, job satisfaction, and rewards.

Recent perspectives and research relating to service encounters are reported by Bitner (1990), Bitner et al. (1990), and Larson (1990).

## Bibliography

Bitner, M. J. (1990). Evaluating service encounters: The effects of physical surroundings and employee responses. *Journal of Marketing*, **54**, (2), Apr., 69–82.

Bitner, M. J., Booms, B. H. & Tetreault, M. S. (1990). The service encounter: Diagnosing favourable and unfavourable incidents. *Journal of Marketing*, **54**, (1), Jan., 71–84.

Carlzon, J. (1987). *Moments of truth*. Cambridge, MA: Ballinger Publishing Co.

Czepiel, J. A., Solomon, M. R. & Surprenant, C. F. (Eds) (1985). *The service encounter: Managing employee–customer interaction in service businesses*. Lexington, MA: Lexington Books.

Larson, L. (1990). Service encounter evaluations: Different perspectives. In E. Langeard & P. Eiglier (Eds), *Marketing, operations and human resources insights into service* (pp. 426–449). First International Research Seminar in Service Management. Aix-en-Provence, France: IAE.

Mudie, P. & Cottam, A. (1993). *The management and marketing of services*. Oxford: Butterworth-Heinemann. Chapter 6.

Palmer, A. (1994). *Principles of services marketing*. Maidenhead: McGraw-Hill. Chapter 7.

Shostack, G. L. (1985). Planning the service encounter. In J. A. Czepiel, M. R. Solomon, C. F. Surprenant (Eds), *The Service Encounter* (pp. 243–253). Lexington, MA: Lexington Books.

BARBARA LEWIS

**service environment**   The service environment (or physical evidence) plays a key role in almost all service production and delivery; exceptions would comprise remote services such as communications and utilities. The service environment includes consideration of the physical environment (both physical design and access aspects, and emotional or atmospheric impact), and also facilitating goods and tangible clues – all of which influence consumers' (and employees') judgements of a services marketing organization. The physical design comprises aspects of space, color, furnishings, temperature, noise, music, decor, layout, and employee dress and provides an atmosphere within which the consumer buys and consumes services. Access includes hours, availability, convenience of location, and privacy. Closely integrated with these are facilitating goods (e.g., cars used by a rental company) and tangible clues (e.g., wrappings for dry cleaning, report folders of accountants) utilized by service organizations to create awareness of and interest in their offerings and to differentiate themselves from competitors. Sometimes the tangible aspects are essential to the provision of the service (e.g., aircraft) and other times much more peripheral and/or of no independent value (e.g., the "freebies" in hotel bathrooms, report folders, check books).

The service environment has been a major focus of research for Bitner (1990 & 1992) who introduces the concept of "servicescapes" which may involve customers only (e.g., in self-service), employees only (as in remote services), or customer–employee interactions as in most service delivery. She discusses the effects of physical settings on both customer expectations, perceptions, and satisfactions, and on employee motivation and ability to work. Perceptions of the environment lead to emotions, beliefs, and in turn behavior. For example, the office decor, furniture, and clothes of a lawyer lead to consumer beliefs about his/her success, cost, and trustworthiness; and to employee opinions about the desirability of the organization and lawyer as employers. Further, pleasurable environments lead to positive customer evaluations of a service and a desire to spend more time and money there, whereas unpleasant servicescapes lead to avoidance.

## Bibliography

Bitner, M. J. (1990). Evaluating service encounters: The effects of physical surroundings and employee responses. *Journal of Marketing*, **54**, (2), Apr., 69–82.

Bitner, M. J. (1992). Servicescapes: The impact of physical surroundings on customers and employees. *Journal of Marketing*, **56**, Apr., 57–71.

Cowell, D. W. (1984). *The marketing of services*. London: Heinemann. Chapter 12.

Mudie, P. & Cottam, A. (1993). *The management and marketing of services*. Oxford: Butterworth-Heinemann. Chapter 4.

BARBARA LEWIS

**service guarantees**  In the provision and delivery of services and service, as customers' expectations and company standards rise, organizations become competitive in the promises they make to customers and there is now increasing evidence of service guarantees in both the public and private sectors: e.g., a hotel chain which offers cash compensation if difficulties are not resolved in 30 minutes; a pizza delivery which becomes free after a certain time delay; telecommunications promises with respect to waiting periods for telephone installations and repair of faults; and the mail services' compensation for late/lost delivery and damaged items. In the public sector there is increasing evidence of service charters and standards, and in financial services codes of practice in which customers are advised of their rights.

Some aspects of service and customer satisfaction cannot be guaranteed, e.g., unconditional on-time arrival of planes, and so promises and guarantees have to be realistic (Hart, 1988). A good service guarantee should be unconditional, easy to understand and communicate, easy to invoke, and easy to collect on. It should also be meaningful, especially with respect to payout which should be a function of the cost of the service, seriousness of failure and perception of what is fair, e.g., 15-minute lunch service in a restaurant or a free meal.

Ideally a service guarantee should get everyone in a company to focus on good service and to examine service delivery systems for possible failure points. However, inevitably, failures may occur and some customers will become dissatisfied of whom (only) a small proportion will complain.

Hart et al. (1990) discuss the additional costs of replacing customers over those of trying to retain customers who may be dissatisfied. They also refer to evidence of customers who complain and who then receive a satisfactory response subsequently being more loyal to an organization, more likely to buy other services/products, and more likely to engage in positive word-of-mouth communication. Reichfeld & Sasser (1990) also discuss the financial benefits of retaining customers and the need, if possible, to monitor defecting customers and their reasons for leaving a company.

Consequently, organizations are encouraging dissatisfied customers to complain, in order to discourage negative word-of-mouth communication, and to retain rather than replace customers. In so doing they are managing service recovery (*see* SERVICE RECOVERY).

**Bibliography**

Hart, C. W. L. (1988). The power of unconditional service guarantees. *Harvard Business Review*, July–Aug., 54–62.

Hart, C. W. L., Heskett, J. L. & Sasser, Jr, W. E. (1990). The profitable art of service recovery. *Harvard Business Review*, **90**, (4), July–Aug., 148–56.

Mudie, P. & Cottam, A. (1993). *The management and marketing of services*. Oxford: Butterworth-Heinemann. Chapter 11.

Reichheld, F. F. & Sasser, Jr, W. E. (1990). Zero defections: Quality comes to services. *Harvard Business Review*, **68**, (5), Sept.–Oct., 105–11.

BARBARA LEWIS

**service personnel**   *see* INTERNAL MARKETING

**service price**  The price of a service is not always readily known or available to the consumer. For example, the consumer may not know the price prior to production and delivery (e.g., dentist, professional services) as the requirement for the service is not fully known at the onset. Even if the consumer has a fair indication of the amount of service required (e.g., painting a house), the price may depend on the skills required from the person of the service provider and in turn the time involved. So the price may then relate to time and speed of delivery and in turn necessitate quotations or estimates to provide information to the consumer prior to production commencing.

Pricing of services is further complicated by the use of various terminologies to reflect how much the consumer pays. Examples include:

● admissions – e.g., to a theater. Consumers do not all pay the same price, which depends on variables such as the place, event, seat location, age of customer, number of customers, time of day, and season.

- charges – e.g., hairdresser, which depend on the skills of the people involved in delivery.

- commission – e.g., estate agent, depends on the amount of business being considered – e.g., value of property.

- fares – e.g., transport. These vary with respect to the company, distance travelled, age of passenger, number of passengers, seat, location, time, and seasonality.

- fees – e.g., professional services, may be a function of an hourly rate, fee for the job, or some more complex method.

- interest – e.g., financial services organizations. This is a charge for the use of money and is a function of the amount borrowed, company policy, and in turn the prevailing interest rates in the economy.

- taxes – levied by both local and central governments for citizen and community services. Tax levels will depend on consumers' income, type and location of home, and government policies; and typically the consumer has no choice with respect to taxation levels.

- salaries and wages – for employment. Levels depend on employee skills, length of service, labor union influence, employee performance, etc.

In setting prices, many service providers take account of the fact that price is one mechanism for balancing fluctuations in supply and demand (*see* SERVICE CHARACTERISTICS) and may participate in one or more types of pricing tactics:

- flexible or differential pricing to build demand at non-peak times, to even out fluctuations in demand, and to decrease perishability;

- discounts – e.g., promotional pricing;

- diversionary – e.g., a basic meal in a restaurant at a low price but with expensive "extras;"

- guaranteed pricing – e.g., estate agents who only charge when a sale is made, and employment agencies who only charge client fees when employee recruitment is completed.

**Bibliography**

Cowell, D. W. (1984). *The marketing of services.* London: Heinemann. Chapter 8.
Palmer, A. (1994). *Principles of services marketing.* Maidenhead: McGraw-Hill. Chapter 11.

BARBARA LEWIS

**service process**   The process of service production and delivery is concerned with operations management issues. Operations management is potentially problematic in services due to problems in managing supply and demand and the variability of services (*see* SERVICE CHARACTERISTICS) and the role of employees in production and delivery (*see* INTERNAL MARKETING); and the incumbent issue of lack of traditional quality standards and control (*see* SERVICE QUALITY).

Nevertheless, service organizations set standards and develop delivery systems which operate efficiently and effectively, and which are responsive and reliable, ranging from systems for car hire pick-up, procedures for providing loans and mortgages, preparing and serving restaurant meals, and integrated reservations systems in the travel industry.

Silvestro et al. (1992) classify service process/ delivery on a continuum ranging from mass services to professional services. Mass services have many customer interactions, limited contact time and customization, a product orientation, and with value added in the back office (e.g., fast food). In contrast, professional services are characterized by few transactions, highly customized services, a process orientation, relatively long provider–customer contact time, and with most value added in the front office. Setting standards and designing systems and processes involves consideration of the service being offered, the extent of organization–customer interaction, the degree of customization, the impact of advanced computer technology (*see* SERVICE DELIVERY), and employee-related issues (*see* INTERNAL MARKETING).

Recent research focused on the service process and the need for dynamic models is reported by Gronroos (1992) and Boulding et al. (1993).

Bibliography

Boulding, W., Katra, A., Staelin, R. & Zeithaml, V. A. (1992). A dynamic process model of service quality: From expectations to behavioural intentions. *Journal of Marketing Research*, **30**, 7–27.

Chase, R. B. & Hayes, R. H. (1992). Applying operations strategy to service firms. In T. A. Swartz, D. E. Bowen & S. W. Brown (Eds) *Advances in services marketing and management* (pp. 53–74). London: JAI Press.

Cowell, D. W. (1984). *The marketing of services*. London: Heinemann. Chapter 13.

Gronroos, C. (1992). Towards a third phase in services quality research: Challenges and future directions.In *Frontiers in Services Conference*, Sept., Chicago: American Marketing Association.

Silvestro, R., Fitzgerald, L., Johnston, R. & Voss, C. (1992). Towards a classification of service processes. *International Journal of Service Industry Management*, **3**, (3), 62–75.

BARBARA LEWIS

**service product**   A service or service product may be defined as "an activity(s) of more or less intangible nature that normally, but not necessarily, takes place in inter-action between the customer and service employees and/or physical resources or goods and/or systems of the service provider, which are provided as solutions to customer problems" (Shostack, 1984). Shostack highlights the fact that the distinction between services and products is not clear-cut, that there are few pure services and products. For example, a car is a physical object and an airline provides a service, but transport is common to both. Shostack (1977 & 1982) provides molecular models which combine product and service elements, and she also offers a continuum of market offerings of products and services with respect to their tangibility (*see* SERVICE CHARACTERISTICS), i.e., tangible elements (*see* figure 1).

A further view of the service product is provided by Gronroos (1987 & 1990) who develops a concept of the service product – the service offering – which is geared to the concept of perceived service quality (*see* SERVICE QUALITY). First, there is the basic or core service package, e.g., a hotel, with facilitating services which are required to facilitate consumption of the service (e.g., reception) together with supporting services which are not required but which enhance the service and differentiate it from competition (e.g., restaurants and bars, leisure and conference facilities). All this is what the customer receives. In addition, one needs to consider how the service is delivered or received which is dependent on the augmented service offering. This includes the accessibility of the service; the extent of customer participation; and interactions/communications between the service provider (its personnel, systems, technology, and environment) and the consumer.

Further aspects of the service product – i.e., service product planning and development – are discussed by Cowell (1984) and Palmer (1994).

Bibliography

Cowell, D. W. (1984). *The marketing of services*. London: Heinemann. Chapter 7.

Gronroos, C. (1987). Developing the service offering: A source of competitive advantage.Sept., Helsinki: Swedish School of Economics and Business Administration.

Gronroos, C. (1990). *Service management and marketing*. Lexington, MA: Lexington Books. Chapter 4.

Palmer, A. (1994). *Principles of services marketing*. Maidenhead: McGraw-Hill. Chapter 6.

Rathmell, J. (1966). What is meant by services. *Journal of Marketing*, **30**, Oct., 32–36.

Shostack, G. L. (1977). Breaking free from product marketing. *Journal of Marketing*, Apr., 73–80.

Shostack, G. L. (1982). How to design a service. *European Journal of Marketing*, **16**, (1), 49–63.

Shostack, G. L. (1984). Designing services that

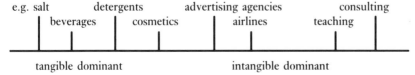

e.g. salt        detergents        advertising agencies        consulting
     beverages     cosmetics     airlines     teaching

tangible dominant          intangible dominant

*Figure 1: The Service Product*
*Source*: Shostack, 1977 & 1982

deliver. *Harvard Business Review*, **62**, Jan.–Feb., 133–139.

BARBARA LEWIS

**service promotion**    The communication and promotion of services presents problems for providers due to the features of services (*see* SERVICE CHARACTERISTICS), in particular intangibility (services cannot usually be presented as physical entities), and variability in their production and delivery – due to the presence and participation of service personnel. In advertising services, organizations may try to: create tangible clues; capitalize on word-of-mouth communication, e.g., feature satisfied customers and persuade them to tell others about the service; demonstrate employees in work roles and situations; and "promise what is possible" (George & Berry, 1981). The last aspect is critical with respect to consumers' perceptions of service quality (*see* SERVICE QUALITY); it is essential for organizations to be able to follow through on what they say or claim about their services, employees, and delivery. They should only promise what can be delivered a very high proportion of the time – in order to foster realistic consumer expectations. A further aspect of promotion in the services sector is personal selling, due to the high levels of interaction and personal contact between the service organization and its employees, and their customers.

**Bibliography**

Cowell, D. W. (1984). *The marketing of services.* London: Heinemann. Chapter 9.

Dobree, J. & Page, A. S. (1991). Unleashing the power of service brands in the 1990s. *Management Decision*, **28**, (6), 14–28.

George, W. R. & Berry, L. L. (1981). Guidelines for the advertising of services. *Business Horizons*, July–Aug., 52–56.

Gronroos, C. (1990). *Services management and marketing.* Lexington, MA: Lexington Books. Chapter 7.

Mudie, P. & Cottam, A. (1993). *The management and marketing of services.* Oxford: Butterworth-Heinemann. Chapter 9.

BARBARA LEWIS

**service quality**    Service quality is critical for all organizations in the services sector (*see* SERVICES SECTOR), and for the manufacturing sector in relation to customer service – before, during, and after sales. The provision and delivery of services and service involves a variety of interactions between an organization and its customers (*see* SERVICE ENCOUNTERS) and, in particular, the organization's personnel are instrumental in the creation and provision of service quality. The concept of service quality is wide and includes service to the customer (providing what is required and being "nice" to the customer), delivery/operations, employees' relationships with customers, and internal relationships between employees and management. In developing service quality strategies and programs, organizations are managing products and services, systems, environment, and people, which brings together marketing, operations management, and human resource management; and service quality programs are increasingly integral to total quality management initiatives within companies.

The need for service quality is driven by customers, employees and a changing business environment:

- Customers, be they individuals, households, or organizations, are increasingly aware of alternatives on offer, in relation to services and provider organizations, and also of rising standards of service(s). Consequently, their expectations rise and they become more critical of the quality of service received. In addition, knowledge of the costs and benefits of keeping customers relative to attracting new ones draws companies' attention to looking after present customers, responding to their needs and problems, and developing long-term relationships (*see* RELATIONSHIP MARKETING). Looking after customers does not conflict with profitability.

- Looking after employees is also an opportunity for an organization. As companies become larger, they may also become anonymous and bureaucratic. Communications may deteriorate and relationships (between customers and customer contact personnel, between customer-contact staff and backroom staff, and between staff and management) may suffer. Further, in a recession climate, cost-cutting exercises and reorganizations can impact on staff morale, motivation, and performance. However, companies are realizing that commitment to employees brings rewards (*see* INTERNAL MARKETING).

- The business environment is characterized by economic, legal, and technological changes. For example, in financial services, the laws resulting in deregulation have increased competition and brought retailers into the industry, thus providing more choice for the consumer. In air travel, deregulation has brought not only competition but also problems of survival. In a competitive environment companies react by emphasizing operations and financial efficiency and/or more focused product and market strategies. Additionally, they can focus on service quality in their corporate and marketing strategies. Superior service quality may be seen as a mechanism to achieve differentiation and a competitive advantage, and so become integral to the overall direction and strategy of an organization.

With a focus on service quality an organization can expect a number of benefits:

- Customer loyalty through satisfaction. Looking after present customers can generate repeat and increased business and may lead to attraction of new customers from positive word-of-mouth communication. Customer retention is more cost-effective than trying to attract new customers. Cost savings also accrue from "getting things right the first time."

- Increased opportunities for cross-selling. Comprehensive and up-to-date product knowledge and sales techniques among employees, combined with developing relationships and rapport with customers, enables staff to identify customer needs and suggest relevant products/services.

- Employee benefits which may be seen in terms of increased job satisfaction and morale and commitment to the company, successful employer–employee relationships and increased staff loyalty, which contribute to reducing the rate of staff turnover and the associated costs of recruitment, selection, and

training activities. Committed and competent employees will also make fewer mistakes (and in turn lead to fewer customer complaints) and so contribute to further costs savings.

- In addition, good service enhances corporate image and may provide insulation from price competition; some customers may pay a premium for reliable service. Overall, successful service leads to reduced costs (of mistakes, operating, advertising, and promotion) and increased productivity and sales, market shares, profitability, and business performance.

*Service Quality Programs*

Service quality initiatives are high priorities in many organizations with expenditure seen as long-term investment for future growth and profitability. The development of service quality programs requires first, an awareness and understanding of the interactions between an organization and its customers and employees (*see* SERVICE ENCOUNTERS) and, in turn, the areas for potential service quality shortfalls (*see* SERVICE QUALITY GAPS). Programs typically involve a number of stages:

- Identifying the key components of service quality (*see* SERVICE QUALITY DIMENSIONS) from internal (employees) and external customer research – their needs and expectations from the company. These relate to the products/services being offered (*see* SERVICE PRODUCT), delivery systems (*see* SERVICE PROCESS and SERVICE DELIVERY), delivery environment (*see* SERVICE ENVIRONMENT), technology (*see* SERVICE DELIVERY), and employees (*see* INTERNAL MARKETING) – which are highly interdependent.

- Measuring the importance of service quality dimensions (*see* SERVICE QUALITY DIMENSIONS and SERVICE QUALITY MEASUREMENT).

- Translating customer and employee needs into appropriate product/service specifications (*see* SERVICE PRODUCT).

- Setting measurable standards and systems for service delivery to include a suitable delivery environment (*see* SERVICE ENVIRONMENT).

- Making the best use of technology in products/services, systems, and environment (*see* SERVICE DELIVERY).

- Developing personnel policies to include recruitment, selection, training, rewards, and recognition (*see* INTERNAL MARKETING).

- Managing the delivery process (*see* SERVICE QUALITY GAPS; SERVICE DELIVERY; SERVICE PROCESS). This includes paying attention to potential failure points, and developing service guarantees and procedures for service recovery (*see* SERVICE GUARANTEES and SERVICE RECOVERY).

- Monitoring service quality initiatives, i.e., developing systems to research and evaluate customer satisfaction and dissatisfaction (*see* SERVICE QUALITY MEASUREMENT) and employee performance (*see* INTERNAL MARKETING).

In order for an organization to be successful with its service quality program there needs to be management commitment to service quality and the creation of an appropriate culture. The organizational culture may require changes to achieve employee orientation to the company and everyone's orientation to the external customer. This change starts at the top: the service quality process begins with senior management commitment to employees and customers, ideally with strong and visible leaders.

### Bibliography

Berry, L. L. & Parasuraman, A. (1991). *Marketing services: Competing through quality.* New York: Free Press.

Brown, S. W., Gummesson, E., Edvardsson, B. & Gustavsson, B. O. (1990). *Service quality: Multi-disciplinary and multinational perspectives.* Lexington, MA: Lexington Books.

Gronroos, C. (1984). A service quality model and its marketing implications. *European Journal of Marketing,* 18 (4), 36–43.

Gronroos, C. (1990). *Service management and marketing: Managing the moments of truth in service competition.* Lexington, MA: Lexington Books.

Heskett, J. L., Sasser, W. E. & Hart, C. W. L. (1990). *Service breakthroughs: Changing the rules of the game.* New York: Free Press.

Lovelock, C. H. (1991). *Services marketing* (2nd edn). Prentice Hall. Chapter 11.

Palmer, A. (1994). *Principles of services marketing.* Maidenhead: McGraw-Hill. Chapter 8.

Zeithaml, V. A., Parasuraman, A. & Berry, L. L. (1990). *Delivering service quality: Balancing customer perceptions and expectations.* New York: Free Press.

BARBARA LEWIS

**service quality dimensions** The dimensions of service quality relate to the products/services being offered, delivery systems, delivery environment, technology, and employees (*see* SERVICE QUALITY), and have been widely conceptualized and researched. Lehtinen & Lehtinen (1982) refer to process quality, as judged by consumers during a service, and output quality judged after a service is performed. They also make a distinction between physical quality (products or support), interactive quality (where the dimensions of quality originate in the interaction between the customer and the service organization), and corporate quality (Lehtinen & Lehtinen, 1991).

Gronroos (1984) discussed the technical (outcome) quality of service encounters, i.e., what is received by the customer, and the functional quality of the process, i.e., the way in which the service is delivered. Functional aspects include the attitudes, behavior, appearance and personality, service-mindedness, accessibility, and approachability of customer-contact personnel. In addition, there exists the "corporate image" dimension of quality which is the result of how customers perceive an organization and is built up by the technical and functional quality of its services. This model was later incorporated with one from manufacturing which incorporates design, production, delivery, and relational dimensions (Gummesson & Gronroos, 1987).

LeBlanc & Nguyen (1988) suggested that corporate image, internal organization, physical support of the service product, systems, staff–customer interaction, and degree of customer satisfaction all contribute to service quality. Further, Edvardsson et al. (1989) present four aspects of quality which affect customers' perceptions:

- Technical quality – to include skills of service personnel and the design of the service system.

- Integrative quality – the ease with which different portions of the service delivery system work together.

- Functional quality – to include all aspects of the manner in which the service is delivered to the customer, to include style, environment, and availability.

- Outcome quality – whether or not the actual service product meets both service standards or specifications and customer needs/expectations.

However, the most widely reported set of service quality determinants is that proposed by Parasuraman et al. (1985 & 1988). They suggest that the criteria used by consumers that are important in molding their expectations and perceptions of service fit ten dimensions:

- Tangibles: physical evidence

- Reliability: getting it right the first time, honoring promises

- Responsiveness: willingness, readiness to provide service

- Communication: keeping customers informed in a language they can understand

- Credibility: honesty, trustworthiness

- Security: physical, financial, and confidentiality

- Competence: possession of required skills and knowledge of all employees, e.g., to carry out instructions

- Courtesy: politeness, respect, friendliness

- Understanding/knowing the customer, e.g., his or her needs and requirements

- Access: ease of approach and contact, e.g., opening hours, queues, phones.

Subsequent factor analysis and testing by Parasuraman et al. (1990) condensed these ten determinants into five categories (tangibles, reliability, responsiveness, assurance, and empathy) to which Gronroos (1988) added a sixth dimension – recovery (*see* SERVICE RECOVERY).

In addition, there is the contribution of Johnston et al. (1990) and Silvestro & Johnston (1990), investigating quality in UK organizations. They identified 15 dimensions of service

quality which they categorized as: hygiene factors – expected by the customer and where failure to deliver will cause dissatisfaction (e.g., cleanliness in restaurant, train arrival on time); enhancing factors – which lead to customer satisfaction but where failure to deliver will not necessarily cause dissatisfaction (e.g., bank clerk addressing one by name); and dual threshold factors – where failure to deliver will cause dissatisfaction, and delivery above a certain level will enhance customers' perceptions of service and lead to satisfaction (e.g., a full explanation of a mortgage service).

## Bibliography

Edvardsson, B., Gustavsson, B. O. & Riddle, D. I. (1989). An expanded model of the service encounter with emphasis on cultural context. Research Report 89: 4. University of Karlstad, Sweden: CTF Research Centre.

Gronroos, C. (1984). *Strategic management and marketing in the service sector.* Bromley, UK: Chartwell-Bratt.

Gronroos, C. (1988). Service quality: The six criteria of good perceived service quality. *Review of Business*, **9**, (3), Winter, 10–13.

Gummesson, E. & Gronroos, C. (1987). *Quality of products and services: A tentative synthesis between two models.* Research Report 87: 3. University of Karlstad, Sweden: Services Research Centre.

Johnston, R., Silvestro, R., Fitzgerald, L. & Voss, C. (1990). Developing the determinants of service quality. In E. Langeard & P. Eiglier (Eds), *Marketing, operations and human resources insights into service* (pp. 373–400). First International Research Seminar on Services Management. Aix-en-Provence, France: IAE.

LeBlanc, G. & Nguyen, N. (1988). Customers' perceptions of service quality in financial institutions. *International Journal of Bank Marketing*, **6**, (4), 7–18.

Lehtinen, U. & Lehtinen, J. R. (1982). *Service quality: A study of quality dimensions.* Working paper. Helsinki: Service Management Institute.

Lehtinen, U. & Lehtinen, J. R. (1991). Two approaches to service quality dimensions. *The Service Industries Journal*, **11**, (3), 287–303.

Parasuraman, A., Zeithaml, V. A. & Berry, L. L. (1985). A conceptual model of service quality and its implications for future research. *Journal of Marketing*, **49**, Fall, 41–50.

Parasuraman, A., Zeithaml, V. A. & Berry, L. L. (1988). SERVQUAL: A multiple item scale for measuring consumer perceptions of service quality. *Journal of Retailing*, **64**, (1), Spring, 14–40.

Parasuraman, A., Berry, L. L. & Zeithaml, V. A. (1990). Guidelines for conducting service quality research. *Marketing Research*, Dec., 34–44.

Silvestro, R. & Johnston, R. (1990). *The determinants of service quality – hygiene and enhancing factors.* Warwick Business School, UK.

BARBARA LEWIS

**service quality gaps** Service quality is variously defined, but essentially it is to do with meeting customers' needs and requirements and with how well the service delivered matches customers' expectations (*see* Lewis & Booms, 1983). The term "expectations" as used in the service quality context differs from the way it is used in the consumer satisfaction literature, where expectations are seen as "predictors" (probabilities) made by a consumer about what is likely to happen during an impending transaction (Oliver, 1981). In relation to service quality, expectations are seen as desires/wants, i.e., what one feels a service provider should offer (rather than what it would offer), and are formed on the basis of previous experience of a company and its marketing mix, competitors, and word-of-mouth communications. Consequently, quality becomes a consumer judgement and results from comparisons by consumers of expectations of service with their perceptions of actual service delivered (*see* Gronroos, 1984; Berry et al., 1985 & 1988). If there is a shortfall then a service quality gap exists which providers would wish to close. However, one needs to bear in mind that: higher levels of performance lead to higher expectations; and to find expectations greater than performance implies that perceived quality is less than satisfactory, but that is not to say that service is of low quality – quality is relative to initial expectations (one of the issues to be taken into account when measuring service quality – (*see* SERVICE QUALITY MEASUREMENT). The concept of service quality gaps has been developed from the extensive research by Berry and his colleagues (Parasuraman et al., 1985; Ziethaml et al., 1988). They defined service quality to be a function of the gap between consumers' expectations of the service and their perceptions of the actual service

delivery of an organization; and suggested that this gap is influenced by four other gaps which may occur in an organization (*see* figure 1).

*Gap 1: Consumer expectations – Management perceptions of consumer expectations*

Managers' perceptions of customers' expectations may be different from actual customer needs and desires, i.e., managers do not necessarily know what customers (both internal and external) want and expect from a company. This may be remedied by market research activities (e.g., interviews, surveys, focus groups, complaint monitoring), and better communication between management and personnel throughout the organization.

*Gap 2: Management perceptions of consumer expectations – Service specifications actually set*

Even if customer needs are known, they may not be translated into appropriate service specifications, due to a lack of resources, organizational constraints, or absence of management commitment to a service culture and service quality. The need for management commitment and resources for service quality cannot be overstated.

*Gap 3: Service quality specifications – Actual service delivery*

This is referred to as the service performance gap and occurs when the service that is delivered is different from management's specifications for service due to variations in the performance of personnel – employees not being able or willing to perform at a desired level. Solutions are central to human resources management (*see* INTERNAL MARKETING).

*Gap 4: Actual service delivery – External communications about the service*

What is said about the service in external communications is different from the service that is delivered, i.e., advertising and promotion can influence consumers' expectations and perceptions of service. Therefore, it is important not to promise more than can be delivered (or expectations increase and perceptions decrease), or to fail to present relevant information (*see* SERVICE GUARANTEES). Success in this area requires appropriate and timely information/communication, both internally and to external customers.

Gaps 1 to 4 together contribute to consumers' expectations and perceptions of actual service (*Gap 5*). Service providers need to identify the gaps prevalent in their organization, determine the factors responsible for them, and develop appropriate solutions (*see* SERVICE QUALITY).

**Bibliography**

Berry, L. L., Zeithaml, V. A. & Parasuraman, A. (1985). Quality counts in services too. *Business Horizons*, **28**, (3), May–June, 44–52.

Berry, L. L., Parasuraman, A. & Zeithaml, V. A. (1988). The service-quality puzzle. *Business Horizons*, July–Aug., 35–43.

Gronroos, C. (1984). A service quality model and its marketing implications. *European Journal of Marketing*, **18**, (4), 36–44.

Lewis, R. C. & Booms, B. H. (1983). The marketing aspects of service quality. In L. L. Berry, G. L. Shostack & G. Upah (Eds), *Emerging perspectives on*

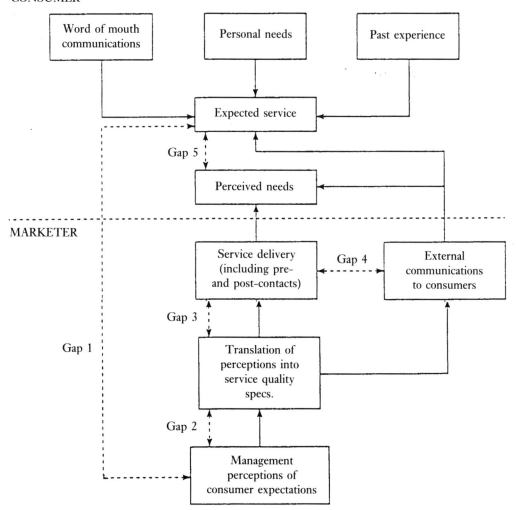

*Figure 1   A Conceptual Model of Service Quality*
*Source: Zeithaml et al., 1988, p. 36*

*service marketing* (pp. 99–107). Chicago: American Marketing Association.

Oliver, R. L. (1981). Measurement and evaluation of satisfaction processes in retail settings. *Journal of Retailing*, **57**, (3), Fall, 25–48.

Parasuraman, A., Zeithaml, V. A. & Berry, L. L. (1985). A conceptual model of service quality and its implications for future research. *Journal of Marketing*, **49**, Fall, 41–50.

Zeithaml, V. A., Berry, L. L. & Parasuraman, A. (1988). Communication and control processes in the delivery of service quality. *Journal of Marketing*, **52**, Apr., 35–38.

BARBARA LEWIS

**service quality measurement**   In measuring service quality, organizations compare consumer expectations of service(s) with their perceptions of actual service delivered (*see* SERVICE QUALITY GAPS), rather than just assessing consumer satisfaction with a particular service outcome. Quality service is believed to exist when perceptions exceed expectations.

Researchers have developed increasingly sophisticated mechanisms to assess levels of consumers' expectations and perceptions with respect to SERVICE QUALITY DIMENSIONS. Many use rating scales that are similar to, or are adapted from, the SERVQUAL (*see* SERVQUAL) instrument. Such scales allow researchers and organizations not only to measure performance against customers' expectations but also to: track service quality trends over time; compare branches/outlets of an organization; measure performance against competition (competitor mapping); measure the relative importance of service quality dimensions; compare service performance with customer service priorities; and categorize customers (*see* Berry et al., 1990; Parasuraman et al., 1990). The relative importance of key service quality dimensions may also be established from rankings, points allocations, and by trade-off analysis Christopher & Yallop, 1990). Christopher & Yallop also provide examples of competitor mapping.

There are various methodological problems associated with measuring service dimensions, relating to the dimensions themselves, variations in customer expectations, and the nature of the measurement tools:

- *Dimensions*. Companies need to be aware that some elements of service(s) are easier to evaluate than others (Parasuraman et al., 1985 & 1988). For example, tangibles and credibility are known in advance, but most elements are experience criteria and can only be evaluated during or after consumption. Some, such as competence and security, may be difficult or impossible to evaluate, even after purchase and consumption. In general, consumers rely on experience properties when evaluating services.

- *Customer expectations* are usually reasonable but vary depending on circumstances and experience, and will rise over time; and experience with one service provider may influence customer expectations of other providers. In addition, consumers have zones of tolerance (Parasuraman et al., 1991a), the difference between desired and adequate expectations. The desired level of service expectation is what they hope to receive, a blend of what "can" and "should" be, which is a function of past experience. The adequate level is what is acceptable, based on an assessment of what the service "will" be – the "predicted" service – and depends on the alternatives which are available. Tolerance zones vary between individuals and companies, with service aspects, and with experience. In addition, if options are limited, tolerance zones may be higher than if many alternatives are available and it is easy to switch service providers.

In addition, it is necessary to realize that as customers are increasingly aware of the alternatives on offer and rising standards of service, expectations may change over time. Higher levels of performance lead to higher expectations. Also, over time the dimensions of service may change, as may the relative importance of such factors. In addition, research and measurement usually focus on routine service situations; organizations also need to consider non-routine service encounters which may have a major impact on consumer (and employee) evaluations and satisfactions – e.g., service recovery situations (*see* SERVICE RECOVERY).

- *Measurement tools*. Problems with SERVQUAL relate to respondent difficulties with negatively worded statements; using two lists of statements for the same items; the number of dimensions of service being assessed; ease of customer assessment; and timing of measurement – before, during, or after a service encounter (*see* Parasuraman et al., 1991b; Babakus & Boller, 1992; Carmen, 1990; Smith, 1992; Lewis, 1993; Lewis, Orledge, & Mitchell, 1994). Parasuraman et al. (1991b & 1993) have addressed some of these issues and made amendments to SERVQUAL; refinements are also discussed by Cronin & Taylor (1992) and Brown et al. (1993).

• Further, rating scales in general raise questions with respect to: verbal labels and the use of extremes; interpretation of the mid-point of unlabeled scales; the propensity to indicate only positive or desirable answers; the number of scale points; and the measurement of desired as against adequate levels of service. There are also cultural differences in attitudes and behavior, and the cultural context of a rating scale assessment and consumer willingness to respond and if necessary criticize companies and service, both of which affect responses.

## Bibliography

Babakus, E. & Boller, G. W. (1992). An empirical assessment of the SERVQUAL scale. *Journal of Business Research*, **24**, May, 253–268.

Berry, L. L., Zeithaml, V. A. & Parasuraman, A. (1990). Five imperatives for improving service quality. *Sloan Management Review*, **31**, (4), Summer, 29–38.

Brown, T. J., Churchill, G. A. & Peter, J. P. (1993). Improving the measurement of service quality. *Journal of Retailing*, **69**, (1), Spring, 127–139.

Carmen, J. M. (1990). Consumer perceptions of service quality: An assessment of the SERVQUAL dimensions. *Journal of Retailing*, **66**, (1), Spring, 33–56.

Christopher, M. & Yallop, R. (1990). Audit your customer service quality. *Physical Distribution and Logistics Management*, **9**, (5), 4–9.

Cronin, J. J. & Taylor, S. A. (1992). Measuring service quality: A re-examination and extension. *Journal of Marketing*, **56**, (3), July, 55–68.

Lewis, B. R. (1993). Service quality measurement. *Marketing Intelligence and Planning*, **11**, (4), 4–12.

Lewis, B. R., Orledge, J. & Mitchell, V. (1994). Service quality: Students' assessments of banks and building societies. *International Journal of Bank Marketing*, **12**, (4), 3–12.

Parasuraman, A., Zeithaml, V. A. & Berry, L. L. (1985). A conceptual model of service quality and its implications for future research. *Journal of Marketing*, **49**, Fall, 41–50.

Parasuraman, A., Zeithaml, V. A. & Berry, L. L. (1988). SERVQUAL: A multiple item scale for measuring consumer perceptions of service quality. *Journal of Retailing*, **64**, (1), Spring, 14–40.

Parasuraman, A., Berry, L. L. & Zeithaml, V. A. (1990). Guidelines for conducting service quality research. *Marketing Research*, Dec., 34–44.

Parasuraman, A., Berry, L. L. & Zeithaml, V. A. (1991a). Understanding consumer expectations of service. *Sloan Management Review*, **32**, (3), 39–48.

Parasuraman, A., Berry, L. L. & Zeithaml, V. A. (1991b). Refinement and re-assessment of the SERVQUAL scale. *Journal of Retailing*, **67**, (4), Winter, 420–450.

Parasuraman, A., Zeithaml, V. A. & Berry, L. L. (1993). More on improving service quality. *Journal of Retailing*, **69**, (1), 140–7.

Smith, A. M. (1992). The consumers' evaluation of service quality: Some methodological issues. In J. Whitelock (Ed.), *Marketing in the new Europe and beyond* (pp. 633–648). Proceedings of the MEG Annual Conference. University of Salford, UK.

BARBARA LEWIS

**service recovery**   The service recovery process is presented by Hart et al. (1990) and Mason (1993). Service organizations typically strive for zero defects in their service delivery, i.e., 100 percent customer satisfaction, to get things right the first time. So they develop their systems and personnel policies accordingly. But problems do occur (bad weather may delay a plane or employees may be sick and absent), and mistakes will happen (e.g., a hotel room not ready on time, a lost checkbook or suitcase). The challenge for service providers is to recover the problem or mistake and get it very right the second time – to turn frustrated customers into loyal ones.

Service recovery may be defined as "a planned process/strategy of returning an aggrieved/dissatisfied customer to a state of satisfaction with a company/service," making a special effort to put things right when something is wrong. This includes focus on critical service encounters (*see* SERVICE ENCOUNTERS) and anticipating and preventing possible failure points. It also includes: identifying service research (e.g., phoning customers to check on services delivered); tracking and analyzing failures; offering rewards for improvement suggestions; and measuring performance against standards (e.g., pizza delivery).

When problems do occur, companies have to expedite service recovery to meet customers' recovery expectations – which may be even higher than initial expectations. It is increasingly accepted that companies should first believe the customer, acknowledge the problem, take responsibility, and avoid defensiveness. They should also apologize, and then fix the problem and recompense explicit and hidden costs if appropriate. Service recovery is "emotional and physical repair." Organizations need to deal with the customer first and then with the problem (Hart et al., 1990).

Service recovery strategies should be flexible, and integral to this is the role of front-line employees and the extent to which they have been empowered (*see* Bowen & Lawler, 1992) to respond to the customer (*see* INTERNAL MARKETING). Employees should have the authority, responsibility, and incentives/rewards to identify, care about, and solve customer problems and complaints. They should be allowed to use their judgement and their creative and communications skills to develop solutions to satisfy customers.

Successful service recovery has economic benefits in terms of customer retention and loyalty. It is also a means to identify organizational problems with respect to all the dimensions of service quality and to improve overall customer awareness and service.

### Bibliography

Bowen, D. E. & Lawler, L. L. (1992). Empowerment: Why, what, how and when. *Sloan Management Review*, Spring, 31–39.

Hart, C. W., Heskett, J. L. & Sasser, W. E. Jr (1990). The profitable art of service recovery. *Harvard Business Review*, **90**, (4), July–Aug., 148–156.

Mason, J. B. (1993). The art of service recovery. *Arthur Anderson Retailing Issues Letter*, **5**, (1), Jan., Texas A and M University.

Mudie, P. & Cottam, A. (1993). *The management and marketing of services*. Oxford: Butterworth-Heinemann. Chapter 11.

BARBARA LEWIS

**services marketing**   Services marketing has evolved as a discipline for a number of reasons, in particular, an increasing acknowledgement that all organizations participate in marketing management (*see* MARKETING MANAGEMENT), and with the growth of service industries in developed economies.

The MARKETING CONCEPT is based on market exchange (*see* EXCHANGE) between buyers and sellers. All organizations have "products" and "markets" and are involved in market exchange and so need to be marketing oriented and to adopt the marketing concept.

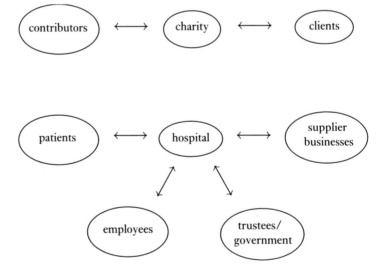

*Figure 1   Services Marketing*

This includes public and private sector organizations, and profit and not-for-profit organizations – where business objectives may relate to social or community orientation. Further, organizations may have more than one market, e.g., charities and hospitals (*see* figure 1).

Charities are involved in exchanges with "donors" who contribute money, material goods, or their time/commitment in return, typically, for "intangible" personal rewards; and also with "clients" who are recipients of help and benefits and who may, for example, be producing products which the charity can sell. Similarly, hospitals which are in the "business" of providing health care to patients are involved in numerous marketing exchanges with patients, employees, trustees, government, suppliers, etc. The concept of multiple customer markets is developed by Payne (1993) and by Christopher et al. (1991).

Charities and hospitals are examples of organizations/businesses which comprise the services sector of an economy (*see* SERVICES SECTOR). As services have become increasingly critical within developed economies, so has the attention to MARKETING MANAGEMENT within the sector due, largely, to the characteristics of services (*see* SERVICE CHARACTERISTICS), and the ensuing implications for managing the marketing mix (*see* MARKETING MIX).

Services are typically seen to be characterized by intangibility, heterogeneity, inseparability, and perishability (*see* SERVICE CHARACTERISTICS). Further, the notion of service encounter (*see* SERVICE ENCOUNTERS) is particular to the services sector and is concerned with interactions between services and their providing organizations and their personnel, and consumers. Service characteristics and service encounters are critical to understanding marketing management in the service sector, and have implications for the MARKETING MIX which includes product, price, place, and promotion (*see* SERVICE PRODUCT; SERVICE PRICE; SERVICE DISTRIBUTION; SERVICE PROMOTION). In addition, Booms & Bitner (1981) talk about an extended marketing mix for the services sector to include physical evidence, process, and people (*see* SERVICE ENVIRONMENT; SERVICE PROCESS; INTERNAL MARKETING).

## Bibliography

Bateson, J. E. G. (1992). *Managing services marketing* (2nd edn). Chicago: The Dryden Press.

Blois, K. J. (1983). The structure of service firms and their marketing policies. *Strategic Management Journal*, 4, 251–261.

Booms, B. H. & Bitner, M. J. (1981). Marketing strategies and organization structures for service firms.In J. H. Donnelly & W. R. George (Eds), *Marketing of services* (pp. 47–51). Chicago: American Marketing Association.

Christopher, M., Payne, A. F. T. & Ballantyne, D. (1991). *Relationship marketing: Bringing quality, customer service and marketing together*. Oxford: Butterworth-Heinemann.

Cowell, D. W. (1984). *The marketing of services*. London: Heinemann. Chapter 2.

Kotler, P. (1979). Strategies for introducing marketing into non-profit organisations. *Journal of Marketing*, 43, Jan., 37–44.

Lovelock, C. H. (1991). *Services marketing* (2nd edn). Prentice-Hall.

Mudie, P. & Cottam, A. (1993). *The management and marketing of services*. Oxford: Butterworth-Heinemann. Chapter 1.

Payne, A. (1993). *The essence of services marketing*. Prentice-Hall. Chapter 2.

BARBARA LEWIS

**services sector**    There is no clear-cut definition of the services sector of an economy but it is generally considered to include all industries other than those involved in manufacturing, and so covers: financial services; tourism and hospitality; health care; leisure, sport and entertainment; professional services; communications and transport; information services; public utilities; government and local authority; education; charities; personal services; household services; industrial and business services, etc. In addition, one can consider the service element in manufacturing industries, e.g., service support provided by computer manufacturers – before and after sales, advisory, technical and maintenance services, etc.

The services sector in developed economies is characterized by continuing growth with respect to output and consumption, employment, and its role in export trade. Many factors contribute to this growth resulting from demographic, social, economic, political, and legal changes, and impact variously on the demand for particular services. The determinants of services industry expansion include (*see* Cowell, 1984; Gronroos, 1990; Palmer, 1994):

- demographic trends, in particular increasing life expectancy and an expanding retired population (with demand for nursing homes, drugs, etc.)

- an increasing percentage of women in the labor force (requiring baby-minding services, house cleaning, etc.)

- more leisure time associated with employment conditions and changing lifestyles (impacting on demand for recreation and tourism, etc.)

- increasing affluence, wealthier societies, and improving quality of life (impact on entertainment, meals outside the home, etc.)

- increasing numbers of new products and greater product complexity (requiring repairs and maintenance)

- greater complexity of life (requiring personal services, e.g., financial)

- greater concern about ecology and resource scarcity

- breakthroughs in computers and information technology, and communications to facilitate exchanges

- development of new towns and regions

- international mobility and travel

- globalization of business

- the size of governments and the development of the European Community.

**Bibliography**

Cowell, D. W. (1984). *The marketing of services.* London: Heinemann. Chapter 1.

Gronroos, C. (1990). *Service management and marketing.* Lexington, MA: Lexington Books. Chapter 1.

Palmer, A. (1994). *Principles of marketing.* Maidenhead: McGraw-Hill. Chapter 1.

BARBARA LEWIS

**SERVQUAL** Parasuraman's five major dimensions of service (tangibles, reliability, responsiveness, assurance, and empathy) – (*see*

SERVICE QUALITY DIMENSIONS) – form the basis for the SERVQUAL questionnaire (Parsuraman et al., 1988).

This has 22 pairs of Likert-type scales. The first 22 items are designed to measure customer expectations of service for a service industry and the following 22 to measure the perceived level of service provided by a particular organization in that industry. For example:

*Service Expectations (E)*: "Customers should be able to trust bank employees."

"Banks should have up-to-date equipment."

| Strongly Agree | | | | | | Strongly Disagree |
|---|---|---|---|---|---|---|
| 1 | 2 | 3 | 4 | 5 | 6 | 7 |

*Service Perceptions (P)*: "I can trust the employees of my bank."

"My bank has up-to-date equipment."

| Strongly Agree | | | | | | Strongly Disagree |
|---|---|---|---|---|---|---|
| 1 | 2 | 3 | 4 | 5 | 6 | 7 |

A quality perception or gap ($Q$) is calculated by subtracting the expectations scale values (E) from the performance scale values (P): i.e., $Q = P - E$. The scale is offered as one with good reliability and validity. Even so, it is limited to current and past customers as respondents need knowledge and experience of the company.

There has been considerable debate over the use and generalizability of SERVQUAL which has led to various modifications (*see* Parasuraman et al., 1991 & 1993).

*See also* **Service quality measurement**

**Bibliography**

Parasuraman, A., Zeithaml, V. A. & Berry, L. L. (1988). SERVQUAL: A multiple item scale for measuring consumer perceptions of service quality. *Journal of Retailing,* **64**, (1), Spring, 14–40.

Parasuraman, A., Berry, L. L. & Zeithaml, V. A. (1991). Refinement and re-assessment of the SERVQUAL scale. *Journal of Retailing,* **67**, (4), Winter, 420–450.

Parasuraman, A., Zeithaml, V. A. & Berry, L. L. (1993). More on improving service quality. *Journal of Retailing*, **69**, (1), 140–147.

BARBARA LEWIS

**shape** Shape is a variable in the design of PACKAGING, and is used in conjunction with different types of packaging materials, e.g., plastic, card, metals. The shape can communicate the nature of a product to the potential customer/consumer/user, e.g., angular packaging may convey an image of strength/power, rounded packaging often conveys softness. However, the shape of packaging should not be too unorthodox as problems may result for resellers in stacking and shelf display, thus reducing turnover/profitability per cubic metre.

**Bibliography**

Dibb, S., Simkin, L., Pride, W. M. & Ferrell, O. C. (1994). *Marketing, concepts and strategies* (European edn). Boston, MA: Houghton Mifflin Co. Chapter 8.

DAVID YORKE

**shopper typologies** These involve a classification that identifies shoppers based upon their purchase behavior, motives, and attitudes. The sciences of DEMOGRAPHICS and PSYCHOGRAPHICS offer measures now widely used to define these shopper groupings. In addition, common lifestyle patterns among consumers can aid the classification process.

A number of shopper groupings have been proposed:

*The convenience shopper* – who tends to be short on disposable time and with a higher-than-average income. Such time scarcity may influence the shopping behavior in terms of the time available, the preferred locations of stores, and the opening hours.

*The leisure shopper* – for whom discretionary time is relatively high and the consumer seeks to fill it with shopping activity. This may include a high number of shopping trips for both purchase and browsing activity often as a form of leisure activity.

*The price-conscious shopper* – who may range from the relatively logical "economic shopper" to the more price-prone "special deal" shopper. For such consumers, pricing is a relatively important consideration and one which may influence the choice of product and outlet more than in other cases.

*The store-loyal consumer* – is seen as one who regularly patronizes a particular retailer when seeking certain goods and who may therefore restrict his/her consideration of competing stores. The reasons for such behavior may include repeated good service and/or a perception that the retailer in question is consistently able to meet his/her needs.

Other types may include the economic consumer, the personalizing consumer, the ethical consumer, and the apathetic consumer (Stone, 1954).

**Bibliography**

Schiffman, L. G. & Kanuk, L. L. (1994). *Consumer behavior* (5th edn). Prentice-Hall..
Stone, G. P. (1954). City shoppers and urban identification: Observations on the social psychology of city life. *American Journal of Sociology*, **60**, 36–45, cited in P. J. McGoldrick (1990). *Retail marketing*. Maidenhead: McGraw-Hill, p. 207.

STEVE WORRALL

**shopping centers** Shopping centers are generally more planned than the traditional high street retailing central shopping areas and have more pedestrian activity. Guy (1994) confines the term to "shopping developments of at least 50,000 sq. ft. gross retail area that include at least three retail units." Bolen (1988) describes a shopping center or mall as: "A group of stores with balanced tenancy – enough of one kind of store to attract traffic but not too many stores of any one type. A shopping center or mall should have adequate parking and a good store visibility from the parking area along with two or more large stores to draw the customer."

*See also* **High street retailing**

**Bibliography**

Bolen, W. H. (1988). *Contemporary retailing*. Englewood Cliffs, NJ: Prentice-Hall.

Guy, C. (1994). *The retail development process.* London: Routledge.

STEVE GREENLAND

**single/multiple sourcing** Traditionally, the ideal in purchasing (*see* PURCHASING PROCESS) has been to use multiple sources for goods and services where the strategic consequences of source failure (e.g., halting production, safety-critical) outweighed the scale economies and operational convenience of single sourcing (Segal, 1989). The use of multiple sourcing to increase the customer's negotiating power was also seen as an important benefit. In practice, even where alternative suppliers were approved, they were not always used, perhaps because of inertia, pressure of work, the strength of established relationships, or perceived switching costs. It is important to recognize that in practical terms changing suppliers can be disruptive, time-consuming, resource-intensive, costly, and even career-threatening for purchasing staff if they make mistakes. To justify change, clear benefits have to be identified to overcome systemic inertia, accumulated personal commitment, alternative work priorities, and switching costs. Most of these factors operate to the advantage of existing suppliers and it takes management determination to maintain a thorough approach to multiple sourcing strategies.

**Bibliography**

Paliwoda, S. J. & Bonaccorsi, A. J. (1994). Trends in procurement strategies within the European aircraft industry. *Industrial Marketing Management*, 23, (3), July, 235–244.

Segal, M. N. (1989). Implications of single v. multiple buying sources. *Industrial Marketing Management*, 18, (3), Aug., 163–178.

DOMINIC WILSON

**skimming pricing** Skimming pricing is the use of high prices (often reflecting large profit margins) for the initial marketing of new products. Such new products will be adopted initially by the least price-sensitive parts of the market. Once demand in these niches falls off, subsequent incremental price reductions may be used to devolve the product to increasingly price-sensitive market areas until demand is replete. Thus, the objective of skimming is to maximize short-term profitability. Skimming pricing contrasts with PENETRATION PRICING in that it adopts a relatively high price compared to the relatively low price of penetration policies.

Skimming policies might be adopted where there is little prospect of a long-term market for offerings (e.g., novelty items), or where organizations perceive only a short-term sustainable differentiation in their offerings (e.g., fashion markets), or where premium pricing is based on strong brands and consumer loyalty (e.g., luxury goods), or by organizations placing a high priority on short PAYBACK periods as a key corporate measure (e.g., where capital costs are high), or by organizations simply seeking to capitalize on the unique benefits of their product (e.g., the sale of distinctive vehicle registrations). The advantages of successful skimming pricing include rapid cost recovery (thereby reducing investment risk), and less commitment to long-term policies to ensure break-even (thereby allowing a more flexible response to market developments and some insurance against forecasting errors). However, skimming strategies can be difficult to manage since an organization may have to defend its offering (e.g., by patent or branding) from any credible imitators that might be attracted by the high profits associated with skimming, but it must also ensure that the corporate image is not tarnished, nor potential demand alienated, by any appearance of profiteering.

**Bibliography**

Dean, J. (1950). Pricing policies for new products. *Harvard Business Review*, 28, (6), Nov–Dec., 45–53.

DOMINIC WILSON

**social change**   *see* DEMOGRAPHICS

**social class** Social class refers to the stratification of members of a society into a hierarchy. Every known human society is stratified, i.e., the hierarchical evaluation of people in different social positions is inherent in human social organizations. Within societies, different occupations, trades, and professions have a more immediate impact on a community and may attract social prestige and authority. Early definitions of social class focused on reputation. For example, Warner et al. (1949) defined social class in terms of how people in a community view one another and place their associates in the social structure, placing an emphasis on status/reputation and participation in the community.

More recently, various "objective" criteria have been used to define and measure social class: e.g., occupation, income level and source, wealth, house-type, area of residence, and educational level. Consequently, various categorizations of social class have been developed: e.g. those referring to typologies such as upper-middle-lower class, and the ABC1 C2DE system developed in the UK by the Joint Industry Committee for National Readership Surveys – based on the occupation of the head of the household. Current typologies are, however, specifically related to lifestyles, e.g., Acorn-types (see LIFESTYLES).

Levy (1964 & 1966) discussed social class in terms of variations which are a combination of a consumer's values, interpersonal attitudes, self-perceptions, and daily life. Such differences find expression in consumer behavior in a number of ways: (1) products and services bought: accumulation of certain products and services can serve as a symbol of class position; (2) use of and reaction to the media, e.g., critical or accepting response to advertisements, questioning of claims; (3) spending, saving, and investment, researched by Martineau (1958a); (4) stores used, again researched by Martineau (1958b); (5) reaction to innovation; (6) entertainment and leisure; (7) consumerism; and (8) use of credit cards and facilities: Mathews & Slocum (1969) considered instalment versus convenience usage of credit cards, and products and services which are acceptable to charge.

Social classes are considered to be relatively permanent and homogeneous. However, the concept of a hierarchy of social class suggests vertical mobility, both upward and downward. This may be a function of: educational mobility, witness the emergence of a "meritocracy" – professional and business leaders who have achieved prominence through intelligence and

hard work; and changes in employment and income, witness the disappearing divisions between white and blue collar consumption habits as economic income levels. However, fundamental social values and attitudes may not change as suddenly as behavior, with increased spending power.

Further, one needs to be aware of the concept of "over/under privilege" within social classes (see Coleman, 1960 & 1983). This is the notion of looking at discretionary income within social class groups, such that certain luxury products and services are targeted at the "over-privileged" across all social classes.

## Bibliography

Coleman, R. (1960). The significance of social stratification in selling. In M. L. Bell (Ed.), Marketing: A maturing discipline (pp. 171–184. Chicago: American Marketing Association.

Coleman, R. P. (1983). The continuing significance of social class to marketing. Journal of Consumer Research, 10, Dec. 265–280. Cited in H. H. Kassarjian & T. S. Robertson (1991). Perspectives in consumer behavior (4th edn). (pp. 487–510). Prentice Hall.

Engel, J. F., Blackwell, R. D. & Miniard, P. W. (1990). Consumer behavior. (6th edn). Orlando, Fla: The Dryden Press. Chapter 4.

Hawkins, D. I., Best, R. J. & Coney, K. A. (1992). Consumer behavior: Implications for marketing strategy (5th edn). Homewood, IL: Irwin. Chapter 4.

Levy, S. J. (1964). Symbolism and lifestyle. In S. A. Greyser (Ed.), Towards scientific marketing (pp. 140–150). Chicago: American Marketing Association.

Levy, S. J. (1966). In J. W. Newman (Ed.), Social class and consumer behavior. On knowing the consumer (pp. 146–160). New York: John Wiley.

Martineau, P. (1958a). Social classes and spending behavior. Journal of Marketing, 23, Oct., 121–130.

Martineau, P. (1958b). The personality of the retail store. Harvard Business Review, 36, Jan.–Feb., 47–55.

Mathews, H. L. & Slocum, J. W. (1969). Social class and commercial bank credit card usage. Journal of Marketing, 33, Jan., 71–78.

Rich, S. U. & Jain, S. C. (1968). Social class and life cycle as predictors of shopping behavior. Journal of Marketing Research, 5, Feb., 41–49.

Schiffman, L. G. & Kanuk, L. Z. (1991). Consumer behavior. (4th edn). Prentice-Hall. Chapter 13.

Solomon, M. R. (1992). Consumer behavior. Needham Heights, MA: Allyn & Bacon. Chapter 12.

Warner, W. L., Meeker, M. & Eells, K. (1949). *Social class in America*. Chicago: Scientific Research Associates.

BARBARA LEWIS

**social marketing**　Social marketing is part of "non-business" marketing (together with NOT-FOR-PROFIT MARKETING) which relates to marketing activities conducted by individuals and organizations to achieve some goal other than ordinary business goals of profit, market share, and return on investment.

Social marketing is concerned with the development of programs designed to influence the acceptability of social ideas, and may be defined to be a set of activities to create, maintain, and/or alter attitudes and/or behavior toward a social idea or cause, independently of a sponsoring organization or person. The purpose may be: to trigger one-time behavior from people (e.g., contribute to a foundation for AIDS research); to change behavior (e.g., to discourage cigarette smoking, drug abuse or drink abuse, unsafe sexual practice, to recycle more newspapers, plastics etc.); or to change attitudes and beliefs (e.g., toward birth control and family planning or toward pollution control).

### Bibliography

Christy, R. (1995). The broader application of marketing. In G. Oliver (Ed.), *Marketing today* (4th edn). (pp. 500–527). Hemel Hempstead, UK: Prentice-Hall. Chapter 24.

Dibb, S., Simkin, L., Pride, W. M. & Ferrell, O. C. (1991). *Marketing* (European edn). (pp. 693–694). Boston, MA: Houghton Mifflin Co.

Kotler, P. (1994). *Marketing management: Analysis, planning, implementation and control* (8th edn). Englewood Cliffs, NJ: Prentice-Hall, p.155.

BARBARA LEWIS

**social responsibility**　The term "social responsibility" most usually refers to an organization's obligation to maximize its long-term positive impact and minimize its negative impact on society. While it is sometimes used interchangeably with the concept of ethics (*see* MARKETING ETHICS), the distinction is generally made that social responsibility is an organizational concern whereas ethics are the concern of the individual manager or business

decision-maker (*see* Carroll, 1981). However, this distinction is by no means universally accepted and debate continues as to whether organizations, given that they are artificial creations, can be said to have social responsibilities at all, or whether the term is only applicable to individuals within the organization. The difference between social responsibility and ethics is further highlighted by Robin & Reidenbach (1987), who define social responsibility as the social contract between business and the society in which it operates, stating that actions society defines as "responsible" in its social contract with business may be found by moral philosophers as ethically unsound (*see also* Steiner, 1972).

Carroll (1981) has identified four specific areas of corporate social responsibility as economic, legal, ethical, and discretionary responsibility – in that order of priority. Davis et al. (1980) similarly represented social responsibility as three concentric circles, again indicating priority: the inner circle referred to the social responsibility aspects of the traditional economic role of business, such as social and ethical issues arising from the performance by business of basic functions; the middle circle contained issues such as ecology, environmental quality, and consumerism; and the outer circle, general social problems that business can help to alleviate.

It has been suggested that what becomes generally accepted as socially responsible will vary in different societies and will also change within society over time. However, a variety of specific social responsibility issues have been recently discussed in marketing literature, including consumer issues; issues of employee welfare; support for minorities; issues of community relations, such as the contribution made by business to the satisfaction and growth of communities by contributing resources to causes such as education, the arts, recreation, or disadvantaged members of the community; and GREEN MARKETING.

While it has been proposed that the long-term value of conducting business in a socially responsible manner far outweighs short-term costs (*see* Stroup et al., 1987), there is some debate as to whether business, on the whole, is becoming more socially responsible in its actions. Robin & Reidenbach (1987) note a trend towards increased social involvement by business; however, Glueck (1980) found little evidence that social responsibility is a significant objective of most businesses, in spite of a good deal of pressure from some societal groups.

*See also* **Marketing concept; Societal marketing**

### Bibliography

Carroll, A. B. (1981). *Business and society.* Boston, MA: Little, Brown & Co.

Davis, K., Frederick, W. C. & Blomstrom, R. L. (1980). *Business and society.* New York: McGraw-Hill.

Glueck, W. F. (1980). *Business policy and strategic management* (3rd edn). New York: McGraw-Hill.

Robin, D. P. & Reidenbach, R. E. (1987). Social responsibility, ethics and marketing strategy: Closing the gap between concept and application. *Journal of Marketing,* **51**, (1), Jan., 44–58.

Steiner, G. A. (1972). Social policies for business. *California Management Review,* Winter, 17–24.

Stroup, M. A., Newbert, R. L. & Anderson, J. W. Jr (1987). Doing good doing better: Two views of social responsibility. *Business Horizons,* Mar.–Apr., 23.

FIONA LEVERICK

**societal marketing**   A major development in the interpretation of the scope of marketing, societal marketing refers to the extension of marketing along its substantive dimension, i.e., the widening of the areas of concern of marketing to focus on the long-term interests of consumers and society. Although the two are often used interchangeably, societal marketing differs from social marketing, the latter referring to the further application of marketing techniques to not-for-profit organizations, such as charitie (*see* Abratt & Sacks, 1989).

*See also* **consumerism; Marketing; Marketing concept; Social responsibility**

### Bibliography

Abratt, R. & Sacks, D. (1989). Perceptions of the societal marketing concept. *European Journal of Marketing,* **23**, (6), 25–33.

FIONA LEVERICK

**source effect**   The source of a MARKETING COMMUNICATIONS message is the sender of information, be it a manufacturer, distributor, other organization, sales person, or another customer. The IMPACT of the MESSAGE depends on a number of factors including the source effect. This has two dimensions, credibility and incongruity.

Credibility comprises dimensions of knowledge and expertness, trustworthiness and likeability. High-credibility sources may add persuasiveness to the communication: e.g., doctors testifying to the benefits of a drug, or a well-known personality endorsing products. Such sources reinforce images or cause attitude change more easily than low-credibility sources, although some people may more easily identify with and be persuaded by sources which they perceive as being similar to themselves.

Source incongruity arises when receivers hold a positive attitude toward the source (e.g., a celebrity) and a negative attitude toward the message (with respect to the product/brand), or vice versa. This is something that organizations would wish to avoid.

### Bibliography

Bauer, R. A. (1965). A revised model of source effect Presidential address of the Division of Consumer Psychology. American Psychological Association Annual Meeting..

McGuire, W. J. (1969). The nature of attitude and attitude change.In G. Lindzey & E. Aronson (Eds), *Handbook of Social Psychology.* Reading, UK: Addison Wesley.

DAVID YORKE

**specifiers**   Specifiers are members of the DECISION-MAKING UNIT (DMU) and are those individuals involved in the technical specification of purchasing requirements. Examples might include design engineers, production engineers, operators, and administrators – in short, anyone with sufficient expertise or experience to be able to recommend the technical parameters of a purchase requirement.

*See also* **Purchasing process**

DOMINIC WILSON

**sponsorship**   Sponsorship is an element of the marketing COMMUNICATIONS MIX and is considered to be the provision of assistance, financial or in kind, to an activity by a commercial organization, for the purpose of achieving commercial objectives.

Reasons for, or objectives of, sponsorship are interrelated and include: keeping the company name before the public; building or altering perceptions of the organization and, therefore, goodwill; portraying a socially concerned and community-involved company; identifying with a target market and, therefore, promoting products and brands; countering adverse PUBLICITY; aiding with recruitment; and helping sales forces with prospects.

Typically, sponsorship is associated with the arts, sports, and community activities, and so companies are seen to be supporting these "events" and would, therefore, claim such support to be an objective of their sponsorship.

Sponsorship monies might finance part of the cost of a community or cultural or sporting event; or assume responsibility for the production of a TELEVISION or RADIO program. Thus, the sponsoring organization aims to establish high visibility and the credibility of being associated with the development and success of the venture.

A recent development with sponsorship is corporate hospitality, in particular at sporting and cultural events.

A major problem with sponsorship is measurement of its cost-effectiveness.

**Bibliography**

Dibb, S., Simkin, L., Pride, W. M. & Ferrell, O. C. (1994). *Marketing: Concepts and strategies* (European edn). Boston, MA: Houghton Mifflin Co. Chapter 15.

Meenaghan, T. (1991). The role of sponsorship in the marketing communications mix. *International Journal of Advertising*, **10**, (1).

DAVID YORKE

**SPSS**   *see* STATISTICAL PACKAGE FOR THE SOCIAL SCIENCES

**Statistical Package for the Social Sciences**   The Statistical Package for the Social Sciences, or SPSS, is a popular package of computer software used to analyze data, including data obtained in MARKETING RESEARCH surveys. The components of the package concern data input, data modification, data analysis, presentation of results, and communication with other packages. The range of statistical procedures that can be specified is very large and includes all types of DESCRIPTIVE STATISTICS, HYPOTHESIS TESTING, UNIVARIATE ANALYSIS, BIVARIATE ANALYSIS, and MULTIVARIATE METHODS (ANALYSIS).

Different versions of SPSS are available: SPSS-X is for mainframe computers; while SPSS/PC+ and SPSS for WINDOWS are for personal computers, with SPSS for WINDOWS being the most user-friendly.

**Bibliography**

Foster, J. J. (1993). *Starting SPSS/PC+ and SPSS for WINDOWS* (2nd edn). Wilmslow: Sigma Press.

MICHAEL GREATOREX

**statistical sources**   In order to monitor and, if possible, forecast environmental change (*see* MARKETING ENVIRONMENT), access to information, in the form of statistics, is vital. In most cases, statistics are presented historically, which means that the user has to make assumptions before extrapolating them into the future. Problems arise, however, in the credibility and comparability of statistics. Government statistics, particularly those in the developed world, have high credibility, but other sources may need careful investigation to discover *how* the information has been collected. A major problem exists when making international comparisons in that the basis for presentation of information may be different for individual reporting countries.

**Bibliography**

Central Statistical Office (1990). *Guide to official statistics*. London: HMSO.

United Nations Yearbook. New York: United Nations.

United States, Bureau of the Census *Statistical Abstract of the United States* (annual). Austin: Reference Press.

DAVID YORKE

**statistical tests** There are many statistical significance tests. The approach to take in a particular set of circumstances depends upon the type of data, the number of samples, whether samples are independent or matched, the type of probability sample, the size of the samples, and whether or not some population characteristics are known (*see also* SAMPLING).

A list of some common tests and the conditions of their use is given in table 1.

In addition, hypotheses (*see* HYPOTHESIS TESTING) concerning the relationships between variables measured on interval scales are studied using REGRESSION AND CORRELATION. Relationships between variables measured on ordinal scales are studied using Spearman's Rank correlation coefficient or Kendall's tau.

There are many more test statistics that are available and can be used according to the circumstances. Some are in direct competition with the ones listed above, others are for circumstances not mentioned.

It is easy to carry out such tests using computer packages such as SPSS, SAS, and MINITAB. However, care must be taken not to misuse these packages by using tests in inappropriate circumstances, e.g., when data are not from probability samples, and when tests that require interval data are used with data that are only ordinal.

**Table 1** Common statistical tests

| Type of data | No. of samples | Independent samples? | Other conditions | Statistical technique |
|---|---|---|---|---|
| Interval | 1 | N.R. | $\sigma$ known | Z test |
| Interval | 1 | N.R. | $\sigma$ unknown | t test |
| Ordinal | 1 | N.R. | | Kolmogorov–Smirnov 1 sample test |
| Nominal | 1 | N.R. | small sample | Binomial test |
| Nominal | 1 | N.R. | large sample | Z test |
| Interval | 2 | Yes | $\sigma$'s known | Z test |
| Interval | 2 | Yes | $\sigma$'s unknown | t test (either pooled or unpooled variance formula) |
| Interval | 2 | No | $\sigma$'s unknown | t test (one sample test of differences) |
| Ordinal | 2 | Yes | | Mann–Whitney test K–S 2 sample test |
| Ordinal | 2 | No | | Sign test, Wilcoxon matched pairs test |
| Nominal | 2 | Yes | | Fisher's Exact test, Z test, Chi-squared test |
| Nominal | 2 | No | | McNemar test |
| Interval | 2+ | Yes | | 1-way ANOVA |
| Interval | 2+ | No | | t tests (as above) of all pairs |
| Ordinal | 2+ | Yes | | Kruskal Wallis 1-way ANOVA |
| Ordinal | 2+ | No | | Friedman 2-way ANOVA |
| Nominal | 2+ | Yes | | Chi-squared test |
| Nominal | 2+ | No | | Cochran Q test |

$\sigma$ is the population standard deviation

**Bibliography**

Tull, D. S. & Hawkins, D. I. (1987). *Marketing research: Measurement and method* (4th edn). New York: Macmillan. Chapter 13.

MICHAEL GREATOREX

**store choice**   This is the decision made by the consumer as to which store to visit. In a highly competitive market place, an understanding of why the consumer chooses a particular store is of great importance. Getting the consumer to cross the threshold and enter a store naturally opens up a number of selling opportunities.

Studies have elicited a large number of reasons as to why consumers choose as they do. The choice factors and the strength of their effects naturally vary from one consumer to another and from one time period to another. Many factors are likely to influence store choice, including consumer perceptions of the price and quality of the merchandise, the internal environment of the store, the helpfulness of staff, ease of access, the product range, and the "image" held by the customer of the outlet or chain.

Given such differences, it is difficult to generalize about the store choice of consumers. The individual retailer is likely to develop an intuitive approach to this question based upon previous experience.

STEVE WORRALL

**store design**   The store is the main retail distribution channel and is perhaps the most powerful medium for communicating with customers; consequently, store design is extremely important. It encompasses the entire store environment including aspects such as layout, ambience, atmospherics, visual aspects of retail merchandising, and retail security. As Levy & Weitz (1995) reveal: "Many retailers like to think of their store as a theater. The walls and floors represent the stage. The lighting, fixtures, and visual communications such as signs represent the sets. And the merchandise represents the show. Like the theater, the store design and all its components should work in harmony to support the merchandise rather than competing with it."

The significance of store design as a competitive weapon and selling tool is frequently overlooked. When implemented properly, however, the design of a retail outlet can influence how successful it is at:

(1) Initially, visually attracting customers to the retailer.
(2) Communicating the desired corporate, store, and product images, differentiating them from those of other retailers.
(3) Creating the most effective balance between products and functions.
(4) Selling, promoting, and advertising products and services, as well as the retailer.
(5) Encouraging the customer to browse around the store and maximize the time spent in it, thereby maximizing the chance of impulse purchase.
(6) Supporting and giving "environmental substance" to media campaigns.
(7) Providing an ergonomically sound environment, freeing more staff time for sales-orientated activities.
(8) Facilitating efficient and quality service delivery.
(9) Developing customer/staff relationships.
(10) Giving user satisfaction, for both staff and customers, aesthetically, emotionally, and in terms of functionality.
(11) Enabling the rapid implementation of any future environment alterations or refurbishment.
(12) Providing an acceptable design life cycle.
(13) Preventing robbery/fraud.
(14) Imbuing staff and customers with confidence in their safety and security. (Greenland, 1994)

Many larger retailers with expansive store networks adopt a centrally controlled, uniform approach to store design. A fully researched, standardized design concept is implemented across the network, projecting a uniform corporate image and enabling considerable equipment/store furniture cost savings to be made through economies of scale and the use of key suppliers.

Stores represent the retailers' frontline physical contact with consumers; accordingly, their design is one of the most important components of retailer image. Store atmospherics and some of the more subtle aspects of its design impact particularly upon customer perceptions and attitudes concerning the retailer. Store design is even more significant in services retailing where there are fewer tangible cues to influence customer perceptions. Here the outlet environment becomes a key transmitter of the institution's image. Financial services retailing is a prime example.

Within stores, the most effective balance between products is developed through research into the space elasticity exhibited by products. Space elasticity is the ratio of the relative change in unit sales to relative change in shelf space (Curhan, 1973). Different products reveal different degrees of space elasticity: e.g., unresponsive products such as salt do not exhibit any significant increase in sales when allocated shelf space is increased; other products do, however (see McGoldrick, 1990). Store layouts, presentation techniques, and the positioning of goods within stores also affect their sales. By emphasizing an item to consumers the retailer enhances the chance of impulse purchase. Store layout patterns and efforts to control the direction and speed of consumers through the store also have similar objectives see Greenland, 1994). Store design is becoming an increasingly scientific subject.

*See also* **Atmospherics; Financial services retailing; Impulse purchasing; Retail distribution channels; Retail merchandising; Retail security**

### Bibliography

Curhan, R. C. (1973). Shelf space allocation and profit maximization in mass retailing. *Journal of Marketing*, 37 (3), 54–60.
Greenland, S. J. (1994). The branch environment. In P. J. McGoldrick & S. J. Greenland (eds), *Retailing of financial services* (pp. 163–196). Maidenhead: McGraw-Hill.
Levy, M. & Weitz, B. A. (1995). *Retailing management.* Chicago: Irwin.
McGoldrick, P. J. (1990). *Retail marketing.* Maidenhead: McGraw-Hill.

STEVE GREENLAND

**straight re-buy**   Robinson, Faris & Wind (1967) suggest a simple division of organizational purchasing into three categories: NEW TASK, MODIFIED RE-BUY, and straight re-buy. This categorization of organizational purchasing is now widely accepted. The most straightforward of these three categories is that of straight re-buy where an existing contract for goods or services from a particular supplier is renewed with little or no change in price, specifications, delivery arrangements, etc. With no significant change involved, straight re-buys can often be managed routinely through standard operating procedures and at a junior level. There can, however, be a danger of overlooking small but significant changes (e.g., in technical specification or delivery arrangements) when an organization has become accustomed to treating particular contracts as "straightforward."

### Bibliography

Robinson, P. T., Faris, C. W. & Wind, Y. (1967). *Industrial buying and creative marketing.* Boston, MA: Allyn & Bacon.

DOMINIC WILSON

**strategic business units**   The term strategic business unit (SBU) allegedly originated in The General Electric Company in the USA, when it analyzed its diversified corporate structure with the assistance of the McKinsey Corporation (McKiernan, 1992, p. 2). There are several approaches an organization can adopt in describing its strategic business units in terms of, for example, segments, geographical markets, products. Generically they will have certain major features: they are discrete units with clearly identifiable costs and revenues (they are, therefore, profit centers) which are either a single business or a collection of related businesses; they have an external market; they have a manager responsible for the SBU; and they have their own competitors. Kotler (1994) argues that ideally they have a distinct mission, and can benefit from STRATEGIC PLANNING. CORPORATE STRATEGY may be concerned with allocating the total resources among the different SBUs so as to meet overall organizational STRATEGIC OBJECTIVES, and various analytical frameworks have been proposed to facilitate the process (*see* BCG MATRIX; PRODUCT PORTFOLIO ANALYSIS).

However, it has been argued by Prahalad & Hamel (1990) that SBUs can be dysfunctional in that the SBU manager adopts a narrow business, as opposed to an organizational, perspective so that skill, knowledge, and other capabilities tend not to be shared and organizationally exploited, to perhaps the long-term detriment of the firm's competitiveness. They propose that organizations instead build on their core competencies.

## Bibliography

Kotler, P. (1994). *Marketing management: Analysis, planning, implementation and control* (8th edn). Englewood Cliffs, NJ: Prentice-Hall. Chapter 3.

McKiernan, P. (1992). *Strategies of growth.* London: Routledge.

Prahalad, C. K. & Hamel, G. (1990). The core competence of the corporation. *Harvard Business Review,* 68, (3), May–June, 79–91.

DALE LITTLER

**strategic control**    Strategic control is a periodic assessment of the effectiveness of the corporate (*see* CORPORATE STRATEGY), business, or Marketing strategy (*see* MARKETING STRATEGY). The concern will be to ensure that strategic objectives are being achieved as planned. More broadly, the aim might be to assess the current strategy in the light of inter alia competitors' performance and the demonstrated ability of the company to capitalize on opportunities. Such assessments may be part of an annual STRATEGIC PLANNING cycle with the results feeding into the next annual cycle. Alternatively, especially in sectors which are experiencing rapid rates of change, they may be undertaken more regularly.

Effective strategic control will enable the organization to take remedial action where there are significant deviations from plan or inadequate performance relative to competitors, and to assess whether or not, inter alia, it is effectively capitalizing on opportunities. Kotler (1994) argues that companies must occasionally undertake a critical review of their overall marketing effectiveness, and suggests two

management techniques: the marketing-effectiveness rating review and a MARKETING AUDIT.

The first essentially involves rating various aspects of the company's marketing activities and arriving at an overall score. A detailed marketing audit is then undertaken where significant weaknesses are identified. This is, in effect, a structured and detailed assessment of a company's or business's environment, objectives, strategies, and procedures, aimed at identifying problem areas and opportunities and making recommendations to improve the marketing performance.

## Bibliography

Bungay, S. & Goold, M. (1991). Creating a strategic control system. *Long Range Planning,* 24, June, 32–39.

Bureau, J. R. (1995). Controlling marketing. In M. J. Baker (ed.), *The marketing book.* Oxford: Butterworth Heinemann.

Kotler, P. (1994). *Marketing management: Analysis, planning, implementation and control* (8th edn). Englewood Cliffs, NJ: Prentice-Hall. Chapter 27.

DALE LITTLER

**strategic decisions**    Ansoff (1965) draws the distinction between three types of decisions: operational, administrative, and strategic. He argues that strategic decisions are primarily concerned with external rather than internal issues of the firm and "specifically with the selection of the PRODUCT MIX which the firm will produce and the MARKETS to which it will sell." Operational decisions, on the other hand, are day-to-day decisions concerned with managing efficiently current operations; while administrative decisions are involved with organizational structure and with the acquisition and development of resources. Some of the key strategic decisions are, Ansoff suggests, those concerned with objectives and goals; diversification strategy; expansion strategy; finance strategy; growth strategy; and the timing of growth.

Various features of strategic decisions have been identified to distinguish them from tactical decisions (Weitz & Wensley, 1983). In particular, they tend to be important (i.e., they are concerned with doing the right thing rather than doing things right); have major resource implications; be taken at the highest levels in the organization; have a longer term impact on the total organization; have less detail, generally being described in broad statements; be typically complex, unstructured, and lacking parallels, whereas tactical decisions are more structured and repeatable; be focused on the environment of the organization, such as competitive activity; and demand creativity and innovation in devising appropriate responses.

Johnson & Scholes (1993) note that strategic decisions are concerned with: the scope of an organization's activities, such as how diversified it should be and whether or not it should enter international markets; ensuring that the organization's activities are compatible with its resources; and matching the organization to its environment. The latter may involve adjustments in its activities to ensure that the organization remains competitive as its environment (see MARKETING ENVIRONMENT) changes.

The distinction between tactical and strategic decisions may not be as clear-cut as is often suggested. Tactical decisions, such as short-term responses to competitors' activities, can have significant long-term and, therefore, strategic repercussions.

### Bibliography

Ansoff, H. I. (1965). *Corporate strategy*. New York: McGraw-Hill. Chapter 1.
Johnson, G. & Scholes, K. (1993). *Exploring corporate strategy* (3rd edn). Prentice-Hall. Chapter 1.
Weitz, B. A. & Wensley, R. (Eds) (1983). *Strategic marketing*. Boston, MA: Kent Publishing.

DALE LITTLER

**strategic marketing**   The essence of strategic marketing is to ensure that the organization's marketing adapts to changes in the external environment (see MARKETING ENVIRONMENT) and that it has the marketing resources to do so effectively. This may be achieved by using STRATEGIC PLANNING, although it may also embrace more opportunistic or entrepreneurial organizational behavior.

DALE LITTLER

**strategic objectives**   Organizations are expected to have objectives, often regarded as part of the strategic plan (see STRATEGIC PLANNING), that act as foci for organizational activities. Such objectives should, according to Quinn (1980), be clear and "state *what* is to be achieved and *when* results are to be accomplished, but they do not state *how* the results are to be achieved." They will tend to be expressed in quantitative terms.

Objectives tend to be shaped by a variety of influences, although the need to satisfy financial stakeholders is understandably likely to be very strong. However, other constituencies, such as employees, consumers, and various pressure groups, may also have an impact. Moreover, as has been noted by many, the separation of ownership from control means that the aspirations of managers can be a significant intervening factor in shaping objectives.

The objectives that emerge will, as Cyert & March (1963) among others have noted, be a balance between the somewhat differing, and on occasions conflicting, requirements of the various organizational constituencies.

Major strategic objectives are likely to be financial: growth in revenue and profitability; growth in earnings per share. There may also be other objectives expressed in terms of, for example, market share. In addition, organizations may establish objectives in terms of, for instance, customer satisfaction levels, or "concern about the environment." However, it could be argued that these may be factors which need to be taken into account in order to achieve the overarching financial targets (to ignore issues of customer satisfaction, for example, may be regarded as having a deleterious impact on the long-term financial health of the organization). They can be seen in essence to be secondary objectives to the primary needs of ensuring that financial objectives are satisfied.

Not all firms emphasize financial objectives, let alone the continued growth in them. The owners of small firms may, for example, be more concerned with maintaining their independence. Many non-profit organizations, such as charities, might be expected to have altruistic concerns, but nevertheless they are increasingly interpreting themselves as businesses with the need to generate selected levels of revenue at targeted margins in order to meet their overall mission. In such cases, though, the financial targets may be defined either in concert with, or subsequent to, the non-financial objectives.

In some cases, the purpose of the organization may be difficult to articulate, so that clear objectives may not emerge. This would be the case in, for example, large bureaucratic bodies, particularly those operating in the public sector. For these, Lindblom (1968) argued that policy-making is a process of incremental steps, often with objectives emerging over time. As with any objectives, they are likely to be adjusted and even redefined in the light of changing circumstances and through acquisition of additional information.

### Bibliography

Cyert, R. M. & March, J. G. (1963). *A behavioral theory of the firm.* Englewood Cliffs, NJ: Prentice-Hall.

Lindblom, C. E. (1968). *The policy making process.* Englewood Cliffs, NJ: Prentice-Hall.

Quinn, J. B. (1980). *Strategies for change: Logical incrementalism.* Homewood, IL: Irwin. Chapter 1.

DALE LITTLER

**strategic planning** Strategic planning is generally regarded as a structured approach to the formulation of corporate or business strategy involving a sequence of stages which embrace: the definition of the STRATEGIC OBJECTIVES and often, in addition, the MISSION STATEMENT or VISION; a SWOT ANALYSIS; the identification and evaluation of the strategic options; and the selection of those likely to yield the optimum return. Increasingly, attention has been directed to the implementation of strategy. Consideration must also be directed to STRATEGIC CONTROL. There may be iterations between these various stages.

In the post-Second World War period, strategic planning was adopted by and became routine in many organizations (*see* e.g., Ross & Silverblatt, 1987), generally because, paradoxically, it was viewed as a means of coping with environmental uncertainties (*see* UNCERTAINTY). Often planning departments were established that were concerned with, inter alia, the formulation of strategic plans, generally

on an annual basis. There were possibly at least two consequences: first, planners and planning became divorced from implementation with the result that elaborate plans were written which may have only a marginal impact on decision-making. Second, the routine strategic planning could result in the extrapolation from previous plans, without taking account of existing or potential environmental discontinuities.

Mintzberg (1990) criticized the structured approach to strategic planning which he termed the "design school." He argued that this is based on three premises: strategy formulation precedes implementation; the process of strategy formulation consists of conscious thought involving senior managers, and more especially the chief executive; and the process and the strategy produced is explicit, simple, and unique. He suggested that the "design school" approach to strategic management can apply only in a minority of cases where the environment is stable; and that thinking and acting are likely to be intertwined, while strategies will tend to be the fruits of experimental trial and error rather than of detached analytical thinking.

Kotler (1994) has argued that strategic plans become obsolete quickly because of intense competition and the rapid dissemination of information using the latest technology. He believes that companies are forced to move from strategic planning to "strategic improvising" and they do this by empowering frontline people to make more of the decisions, subject, of course, to certain parameters.

### Bibliography

Kotler, P. (1994). Reconceptualising marketing: An interview with Philip Kotler. *European Management Journal*, **12** (4), December.

Mintzberg, H. (1990). The design school. Reconsidering the basic premises of strategic management. *Strategic Management Journal*, **11**, (3), Mar.–Apr., 171–195.

Ross, J. E. & Silverblatt, R. (1987). Developing the strategic plan. *Industrial Marketing Management*, **16**, 103–108.

DALE LITTLER

**strategic styles** It has been suggested that organizations can be categorized according to their broad strategic style. For example, Mintzberg (1973) suggests that there are three main approaches to (or modes of) strategy-making: the adaptive; entrepreneurial; and planning (see ADAPTIVE STRATEGY; ENTREPRENEURIAL STRATEGY; and PLANNING STYLE). Goold & Campbell (1987) in a study of 16 major diversified companies classified them according to how the "center" (i.e., the headquarters) controlled and measured performance. They identified three major types: strategic planners, where the "center" makes crucial decisions for subsidiaries; strategic controllers, in which the center's role is to review the plans formulated by subsidiaries; and the financial controllers, in which the strategic decisions are made by the subsidiaries, with the center judging performance by numbers.

Littler & Leverick (1994), in an analysis of the strategies employed by firms entering the mobile communications sector, identified four major styles, all of which exhibited to different degrees opportunistic behavior: the "visionaries" which had a clear view on how they wanted the market to develop; the "calculated gamblers," attracted by the potential of high profits while minimizing downside risk; the "incrementalists," which saw entry into the market as a natural extension of the current portfolio of product interests; and the "bureaucrats," which entered the market after a detailed analysis and the use of formal planning procedures. They also identified three major styles of strategic management followed by these companies after they had entered the mobile communications market: the "ad hoc," with an emphasis on operational management rather than on longer term strategic issues; the "lodestar," which emphasized the articulation of clear targets but which lacked detail on the means by which these were to be achieved (see UMBRELLA STRATEGY); and the "conformists," which were bureaucratic, relying on formal STRATEGIC PLANNING and analyses.

### Bibliography

Goold, M. & Campbell, A. (1987). *Strategies and styles: The role of the centre in managing diversified corporations.* Oxford: Basil Blackwell.

Littler, D. & Leverick, F. (1994). Marketing planning in new technology sectors. In J. Saunders (ed.), *The marketing initiative* (pp. 72–91). Prentice-Hall.

Mintzberg, H. (1973). Strategy making in three modes. *California Management Review*, 16, (2), Winter, 44–53.

DALE LITTLER

**strategy**  Strategy is derived from the Greek "strategia" meaning generalship. Von Clausewitz (1976) wrote the classic military strategy. The widespread use of the term in business occurred after the Second World War although businesses, in particular the Pennsylvania railroad, employed strategy in the 19th century. Zinkham & Pereira (1994) suggest that the notion of strategy was first introduced to the management literature in 1944 by Von Neumann & Morgenstern in their classic work on the theory of games which essentially focused on situations of conflict. Following on from this, there was a series of major contributions on strategy such as those of Selznick (1957), and Chandler (1962). Ansoff's comprehensive text *Corporate Strategy*, published in 1965, firmly established strategy in the management lexicon. The military connotations of strategy undoubtedly appeared apt given the traditional perspectives of competition in which firms were seen as "fighting for market share," engaging in "price wars" and embarking on advertising "campaigns." The military analogy was extended to MARKETING (James, 1985; Kotler & Singh, 1980). However, Liddell-Hart (1967) was critical of the view, put forward by Von Clausewitz, that: "The destruction of the enemy's main forces on the battlefield constitutes the only true aim in war." He suggested that: "The 'object' in war is a better state of peace, even if only from your own point of view." Contemporary management theory is much more likely to identify a spectrum of strategies, ranging from the extreme competitive (see COMPETITIVE STRATEGY) through to various forms of cooperation. Indeed, many companies now regard strategic alliances, which may be formed for some markets with firms that are competitors in others, as strengthening their competitive position.

There are many definitions of strategy, but in general it is regarded as embodying the joint selection of the product market arenas in which the firm is or will compete and the key policies defining how it will compete Rumelt et al.,

1991). The Walker et al. definition (1992) suggested that an effective strategy would embrace: what is to be attained; which product markets should be the focus; and how resources and activities will be allocated to each product market to meet environmental OPPORTUNITIES and THREATS. Johnson & Scholes (1993) define strategy as: "the direction and scope of an organisation over the long term: ideally, which matches its resources to its changing environment, and in particular its markets, customers or clients so as to meet stakeholder expectations" (p. 10).

In general, a strategy encompasses the goals, regarded as a general statement of aim or purpose, and objectives, and the means by which these are to be achieved. It can apply at several levels: the organizational or corporate; the business (see STRATEGIC BUSINESS UNITS); and the product. Strategy may also be associated with certain activities. Thus, for example, there is reference to PRICING strategies and NEW PRODUCT DEVELOPMENT strategies. There is much debate about whether or not strategy can be clearly formulated in advance of being applied. However, as Mintzberg (1990) argues, managers may often define strategy in terms of past actions, rather than in terms of intentions. Moreover, a consciously conceived strategy may not be easily realized because of the intervention of, inter alia, UNCERTAINTY.

*See also* **Strategic decisions; Strategic planning**

### Bibliography

Ansoff, H. I. (1965). *Corporate strategy: An analytical approach to business policy for growth and expansion.* New York: McGraw-Hill.

Chandler, A. D. Jr (1962). *Strategy and structure.* Cambridge, MA: The MIT Press.

James, B. G. (1985). *Business wargames.* Harmondsworth: Penguin.

Johnson, G. & Scholes, K. (1993). *Exploring corporate strategy* (3rd edn). Prentice-Hall.

Kotler, P. & Singh, R. (1980). Marketing warfare in the 1980s. *Journal of Business Strategy*, 1, (3), 30–41.

Liddell-Hart, B. H. (1967). *Strategy.* New York: Praeger.

Mintzberg, H. (1990). The design school: Reconsidering the basic premises of strategic management. *Strategic Management Journal*, 11, (3), 171–195.

Rumelt, R., Schendel, D. & Tece, D. (1991). Strategic management and economics. *Strategic Management Journal*, 12, 5–29.

Selznick, P. (1957). *Leadership in administration.* New York: Harper & Row.

Von Clausewitz, C. (1976). *On war* (translated by M. Howard & P. Paret). Princeton University Press.

Von Neumann, J. & Morgenstern, O. (1994). *Theory of games and economic behavior.* Princeton University Press.

Walker, O. C., Boyd, H. & Larreche, J. (1992). *Marketing strategy: Planning and implementation.* Homewood, IL: Irwin.

Zinkham, G. M. & Pereira, A. (1994). An overview of marketing strategy and planning. *International Journal of Research in Marketing*, 11, 185–218.

DALE LITTLER

**structural equation models** Structural equation models bring together research methods in a holistic way. Hypothetical relationships between variables are represented in a network of causal and functional paths. The variables may be latent constructs related to directly measurable variables in a way that is part of the specification of the structural equation model. The computation procedures are such that the empirical estimation of the relationships between the latent variables and their specified manifest variables and the estimation of the specified relationships between the latent variables are carried out jointly, using a common objective, rather than as separate activities each using a separate objective. Some multivariate methods (*see* MULTIVARIATE METHODS (ANALYSIS)) can be seen as special cases of structural equation modeling.

Structural equation models can be used throughout MARKETING RESEARCH, for instance studying the links between advertising, attitudes towards brands, intentions, and purchasing. They have also been used to test for RELIABILITY and VALIDITY in a number of studies.

Structural .equation modeling using latent variables is becoming a popular tool in marketing research, being seen as a comprehensive tool capable of replacing older and more elementary multivariate methods. To assist this development, computer programs have been developed. Among the well-known programs are LISREL, now incorporated in the STATISTICAL PACKAGE FOR THE SOCIAL SCIENCE or SPSS, and the PROC CALIS procedure in SAS and EQS, now available in a PC version.

## Bibliography

Bagozzi, R. P. (1994). Structural equation models in marketing research: Basic principles.In R. P. Bagozzi (Ed.), *Principles of marketing research*, (Chapter 9). Cambridge, MA: Blackwell.

MICHAEL GREATOREX

**suppliers**   It is an axiom of marketing that suppliers are CUSTOMERS too (Kotler & Levy, 1973). A graphic illustration of this point is provided by the Mandarin words for "buy" and for "sell" which are virtually identical – the difference being in intonation. It is self-evident that any marketing transaction requires a "supplier" as well as a "customer" but the logical extension of this into "supplier strategies" as well as "customer strategies" has been given much less attention in the marketing literature until relatively recently. Now there is widespread recognition of the importance of fostering long-term relationships with suitable suppliers and there is considerable research into such crucial issues as: understanding marketing strategy in terms of a NETWORK of suppliers (Håkansson & Snehota, 1989); the management of customer/ supplier relationships (Han et al., 1993); and the advantages and disadvantages of long-term "partnership" between customers and suppliers (Lamming, 1993; Matthyssens & Van den Bulte, 1994). Rather less attention has been given to the costs and problems involved in collaborative relationships between suppliers and customers, and to the situations when such relationships may be less appropriate (i.e., when the risks of providing a supplier with privileged access may exceed the potential benefits).

*See also* **Relationship marketing**

## Bibliography

Kotler, P. & Levy, S. J. (1973). Buying is marketing too. *Journal of Marketing*, 37, (1), Jan, 54–59.
Håkansson, H. & Snehota, I. (1989). No business is an island: The network concept of business strategy. *Scandinavian Journal of Management*, 4, (3), 187–200.
Han, S-L., Wilson, D. T. & Dant, S. P. (1993). Buyer–supplier relationships today. *Industrial Marketing Management*, 22, (4), Nov., 331–338.
Lamming, R. (1993). *Beyond partnership*. Prentice-Hall.
Matthyssens, P. & Van den Bulte, C. (1994). Getting closer and nicer: Partnerships in the supply chain. *Long Range Planning*, 27, (1), Feb., 72–83.

DOMINIC WILSON

## survey research

*Introduction*

Survey research is one of the four main sources of PRIMARY DATA, the others being OBSERVATION, QUALITATIVE RESEARCH, and experimental research. Surveys can provide information on past and intended behavior, attitudes, beliefs, opinions, and personal characteristics. While the data provided by surveys are basically descriptive, appropriate analysis of the survey data can provide evidence of association between variables.

Surveys involve asking people (respondents) questions, either verbal or written. The term sample survey indicates that survey data have been collected from a sample of a population. Data are collected with the aid of questionnaires through the mail or by means of computers or administered to individuals or groups in face-to-face interviews in the home or in the street or using the telephone.

In cross-sectional studies, data are collected at a single point in time from a cross-section of the population. Typical analysis of cross-sectional surveys involves attempting to measure characteristics of the population as a whole and/or breaking down the sample into subgroups and seeing if behavior, opinions, etc. vary between the groups.

In longitudinal studies, respondents are studied at different moments in time in order to examine trends and changes, if any, over time.

*Types of Surveys*

Surveys usually involve the use of structured interviews with the interviewer or respondent following the wording and order provided on a questionnaire. Survey methods are usually classified by mode of administration, the three main modes being personal, telephone, and postal interviewing.

*Personal interviews.* Personal interviews usually take place either in the home of the respondent or in a public place such as the street or a shopping mall.

In face-to-face interviews in the home, it is the interviewer's job to contact the respondent, often selected by the research director using some form of probability sampling (*see* SAMPLING), pose the questions, and record the answers. Lengthy interviews are possible and the interviewer can use physical stimuli as part of the interviewing process. The respondent is able to seek clarification of confusing questions or terms and the interviewer is able to observe the respondent, for instance, to see if the questions have been understood. In-home, or door-to-door, interviewing is expensive and its use is declining.

Street or shopping mall intercept interviews are the commonest type of personal interview. Interviewers intercept passers-by and either question them on the spot or take them to a nearby facility to conduct the interview. It is possible to get a random sample of passers-by by selecting every nth passer-by. However, it is unlikely that the population of interest will pass by the places where interviewers are located. For this reason mall intercept surveys are rarely statistically representative of the required populations and rely on quota sampling procedures to ensure some amount of representativeness. They are cheaper than door-to-door interviews and it takes less time to complete an intercept survey.

In direct computer interviewing, the computer presents the questions to a respondent on a screen and the respondent uses a keyboard or a mouse to answer. These are often used in shopping malls or at conferences and trade shows. For some surveys, respondents are selected by interviewers as in other types of personal interviewing research; in other surveys the computer is placed in a prominent place and interested passers-by select themselves as respondents. As well as freeing the interviewer from posing the questions and recording the answers and reducing data inputting time and expenses, this method has an extra advantage in that interviewer bias is low.

*Telephone interviews.* Telephone interviewers, stationed at a central location, present their questions using the telephone to interviewees over a wide area. Computer-assisted telephone interviewing (CATI) is growing quickly. As in other computer assisted interviewing methods the questionnaire is programed into the computer. The interviewer reads the questions from the screen and records the answers directly into the computer. The computer can be programed to make the calls, for instance using random digit dialing, and subsequent recalls can be made when initial calls are unanswered.

Flexibility is the main advantage of computer-presented questionnaires. The questions can be varied according to earlier answers, e.g., buyers of a brand may be asked one set of questions and non-buyers a different set. Also, order problems caused in some closed questions where possible answers are presented to respondents can be averted by the computer varying the answers from respondent to respondent.

Low cost and the speed with which a survey can be carried out are two other advantages of telephone interviews. Interim results and updates are easy to obtain as the data are recorded immediately. Interviewer bias is low, respondents can feel that their anonymity has been maintained, and sensitive questions can be posed with less embarrassment than in face-to-face interviews. On the other hand, it is difficult to use physical stimuli as part of the interview although the use of fax machines can ease this problem. The fact that not every household has a telephone, that some numbers are ex-directory, and that an individual member of a large household has a smaller chance of being chosen than a member of a small household, means that a sample may not be truly representative of a specified population.

*Postal surveys.* Questionnaires are delivered to the respondents who return completed questionnaires by post to the researcher. Postal interviews are widely used. They allow a large sample to be contacted very cheaply and the absence of an interviewer cuts out interviewer bias. On the other hand, complex questionnaires are unsuitable and the questionnaire has to be carefully constructed. The major disadvantages of postal surveys are the high level of non-response and the length of time allowed for respondents to reply.

Non-response is a problem for all types of surveys but especially so for postal surveys. Non-response can be reduced in the first place through pre-notification, by offering monetary inducements including a free entry to a prize draw, by use of reply-paid envelopes, by making the questionnaire interesting, etc. Follow-up contacts can be used to increase the overall response rate.

The critical issue concerning non-response is the extent to which the respondents and non-respondents are alike on the important variables. Among the ways of assessing this is to make comparisons of successive waves of respondents and to subsample intensively non-respondents for comparison with the original respondents. Unless care is taken to assess the effects of non-response on representativeness of the sample obtained, results from postal surveys should be treated cautiously.

*Conclusion*

Two problems of interviewing include the responses to sensitive questions and biases caused by interviewer effects. Since face-to-face interviews and, to a lesser extent, telephone interviews involve social interaction between interviewer and respondent, it is possible that respondents will answer sensitive questions with socially acceptable, rather than truthful, answers. Postal and computer surveys, which do not suffer from this social interaction, may yield more accurate answers to sensitive questions.

Interviewers may vary the way that they pose the questions, by changing the wording or simply altering their tone of voice or body language, from interview to interview, with the result that each respondent has a slightly different interview, a disadvantage in survey research. The interviewer's age, sex, appearance, social class, etc. may affect the answers as respondents seek to give answers that they believe will be acceptable to the interviewer. The recording of answers to open-ended questions may be biased by the interviewer's opinions. These interviewer effects will be most pronounced in personal interviews, least pronounced in computer and postal interviews, with telephone interviews somewhere in between.

### Bibliography

Malhotra, N. K. (1993). *Marketing research: An applied orientation.* Englewood Cliffs, NJ: Prentice-Hall. Chapter 7.

Tull, D. S. & Hawkins, D. I. (1987). *Marketing research: Measurement and methods* (4th edn). New York: Macmillan. Chapter 4.

MICHAEL GREATOREX

**SWOT analysis** As part of the STRATEGIC PLANNING process, it is generally prescribed that organizations undertake an INTERNAL AUDIT, aimed at identifying their major skills, technologies, and resources, and existing and possible future vulnerabilities; and an ENVIRONMENTAL ANALYSIS aimed at identifying inter alia existing and future societal (e.g., demographic), technological, legal, and economic developments. The major purpose is to identify the strengths and weaknesses of the organization, and the major opportunities and threats opened up by what is happening and likely to happen in its environment; hence, SWOT. The purpose of the STRATEGIC PLANNING exercise, then, is to build on the strengths, and where possible overcome or avoid the weaknesses, by exploiting opportunities in the environment as well as defending the organization against possible threats, or even converting so-called threats into opportunities.

In the positivist tradition, this analysis is presented as though objective data about the organization and its environment are present to be discovered, ignoring the fact that individuals have their own values, prejudices, and motives which can affect their perception of the environment. Thus, there can be differing perspectives on, say, the competencies of an organization because of the intrusion of, for example, selective perception.

### Bibliography

Littler, D. & Leverick, F. (1994). Marketing planning in new technology sectors. In J. Saunders (ed.), *The marketing initiative* (pp. 72–91). Prentice-Hall.

Sanderson, S. M. & Luffman, G. A. (1988). Strategic planning and environmental analysis. *European Journal of Marketing*, **22**, (2), 14–27.

DALE LITTLER

**systems marketing**   Especially in organizational markets (*see* ORGANIZATIONAL MARKETING), businesses have developed the capability to provide what might be termed "total solutions" to customer "problems" or requirements. Thus, suppliers of computerized businesses systems will design, develop, and implement, including the training of users, a management information system to meet the information requirements of customers; or process plant contractors might be involved in the design, construction, and commissioning of chemical plant. These suppliers may have all the resources in house to provide the total "package" or they may, as appropriate, subcontract to others. In some cases, there are firms, such as consultant engineers, which act as coordinators based on their skills in planning and managing the various activities required.

In many MARKETS, such as defence or where complex plant and equipment is required, there is a tradition of providing "systems." The purchaser often solicits tenders from what are termed prime contractors which are responsible for bidding and assembling the different activities necessary to supply what the customer wants. These prime contractors provide a "turn-key" operation, so called because the customer simply turns one key to obtain what is sought.

DALE LITTLER

# T

**target market** This is a group of potential users or consumers which is the focus of the business's marketing effort for a particular product or service, usually identified by means of MARKET SEGMENTATION.

FIONA LEVERICK

**targeting** *see* MARKET SEGMENTATION; POSITIONING

**technological environment** The technological environment is one of the elements of the MARKETING ENVIRONMENT. This aspect is concerned with developments and trends in technology not only in terms of customer offerings but also with respect to the technology of production and distribution. For example, there have been important developments in aspects of technology relevant to marketing itself – such as the use of relational databases, barcode scanning, electronic data interchange, personal mobile communications, computerized animation, interactive multi-media systems, and telephone shopping.

*See also* **Environmental analysis**

DAVID YORKE

**telemarketing** Telemarketing (or telephone selling) systematically uses a DATABASE of actual and potential customers to define and sell to customers with a high probability of purchase. Greater efficiency is achieved by: avoiding expensive sales visits; widening the range of possible contacts, particularly for smaller orga-

nizations: and responding more quickly to customer requests or complaints. Disadvantages, if not managed properly, are: a possible breakdown in coordination between the inside and outside SALES FORCE, if both are used; too much harassment of customers; the creation of the impression that it is a cost-cutting and less personal substitute for a field sales force; and lack of coordination of customer selling and service.

**Bibliography**

Dickson, P. R. (1994). *Marketing management.* Fort Worth: The Dryden Press. Chapter 11.
Moncrief, W. C., Shannon, S., Lamb, C. W. Jr & Cravens, D. W. (1989). Examining the roles of telemarketing in selling strategy. *Journal of Personal Selling and Sales Management,* Fall, 1–12.
Winter, C. de (1988). *Telephone selling.* London: Heinemann.

DAVID YORKE

**teleshopping** *see* TV-BASED HOME SHOPPING

**television** Television is a communications medium (*see* MASS MEDIA) combining sound and visibility with animation. Its availability is widespread in developed countries, enhanced by the development and growth of cable networks and satellite channels. Television is a major ADVERTISING medium, its main advantages being: national or selective coverage; intrusiveness; an ability to build awareness quickly; a family medium; a capacity to stimulate INTERPERSONAL COMMUNICATIONS; and availability of accurate audience audit/market research data.

However: television areas may be too large for potential advertisers; coverage may be restricted; potential targets may be light viewers; and the attention of the viewer may not be guaranteed due to choice of channels, fastforwarding of video recorders during commercial breaks, and channel switching between these breaks. Consequently, although measures of REACH and FREQUENCY are known, the cost-effectiveness of television advertising is difficult to evaluate.

DAVID YORKE

**tender**  *see* BIDDING

**test marketing**  Test marketing involves the marketing of the product using the proposed marketing policy in a limited area that is representative of the total market. The ratio of the marketing effort for the test region to that agreed for the total market must be approximately the same as the ratio of the size of the test market to the total market.

Test marketing will generally be employed to predict the results of a full national launch. It is also a means of testing the implementation and management of the launch.

Although test marketing may be expensive, it will incur a lower cost than a full national launch, while information received during the test may be used to modify or even significantly alter the marketing program before a full national launch. It is an attempt to reduce risk.

There are a number of advantages of test marketing, such as the detection of possible weaknesses with the marketing mix and the experimentation of alternative marketing mixes in different test areas to assess brand awareness, brand loyalty, and repeat purchases that may result from variations in the marketing mix.

However, test marketing can alert competitors of an impending product launch. They may decide to develop a rival product which benefits from observations made of the test marketing exercise. Test marketing in any case gives competitors time to develop and launch their own product. In addition to competition, other conditions may also change, resulting in, for example, lost opportunities flowing from the decision not to market fully earlier.

Another risk is that other companies marketing products, which in some way compete with the new product, may take actions to disrupt the test market. They may increase advertising and promotion, introduce special offers, or temporarily cut prices. Meaningful conclusions on the performance of the new product will consequently be difficult to make.

The decision to test market is then a result of a careful balancing of the opportunity costs against the benefits of lowering risk and possibly improving the full market launch.

*Stages in Planning a Test Market*

There are several stages involved in planning a test market exercise:

– *Establish Aims*
In general, the aim will be to predict the sales that are likely to be obtained if the product was marketed in the total market. Moreover, since it is in effect a rehearsal of the national launch, the company will also be interested in evaluating the operation of the test marketing exercise.

– *Select of a Test Market Representative of the Total Market*
For many products, the area selected should be a microcosm of the national market in terms of demographic structure, number and size of retailing outlets, employment and socio-economic factors. This may be difficult to guarantee, and some approximations will have to be made. Where specialized market segments form the target, and/or where television advertising is not a component of the marketing program, more limited areas, including towns or areas of cities, may be selected.

– *Decide on the Duration of the Test*
In general, companies will strive to obtain an indication of the "equilibrium" market share, while at the same time having as short a test market period as possible so as not to give competitors time to develop and market competitive products before the test marketer decides to go national. In order to gain a realistic insight into the acceptability of the

product, marketers may wish to observe at least one repeat purchase cycle – particularly in the case of convenience products where it is the extent to which customers will purchase the product again (and again!) that is relevant. In deciding on the duration of the test, the following should be borne in mind: initial demand for a new product will inevitably involve much trial and experimentation; many of the initial users will, for various reasons, often not repurchase; and eventually sales will fall to some reasonably stable level that reflects the degree of repeat purchasing behavior.

– *Decide on the Marketing Research to be Undertaken*
Careful consideration should be paid to the sorts of information that ˙need to be collected before, during, and after the test marketing *prior to* the start of the test. Companies may decide to measure retail sales achieved during the test marketing, the awareness of an attitude towards the advertising, the level of distribution, the sales per outlet, and so on.

The test market data may not, however, be a true indicator of the results to be obtained from a full national launch. There are a number of reasons why this might be the case:

– The test market may not be fully representative of the national market.
– There may be "learning effects" as a result of experience gained from the test market.
– The environment may change between the test marketing and the full launch; e.g., new competition may emerge, and economic conditions may alter.
– Competition may have disrupted the test marketing by engaging in exceptional marketing activity (such as severe price cutting, and dramatic promotional offers).

### Bibliography

Dibb, S., Simkin, L., Pride, W. & Ferrell, O. C. (1994). *Marketing: concepts and strategies* (2nd European edn). Boston, MA: Houghton Mifflin Co.
Kotler, P. (1984). *Marketing management: Analysis, planning and control* (5th edn). Englewood Cliffs, NJ: Prentice-Hall.

Littler, D. A. (1984). *Marketing and product development*. Oxford: Philip Allan.
Urban, G. L. & Hauser, J. R. (1993). *Design and marketing of new products* (2nd edn). Englewood Cliffs, NJ: Prentice-Hall.

MARGARET BRUCE

**threats**   *see* SWOT ANALYSIS

**trade journals**   Trade journals are a range of journals which are aimed at specific industries e.g., footwear, and at "trades" (e.g., *The Caterer*). They provide a conduit to a clearly defined target audience for both advertising and publicity. It is suggested (e.g., by Martilla, 1971) that they comprise a medium which may be a valuable source of information to OPINION LEADERS or GATEKEEPERS in organizational markets (*see* ORGANIZATIONAL BUYING BEHAVIOR).

### Bibliography

Martilla, J. A. (1971). Word of mouth communication in the industrial adoption process. *Journal of Marketing Research*, 8, May, 173–178.

DALE LITTLER

**transaction**   This is the transfer of ownership or use of a product or service from one party to another in return for a payment of some kind. For a transaction to occur, a number of conditions would usually have to be satisfied: the existence of two things of value, agreed-upon conditions, a time of agreement, and a place of agreement. A transaction can be seen as being distinguishable from a transfer, the latter describing a situation where one party gives to another but receives nothing in return.

FIONA LEVERICK

**transfer pricing**   Transfer pricing refers to the pricing of internal movements (or "transfers") of goods and services between cost centers within an organization and is an important aspect of cost control (Ward, 1993). Transfer pricing is a necessary aspect of management accounting but can be unethical or even illegal where it is used to evade corporate taxation, perhaps in the movement of goods between organizational subsidiaries operating within different taxation regimes.

**Bibliography**

Crow, S. & Sauls, E. (1994). Setting the right transfer price. *Management Accounting*, **76**, (6), Dec., 41–47.
Ward, K. (1993). Gaining a marketing advantage through the strategic use of transfer pricing. *Journal of Marketing Management*, **9**, July, 245–253.

DOMINIC WILSON

**trial**  A trial is an element in the CONATIVE STAGE of the INNOVATION-ADOPTION MODEL of MARKETING COMMUNICATIONS. A potential customer may wish to use a certain product for a trial period in order to evaluate its ability to satisfy a particular need, thereby reducing the PERCEIVED RISK of purchase.

**Bibliography**

Kotler, P. (1994). *Marketing management: Analysis, planning, implementation and control* (8th edn). Englewood Cliffs, NJ: Prentice-Hall. Chapter 22.
Rogers, E. M. (1962). *Diffusion of innovations.* New York: Free Press. (pp. 79–86).

DAVID YORKE

**TV-based home shopping**  Television-based home shopping involves the purchase of products advertised on television programs and commercial breaks by telephoning orders through to the advertised number. Berman & Evans (1995) indicate that this channel represents approximately 10 percent of the US consumer goods market. Whitford (1994) discusses the advantages afforded to the retailer by the home shopping channel, namely, wide audience reach, the equivalent of free advertising, instant market feedback, high short-term volume of sales, and immediate results. The increasing number of television channels, introduced via cable and satellite television networks, is likely to increase the proportion of retail sales generated by this retail distribution channel.

*See also* **Retail distribution channels**

**Bibliography**

Berman, B. & Evans, J. R. (1995). *Retail management.* Englewood Cliffs, NJ: Prentice-Hall.
Levy, M. & Weitz, B. A. (1995). *Retailing management.* Chicago: Irwin.
Rosenbloom, B. (1991). *Marketing channels.* Chicago: The Dryden Press.
Whitford, D. (1994). TV or not TV, Inc. INO, **16**, (6), 63–68.

STEVE GREENLAND

**two step flow model**  The two step flow model is concerned with the flow of MARKETING COMMUNICATIONS from the MASS MEDIA, in particular ADVERTISING, via OPINION LEADERS to customers, or opinion "followers." Opinion leaders are portrayed as direct receivers of information from impersonal mass media sources, and they interpret, legitimize, and transmit this information to customers, i.e., they are middlemen.

This theory assumes that mass media influence on mass opinion is not direct, i.e., that the mass media alone cannot influence the sales of products; that mass media communications are mediated by opinion leaders; that opinion leaders are more exposed to mass media than those they influence; and that opinion leaders may alter communications messages (i.e., they are GATEKEEPERS).

However, this is not an accurate portrayal of the flow of information and influence. Modifications to the theory accept that: mass media and interpersonal channels of communications are complementary not competitive, i.e., that mass media may inform both opinion leaders and followers; and opinion leadership is not a dichotomous trait, i.e., that INTERPERSONAL COMMUNICATIONS can be initiated by both leaders and followers, e.g., receivers are not passive and may request information/advice from opinion leaders, or seek it directly from the mass media.

*See also* **Interpersonal communications; Opinion leaders**

**Bibliography**

Lazarsfeld, P. F., Berelson, B. & Goudet, H. (1948). *The people's choice* (2nd edn). New York: Columbia Press.
Schiffman, L. G. & Kanuk, L. L. (1991). *Consumer behavior* (4th edn). Prentice-Hall, p. 502.

BARBARA LEWIS

**types of measure**  Measurement involves assigning numbers to characteristics of objects or events in such a way that the numbers reflect reality. Essentially, there are four different types of measurement scales: nominal (or categorical), ordinal, interval, and ratio. As we move from categorical to ratio so the arithmetic powers of the measures increase. The selection of the appropriate descriptive statistical measure and/or test statistic depends upon, among other things, the type(s) of scales used to measure the variables of interest.

*Nominal measurement scales* use numbers to categorize objects or events. Thus, for a variable called gender the number 1 can be used as a label for males, the number 2 as the label for females. Again for a variable such as occupation doctors can be labeled 1, teachers 2, students 3, market researchers 4, and so on. The numbers are being used as shorthand to identify categories, and the numbers are replaceable by fuller descriptions or labels at any time. There is no suggestion that males precede females just because in everyday arithmetic 1 comes before 2, or that one female is worth two males because 2 is twice 1, or that adding a doctor to a teacher gives a student just because 1 plus 2 equals 3. The well-known rules of arithmetic do not apply to these numbers for obvious reasons.

*Ordinal scales* use numbers to rank items in order. As with nominal scales, cases are given the same number as other cases that share the same characteristic but the order of the given numbers reflects the order in reality. Thus, respondents may be asked about their level of agreement or disagreement with a statement. For such a variable, respondents who "agree strongly" may be given the number 1, those "agreeing" given 2, those "neither agreeing nor disagreeing" given 3, those "disagreeing" given 4 while those "disagreeing strongly" are given 5.

The numbers reflect the relative position of the responses but not their magnitude. There is no suggestion that the difference between the categories "agreeing" and "agreeing strongly" is necessarily the same as the difference between the categories "neither agreeing nor disagreeing" and "agreeing" despite the fact that, in other circumstances, the differences between 2 and 1 and between 3 and 2 are the same.

Much MARKETING RESEARCH involving the use of questionnaires to measure the attitudes, opinions, preferences, etc. of consumers is based on ordinal measurement scales. Ordinal measures are better than nominal measures in that with ordinal scales the order of the numbers reflects a real life order of the categories while nominal measures are used when such real life ordering is not possible.

*Interval measurement scales* have the property that equal distances on the scale represent equal differences in the characteristic being measured. Thus, temperature can be measured on interval scales, the difference between 10 and 15 degrees is the same as the difference between 25 and 30 degrees. An improved form of interval scale, *the ratio scale*, has the additional property that it is possible to compute and compare ratios. Thus, the difference in price between 1 and 2 is the same as the difference between 8 and 9 but also the ratio of 10 to 5 is the same as the ratio of 6 to 3. Many variables can be measured on scales with these properties; examples are height, weight, incomes, revenues, sales, prices, profits, ages, etc. Such scales have all the properties of nominal and ordinal scales, indeed it is possible to convert ratio/interval scales into ordinal scales which themselves can be converted to nominal scales, in each case with some loss of information.

The first question to be asked when a statistician begins to analyze a set of data is what type of scale is used to measure each variable. Only then can a decision be made as to which statistics and tests are appropriate.

**Bibliography**

Malhotra, N. K. (1993). *Marketing research: An applied orientation*. Englewood Cliffs, NJ: Prentice-Hall, pp. 275–81.

MICHAEL GREATOREX

# U

**umbrella strategy** An organization is said to have an umbrella strategy when there is a clear definition of strategic goals, and even the general strategic direction, by the chief executive (or senior management), but the detail of how these goals are to be achieved has yet to be decided. Within these established boundaries, the various actors (such as functional managers) have the flexibility, often through a process of iteration and consensus building that will involve senior management, to develop the substance of the STRATEGY, i.e., the means by which the strategic goals are to be realized. The strategy has also been termed "deliberately emergent" (Mintzberg & Waters, 1985) as the leadership purposefully allows others the flexibility to devise strategic content.

*See also* **Emergent strategy**

**Bibliography**

Mintzberg, H. & Waters, J. A. (1985). Of strategies, deliberate and emergent. *Strategic Management Journal*, 6, (3), July–Sept., 257–72.

DALE LITTLER

**uncertainty** Uncertainty has traditionally been defined in terms of its difference from risk, the classic distinction between the two being made by Knight (1921). He suggested that "risk" applies to those instances where the outcome(s) can be measured, i.e., where some value (or probability) can be ascribed to the possibility of some particular event occurring. Uncertainty, on the other hand, applies when it is not possible to do this. Hague (1971) adopts a slightly different terminology, distinguishing between "insurable" and "non-insurable" risk.

The former, he suggests, refers to situations where it is possible to assess the likelihood of a particular occurrence based on statistical analysis by experts such as actuaries. "Non-insurable risk" applies when it is difficult to predict the outcome, which is the case, so Hague contends, in most business investment decisions. Shackle (1970) suggested that uncertainty exists when "there can be no knowing for certain what will be the consequences of action" (21).

Some, e.g., Freeman (1974), have argued that in the case of technological INNOVATION, where there is generally considerable uncertainty about the outcome, uncertainty can be an aggregation of at least three different types: market, technological, and general business uncertainty. Market uncertainty arises from the difficulties in predicting competitors' actions and the market reaction at different prices. Technological uncertainty occurs because of the difficulties involved in predicting whether or not the initial technical specifications will be achieved at a cost which will enable the company to set a price acceptable to customers and at the same time make a satisfactory return. In many cases, product development may be attended by increasing costs of development as unforeseen technical hurdles arise demanding, sometimes, novel technical solutions. Finally, general business uncertainty surrounds all major investment decisions, and stems from the possibility of random events.

Uncertainty can have a profound impact on decision-making, and especially that related to significant changes. It undermines many of the assumptions surrounding the "design school" of strategy formation (Mintzberg, 1990) (*see* IMPLEMENTATION of strategy), and suggests the need for flexibility and CONTINGENCY PLANNING.

## Bibliography

Freeman, C. (1974). *The economics of industrial innovation.* Harmondsworth: Penguin. Chapter 7.

Hague, D. C. (1971). *Managerial economics.* Harlow: Longman. Chapter 7.

Knight, F. H. (1921). *Risk, uncertainty and profit* (2nd edn). Boston, MA: Houghton Mifflin Co.

Mintzberg, H. (1990). The design school: Reconsidering the basic premises of strategic management. *Strategic Management Journal,* 11, (3), Mar–Apr, 171–195.

Shackle, G. L. S. (1970). *Expectation, enterprise and profit,* London: Allen & Unwin.

DALE LITTLER

**univariate analysis** Univariate analysis is concerned with the quantitative analysis of data where each variable is analyzed in isolation. The preliminary analysis of a survey often begins with a univariate analysis of the data. Data for a series of variables, one variable at a time, for the whole of a sample can be summarized into a frequency distribution for each variable with a suitable accompanying GRAPHICAL REPRESENTATION, such as a pie diagram, bar chart, histogram, ogive, etc. Alternatively, DESCRIPTIVE STATISTICS such as measures of average, variation, skewness, and kurtosis may be calculated for each variable.

Point estimates of population characteristics, such as population proportions or population means and totals, can be made, and CONFIDENCE INTERVALS based on the normal or t-distributions are easily computed. Hypothesis tests (*see* HYPOTHESIS TESTING) concerning population parameters for each variable, such as population proportions, population average, or standard deviation, are well known and include the z-test and t-test for interval data, the binomial test and one sample chi-square test for nominal data, and the Kolmogorov-Smirnov test for ordinal data.

## Bibliography

Tull, D. S. & Hawkins, D. I. (1987). *Marketing research: Measurement and method* (4th edn). New York: Macmillan. Chapters 12 & 13.

MICHAEL GREATOREX

**users** Users are members of the DECISION-MAKING UNIT (DMU) and are those individuals working in an organization who are directly involved in the use of the goods and services purchased by the organization. For example, a welder could be a user of his/her organization's welding machinery, protective clothing, canteen, first-aid station, training courses, pension scheme, etc. It is important to involve users in the PURCHASING PROCESS to ensure that whatever is eventually purchased will be practicable and readily integrated in organizational systems. Users can be influential in the early stages of the purchasing process where they may initiate a purchasing process through identifying a particular need and specifying what is necessary to meet that need. They can also be involved in later trials and quality monitoring.

*See also* **Organizational buying behavior**

DOMINIC WILSON

**utility** Businesses, in providing products and services through their production and marketing activities, create a number of kinds of economic utility to consumers. These economic utilities (of form, task, time, place, and possession) enable an organization to provide consumer satisfaction.

Form utility is created by converting raw materials into finished goods that meet consumer needs, e.g., producing a tennis racket. Task utility is provided when someone performs a task for someone else, e.g., a bank handing financial transactions. But just producing tennis rackets or handling bank accounts does not result in consumer satisfaction; the product (or service) must be something that consumers want or there is no need to be satisfied and, therefore, limited utility. Consumers will not be satisfied until possession, time, and place utilities are also provided.

Possession utility means facilitating the transfer of ownership or use of a product/service to the consumer. Thus, the consumer obtains a good or service and has the right to use or consume it; customers usually exchange money or something else of value for possession utility.

Time utility is created by having goods/services available when consumers want them, and relates to opening hours of retail outlets, 24-hour telephone lines for banking and/or advice services, etc.

Place utility is created by making goods/services available where consumers want them, e.g., moving products from warehouses or producers to a location where consumers want to buy them, and having services available where consumers want to consume them.

## Bibliography

Dibb, S., Simkin, L., Pride, W. M. & Ferrell, O. C. (1991). *Marketing*. (European edn). Boston, MA: Houghton Mifflin Co.. Chapter 1, p. 326.

McCarthy, E. J. & Perreault, W. D. (1993). *Basic marketing* (11th edn). international student edition. Homewood, IL: Irwin. Chapter 1, p. 5.

BARBARA LEWIS

# V

**validity**  A scale or a measure is valid if it measures what it is intended to measure. Validity is established by considering the following criteria: face validity, reliability, criterion validity, and construct validity.

*Face* or *content validity* is the degree to which a measure captures the characteristics of a concept one desires to measure. It is a subjective assessment of the correspondence between the theoretical concepts under study and the measurements being constructed.

High RELIABILITY is essential for validity but does not ensure validity. A measure may be reliable but not valid when errors are consistent or systematic.

*Criterion validity* considers whether or not the scale performs as expected in relation to other variables, the criterion variables. The criterion variables may be selected attitudinal, behavioral, socioeconomic, or psychographic variables. Concurrent validity is assessed when the scale being evaluated and the criterion variables are measured at the same time. Predictive validity is assessed when the data on the scales are collected at one point in time and used to predict values of the criterion variables which are measured at a later point in time.

*Construct validity* involves understanding the concepts that the constructs are measuring and their interrelationships. Is a constructed measure highly positively correlated with other measures of the same construct (convergent validity), not correlated with theoretically unrelated constructs (discriminant validity), or correlated in an expected way with different but related constructs (nomological validity)? A construct is valid if it behaves as expected in relation to other constructs.

Bibliography

Tull, D. S. & Hawkins, D. I. (1987). *Marketing research: Measurement and method* (4th edn). New York: Macmillan, pp. 225–228.

MICHAEL GREATOREX

**VALS**  *see* LIFESTYLES; PSYCHOGRAPHICS

**value added**  The notion of value added refers to the principle that value is added cumulatively to a product or service by successive participants in the VALUE CHAIN. Thus, value added at any particular stage of the chain can be estimated as: value of output less cost of input (not including labor). Value added analysis can provide a useful input to internal productivity calculations (e.g., value added per person or per work group) and can also, of course, be an important basis for taxation.

For the purposes of PRICING decisions it is important to assess value in terms of the user at the next stage in the value chain. In other words, in a competitive market, value should be determined by the "customer perspective." The concept is also particularly useful in competitive analysis where organizations can examine their own activities to ensure that they only engage in operations where they are able to add significant value, leaving other aspects of their activities (e.g., distribution, design) to specialist subcontractors.

DOMINIC WILSON

**value chain**  The value chain embraces the various activities aimed at creating value for the customer and the margin that the firm obtains. It was first articulated by Porter (1985). The value activities can be divided into two main categories: support activities, which include firm infrastructure, human resource management, technology development and procurement; and the primary activities of inbound logistics, operations, outbound logistics, marketing and sales, and service. It provides a framework for analyzing not only how the organization currently provides value but also how value can be enhanced. Organizations may strive to secure synergies with, e.g., suppliers by, e.g., developing inbound logistics systems that provide mutual benefits. Although an interesting concept, its practical usefulness remains to be demonstrated.

**Bibliography**

Porter, M. E. (1985). *Competitive advantage: Creating and sustaining superior performance.* New York: Free Press.

DALE LITTLER

**vertical integration**   This is regarded as an integrative growth strategy (Kotler, 1994), although it can be employed to defend the organization against powerful competitors, suppliers, and customers (*see* COMPETITIVE STRATEGY). It generally involves the acquisition of suppliers and/or customers, thereby inter alia providing security of supply or of access to the market. There are also vertically integrated systems in which there may not be complete ownership, but in which cooperation is founded on, e.g., agreements or minority stakes by the various parties in each other. Such systems may be effectively coordinated or administered by one dominant organization.

*See also* **Horizontal integration**

**Bibliography**

Kotler, P. (1994). *Marketing management: Analysis, planning, implementation and control* (8th edn). Englewood Cliffs, NJ: Prentice-Hall. Chapter 3.

DALE LITTLER

**vision statement**   The vision statement is a relatively recent introduction to the lexicon of strategic management and is generally regarded as encapsulating the desired-for future for the organization, usually as expressed by the chief executive. Vision is also regarded as an element in the MISSION STATEMENT.

**Bibliography**

Hamel, G. & Prahalad, C. K. (1994). Competing for the future. *Harvard Business Review*, 72, (4), July–Aug., 122–128.

DALE LITTLER

# W

**wealth** A person's purchasing power derives from DISPOSABLE INCOME and DISCRETIONARY INCOME, resulting from both employment and other sources. An increasingly important source is that of wealth, i.e., the ownership of assets such as property savings, shares, etc. which themselves yield an income and which help to create a lifestyle (*see* LIFESTYLES). The second half of the 20th century has seen an increase in wealth among large numbers of people in economically developed countries, but as the populations of such countries age, and the state is unable or unwilling to support those in retirement, the income from wealth may not be spent in the short term but may be reinvested for the future.

## Bibliography

Central Statistical Office. *Family Spending* (annual). London: HMSO.
Dibb, S., Simkin, L., Pride, W. M. & Ferrell, O. C. (1994). *Marketing, concepts and strategies* (European edn). Boston, MA: Houghton Mifflin Co. Chapter 2.
United States, Bureau of the Census. *Statistical abstract of the United States.* Austin: Reference Press.

DAVID YORKE

**wheel of retailing** This is a theory suggesting that entrants to a new retail market will begin trading as cut-price, low overhead, low margin, and low status operations (McNair, 1958). Over time, these traders will increase their overheads by offering additional services and product lines, perhaps in better locations, smarter premises and with more sophisticated marketing communications. These retailers are then more vulnerable to new low cost entrants to the market who may be able to undercut the original retailer's prices. The retail cycle will then have come full circle.

The wheel theory is a generalization that may not hold true in all cases. Retailers entering new markets may be tempted to copy the trading format of established retailers which may require sophisticated trading patterns from the start. In other cases, such as times of recession, retailers may attempt to cut costs and even reduce some services, thus moving in the opposite direction to that which is suggested by the wheel theory.

## Bibliography

McNair, M. P. (1958). Significant trends and developments in the post war period. In A. B. Smith (Ed.), *Competitive distribution in a free high level economy and its implications for the university* (pp. 1–25). University of Pittsburgh Press.

STEVE WORRALL

**wholesalers** Wholesalers form the part of the marketing channel between producers/manufacturers and the retailer. Wholesalers buy and sell in large quantities direct to the retailer and generally do not sell goods direct to the public.

*See also* **Retail distribution channels**

## Bibliography

Lewison, D. (1994). *Retailing.* New York: Macmillan.

STEVE GREENLAND

**word-of-mouth communications** Word-of-mouth communication is a non-commercial form of marketing communication where the

sender of the MESSAGE is assisted by intermediaries in attempting to REACH the target
buyer/customer/consumer. Opinion leaders (*see*
OPINION LEADER) may benefit an organization
with positive word-of-mouth communications
but there is a danger that word of mouth may be
detrimental to the organization and its products
or services as a result of poor experiences of the
intermediary.

*See also* **Interpersonal communications;
Marketing communications**

DAVID YORKE

# —— INDEX ——

Compiled by Meg Davies (Registered Indexer)